Prim **ary Geography Handbook** SECOND EDITION **ok**

Primary Geography Handbook

Children from Woolmore School, Tower Hamlets, out on fieldwork. **Photo** | *Jonathan Barnes.*

Primary Geography

Handbook
REVISED EDITION

Edited by Stephen Scoffham

Geographical Association

Acknowledgements

A handbook of this kind is a team effort involving many authors and contributors. The production too is a complex process which depends on the publisher, editor, designer, illustrator and printer. I am indebted to all those who have given their time and professional expertise so unstintingly to such good effect. Revising and updating a text is a rather unglamorous task and I am grateful to all the authors for the way they have responded. In addition, I would like to acknowledge the support of Geographical Association staff, especially Ruth Totterdell for her support for the project, Wendy North for her immense help with illustrations and Nicola Donkin for her careful proof reading. We are also most grateful to all the schools and pupils whose work is featured.

This edition of the *Primary Geography Handbook* is based on an earlier version published in 2004, which was itself reworked from the handbook produced in 1998. The 1998 book, edited by Roger Carter, provided firm foundations on which to build. Fran Royle made huge contributions to these earlier publications in her role as GA Publications Manager. Now as a freelance editor she has brought her experience, wisdom and common sense to this present publication. In addition, she has negotiated with myself and other authors with extraordinary understanding and good humour. Thank you Fran for everything you have done and for making our work such a pleasure. Finally, I would like to offer thanks to all those friends and colleagues within the Geographical Association and in the Faculty of Education at Canterbury Christ Church University who have supported me in my role as editor. Being able to draw on their enthusiasm, support and expertise and belonging to a community of geographers has been invaluable.

Stephen Scoffham
July 2010

© Geographical Association, 2004, 2010

ISBN 978-1-84377-297-2
First published 2004
Revised and updated 2010
Year 2014 2013 2012 2011 2010

Published by the Geographical Association, 160 Solly Street, Sheffield S1 4BF.
Company no 07139068.
Website: *www.geography.org.uk*
Email: *info@geography.org.uk*
The Geographical Association is a registered charity: no 1135148.

Founded in 1893, the GA is an independent charity with a core objective of furthering the learning and teaching of geography. The GA promotes and supports geography teaching by producing acclaimed resources for teachers, holding quality CPD events and lobbying government. As a membership organisation it is the members who give the GA its strength. We would be happy to hear from potential authors who have ideas for geography books. Find out more at *www.geography.org.uk*.

Edited by Fran Royle

Designed and typeset by PrintPod, Huddersfield

Illustrations by Dan Parry-Jones and Linzi Henry

Printed and bound in China through Colorcraft Ltd, Hong Kong.

Foreword

Over the last few years, the long and enduring staple crop of history-led television programmes have given way to a dizzying spread of geographical fodder. What began as a twinkle in Michael Palin's eye, grew with the indigenous wanderlust of Bruce Parry and the homegrown beachcombing of the *Coast* team, and has taken root with the latitudinal travelogues of Simon Reeve and the expeditionary zeal of programmes like *Operation Borneo* and *Land of the Jaguar*. Add to that the glossy specials like

Iain Stewart.

Planet Earth, Earth: The Power of the Planet and *How Earth Made Us* and you realise that a new star has been born in popular culture: the planet.

I'm never sure if the mass media drives or is driven by the public mood, but this burst of primetime entertainment drawn from the world around us seems to me to be firmly rooted. Global geopolitical issues that have gestated in geography classrooms around the country for decades have now crept into homes and workplaces, as questions about climate, hunger, resources, population, and migration become the everyday conversations. Folk for whom geography once meant a bemused recollection of oxbow lakes are now routinely debating the merits of recycling, the efficacy of renewable energy sources, and the legitimacy of government carbon emission or immigration policies.

It is clear to me that geography is no longer the blue trivial pursuit but something with real currency in modern society. Not everyone will want to study it, but with geographical issues being among society's most pressing concerns, our future depends on those who will. And of course, it all starts with you.

Teaching geography in primary schools helps young people make sense of the abundance of information that they acquire from the television, the media, from conversations at home and from their own observations. Geography helps young people to become more aware of their planet and develop into informed individuals in an increasingly challenging and unpredictable world. This book offers fantastic support that will enable you to help your pupils on this journey.

Iain Stewart
July 2010

Iain Stewart is a Professor of Geosciences Communication in the School of Geography, Earth and Environmental Sciences at the University of Plymouth. He has presented television series including *Journeys From the Centre of the Earth, Earth: The Power of the Planet, Hot Rocks, 10 Things You Didn't Know About...* and *How Earth Made Us.*

Contents

Contents

Introduction   *Stephen Scoffham*   **9**

Section 1: Geography and learning
Chapter 1   Young geographers   **14**
                Stephen Scoffham
Chapter 2   Geography, creativity and place   **24**
                Jonathan Barnes
Chapter 3   Geography and the emotions   **34**
                Julia Tanner, with contributions from Stephen Scoffham
Chapter 4   Making geography fun   **48**
                Kathy Alcock, with contributions from Ruth Potts and Janie Whittle
Chapter 5   Young children making sense of the world   **62**
                Fran Martin and Paula Owens
Chapter 6   Understanding and developing primary geography   **74**
                Simon Catling

Section 2: Geographical skills
Chapter 7   Enquiries and investigations   **94**
                Geoff Dinkele, with contributions from Stephen Scoffham
Chapter 8   Mapwork skills   **104**
                Colin W. Bridge
Chapter 9   Using photographs, diagrams and sketches   **120**
                Margaret Mackintosh
Chapter 10   Fieldwork and outdoor learning   **134**
                Paula Richardson
Chapter 11   Geography and language development   **148**
                Liz Lewis
Chapter 12   Geography and ICT   **164**
                Kate Russell

Section 3: People and places
Chapter 13   Using the school locality   **180**
                *Angela Milner and Terry Jewson, with contributions
                from Stephen Scoffham and Philip Maudsley*
Chapter 14   Contrasting localities   **194**
                Greg Walker, with contributions from Gemma Kent
Chapter 15   The wider world   **204**
                Maureen Weldon, with contributions from Stephen Scoffham
Chapter 16   The global dimension   **216**
                Mary Young

Section 4: Themes and topics

Chapter 17	Weather and climate	230
	Rachel Bowles	
Chapter 18	Rivers, coasts and the landscape	246
	Liz Lewis	
Chapter 19	Settlement	260
	John Halocha	
Chapter 20	Environmental geography	272
	Liz Essex-Cater and Steve Rawlinson	
Chapter 21	Citizenship and primary geography	288
	Elaine Jackson	

Section 5: Managing the curriculum

Chapter 22	Planning the curriculum	302
	Paula Richardson	
Chapter 23	Assessment for learning	312
	John Kenyon, with contributions from Stephen Scoffham	
Chapter 24	Inclusion and special needs	322
	David Blow, with contributions from Stephen Scoffham	
Chapter 25	The subject leader	334
	Jeremy Krause and Jane Millward, with contributions from Anthony Barlow	
Chapter 26	The inspection and accreditation of geography	348
	Marcia Foley	

| **Resources** | 358 |
| **Index** | 361 |

Contributors

Stephen Scoffham is the author of many books on primary geography, atlas consultant, Honorary Publications Officer of the Geographical Association, and Principal Lecturer at Canterbury Christ Church University.

Kathy Alcock, formerly a teacher and lecturer in primary geography with a strong interest in the environment, now lives in southern France where she helps to run her small holiday business.

Anthony Barlow is a teacher from Bolton who has a passion for 'under-your-nose' geography. He is Vice-Chair of the GA Early Years and Primary Phase Committee and a Geography Champion.

Jonathan Barnes is Senior Lecturer in Primary Education at Canterbury Christ Church University and teaches, researches and writes about cross-curricular and creative teaching and learning.

David Blow, once a Senior Lecturer in Education, worked for thirty years in residential and mainstream special education.

Rachel Bowles, lately of the University of Greenwich, is co-ordinator of the Register of Research in Primary Geography and an ex-officio member of the GA Early Years and Primary Phase Committee.

Colin W. Bridge, an ex-headteacher, is a keen environmentalist who has contributed regularly to *Primary Geographer* over many years and co-authored numerous primary geography texts.

Simon Catling is Professor of Primary Education at Oxford Brookes University and was President of the Geographical Association 1993-4. He teaches and researches in primary geography.

Geoff Dinkele was Hampshire's County Inspector for Geography and a teacher trainer. He now serves and smiles in Abbotts Ann village shop near Andover.

Liz Essex-Cater, Senior Lecturer in Geography Education at Northumbria University for 14 years, sadly died in 2008. Her contribution to this book is part of her legacy.

Marcia Foley, formerly Geography Adviser for Kent, is a freelance primary geography consultant, author and GA Primary Geography Quality Mark Moderator.

John Halocha is Reader in Geography Education and Head of Geography at Bishop Grosseteste University College, Lincoln. He was President of the Geographical Association 2009-2010.

Elaine Jackson, formerly a primary school headteacher, is now Chief Adviser (Primary) for Trafford LA and author of numerous books including the Barnaby Bear range of big books.

Terry Jewson was a primary school headteacher for many years and part of an author team that has written numerous primary geography texts.

Gemma Kent is Geography Co-ordinator at The Lyceum School, London and a Geography Champion in the London region.

John Kenyon, formerly headteacher of Middlewich Primary School, Cheshire, is a member of the GA Early Years and Primary Phase Committee.

Jeremy Krause, formerly Senior Geography Adviser in Cheshire and President of the Geographical Association 2001-2, is currently Senior School Improvement Adviser, National Strategies SW.

Liz Lewis, formerly Senior Lecturer in Geography Education in the Universities of Sunderland and Durham, is a long-term contributor to GA primary publications, including the Barnaby Bear range of little books.

Margaret Mackintosh taught in Nigeria and Humberside before joining the University of Plymouth. She was Honorary Editor of *Primary Geographer* 1995-2005 and is now retired.

Fran Martin is Senior Lecturer at Exeter University where she specialises in Early Years, Geography and Global Education. Honorary Editor of *Primary Geographer* 2005-2010, she will be GA President in 2011.

Philip Maudsley is Deputy Headteacher at Coatham CE Primary School, Redcar and Cleveland.

Jane Millward, is currently employed by Ofsted as an HMI and was previously a senior officer for a local authority.

Angela Milner was formerly Senior Associate Dean in the Faculty of Education at Edge Hill University.

Paula Owens is Curriculum Development Leader (Primary) for the Geographical Association. Formerly a Deputy Head, her specialisms are Early Years, Geography and ESD.

Ruth Potts is a Geography/History coordinator (primary) and a member of the GA Early Years and Primary Phase Committee.

Steve Rawlinson is Principal Lecturer in Geography Education at Northumbria University, Chair of the *Primary Geographer* Editorial Board, and a Geography Champion.

Paula Richardson, former teacher, LA adviser and geography inspector, is an independent geography adviser, Geography Champion, author and member of the GA Publications Board and LOtC fieldwork group.

Kate Russell is Staffordshire's Senior Adviser for Geography. She is editor of the Staffordshire Learning Net for geography (*www.sln.org.uk/geography*) and a long-standing member of the GA ICT Working Group.

Julia Tanner is Dean of the Faculty of Education at Leeds Trinity University College. She has a particular interest in the role of emotions in learning.

Greg Walker, lately Senior Education Lecturer and Primary Humanities Coordinator at Roehampton University, has particular interests in children's understanding of distant places and producing primary geography resources.

Maureen Weldon, formerly an Advisory Teacher for Geography in Lincolnshire and a primary headteacher in Peterborough, is Chair of the GA Publications Board

Janie Whittle started her career as geography co-ordinator at Edwalton Primary School, Nottingham, and she now teaches the IB Primary Years Programme in Italy.

Mary Young is a freelance trainer and writer on global citizenship and a former Education Adviser with Oxfam.

Introduction

Geography matters! The events that affect us as individuals do not occur in isolation, they happen in a context. Pick up a newspaper, watch the television news or listen to people's conversations and you will quickly discover how crucial places are to our lives. Understanding the world around us, making sense of the way it is inter-related and considering how it might change in the future stand at the heart of geography.

Tracing the word 'geography' back to its linguistic roots reveals two key aspects of the subject: 'geo' means 'earth' and 'graphia' means 'writing'. Of course geography as an academic discipline has developed dramatically since the term was first coined in the museum of Alexandria around 300BC. However, geography's role in describing and interpreting our surroundings, both local and distant, is as valid today as it was over 2000 years ago.

Traditionally, there are two main branches of geography. Physical geography focuses on the earth's surface and the processes that shape it, and covers topics including landscapes, rocks, oceans, climate and habitats. Human geography is the study of people and places. By exploring themes such as settlement, population, transport, agriculture, trade and industry, geographers investigate the way we live our lives. They look for patterns and connections and try to identify future trends. However, a focus of particular interest and concern now is the state of the natural environment. Environmental issues, which are inextricably bound up with the relationship between people and their surroundings, are central to geography.

Finding out about the world is not just a matter of being an objective observer, recording and analysing phenomena. Modern thinking recognises that our experience and emotions colour the way we respond to places and events. Michael Palin (2008) hints at this when he observes that geography is 'a fusion of the power of the imagination and the hard truths of science'. Indeed there is a sense in which, as we investigate the external world, we are also embarking on a journey of self discovery. No wonder, then, that geography excites so much interest and attention. As Andrew Goudie (DfEE/QCA, 1999) asks rhetorically, 'What other subject tells us so much about the great issues of the age?'

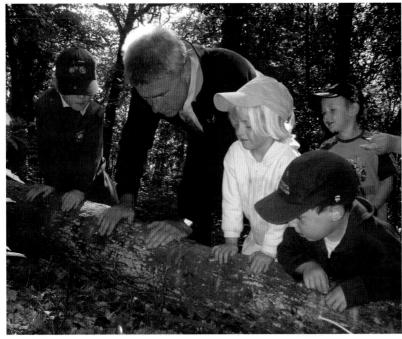

Photo | Paula Owens.

The aims of primary geography

In devising your school geography curriculum there is plenty of content to choose from. Indeed the challenge is to decide what to leave out, especially given the pressure on curriculum time. Your choice could be guided by the aims for primary geography identified when the national curriculum was first devised, which are just as relevant today. These highlight environmental issues and suggest opportunities for links with other subjects; they also include a strong focus on values. They are:

- to stimulate pupils' interest in their surroundings and in the variety of physical and human conditions on the earth's surface

- to foster their sense of wonder at the beauty of the world

- to develop an informed concern about the environment

- to enhance their sense of responsibility for the care of the earth and its peoples.

(DES/WO, 1990, p. 6.)

Geography in the curriculum

As we go to press it is unclear what the government will decide and there are uncertainties surrounding all primary school subjects, although two major reviews – the Rose Review (DCSF, 2009) and the Cambridge Review (Alexander, 2010) – have both recommended more cross-curricular work. What we offer here are the essential components of primary school geography, exemplified in good practice. We believe the suggestions and ideas in the following pages provide a fresh and vibrant interpretation of geography that will stand the test of time and endure in changing circumstances.

For up-to-date information and guidance, visit the GA website – *www.geography.org.uk/primaryhandbook* – where we will try to keep you informed on the most recent legislation and initiatives.

About the handbook

This book is about how to teach geography in primary schools. It has been written by a volunteer team from around the country and brings together in a single volume their collected wisdom, which draws on well over five hundred years of teaching experience! The book is divided into five sections covering learning, skills, places, themes and curriculum management. Some themes, such as fieldwork, enquiries and progression, recur throughout: others, such as inspection and schools linking, are concentrated in just a few chapters. The navigator opposite is intended to help you locate the material you need as quickly as possible. For more detailed searches use the index at the back.

This handbook is intended to inspire. There are chapters on topics as diverse as emotional geography, creative thinking and global citizenship. Enthusiastic and motivated teachers are the best guarantee for vivid and vibrant classroom practice. Geography has always needed ambassadors who will speak up and argue its case. This is as vital as ever at the moment when there are so many pressures on curriculum time and such a strong focus on measurable achievements.

Since the previous edition of the *Primary Geography Handbook* (Scoffham, 2004) there have been many new educational initiatives. These include Every Child Matters, Community Cohesion, Sustainable Schools, SEAL (Social and Emotional Aspects of Learning), the Learning Outside the Classroom Manifesto and the creative curriculum. Primary languages has emerged as a new subject and ICT has developed almost beyond recognition. In making changes we have referred to key documents where appropriate. We have also incorporated the latest findings from educational research, updated the photographs and listed current websites.

Some of today's pupils will still be alive at the end of the century. We can only guess at the challenges they will confront. What we can try to ensure, however, is that their primary school education gives them the understanding they need for the present and prepares them for a future in which they will continue to learn and develop. Geographical perspectives are an essential part of this foundation. We need to see that children are proficient in basic skills such as communicating information, way-finding and interpreting the environment. We have a duty to attend to their psychological and emotional well-being and to nurture the formation of positive attitudes to themselves, each other and the environment. In addition we need to help pupils of all abilities and backgrounds – tomorrow's adults – to play their part in a shrinking world. This book is designed to help you achieve these objectives and enable your pupils to live fulfilling lives.

Stephen Scoffham, July 2010

Theme and chapter navigator

Theme	Chapter number																									
	1	2	3	4	5	6	7	8	9	10	11	12	13	14	15	16	17	18	19	20	21	22	23	24	25	26
Assessment					•			•															•		•	•
Citizenship		•											•		•					•	•					
Concepts	•				•	•					•															
Creativity		•	•	•																			•		•	
Cross curricular links		•	•	•	•	•							•								•					
Differentiation												•												•	•	
Distant places	•	•	•	•											•	•	•				•					
Enquiries							•				•	•	•				•	•	•	•						
Environment			•					•					•			•										
Europe				•										•	•											
Fieldwork										•	•		•	•		•	•	•	•	•				•		
Futures		•								•						•			•							
Games/play				•	•													•								
Good practice					•	•						•				•						•		•	•	•
History		•											•						•							
ICT								•	•			•								•						
Identity	•		•		•																					
Inclusion/SEN		•	•	•									•											•		
CPD/INSET											•														•	•
Inspection																									•	•
Issues		•	•				•											•	•	•				•		
Learning theory	•		•	•	•					•																
Literacy/stories											•					•		•	•		•	•				
Local area	•		•						•	•			•					•								
Mapwork	•	•							•	•				•	•											
Misconceptions											•				•	•	•	•		•	•					
Photographs		•							•	•		•			•	•										
Planning					•	•					•			•	•	•						•	•		•	
Progression							•	•	•		•	•						•	•			•	•	•		
Questions							•	•	•		•							•	•							
Schools linking															•	•	•									
Transition					•																•				•	
Vocabulary								•			•							•	•							

References

Alexander, R. (2010) *Children, Their World, Their Education*. London: Routledge.

DCSF (2009) *Independent Review of the Primary Curriculum*. Nottingham: DCSF.

DES/WO (1990) *Geography for Ages 5 to 16*. London: HMSO.

DfEE/QCA (1999) *The National Curriculum: Handbook for primary teachers in England*. London: DfEE/QCA.

Palin, M. (2008) 'Geography action plan at Speaker's House', *Mapping News*, 33, pp. 4-5.

Geography and learning

Chapter

1. Young geographers

2. Geography, creativity and place

3. Geography and the emotions

4. Making geography fun

5. Young children making sense of the world

6. Understanding and developing primary geography

Young geographers

> *'Our present-day knowledge of the child's mind is comparable to a fifteenth-century map of the world – a mixture of truth and error ... vast areas remain to be explored'*
>
> **Arnold Gesell,
> cited in Fisher, 1995.**

Over the past few decades there has been a growing interest in primary geography research and the misconceptions which many children hold about the world around them. The way in which children learn about places is complex and researchers are only slowly piecing together the story. Part of the problem is that there is no entirely logical or inevitable sequence of events. Learning is for many people a surprisingly idiosyncratic process in which ideas are acquired in an apparently random manner. Most people do not become systematic thinkers until they reach adolescence or even later.

It is also remarkably difficult to discover what is actually going on inside a child's head. We were all young once, but it is impossible to recapture the sense of awe and wonder which children experience on doing something for the first time. Adults can often only observe and deduce what seems to be happening from the outside.

Despite these complexities there is, however, one clear message: the skills and competencies of young children appear to have been consistently underestimated. In part this is due to an uncritical acceptance of Piaget's theories. Few people nowadays would contest Piaget's central thesis that children pass through developmental stages as they grow older. However, the age at which this happens, and children's ability to operate at different levels of understanding, is much more variable than was first thought. The more we find out about different aspects of geographical learning the further the roots go back into childhood.

Spatial awareness

Children first begin to discover the location of objects as they play with toys in their cots. Initially, taste and touch provide the main clues, but after about three months their vision improves and they become capable of focusing more sharply on objects. From about ten months onwards children begin to actively explore their environment. As they develop the ability to crawl, and then walk, the scope and range of the places they can visit expands enormously, though parents usually restrict these early forays for fear of dangers. However, as youngsters grow in ability and confidence, so they are allowed to go further afield. This introduces them to the environment beyond the front door.

Maps are essential tools in the discovery process, but how do young children learn to use maps and find their way from place to place? Palmer and Birch (2004) describe an investigation by Bluestein and Acredolo which provides some interesting insights. Sixty 3-5 year-olds were asked to find a toy elephant hidden in a room. They were given a map that showed the layout of the furniture with the position of the toy marked with a cross. The results were impressive. Half the three-year-olds, three-quarters of the four-year-olds and all the five-year-olds were able to find the toy. Generally the children had little difficulty interpreting the map and appeared to understand that the room, furniture and toy were shown symbolically. Subsequent investigations showed the importance of aligning the map. When the map was rotated by 180 degrees only the oldest children were able to use it correctly and even they had difficulty.

Figure 1 | *Drawings of the route taken by the wolf in 'The Three Little Pigs' by reception, year 1 and year 2 children.*

Other researchers investigated cross-cultural issues. One study considered the mapping abilities of four-year-old children in a number of different countries. After discussing the features on a vertical aerial photograph, the children were asked to trace a route from one house to another. Not only were the majority of the children able to complete the task successfully, they all demonstrated an ability to interpret the photograph whatever their cultural background.

Further evidence that spatial reasoning is universal and not related to cultural background comes from a study in rural Kenya conducted by Matthews (1995). Here pupils aged seven to thirteen were asked to draw a map of their village. Despite being almost completely isolated from Western influences and never having seen a formal map, the majority of the pupils completed the exercise successfully. Furthermore they recalled their environment in vivid terms using plan views and other relatively sophisticated representations.

Another issue which has occupied many researchers is whether there is a difference in spatial ability between boys and girls. Wiegand (2006) provides a useful summary of the research, concluding that boys tend to draw maps which are spatially more accurate than those drawn by girls. Boys' maps are also better organised and contain more route information. However, Wiegand also notes that spatial ability is a complex term which encompasses a number of qualitatively different abilities, so research studies into mapwork and gender often yield contradictory results.

One question to emerge from this research is whether gender differences in mapwork are innate or whether they reflect social and cultural influences. In the past, primary age boys were allowed considerable freedom to explore their surroundings which may have helped to develop their spatial understanding. By contrast, girls were allowed out less often and not permitted to go so far. It remains to be seen how changing social attitudes and modern technology will impact on the quality of children's maps.

In general, research provides compelling reasons for introducing children to mapwork from an early age. Many infant school teachers already take the opportunity to create 'pictures' to show journeys associated with stories and fairy tales. The route taken by the wolf in 'The Three Little Pigs' is a typical example (Figure 1). However, the fact that children seem to draw maps spontaneously long before they learn to read or write suggests that spatial awareness is a fundamental skill which should be developed in nurseries and other pre-school groups as a basic educational entitlement.

Exploring the local environment

Most of us remember the place where we were brought up in some considerable detail and often recall it with fondness. These first impressions of the outside world stay with us throughout our lives and provide a rich source of experience. Authors such as Laurie Lee, Virginia Woolf, George Orwell and Marcell Proust recall their early memories with great sensitivity in their novels. Our sense of identity, it seems, derives in some part from the social and physical environment in which we spend our childhood.

The way children interact with their immediate surroundings is important not only for their psychological well-being, it also promotes their educational development. Many play activities involve rehearsing or re-enacting previous events and situations. Through imitation children are able to give full reign to invention and fantasy. Piaget argues that make-believe play allows children to assimilate knowledge and forms the basis of a child's thought even before it can speak. Certainly the opportunity to model and manipulate experiences seems to be an essential part of the learning process.

Several researchers have attempted to find out more about children's private geographies. The classic study was undertaken by Hart (1979) who made a detailed investigation of a New England township over a two-year period. Hart discovered that the children put a particularly high value on water features such as rivers, lakes and ponds. They also favoured trees for climbing and hiding games. The places they feared matched the archetypal scary places of children's literature – attics, cellars and abandoned buildings, and bedrooms and garages at night. Very few of the children selected places for their aesthetic qualities alone. Hart comments on the way children treasure informal routes and pathways which they often use as 'shortcuts' even when they are actually longer. Other researchers, too, remark on children's affinity for secret routes and alleyways. As they explore their surroundings children construct private geographies which meet their physical and emotional needs.

The names they invent for their favourite places offer further insight into children's thinking. In activities such as rollerblading, Ross (2005) reports how children give special names to hills and playing spaces, along with minor details such as 'the gap in the hedge'. These personal

Figure 2 | *Exploring their environment helps children develop their sense of attachment and identity.* **Photo** | *Diane Wright.*

names usually denote the activities that can be done in a particular spot rather than its physical appearance. This preference for functionality was also noted by Owens (2003) who describes how a metal bar used for fastening a door was variously identified by reception class pupils as a meeting place, something you can lean and swing on and something you must not touch.

In thinking about pupils' perceptions of the environment it is important to recognise that their experience may be limited and not to make assumptions. For example, Owens (2003) discovered through discussion with reception class pupils that many of them had no idea that there was a field attached to their school. Similarly, there are adolescents living in London who have never travelled by bus or underground or ventured across the River Thames and those from the Channel ports have never been to mainland Europe.

At the same time children are naturally curious and inventive. They invest their surroundings with personal meaning and interpret them according to their needs. It is worth remembering in this context that the most intensively used play areas are often small patches of dirt rather than designated facilities. Children also need places where they simply loiter or daydream (Figure 2). Edmund Gosse, the Victorian naturalist, is one of many authors who have left us with a description of their childhood pleasures:

> *By the side of the road, between the school and my home, there was a large horse pond. Here I created a maritime empire – islands, a seaboard with harbours, lighthouses, fortifications. My geographical inventiveness had its full swing. Sometimes, while I was creating, a cart would be driven roughly into the pond, shattering my ports with what was worse than a typhoon. But I immediately set to work, as soon as the cart was gone and the mud had settled, to tidy up my coastline again and scoop out anew my harbours.* (Gosse, 1965, p. 136)

It is through transactions of this kind that children come to invest their environment with meaning. The attachment to places which we develop as adults is derived from these childhood interactions. We identify with our home area in lots of different ways. Some people support their local football team, others become involved with local history or trace their family tree. Historically people used to believe they belonged to the soil of a particular place in an organic and religious relationship. The Romans recognised the spirit or essence of a locality (its *genius loci*) by setting up shrines to local deities. Anthropologists have recorded similar beliefs among the original inhabitants of Australia and North and South America.

These studies remind us that the quality of an environment is a very complex issue. As well as quantifying physical and human processes, geographers seek to take account of subjective and personal responses. What a place is like is not simply a matter of fact. It depends equally on how we perceive it and what we feel about it. Contemporary concerns over personal security and the relentless growth of road traffic are serving to erode children's personal freedom and their links with the environment. Malone (2007) argues that today, in westernised countries around the world, many parents are restricting children's movement to such an extent that it is damaging their social, psychological, cultural and environmental development. The 'bubble-wrap' generation is being deprived of opportunities to take initiatives, learn survival skills, develop a sense of adventure, gain self esteem and accept responsibility for their actions. In addition, children are failing to keep physically fit and healthy.

Restoring this richness to children's lives is a challenge which schools cannot expect to meet on their own. However, they can at least promote pupils' awareness and provide some form of environmental experience. Geographical fieldwork has a unique contribution to make to this process. On one level fieldwork can consist of environmental walks and simple data collection activities in and around the school buildings. It can also involve work in local streets and journeys to nearby places. In addition many schools organise some form of residential experience or school journey.

It may also be possible to make better use of the daily journey from home to school. In a study of 150 key stage 1 and EYFS pupils, Large (2004) found that those who talked to an adult about their journey were much more aware of the route than those who did not, even if they travelled by car. Parental involvement was the crucial factor in turning children from passive participants to active learners. Equally, teachers can encourage pupils to engage with their surroundings by setting them challenges such as identifying the nearest postbox or making a survey of front door colours.

Distant places

Children's ideas about distant places develop alongside their knowledge of the local area. Fairy tales and picture books often provide settings which are way beyond a child's immediate experience. Some stories involve journeys to the other side of the world. Others describe adventures in mountains, forests or deserts. Birds and animals provide much of the interest in young children's literature. Pictures of lions, tigers and other creatures frequently decorate the walls of toddlers' bedrooms and many children first learn about Africa and Australia through wildlife.

At the same time, images of the wider world are beamed into our homes through the media. Satellite images and scenes from foreign lands appear regularly on our televisions. Soap operas, with their focus on people and strong storylines, are a particularly powerful influence, although they give a surprisingly limited impression of places. Advertisements and magazines are another source of images and information. Children's natural curiosity about distant places feeds off these stimuli. At first they may not be too sure about the difference between real and fictitious places. They will probably also be very confused about distances. However, as they grow older they gradually begin to sort out their ideas into a more logical framework.

As well as being exotic and exciting, some psychologists have postulated a deeper reason for children's interest in faraway lands. It is suggested that infants try to cut loose from the restrictions of family and neighbourhoods by thinking about imaginary or distant locations. In this way they begin to acquire detailed information about specific places such as villages, harbours and small islands. As well as being reassuring, a knowledge of the boundaries of the world builds up children's self-confidence and helps to

Photo | *Paula Richardson.*

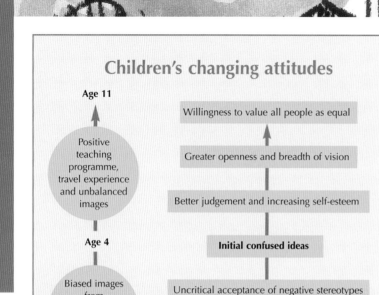

Children's changing attitudes

Age 11 ↑

Positive teaching programme, travel experience and unbalanced images

Age 4

Biased images from advertisements, the media, parents and peers

Age 11 ↓

Willingness to value all people as equal

Greater openness and breadth of vision

Better judgement and increasing self-esteem

Initial confused ideas

Uncritical acceptance of negative stereotypes

Tendency to generalise about people

Prejudice and racism

Figure 3 | Positive images of the developing world are best developed in the primary years before attitudinal rigidity sets in.

develop their sense of individuality. What then are the images of the Earth which young children carry around in their heads? Wiegand (2006) reports on a number of studies. In one of these, primary school pupils were asked to write down the names of all the countries that they knew. The seven-year-olds typically named about five countries, focusing especially on the larger land masses such as America, Africa, India and Australia. By age 11 the pupils' knowledge had expanded and they were on average able to name 15 countries. Generally they appeared to have a good knowledge of Western Europe but the countries of Africa and many other parts of the developing world still did not feature significantly on their mental maps.

What children think about a country is of course more important than the ability to name it. In recent years numerous activities have sought to reveal their images and ideas. Generally it appears that infants and lower juniors tend to associate countries with food and animals but are likely to be confused. Older children exhibit a wider range of responses but also include an increasing number of negative images such as war, famine and poverty.

Disney (2005) conducted a detailed study of children's perceptions of other countries. During the early stages of a schools linking project, two classes of year 5 children in Nottinghamshire were asked to draw pictures showing how they imagined the locality of their Indian partner school. The drawings fell into roughly four categories:

■ *stereotypical images* – traditional villages with straw or mud huts, animals and people carrying baskets on their heads

■ *exotic images* – fairy-tale images of domed buildings, snake charmers and scenes from stories such as the Arabian Nights

■ *undifferentiated images* – this (rather uncommon) response was characterised by drawings of supermarkets, roads and houses which could have been in England

■ *complex images* – palm trees, markets, blocks of flats which appeared to be based on some knowledge but also included traditional stereotypes.

Disney concludes that these representations are fairly consistent with previous research. When Graham and Lynn (1989) invited groups of pupils to discuss photographs of the economically developing world they found 'a large proportion of infants and many less mature upper juniors associated the scenes in Bengal and Bangladesh with hunter-gatherer lifestyles,

Figure 4 | *We can help children to relate to people in other parts of the world by stressing common human needs and emotions.* **Photo** | *Stephen Scoffham.*

one declaring "They sleep on skins from the bears they've killed with spears"'. Over twenty years later, Martin's work on children's ideas about The Gambia (cited in Maddern, 2010) discovered similar responses. It appears that Western children associate life in economically developing countries with primitive customs and are quick to adopt negative stereotypes.

Teachers need to be aware of these findings so that they can provide classroom activities which will broaden pupils' thinking. If left unchallenged, crude stereotypes can easily harden into prejudices, especially when reinforced by peer or group pressure. Infants, it appears, learn attitudes in the same way that they learn facts. Stereotypes are thus fairly easy to dislodge at this age. By the time pupils reach secondary school their attitudes are much more entrenched and difficult to modify (see Figures 3 and 4).

Teaching strategies

The fact that children develop their geographical understanding from an early age has significant implications for teachers. To begin with, it is important to discover what pupils already know before teaching them something new and to engage with their personal experiences, which are often highly individual. Not only does this serve to eliminate repetition, it also helps with lesson planning. New knowledge, as Bruner has pointed out, is much more secure if it is keyed into existing patterns of understanding. Conversely, misconceptions can obstruct even the best-planned lesson, confusing pupils as they seek to grasp new ideas.

Figure 5 | *Primary geography involves studies of both the local area and distant places from the earliest years.*

Regarding curriculum content, there are strong reasons for introducing children to geography from the earliest ages upwards. Children are naturally curious about their surroundings and we can harness this energy to enhance their knowledge and understanding. One of the aims of curriculum planning is to ensure that pupils have a reasonable balance of topics and are introduced to new ideas in a logical and progressive manner. Blyth and Krause (1995) have proposed a model of progression in geography which is particularly compelling.

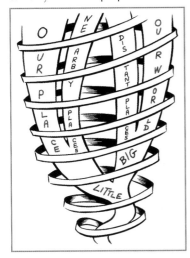

They see the curriculum in terms of four main strands:
1) the local area
2) nearby places
3) distant places
4) the wider world.

Basing their ideas loosely on Bruner's spiral curriculum, they argue that all four strands need to represented at each stage of development. However, as children grow older they will revisit the strands in increasing breadth and complexity. One of the strengths of this model is that it acknowledges how the local and the distant are intertwined. Another advantage is that it acknowledges that pupils need to consolidate their learning by revisiting it in a number of different ways (Figure 5).

In recent years there have been a number of new developments which have further illuminated our thinking about primary geography. Perhaps the most profound comes from research into the workings of the brain.

Using radioactive trackers, neuroscientists are able to identify which areas of the brain 'light up' when we do particular tasks. Not only has this shown that very simple activities can involve complex brain operations, but also that almost everything that we do involves both an emotional and intellectual component. It seems our 'thinking' and 'emotional' brains work in tandem and cannot easily be separated.

One of the reasons why the emotions are so crucial is because they focus our attention which in turn drives our learning and memory systems. Deep and meaningful learning can only occur when we are emotionally engaged. This in turn depends on a secure and affirmative classroom environment.

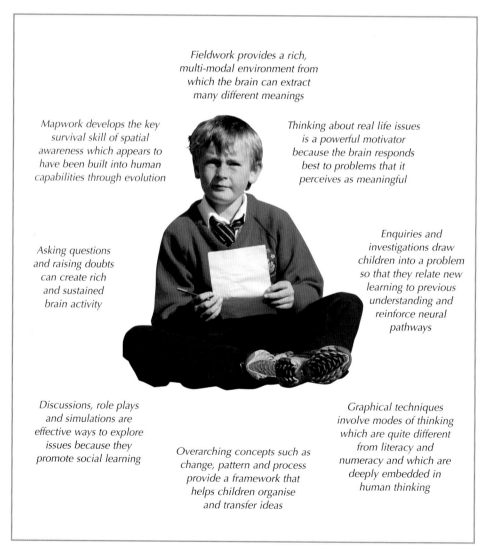

Fieldwork provides a rich, multi-modal environment from which the brain can extract many different meanings

Mapwork develops the key survival skill of spatial awareness which appears to have been built into human capabilities through evolution

Thinking about real life issues is a powerful motivator because the brain responds best to problems that it perceives as meaningful

Asking questions and raising doubts can create rich and sustained brain activity

Enquiries and investigations draw children into a problem so that they relate new learning to previous understanding and reinforce neural pathways

Discussions, role plays and simulations are effective ways to explore issues because they promote social learning

Overarching concepts such as change, pattern and process provide a framework that helps children organise and transfer ideas

Graphical techniques involve modes of thinking which are quite different from literacy and numeracy and which are deeply embedded in human thinking

Figure 6 | *Many of the strategies used in primary geography teaching are compatible with our new understanding about the working of the brain.* **Photo** | *Shaun Flannery.*

Fortunately geography, because it is such a rich and varied subject, provides young children with a great number of entry points, any one of which can harness their enthusiasm. In addition, geography teachers have a long tradition of linking classroom learning with the outside world which makes it more personal and meaningful. They have also promoted methods of learning that encourage pupils to ask questions, test hypotheses and transfer ideas from one situation to another. These different approaches, which practitioners know are effective from long experience, are increasingly being validated by empirical evidence from the new science of learning (Figure 6).

Investigating the quality and character of different places is an essential component of any worthwhile geography curriculum. Children are uniquely equipped to undertake these studies as they have a freshness of vision and a strong natural desire to explore their surroundings. As the 19th-century educationalist Friedrich Froebel put it, children 'seek adventure high and low' in their 'desire to control the diversity of things' and 'see individual things in their connection with the whole' (Lilley, 1967). We need to encourage them in this endeavour from an early age.

References and further reading

Ballin, B. (2010) 'Making connections through school partnerships', *Primary Geographer*, 71, pp 26-28.

Blyth, A. and Krause, J. (1995) *Primary Geography*. London: Hodder and Stoughton.

Disney, A. (2005) 'Children's images of a distant locality', *International Research in Geographical and Environmental Education*, 14, 4, pp. 330-335.

Gesell, A. (1949) 'Pediatrics and child psychiatry', *Pediatrics*, 4, 670-676. Quoted in Fisher, R. (1995) *Teaching children to think*. Cheltenham: Nelson Thornes.

Gosse, E. (1965) *Father and Son*. London: Heinemann.

Goswami, U. (2008) 'Principles of learning, implications for teaching: a cognitive neuroscience approach', *Journal of Philosophy of Education*, 42, 3-4, pp. 381-399.

Graham, J. and Lynn, S. (1989) 'Mud huts and flints: children's images of the third world', *Education 3-13*, 17, 2, pp. 29-32.

Hart, R. (1979) *Children's Experience of Place*. New York: Irvington.

Large, J. (2004) 'Watch how you go', *Primary Geographer*, 53, pp. 56-7.

Lilley, I. (ed) (1967) *Friedrich Froebel: A selection of his writings*. Cambridge: CUP.

Maddern, K. (2010) 'Tie-ups with developing world leave children with 'neocolonialist' views, research shows', *Times Educational Supplement*, 5 March. Available online at *www.tes.co.uk/article.aspx?storycode=6038085* (last accessed 21 June 2010)

Malone, K. (2007) 'The bubble-wrap generation: children growing up in walled gardens', *Environmental Education Research*, 13, 4, pp. 513-527.

Matthews, M. (1995) 'Cultural, environmental experience and environmental awareness: making sense of young Kenyan children's views of place', *The Geographical Journal*, 3, 161, pp. 285-295.

Owens, P. (2003) *Fields of Meaning: The construction of environmental meaning and value in the early years*, unpublished PhD thesis. Canterbury: Canterbury Christ Church University.

Palmer, J. and Birch, J. (2004) *Geography in the Early Years*. London: RoutledgeFalmer.

Ross, N. (2005) 'Children's space', *International Research in Geographical and Environmental Education*, 14, 4, pp. 336-341.

Wiegand, P. (2006) *Learning and Teaching with Maps*. London: Routledge.

Geography, creativity and place

Figure 1 | *Ed makes a detailed and poetic description of the physical properties of an old wall.* **Photo** | *Rhian Langford.*

Geography and creativity are not words that are usually associated with each other. Etymologically speaking, 'geography' comes from the Greek word *geographia* meaning 'Earth writing'; a concrete and clear-cut activity if ever there was one. During the last century, geography was considered to be a subject dealing with hard facts about our world, such as the names of continents, capitals and countries, and descriptions of landscapes, rivers and economies. Today, definitions of the subject are much wider, and include social perspectives and broad concepts about the world. These concepts include change, sustainability, environment, interdependence, character, fieldwork (Figure 1), environmental improvement and futures education. Geography has always been imbued with creative potential, but as the curriculum has become more sensitive to the way that children learn, its potential is significantly increased. Creativity involves imagination and activity to produce an outcome which is both original and of some value. While creativity varies in degree and impact, it always involves making connections between two previously unconnected items or ideas.

Creativity may range from exceptional insights which permanently change our thinking to everyday flashes of inventiveness that are only valuable for a moment. However, it is important to recognise that creativity is much more than just inspiration; it also involves the rigorous testing and evaluation of ideas. From an educational point of view, creativity is therefore closely associated with thinking and learning skills.

Contrary to popular belief, one of the other features of creativity is that it can be taught. Creativity does not automatically imply talent, nor is it something that is fixed. Everyone is capable of creative activity and achievement and everyone can improve their performance. It follows that teachers can provide the conditions for everyday creativity, by providing multiple opportunities for lateral thinking, reflection, imagination and the sharing of ideas. A creative education might be expected to be personal, imaginative, value-rich, individually configured and emotional. It is no coincidence that these are precisely the qualities which Britain will depend on both economically and socially as the 21st century develops (Robinson, 2001; Claxton, 1998).

Figure 2 | *There are many different entry points to learning.* **Photo** | *Shaun Flannery.*

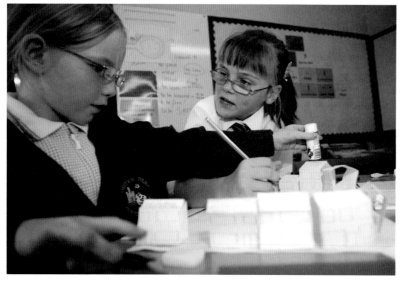

A creative view of geography

Teachers today have the opportunity to adopt an enlightened approach to teaching geography, following advice from the government and the Geographical Association, which has highlighted the importance of curiosity about places, sensitivity towards the environment, open-mindedness towards peoples or cultures and questioning what might happen in the future. Official guidance such as the Roberts report (Roberts, 2006) and inspection findings (Ofsted, 2010) endorse this approach. By adopting a more personal, emotional and creative approach to their subject teachers can ensure that geography thrives on the 'information revolution', offering pupils a good deal more than the diet of facts and simple data that is now available to them via the internet (see Figure 2). This approach can be seen as a way of integrating the following:

- The factual and the imaginative
- The analytical and the emotional
- Objective truth and personal values
- The global and the local.
- The general and the unique

What follow are examples of actual lessons which illustrate a 'creative approach' to geography in the context of the above pairings.

Lesson 1: The factual and the imaginative

Harvey's nursery class is listening to a counting story, but the words do not seem as important to the pupils as the bold and interesting illustrations in the book. The book, *Over in the Jungle* (Berkes and Canyon, 2007), contains a series of illustrations of rainforest creatures. The pupils are eagerly telling Harvey what they can see in the pictures. As Harvey observed afterwards, 'The influence of the illustrations was such that the storyline took a back seat in their learning'.

Through this activity pupils as young as three and four years old are engaging with some of the core components of geography: describing environments; observing and discussing change in the environment; coming to conclusions about what counts for quality in the environment; and thinking about damaged environments and how we might improve them.

After focused discussion Harvey suggests making a painting of the rainforest. The pupils begin the task with real gusto, eager to put down in picture form their thoughts and new understandings (Figure 3).

Harvey has taken the pupils on a journey that has led to a demonstrable sensitivity to a quite distant world. At least in the short term, attitudes seem to have changed. He reports 'By the

Objectives	Transcribed conversation
Understand key vocabulary associated with landscape	Teacher: Wow that looks great! Is that the sea? Pupil: Yeah and I got sand too. And lots of monkeys. Teacher: What else have you painted? Pupil: Birds and flowers and lots of nice birds.
Compare and contrast with home area	Pupil: I've got a tree in my garden. Teacher: Have you? Does it look like the one in the picture? Pupil: Yeah, it does, but mine's smaller; those are massive. I like my tree though. They look nice too. I can climb my tree to the top. Those are really big!
Interpreting pictures	Teacher: What are you painting? It looks like a rainforest. Pupil: Yes. Teacher: Can you tell me what's in your picture? Pupil: It's a forest with creepers and vines and lots of trees. Teacher: What's the brown for? Pupil: That's the mud.
Knowledge of distant places	Teacher: What do you think the climate will be like in the rainforest? Pupil: Climate ...? Teacher: Will it be cold? Pupil: No! It's hot, wet and hot, really hot and sweaty!

Figure 3 | *The thinking behind the artwork.*

end of the scheme of work the pupils' misconceptions about the jungle had disappeared and been replaced by positive, geographically valid ideas. They were fascinated by the creatures, and wanted to know more about them and the plants that live there. Their enthusiasm carried over into dance and drama where the children each adopted an animal and imitated it to appropriate music.' This project started with the use of the image and imagination to engage and motivate children, but led to deeper thought and cross-curricular activities. Essentially, the painting exercise gave pupils time to dream and reflect; creative activity was the door to deeper engagement and transferable geographical learning.

Lesson 2: Objective truth and personal values

Cherry wants to teach her class about a place in India. The pupils in her year 3 class have severe learning difficulties. She knows that they learn better through their senses (touch, sound, taste, smell, sight and movement) than they do by listening to her speak. She knows too that they concentrate particularly hard when they are involved in their favourite activities, such as singing, making music and cooking.

Figure 4 | *Music used as a way in to a distant locality.* **Photo** | *Cherry Barnes.*

Cherry has visited India and collected a wide range of teaching resources. She starts her lesson by singing a gentle Indian melody against a silent video of a street market. The pupils participate by tapping small bells and drums (Figure 4) that instantly give the song an Indian flavour. Cherry tells the pupils they are going to find out about living in a faraway place, and helps them dress in local costumes – saris, dhotis, and headscarves. While they are dressing, Cherry plays a CD of Indian tabla and sitar music. Once in their Indian clothes, the pupils are helped to board an imaginary plane, holding passports and luggage. Their flight (with an appropriate flying song) takes them on the long journey to Chennai, the capital of Tamil Nadu.

The school's sensory room represents Chennai for the pupils. The room is lit with twinkly colours and hung with oriental fabrics. Hot-air blowers and fine water sprays produce a warm, damp atmosphere. The humid air is filled with the smell of spices. Cherry asks the pupils what it feels like now they have arrived in Chennai. Some are able to answer 'hot and sweaty'; others are engrossed in the video which is now showing pictures of traffic and congestion in a busy Indian city.

Photo |
Shaun Flannery.

Meanwhile, Bandana, a school volunteer, has arrived in the classroom to cook some Indian food. When the pupils return, their room is already filled with different smells and the sound of spices being crushed in a granite mortar. The pupils help to crush cinnamon, cardamom and anise and pass the powders around to each other to smell. While they are helping with the cooking, Cherry and a teaching assistant have laid out a market stall behind the group. Fruit, vegetables, brushes and sacks of rice are arranged on the floor to represent a street market and the pupils are invited to come and shop. They want to ask their friends from the next door classroom to come too. Tomorrow they will learn an Indian dance.

Activities like these would be exciting for any pupils, but Cherry feels that they also promote the learning of information and teach positive values. Pupils in her class are learning that difference is not necessarily threatening, that unusual sounds, tastes and smells can be good, that people from other cultures are the same as them and that diversity is interesting. Cherry can tell instantly through facial expressions and individual sounds that the pupils are enjoying experiences like these; she knows the lesson has enriched their lives. The fact that the pupils wanted to share the experience with other classes was strong evidence that the session had affected their values.

This lesson highlights some key issues for primary geography. As children become increasingly aware of our global interdependence, they realise that what they regard as 'true' or 'right' may not be the same for all other people. This is so within complex multicultural societies like ours; recognising it helps us appreciate why it is so difficult for multinational organisations like the UN and EU to come to unanimous decisions. The government has always included statements of values in the national curriculum. Values which are particularly relevant to geography include the contributions of a diverse range of people, cultures and heritages to our society and the need to protect the environment as the basis of life and a source of wonder and inspiration. More specifically, we should:

▮ Refuse to support values or actions that may be harmful to individuals or communities
▮ Respect religious and cultural diversity
▮ Contribute to, as well as benefit fairly from, economic and cultural resources
▮ Accept our responsibility to maintain a sustainable environment for future generations
▮ Understand the place of human beings within nature
▮ Ensure that development can be justified
▮ Preserve balance and diversity in nature wherever possible
▮ Preserve areas of beauty and interest for future generations
▮ Repair, wherever possible, habitats damaged by human development and other means.

Figure 5 | *Canterbury through history. Work by year 5 pupils at St Peter's Methodist Primary School, Canterbury.*

Lesson 3: The general and the unique

Looking for patterns in the weather, landscape, human activity and environment has been a key geographical activity for generations, but Richard wanted to help his pupils understand local geography in a more personal and meaningful way. Since part of the town centre was being redeveloped as a shopping centre, Richard invited his year 5 class to think about continuity and change in their locality (Rogers and Barnes, 2003). The pupils had already learnt about the history of the area by visiting the archaeological excavation being undertaken at the redevelopment site. They had met executives from the development company and seen films and projections of what the site would look like in the future. Richard set about collecting all the maps he could find which showed this area of the town at different periods. He found copies of maps made in 1640, 1750, 1801, the 1870s, 1912 and the 1950s to add to the school collection of modern maps. He then used the photocopier to reduce or enlarge each map to a similar scale. His lesson used the map reading skills the pupils had been taught earlier in the term.

Richard divided the pupils into groups of four. Each group was given a map of the redevelopment area, but from a different historical period. The first task was to note down the main features shown on the map. Bringing this information together after ten minutes it became obvious that certain features were the same whatever the date. For example, the city wall, the burial mound, the cathedral, the flint church, the pub and piece of open land all remained constants. The class was then briefly reminded about the orientation exercises they had done while on a weekend adventure holiday. In their groups they were asked to work together to imagine what the views would have been like to the north, south, east and west from a central point at the time their map was made. This activity generated a great deal of talk as the groups formed their ideas using direction, map symbols, scale and historical knowledge. The views were drawn as borders around the edge of their photocopied maps (Figure 5) and displayed. Change and continuity were depicted strongly in the different scenes shown in the frames. The work made a strong impression on each of the participants and they remembered the detail and implications very precisely when they were interviewed months later.

The experience of provoking imagination through studying maps was to become even more personal. In the following lesson Richard asked the class to imagine the future, after the new shopping centre was built, after the saplings had matured, even perhaps after the motorcar had been superseded. Each pupil used a base map of familiar streets to demonstrate their own understanding of what might be visible from the same place in 2050. The results were startlingly individual, but also displayed the internalisation of the idea of change and continuity and feelings about what it was important to preserve in the context of a specific place.

The world is full of patterns and processes. Learning in geography is very much about identifying, analysing and evaluating them. We should never lose sight of the fact that the patterns geography exposes and the processes it describes help us to make sense of a world

Photo | *Paula Richardson.*

that might otherwise seem chaotic. Geographical patterns and processes are nonetheless thoughtful generalisations and teachers need to help pupils construct such generalisations, starting by helping pupils to see the patterns and processes in the place where they are.

Lesson 4: The analytical and the emotional

A year 4 class is working with their teacher, Kirsty, beside a river and an old building behind the school. They have been given a diagram and asked to label it. The river bank slopes gently where the pupils are standing, but on the opposite side, where the water is travelling faster, some pupils have noticed that the bank is steep. They are excited by this observation and are discussing whether it might be more dangerous to stand on the far side:

Pupil A: 'If you stood there you'd fall right in.'
Pupil B: 'No you wouldn't, it's safe.'
Pupil A: 'The bank would fall down, 'cos it's just soil.'
Teacher: 'That's interesting, do you think the steep bank has got anything to do with the fast water?'
Pupil B: 'It might be wearing it away. Look' (points to a large twig scraping the river bank).

This discussion is typical of those that happen repeatedly when pupils learn in an educational setting which truly promotes thinking. Fieldwork instantly puts pupils in a context that provokes and interests them because natural and built environments beyond school are automatically richer and more generative than even the most stimulating classrooms.

The lesson continues and the pupils go on collecting words and making descriptions of the river. The little drawings and diagrams they produce involve a relatively low level or 'everyday' creativity, but the atmosphere changes when Kirsty asks them to sit on the grass with their eyes closed and listen to the water. After a full four minutes of silent listening with (she hopes) open minds, Kirsty very quietly asks the pupils to say the words which have come into their heads. She writes them down – rustling, wind, tweeting, brrr, swirling, silent, swishing, quiet, click, crunch of twigs, shimmering, lapping, tinkling. As the responses are beginning to slow down Kirsty reminds the pupils of the Japanese poems they had been reading and learning about the day before. She asks the pupils to find their own space to try to write a simple poem in the same style. Here are two examples:

Photo |
Diane Wright.

Walls with small bumps
Plaster pointed lumps
River flowing at a lazy pace
Water ripples and weaves around columns
Swirling and whirling as if fine lace.
(Jonathan)

Photo | *Diane Wright.*

Water swirling across stones sticking up
Very silent swishing
The water bed covered with little pebbles
A dark browny colour the water is
Bright green leaves shining in the water.
(Dorothy)

This may be described as a literacy activity, but it has arisen out of a geography field trip, so is it now geography? It does not matter of course. What Kirsty and her pupils have discovered is that real experience cuts across subject disciplines all the time. The poems which Dorothy and Jonathan wrote employ skills from both literacy and geography. Their work exhibits imagination, intuition, analysis and evaluation in full measure and it is clear that lasting learning has taken place. Geographical truths came via physical and emotional engagement. The mind, spirit, body and senses combined to effect attitude change. These pupils will not feel the same about this river again.

Lesson 5: The global and the local

Stephen is teaching a year 6 class about Tanzania as part of the school's Africa Week. He has explained how he visited Tanzania the previous summer and visited the village of Vunta in the Pare Hills where aid dependency is a serious problem. He has also provided pupils with information about the climate, landscape and people who live in the area. Now the pupils are working in small groups on a number of detailed (and real) farm plans. They have already learned how to interpret a map and are used to reading climate statistics. They have also examined real artefacts from Tanzania in a previous session.

It is clear that the pupils have made sense of and identified with the four hectares of steeply sloping and fragmented farmland which has been allocated to them. Each group has also been allocated 5000 Tanzanian shillings (about £50) to spend for the year ahead and is responsible for feeding, caring for and educating the rest of their 'family' (eight people). In addition to these meagre funds, they can plan to use their own physical resources to improve their particular plot of land and make it profitable. The conversations around the farm plans are revealing:

- 'We can't build a fishpond here, it would just dry up. There's no shade.'
- 'Can't we just sell off that extra bit of land over there, I'm sure Njogu's family would buy it, and then we could buy one of those big cows that give lots of milk. You know, those Friesian ones.'
- 'Yeah, then we could sell it at the market.'
- 'I wish we had even a little stream. Couldn't we all work together and build a channel which could water three farms?'
- 'How are we going to pay the workers?'

The situation seems very real to the pupils, and their individual contributions are focused and thoughtful. However, this imaginative activity is more than just emotionally engaging, it introduces pupils to development issues in a meaningful way. The problems they are discussing are similar to those which face poor farmers in all parts of the economically developing world. Pupils in this class are learning from the inside about the complexity of development, about the need for small-scale appropriate solutions and about the difference working in teams can make. At the same time the work gives pupils the opportunity to apply some of the key skills of geography and to show the degree to which they understand and can use tables, maps, graphs and climate statistics. Finally, they are relating the problems of the economically developing world to their own situation and circumstances. We all need food, water and shelter: the question is, how can people best meet these needs in different parts of the world?

In his assessment of individual responses to this task Stephen is convinced that 80% of his pupils can readily transfer these skills to other situations. Metacognitive learning of this kind has enduring value. Such life skills are best taught in a shared context, and pupils may develop individual insight and attitudes through their part in powerful and informed role play.

What do these examples show?

Each of the examples above illustrates how primary geography lessons can be both creative and combined with other subjects. They also show how to teach or extend key geographical skills, including mapwork, fieldwork, the use of photographs and geographical vocabulary, and recording and expressing geographical views.

All the lessons have built up a knowledge and understanding of places and have identified patterns and processes. Most have helped pupils to understand the notion of environmental change and consider sustainable development. Such activities deal in facts and specialised understandings that would be familiar to geographers anywhere. These lessons also illustrate another important principle; that traditional and creative approaches in geography are not necessarily opposed.

- An imaginative stimulus generated an atmosphere in which geographical vocabulary and facts were easily internalised by nursery-aged children
- Positive images of India resulted from an imaginary visit linked to video footage of a market and supported by food and smells
- Discussing a map of a well-known area in a group setting resulted in a highly individualised but informed view of both the past and the future of the area
- Feelings about places and environment arose from a fieldwork trip to a river
- Role playing an African farmer gave rise to personal responses and led to an understanding of global issues in development education, and transferable geographical skills

Why is place so important?

The skills, knowledge and understandings of geography cannot be fully understood unless applied to actual places. Place is a central concept in geography, but why should we use a place to stimulate creativity? Here are a number of reasons:

- The place where we work is ours. We have an inbuilt emotional involvement with these unique environments and since learning requires an emotional involvement this makes a good starting point.
- Our place of work is, or should be, safe, and a feeling of emotional and physical safety is

essential because our brains have evolved so that emotional or physical survival overrides all other considerations.

▓ The school grounds and buildings round about us are multi-faceted. They represent a fusion of art, design, technology, science, philosophy, geography, history, mathematics, language, culture and creativity.

▓ The local area, whether inner city, suburban or rural, provides a rich environment; authentic, multi-sensory, not imagined and easily related to other knowledge.

▓ Our places are (sometimes literally) concrete, but our pupils spend much of their time being asked to consider abstract answers to abstract problems when we know that many of them have real difficulty in abstract thought. Our 'survival oriented' brains are good at fine discrimination, categorising, handling and sensing but need metaphors and external prompts to help them develop and handle new thoughts.

We know environments, like our minds, are plastic; they are always changing, but we can have some say over those changes. If either our places or minds are not supple, they become ineffective, inappropriate and ultimately useless. Personal and community inventiveness has a big part to play in keeping mind and place flexible. There is a strong metaphorical and practical link between our minds and our places. All places are shaped by people, through history, culture, community and technologies. In a modern and fast-changing world where the total information available to us doubles every two years (Robinson, 2001), we can no longer teach geography as a rigid body of knowledge, but must consider it as a disciplined but imaginative process which deepens our understanding of the places we share.

References and further reading

Baker, J. (1989) *Where the Forest Meets the Sea*. London: Walker Books.

Barnes, J. (2007) *Cross-Curricular Learning 3-14*. London: Chapman.

Berkes, M. and Canyon, J. (2007) *Over in the Jungle: A rainforest rhyme*. Nevada City: Dawn Publications.

Claxton, G. (1998) *Hare Brain Tortoise Mind*. London: Fourth Estate.

Craft, A. (2005) *Creativity in Schools: Tensions and dilemmas*. London: Routledge.

Craft, A. Cremin, T. and Burnard, P. (eds) (2008) *Creative Learning 3-11*. Stoke on Trent: Trentham.

Csikszentmihalyi, M. (1996) *Creativity, Flow and the Psychology of Discovery and Invention*. New York: Harper Collins.

Fisher, R. (2005) *Teaching Children to Think*. Cheltenham: Nelson Thornes.

Gardner, H. (2006) *Five Minds for the Future*. Boston: Harvard Business School.

Ofsted (2010) *Learning: Creative approaches that raise standards*. London: Ofsted.

Roberts, P. (2006) *Nurturing Creativity in Young People: A report to government to inform policy*. London: DCMS.

Robinson, K. (2001) *Out of Our Minds*. Oxford: Capstone.

Robinson, K. (2009) *The Element*. London: Allen Lane.

Rogers, R. and Barnes, J. (2003) 'Past, present, future', *Primary Geographer*, 50, pp. 22-3.

Websites

Philosophy for children *www.sapere.org.uk*

TeacherNet philosophy *www.teachernet.gov.uk/teachingandlearning/subjects*

See also the 'Geography & Creativity' articles in the EY and Primary section of the GA website *www.geography.org.uk*

CHAPTER COVERAGE:
CREATIVITY • CROSS-CURRICULAR LINKS • DISTANT PLACES • ENVIRONMENT • IDENTITY
• INCLUSION/SEN • ISSUES • LEARNING THEORY • LOCAL AREA • PHOTOGRAPHS

Geography and the emotions

Geography is about places, and places can provoke powerful emotional reactions. Dramatically beautiful places evoke feelings of awe and wonder and harsh environments a sense of fear or alienation. People feel affection for otherwise ordinary places which have personal significance. Environmental issues, too, can arouse strong passions, as witnessed by any proposal to build a new bypass, demolish an attractive building, limit car usage or cut carbon emissions.

The term emotional literacy was first used by Claude Steiner. He suggests emotional literacy has three elements: 'the ability to understand your emotions, the ability to listen to others and empathise with their emotions, and the ability to express emotions productively' (Steiner and Perry, 1997, p. 11).

The term emotional intelligence has been popularised by Daniel Goleman, who argues that emotional intelligence may be more important than intelligence quotient (IQ) for success in life (Goleman, 1996). Building on Howard Gardner's work on multiple intelligences (Gardner, 1983), Goleman suggests that emotional intelligence involves five main domains. The first three of these relate to what Gardner refers to as intrapersonal intelligence, whereas the last two relate to the interpersonal aspects of emotional quotient (EQ):

1. Knowing one's emotions involves self awareness and recognising feelings as they happen, and is the keystone of emotional intelligence.
2. Managing emotions is concerned with self regulation and handling feelings in an appropriate way.
3. Motivating oneself is concerned with goal achievement and so is essential for maintaining attention, self-motivation, and creativity.

4. Recognising emotions in others involves understanding others and developing empathy, and is a fundamental interpersonal skill.
5. Handling relationships is concerned with social competence and is therefore related to the ability to influence others, communicate well, manage conflict and work collaboratively.

Goleman has created worldwide interest in the concept of emotional intelligence, arguing that teaching pupils the skills of emotional literacy is as important as teaching other forms of literacy:

'In navigating our lives, it is our fears and envies, our rages and depressions, our worries and anxieties that steer us day to day. Even the most academically brilliant amongst us are vulnerable to being undone by unruly emotions. The price we paid for emotional illiteracy is in failed marriages and troubled families, in stunted social and work lives, in deteriorating physical health and mental anguish' (Goleman, 1996, p. 43).

The two concepts are closely related, and are often used interchangeably. Emotional literacy appears to be a broader term, increasingly used in education, while emotional intelligence is more associated with business and leadership.

To nurture emotional literacy and emotional intelligence we need to attend to children's feelings and reactions. Emotionally literate people are able to recognise and manage their own feelings and build constructive and effective relationships with others. It is now widely recognised that emotional intelligence is crucial for success in personal and professional life (Goleman, 1996). The difference between emotional literacy and emotional intelligence is explored in Figure 1.

Geography has a particular contribution to make to the development of emotional literacy because the study of real places, real people and real-life issues is at its core. In investigating places, people and issues, primary age pupils can explore the significance of the affective domain in relation to place, space and the environment.

Figure 1 | *Emotional literacy and emotional intelligence.*

It amplifies the thinking in a number of influential government initiatives such as *Excellence and Enjoyment* (DfES, 2003), *Every Child Matters* (DfES, 2004), the SEAL programme (DCSF, 2005) and the Healthy Schools agenda. It also reflects the increased importance attached to children's happiness and well-being in the national curriculum.

Education and the emotions

There is a long tradition of interest in the role of education in promoting emotional development which may be traced back to the work of John Dewey and other progressive educators. But, as Suzie Orbach, a psychoanalyst and co-founder of Antidote (a national charity devoted to promoting emotional literacy) has argued, the relentless focus on raising standards and on targets, tests and league tables has meant that 'it has been difficult for arguments about the importance of emotional development in schooling to find a place on the agenda' (Orbach, 1998). Indeed the philosophical underpinning for the national curriculum derives ultimately from the work of thinkers such as Kant and Descartes who specifically separated the affective and the intellectual.

Recent developments in neuroscience suggest that strong links exist between emotions and thinking as well as between feeling and understanding. Studies of patients whose brains have been damaged in the areas specifically associated with the emotions have established that a lack of affective input severely compromises social interactions and judgements. In other words, damage to the brain's emotional circuits restricts our ability to live a meaningful life. As far as learning is concerned, it appears that the emotions, either conscious or unconscious, provide a platform for cognitive thought (Immordino-Yang and Damasio, 2007). They are also crucial in generating motivation, a crucial ingredient in the learning process. Neuroscientist Usha Goswami (2008) believes that a number of principles can be 'safely' applied to education. These include the value of multi-sensory teaching and the importance of safe and secure environments. Such principles may appear to support what teachers already know, but it is significant that neuroscientists now have empirical evidence to validate them.

On a general level our new understanding of the significance of the emotions in learning suggests that paying more attention to the affective domain may help to raise standards across the curriculum. This applies equally to slow learners and gifted and talented pupils. McCarthy and Park (1998) summarise the key arguments for emotional learning as follows:

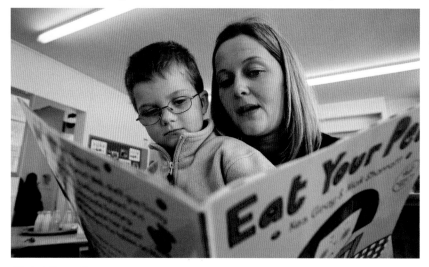

Photo | Shaun Flannery.

- understanding emotions is directly connected with motivation and with cognitive achievement
- dealing with emotions helps to develop better relationships and a sense of psychological and mental well-being
- emotionally developed young people are better equipped to live with difference
- our moral outlook and value systems are deeply shaped by our attitudes and feelings; and
- our sense of meaning and purpose is derived as much from feeling as from understanding.

Emotional literacy in the school curriculum

In terms of the wider curriculum framework, emotional literacy and intelligence have particularly strong links with physical health and well-being, as the SEAL programme acknowledges. This area of the curriculum is concerned with preparing children for life now and in the future. It is about developing their self-knowledge, their ability to understand and manage their feelings, to build relationships with other pupils and adults, and to understand their local community and national society. As Elaine Jackson has comprehensively demonstrated, there are strong natural connections between primary geography and physical and emotional development. Both provide opportunities to express opinions; to develop an understanding of the place of the individual in society, and of collective rights and responsibilities; to develop empathy, and an awareness of the points of view of others, and cultural understanding of other societies. In addition, active learning in geography requires purposeful pupil interaction, group activities, co-operative working, collaboration, reasoned debate, negotiation and informed decision-making. (Jackson, 2000, p. 34)

Some years ago, Frances Slater suggested that geography education should seek to develop both reason and feeling (Slater, 1994), echoing a persistent argument that really meaningful learning in any subject engages both the intellect and emotions. Geography offers three major opportunities for developing emotional literacy:

- It helps children to recognise and express emotions associated with places and environmental issues;
- It provides opportunities to develop empathetic understanding of others' feelings and views; and
- It develops interpersonal skills through the active learning approaches required by meaningful geographical enquiry.

Attachment to place

It is well known that secure attachment to significant people is important for young children's psychological growth and health. It is also argued that attachment to place can be equally significant, for as Spencer (2005) argues, the emotional bonds that we form with places are part of our identity. Identification with and attachment to place is expressed in many ways, such as supporting a local football team, identifying oneself as a Yorkshirewoman, campaigning to preserve a locally significant building, or studying local history. Most people appear to be interested in and care about the place they live, and this attachment to place seems to have its roots in childhood experiences.

For many adults some of their strongest memories and recollections of childhood relate to places. Most of us recall in some detail, and often with affection, the homes where we were raised, the buildings in which we were educated, and the places we played in. While I was writing this chapter I drove every day past the site where a gracious but outdated Edwardian school was being replaced. Several weeks before the site was due to be vacated, a large sign appeared outside inviting people to 'Say goodbye to the old buildings'. This invitation represents an acknowledgement that former pupils, teachers and local residents may have feelings of sadness when a locally significant landmark is demolished. In her study of adults' memories of childhood places, Louise Chawla found that affectionate memories were associated with 'places to which we trace our roots, which are associated with happiness and security … there is a parallel between the warmth of feeling for the place and people in it' (Chawla, 1986, quoted in Titman, 1994, p. 7).

Simon Catling argues that children's experience of places is a vital part of their lives, contributing to their sense of self, identity and self-esteem (Catling, 2003). It is also often said that young children are natural geographers (Scoffham, 1998). From early infancy, they start to learn about their surroundings through direct first-hand experience, and so become familiar with 'their place'. Through secondary sources of information such as television, books, photographs and pictures, they also begin to form perceptions about 'other places' beyond their experience. Both known places and (as yet) unvisited places evoke feelings in, and have meaning for, children and inform their developing sense of place. As Noddings (2003) puts it: 'place figures prominently in the happiness of individuals, and is also central to creative work' (p. 33). Bonnett (2004) makes a similar point in a different way when he declares that our relationship with nature, whatever its kind, sets 'the contours of what can count as human flourishing' (p. 30).

By the time they enter school, children will already have developed knowledge of their familiar environments, and will also have feelings about them. Their environments will be, as Catling points out, not only physical places but also 'affective places, places for fun and enjoyment with freedom of movement or places of limits, exclusions and, perhaps, fears' (Catling, 2003, p. 173). During their primary years, children's experience of known places extends as they are given or take greater freedom to move unsupervised around the local area. Furthermore, these early childhood experiences have an impact which carries through into adult life. Many of today's environmental activists, for example, can point to first-hand experiences in the natural world that nurtured their later enthusiasm and interests (Palmer, 1998). The importance of 'significant life experiences' of this kind is also recognised in many biographies.

Titman (1994) too notes that children consistently express strong positive reactions to relatively 'natural' areas. She found that although they were keenly aware of the intrinsic value of the environment and of the need to care for the natural world as the home of all living things, children also valued natural places because of the way they made them feel. Natural places were judged to be peaceful, but were also associated with freedom, adventure and challenge. Environmental elements seen positively included natural colour, trees, woods, shady areas, big grassy areas, places with different levels, places where you can climb/hide/explore/make a den, places that have 'millions of bits', and places with wildlife.

Special places

Pupils in a year 5 class were asked by their teacher to think about places which were special to them. Many produced carefully executed pictures to show their special place, and wrote about why it mattered to them, and how they felt about it when in it.

Of the 30 pupils, 16 (both boys and girls) nominated their own bedroom as their special place. Many described their bedroom in great detail and explained what they enjoyed doing in it. Bedrooms were referred to as places of safety, where they could relax and 'be themselves'.

'I can have a happy time reading. I am relaxed and calm, especially when I read one of my books or magazines. My bed is very cosy and comfortable and warm. It is blue with daisies all over. I have lots of cuddly toys in my bed and I feel safe.'

'Because nobody shares it me with me – it's always there to turn to when I am sad and weary.'

Several others reported that they valued their bedroom as a place where they could withdraw from family life, especially contact with siblings: 'What I like best is that my brother can't come in'. Friends, however, were welcome in many bedrooms, as their presence was associated with fun. One pupil offered a particularly detailed picture of her bedroom and what it meant to her:

'My special place is a corner of my room. It has got a bean bag, books, a CD player, games, a cuddly toy, cushions and a lamp. It's special to me because I can have some space and just chill out. I normally just sit down, put my music on low and read a book. It really helps when I do that. If I have just fallen out with my mum and dad, I can relax and get it all out of my system. What I like best is the space to do whatever I want. It really annoys me when people break the atmosphere by knocking on my door, just to ask a stupid question'.

A wide range of other types of places were nominated by the pupils as particularly special to them. These included the local park, a tent, a shed in the garden, a shop owned by parents, a grandma's house, Disneyland Paris, the London Eye, an Indian beach, a fast-food restaurant in India and an aqua park in Corfu.

In many cases these places were associated with enjoyable activities, happy memories, or with people to whom the pupils were attached. The girl who chose the local park said:

'I like this place because I made my first best friend there. I also meet my friends there sometimes, we have lots of fun. It also brings back memories like the time my brother was playing football with his friends and I was the commentator. I feel very relaxed, especially with my friends, and cheerful and glad too. The thing I like best is that you feel free and have a lot of fresh air. The park will always be my special place even if I move away'.

Animals were significant for two girls, one who enjoyed going to her grandma's to play with the dog, and the other to the shed where she kept guinea pigs:

'My special place is in my shed because my guinea pigs comfort me when I'm down, and when my parents tell me off I feel safe and secure when I'm around my guinea pigs and I enjoy stroking them'.

Only one of the year 5 pupils, a girl, nominated a fantasy place; 'a secret hidden away beach' which she can imagine 'really easily', and where she goes (in her imagination) when she feels down or bored, because 'it feels safe'.

Figure 2 | *Special places – a year 5 case study.*

Dirt, pollution, rubbish, litter, damaged things, unnatural colour, tarmac, places where you can't climb/hide/explore/make a den, and places that were 'boring' or 'too open' were all viewed negatively by children in the study.

Working with feelings

One way of helping children to recognise and acknowledge their feelings about their surroundings is by asking them to think about their favourite places. What parts of their home, school and immediate locality do they value and why? Key stage 1 pupils can conduct a survey of the most liked and disliked places in the school grounds or local area, and discuss the results. This will enable them to explore why people tend to feel more positive about some features or areas than others. The study of a contrasting locality, whether in the UK or overseas, should provide opportunities for children to consider the questions 'How do I feel about this place?', and 'How do other people, including those who live there, feel about it?'. As a broader perspective is developed in key stage 2, pupils can consider their responses to different types of environment – urban, rural, wild and pockets of one within another, e.g. open spaces in an urban area, traditional buildings in rural landscapes. They should be encouraged to attend more deeply to their feelings for the places studied, and to try to understand, articulate and explain them (Figure 2).

At any age, children can be encouraged to express and communicate their affective response to places, spaces and environments in a variety of ways. Many of the oral strategies used in circle time to explore feelings can be successfully adapted to give them a geographical

Photo | Paula Richardson.

focus. For example, the activity 'Someone else's shoes' provides a structure for developing empathy, and would be a useful way of explaining differing views and opinions about an environmental issue. Creative visualisations are another excellent device for focusing on different places, such as a beach or part of the Amazon rainforest.

In addition to communicating through language, teachers can make meaningful cross-curricular links by using the creative and expressive arts. Drama, dance and movement, music and art are all traditionally associated with personal and social development. The way that children, who may be otherwise reticent and withdrawn, take on new persona when placed in a role is well attested. This can be an excellent way of exploring the impact of changes and local issues. Such approaches encourage children to express their feelings about places and issues creatively, and helps them to develop empathy for others' emotions and opinions.

Places as contexts for learning

The school grounds

In recent years, a great deal of attention has been paid to the way school grounds and the environment can be developed for learning and play. Many schools have sought to improve their grounds by setting up ponds, wildlife areas, fitness trails, vegetable and herb gardens, murals, areas for different types of play activity, hedge and tree planting. School grounds improvement projects provide an excellent opportunity for pupils to participate in real-life decision making and environmental enhancement, and experience the roller-coaster of emotions that often accompanies such initiatives. Yet, as Catling (2005) points out, the wider school environment has been largely ignored as a learning resource.

A fascinating study undertaken by Wendy Titman (1994) confirms that the school grounds are very significant places to primary age children. Titman found that pupils had a well-developed concept of their ideal school grounds which would offer plenty of opportunities for them to 'feel' and 'be' as well as 'do' and 'think'. In Titman's words they wanted the school grounds to offer:

> *A place for feeling – which presented colour and beauty and interest, which engendered a sense of ownership and pride and belonging, in which they could be 'small' without feeling vulnerable, where they could care for the place and people in it and feel cared for themselves … [and] … a place for being – which allowed them to be themselves, which recognised their individuality, their need to have a private persona in a public place, privacy, being alone and with friends, for being quiet in noise, for being a child* (Titman, 1994, p. 58).

The local area

The study of the local area is the bedrock of primary geography. It is important to study the school grounds and the immediate locality partly because, in geography, as in other subject areas, we should build on what pupils already know. However, it is also important because through this work, we demonstrate to pupils that where they come from matters and is worthy of study. This in turn helps to create a sense of personal worth. The investigation of local streets, buildings, landmarks and open spaces can enable pupils to really 'see' them for the first time and to appreciate their inherent interest and qualities.

In all key stages, pupils should have opportunities to notice and think about buildings or features of the local area which they or other people value, and which are worthy of care and preservation. Some of these may be of purely local significance, and valued for their amenity value, historical origins, or aesthetic qualities. In every locality there will also be areas or buildings which are in need of improvement or repair or could be better cared for. In addition, many schools will have easy access to an officially recognised 'special' place. There are over 500,000 buildings in the UK listed for their architectural or historical merit, nearly 30,000 monuments and 10,000 conservation areas. Identifying these and considering how they can be used in your geography could be a stimulating early evening INSET session involving the whole staff.

To nurture emotional literacy through local study, teachers can encourage pupils to consider questions such as:

- Where is special in our local area?
- What makes it special?
- How do I feel about this place, building or feature?
- How do other people feel about it?
- How can we encourage everyone to look after it and preserve and enhance its special qualities?

Photo | *Alessandro Vannucci.*

Finding out about the character of different places is central to geography. The best way to do it is through first-hand enquiries and observations.

Distant places

The study of more distant places, within and beyond the UK, also offers opportunities for pupils to attend to their feelings about places and develop empathy for the people who inhabit them. They can be asked to consider a parallel set of questions to those about the local area noted above, for example:

- What is special about this place?
- How do I feel about it?
- How do the people (children/adults, men/women, richer/poorer people) who live there feel about it?
- What could be done to look after this place, and enhance its special qualities?

Learning about a range of places around the world can also help to allay children's natural fears and uncertainties. We all tend to be wary of the unknown and approach it with a mixture of suspicion and excitement. By teaching children about distant places we can help them to develop more complete and balanced images which are based on fact rather than the incomplete, stereotypical and limited images they may pick up from elsewhere.

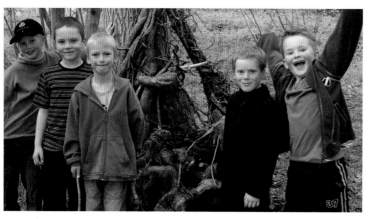

Field trips have huge potential for building engagement and well-being. **Photo** | *Sharon Witt.*

Environmental issues

The study of local and more distant environmental issues also offers pupils the opportunity to express their own feelings and opinions. As they get older and develop a less egocentric view of the world, children are increasingly able to understand that other people may feel differently from themselves, and that there might be a range of legitimate perspectives on environmental issues or problems.

Topical, real-life, local environmental issues can arouse strong feelings, as reading the letters page of any local paper will testify! The study of local issues is very motivating, particularly if it engages pupils in debate with local residents or officials, or leads to action for change. In most communities there is a wide range of issues which could be tackled:

- Poor public transport provision
- Lack of safe places for children to play
- Problems with traffic congestion and parking
- Pedestrian safety
- Protection of open spaces, attractive buildings or significant trees
- Provision of recycling facilities
- Vandalism and graffiti
- Footpath maintenance
- Planning applications for demolition, extensions, or change of use.

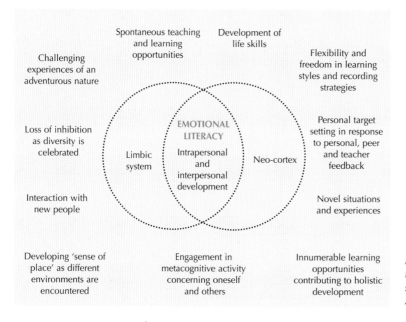

Figure 3 | *Visual framework for the development of emotional skills through residential fieldtrips. After Chantler, 2004.*

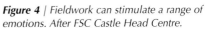

Figure 4 | *Fieldwork can stimulate a range of emotions. After FSC Castle Head Centre.*

At one school in a village on the edge of Leeds, pupils investigated traffic problems and then wrote to the City Planning Department about their concerns. In an inner city school, year 2 pupils lobbied local residents and Councillors about the problem of dog mess in the adjacent park – the only open space in the area. In a third school the parking problems caused by parents driving their children to school led to the establishment of a Walk to School campaign committee. In all these examples, pupils' interest and motivation was high, and very high quality work was completed because both their emotions and intellect were fully engaged. This point has been noted in many HMI and Ofsted reports. In their annual report for 2001/2, for example, the Inspectors noted that 'some of the best work involved pupils in practical activities linked to relevant and real issues' (Ofsted, 2003).

Promoting empathy and interpersonal skills in different contexts

Geographical learning in the primary school provides a valuable context for developing the interpersonal aspects of emotional intelligence. The enquiry approach in particular requires collaborative and co-operative work, through which pupils develop their ability to handle relationships, exercise responsibility and initiative, and work in teams. Fieldwork too usually demands group work with peers and may involve interaction with adults including members of the public.

Fieldwork

Fieldwork is a core element in primary geography. It brings pupils into contact with the natural and built environment, helps to develop their sense of place and encourages their notion of stewardship and care for the environment. For many pupils, it offers the chance to experience places where they would not otherwise go. Fieldwork entails many opportunities for pupils to notice, attend to and communicate their emotions and feelings. Figure 3 suggests ways in which fieldtrips may develop children's emotional literacy.

An excellent resource developed and produced by the staff of the Field Studies Council is a sheet of cartoon faces humorously illustrating seventy alphabetically organised emotions that could be experienced during fieldwork (Figure 4). These range from anxious, bored and exhausted to curious, satisfied and ecstatic. One innovative use of the sheet involves asking pupils to draw the faces to complete a 'feelings graph' to show how they feel at various times during a day visit to Box Hill. This approach could easily be adapted for fieldwork in the local area.

Figure 5 | *Road with Cypresses, 1890
(oil on canvas). Gogh, Vincent van (1853-90)
/Rijksmuseum Kroller-Muller, Otterlo,
Netherlands.*

Paintings and photographs

Many great artists have been moved to interpret the places they cared about through their art, and numerous well-known works of art are representations of places. Painters such as Constable, Van Gogh and Cézanne have left us with enduring images and transformed our perception of the landscape (Figure 5). You can encourage pupils to talk about their feelings using on-screen images of these scenes. Useful starting points for discussion include:

▥ How do you feel when you look at this picture?

▥ Why do you think that artist chose to paint/draw this place?

▥ How do you think s/he felt about the place?

▥ What feelings did s/he want to provoke in people looking at the picture?

▥ How does s/he encourage these feelings?

Questions like these will provide an excellent focus for discussing the feelings associated with places, and for recognising that different people may respond differently to the same place. Using similar materials, techniques or style to the artist to create a representation of the local area or other place will also help develop their sensitivity to the affective impact of visual images.

Photographs of known or unfamiliar places can also provide a successful stimulus for exploring emotional response.

▥ Pupils can be asked to consider how selected photographs make them feel, using a feeling word list as a prompt if appropriate.

▥ A set of striking photographs can be displayed and the class provided with small coloured stickers to represent different emotions, e.g. red for angry, blue for sad, yellow for happy. Pupils can then be invited to place their stickers against any photographs which make them feel that emotion. The pattern of response can then be discussed, e.g. 'Why did this photograph make so many of us feel sad?', and individuals invited to explain their response: 'I felt happy when I looked at this photograph because …'.

▥ Pupils can draw themselves on a post-it, and then 'put themselves in the picture' by placing the post-it on a photograph. Ask the children to imagine themselves in the photograph and to say what they can see, hear, touch etc., and how they feel about being in that place.

. . . to the remains of the city of Machu Picchu hidden in the Andes Mountains.

Figure 6 | *Babar and Celeste visit Machu Picchu. Babar's World Tour*
© *2005 Laurent de Brunhoff, published by Abram Books.*

▓ High-quality photographs of children in the distant localities studied can be used to develop empathy by considering questions such as 'What was he/she doing when the photograph was taken?' 'What do you think he/she was thinking?' 'How do you think he/she was feeling?'.

▓ Carefully selected photographs can also provide a stimulus for role play or drama, e.g. by role playing an interview with someone in a photograph, or acting out what happened the moment after the photograph was taken.

Story and fiction

Picture and story books and fiction offer many opportunities for developing a sense of place, for exploring feelings about places and issues, and for developing empathy for characters. Many primary teachers are skilled in using fiction in this way, and many of the ideas in this chapter can be developed in relation to picture and story books. Fiction offers children the opportunity vicariously to experience otherwise inaccessible experiences, places, events and situations, and to explore and articulate the emotions associated with them (Figure 6). *Babar's World Tour* (Brunhoff, 2005) is a delightful journey around famous cities and sights by the popular elephant family. In a more serious vein *The Silence Seeker* (Morley, 2009) is about a boy's search for quiet and personal space. Both books explore our relationship to places, but in very different ways.

Conclusion

An emotionally literate geography education provides the opportunity for primary age children to:

- Recognise and acknowledge attachment to personally significant places
- Understand the power of place to provoke affective responses
- Recognise and express emotions about known and unknown places
- Listen to, understand and acknowledge others' feelings about places
- Develop empathy for others' feelings about places
- Know that affective response to places may be represented through different media, e.g. 3D and textile art forms, music, photographs, dance and movement
- Represent and communicate feelings about places in a variety of ways
- Understand that environmental issues may arouse strong feelings
- Express their own emotions associated with environmental issues appropriately.

Many children growing up today have fractured families and disrupted home lives and are thus likely to have experienced greater change and be more rootless than their predecessors. The fear of strangers and exaggerated worries about safety are also causing parents to be more vigilant. The result is that more and more children are restricted in where they can go independently and are ferried from place to place by car. Not only are children going out less, they also now have televisions in their bedrooms or spend hours staring at a screen as they surf the internet, with well-documented adverse consequences for their physical and social development (Palmer, 2007).

Geography can make a significant contribution to the development of emotional literacy. Fully rounded studies of the local area and other localities will provide children with opportunities to attend to, acknowledge and express their feelings about places. At a time when education is dominated by standards, accountability and measurable outcomes, it is particularly important to keep sight of the ultimate goal. If we can help our pupils to lead more complete, fulfilling and balanced lives we will have achieved something really worthwhile. If we can lead them to reflect on the needs of others and contribute positively to the world, both locally and globally, the benefits will be even greater. Geography can be and should be part of this vision.

References and further reading

Bonnett, M. (2004) *Retrieving Nature: Education for a post-humanist age*. Oxford: Blackwell.

Brunhoff, L. de (2005) *Babar's World Tour*. New York: Abrams.

Catling, S. (2003) 'Curriculum contested: primary geography and social justice', *Geography*, 88, 3, pp. 164-210.

Catling, S. (2005) 'Children's personal geographies and the English primary school geography curriculum', *Children's Geographies*, 3, 3, pp. 325-344.

Chantler, L. (2004) *What Effect does Residential Fieldwork in Geography Have on Children's Emotional Development?* Unpublished dissertation. Canterbury: Canterbury Christ Church University.

DCSF (2005) *Social and Emotional Aspects of Learning*. London: DCSF.

DfES (2003) *Excellence and Enjoyment*. London: DfES.

DfES (2004) *Every Child Matters: Change for children in school.* London: DfES.

Gardner, H. (1983) *Frames of Mind: The theory of multiple intelligences.* New York: Basic Books.

Goleman, D. (1996) *Emotional Intelligence: Why it can matter more than IQ.* London: Bloomsbury.

Goswami, U. (2008) 'Principles of learning, implications for teaching: a cognitive neuroscience perspective', *Journal of Philosophy of Education*, 42, 3-4, pp. 381-399.

Immordino-Yang, M. and Damasio, A. (2007) 'We feel therefore we learn: the relevance of affective and social science to education', *Brain, Mind and Education*, 1, 1, pp. 3-10.

Jackson, E. (2000) 'Personal, social and health education' in Grimwade, K. (ed) *Geography and the New Agenda.* Sheffield: Geographical Association.

Matthews, M. (1992) *Making Sense of Place.* Hemel Hempstead: Harvester Wheatsheaf.

McCarthy, K. and Park, J. (1998) *Learning by Heart: The role of emotional learning in raising school achievement.* London: Calouste Gulbenkian Foundation.

Morley, B. (2009) *The Silence Seeker.* London: Tamarind.

Noddings, N. (2003) *Happiness and Education.* Cambridge: CUP.

Ofsted (2003) *Geography in Primary Schools: Ofsted subject reports 2001/02.* London: Ofsted.

Orbach, S. (1998) 'Emotional literacy', *Young Minds*, 3, pp. 12-13.

Palmer, J. (1998) *Environmental Education in the Twenty First Century.* London: Routledge.

Palmer, S. (2007) *Toxic Childhood.* London: Orion.

Robinson, A. and Young, A. (2009) *Mohammed's Journey.* London: Frances Lincoln.

Scoffham, S. (1998) 'Places, attachment and identity' in Scoffham, S (ed) *Primary Sources: Research findings in primary geography.* Sheffield: Geographical Association.

Slater, F. (1994) *Learning Through Geography.* Oxford: Heinemann.

Spencer, C. (2005) 'Place attachment, place identity and the development of the child's self-identity: Searching the literature to develop an hypothesis', *International Research in Geographical and Environmental Education*, 14, 4, pp. 305-9.

Steiner, C. and Perry, P. (1997) *Achieving Emotional Literacy.* London: Bloomsbury.

Titman, W. (1994) *Special People, Special Places.* Godalming: WWF UK/Learning Through Landscapes.

See also the think piece 'Geography and Happiness' on the GA website *www.geography.org.uk/gtip/thinkpieces* and *Primary Geographer*, 65, Spring 2009, which focused on the geography of happiness.

Websites

Antidote *www.antidote.org.uk*

Valuing Places *www.geography.org.uk/projects/valuingplaces*

World happiness map *www.happyplanetindex.org/explore/global*

with contributions from Ruth Potts and Janie Whittle

CHAPTER COVERAGE:
CREATIVITY • CROSS-CURRICULAR LINKS • DISTANT PLACES • EUROPE
• GAMES/PLAY • INCLUSION/SEN • LEARNING THEORY

Making geography fun

Look around the world we inhabit, glance out of the window, switch on the television, look at a newspaper. There are places which are flat, mountainous, dry, wet, barren, cultivated, empty, covered with buildings, teaming with human life, totally desolate, safe, dangerous, dull, interesting … the list could go on. Bring to mind some of the people you know and their characteristics, the jobs they do, the languages they speak, the colour of their skin, the leisure activities they engage in. Now extend that to the people you meet and interact with indirectly through the media, through travelling, through surfing the internet and so on. Reflect on some of the issues with which geography engages. They affect almost every aspect of our lives and those of the people living across the world now and in the future.

Have you ever wondered why, with all this diversity and variety, geography is not top of the popularity list for school subjects? How is it that pupils and adults both within education and outside it fail to find geography riveting, captivating, mind-blowing and all the other superlatives people associate with subjects which inspire them? We cannot blame the raw material with which we operate. We could suggest that the pupils have some part to play, but it is my belief that it is the way the material has been, and often still is, presented within our schools which is the root cause of any disaffection. As Kirchberg writes:

> *The didactics of geography do not need to be redesigned, but new paths have to be followed, with new contents, methods and lesson procedures that are better adapted to today's children and adolescents.*
> (Kirchberg, 2000, p. 5)

If geography educators are to become more effective they need to learn lessons from the plethora of recent research about learning and apply appropriate strategies in their teaching. To use words attributed to Mahatma Gandhi: 'Be the change you want to see in the world' (Gilbert, 2002). It is my passion, and one I know is shared by many

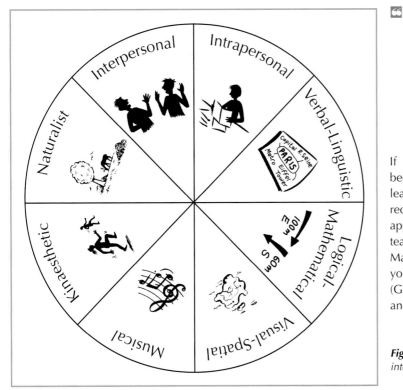

Figure 1 | *Diagram to show multiple intelligences. Based on Gardner (2000).*

others, that young people should be introduced to geography in ways that will motivate them to discover more for themselves: to enquire, investigate and search for answers; to enjoy their learning and pass on positive rather than negative messages. We can use the enthusiasm and interests of the pupils. We can find out how they learn, what they know, want to know, enjoy doing, question, don't understand, what is going to be useful to them. We can vary the teaching strategies employed.

If teachers wish to be truly inclusive, they must ensure they take account of differences, be aware of the need for versatility and design activities which take account of specific needs – it is my premise that there are few geographical experiences which cannot be enjoyed and provide learning opportunities for all. Many of the ideas offered in this chapter are open ended, offering potential for gifted and talented pupils to be adequately challenged. They can also be used, easily adapted or modified to cater for pupils with specific needs.

If we, as teachers, can engage with geography in a positive way and develop our own vision of what the subject encompasses it is likely that our teaching will be enriched, leading to improvement in the learning of the pupils with whom we work. If we are having fun, they are likely to have fun too.

Different ways of thinking

The way in which a topic is introduced can determine the attitude pupils have to the rest of the work. Howard Gardner's multiple intelligence theory (Gardner, 2000) suggests that the human mind, rather than being a unified entity, is better considered as a community of separate intelligences. In daily life these intelligences usually work in harmony so their individual characteristics are not apparent. In teaching, however, we need to be aware of these different modes so we can develop each one to its full potential. Howard Gardner argues that the human mind consists of different forms of intelligence each of which is equally valid (Figure 1).

We need to take account of these various 'intelligences' when we begin any new topic, as well as throughout a unit of work. For example, if you are introducing work on the local area to your class, whether through a published scheme or a school-specific plan, you could use one of the activities in Figure 2 to 'get pupils interested and alert' each lesson. It is envisaged that these activities will last for ten minutes maximum. Other 'starter' activities are suggested later in this chapter.

Photo | *John Collar and Kathy Alcock.*

Figure 2 | *Suggestions for 'starter' activities about the local area that tap into different forms of intelligence.*

Interpersonal

Divide pupils into groups of two or three and ask them to talk for about three minutes about the places they like going to in their local area. Then get the pupils to change groups and discuss people they know who work in the area, again for three minutes. The final discussion, in another group, could relate to an issue in the local area which the pupils believe is important.

Intrapersonal

Present the class with a number of statements about the place they are studying. They have to rank the statements in order depending on how important they are to them, thus making value judgements. Examples might include: 'There are too many new houses being built here' or 'The proposed waste disposal site should be allowed'. In this exercise it should be stressed that all opinions are valued and it may be better not to share results.

Verbal/linguistic

Ask pupils to work with a partner and to put the name of the place in the centre of a large sheet of paper. They then write around it all the words and phrases they associate with that place. Alternatively, give the pupils an initial letter and tell them to think of all the words associated with the place beginning with that letter. After about one minute change the letter, and so on.

Logical/mathematical

Give pupils a pie-chart showing the different shops and services available within the chosen area. What can they deduce from studying the chart?

Visual/spatial

Give pupils a map of the local area drawn to an appropriate scale. Display a series of pictures around the room. Ask the pupils what they think the pictures show, where they are found on a map, and to identify each location with a mark. You could also ask them to devise a key.

Musical

As the lesson begins, play music associated with the local area. This could be music from the local place of worship, sounds which might be heard in the streets, or music which evokes a sense of the place, e.g. traditional sea shanties or part of Beethoven's 'Pastoral Symphony'.

Kinaesthetic

Allow pupils to walk around the school grounds (or the school building if more appropriate) and look at what they can see of the local area from a variety of viewing points. If possible the class should be divided into small groups (two or three pupils) to facilitate discussion.

Naturalist

Set up a classroom display of wildlife specimens (leaves, grasses, plants) that are found in the area. Ask pupils to identify them and say where they might be found.

Fun and games in geography

'Research has shown that mental limbering up makes for more effective learning' (Gilbert, 2002, p. 119).

Start a geography lesson by saying 'we'll start off with a game' and you will engage many pupils immediately. This strategy is equally successful in the middle of a lesson, when their attention may be flagging. If you finish off with a game, they may not want the lesson to finish! Some websites featuring geographical games are listed at the end of this chapter.

Photo | *Anne Keeling.*

Quizzes and puzzles

The numerous quiz shows on TV and radio have great potential as fun ways of learning, or assessing knowledge and understanding. Try these:

```
            B   E
A M S T E R D A M
            R   I   U
            L   N   N
            I   B R I S T O L
            N   U       C
            R   H
            G
            H
```

Present geographical words or phrases as anagrams – a good way of warming up the brain:

IVRSER AYM DOLFO NI AVHEY NRIA

Put one word on the board and see how many other words of three letters or more can be made from it – find 20 in five minutes:

AFGHANISTAN

Write the name, for example, of a European country or city on the board or a large sheet of paper and challenge the class to create a crossword as quickly as possible. How quickly could you get to 15 European cities? Keep the crossword accessible so that pupils can devise the clues during the following week, possibly in free time.

Globe games

Use an inflated or soft globe and let the class throw and catch it. Have a letter spinner or set of alphabet cards and a set of geographical 'category' cards. One pupil at a time chooses the initial letter and another the category so that when the globe is caught the pupil (or pair of pupils if that is more appropriate) has to say the name of a place or feature beginning with that initial letter. For example letter 'E', category 'mountain'. What would you say? These games can be adapted by adding 'Ask a question about ...' or 'Say anything you know about ...' or 'Find this place on the globe ...'.

Map cards and games

Pupils will learn from and enjoy playing the Mapzone games (*http://mapzone. ordnancesurvey.co.uk*) but you can devise your own. Here are some ideas to get you started:

Make or buy a set of individual Ordnance Survey map symbols flashcards. Now make a second set of cards with the corresponding names of the features from the symbol cards. Divide the class into groups and take it in turns to 'say the symbol' or 'sketch it'. Share the cards out and make up a story which includes the features on the cards. As you say the word the pupil with that symbol stands up and holds up the card. Make it really fun by increasing the frequency with which these words appear. As pupils get more proficient get them to tell their own story for the rest of the class to react to. A further variation can involve the pupils creating a class set of geographical feature cards (Figure 3).

Figure 3 | *River Snap. Work by Y5/6 pupils, Shelley Primary School, Horsham.*

Using maps

If you have access to a range of 1:50,000 OS maps, ask pupils to select a map, then a place on the map they would like to visit for a holiday. Give them a set time (say three minutes) to use the map evidence – contours, symbols, place names and so on – to 'pack' a rucksack or a case with clothes and equipment which they might need during their holiday. Pupils can record their answers visually in a pre-drawn rucksack or case outline, or verbally in pairs.

Initial letter, word and guessing games

In small groups, ask pupils to think of all the features beginning with a certain letter they might find, for example, in the countryside, a town, or a named area. For example, how many features can you think of that you might see at the seaside beginning with s? Then ask pupils to make up a story using the words identified. With younger pupils you might ask them for just one or two things then change the letter. Alternatively, play a version of 'I spy' with the teacher or pupils taking it in turn to identify the themes, e.g. building, mode of transport, physical feature. A similar game involves the pupils in asking questions. You say, for example, 'I am thinking of something I can see at the seaside' and write the word or draw the picture on a whiteboard which the pupils can't see. They ask questions until they find the right answer. This could be made more challenging by restricting the pupils to asking questions that can only be answered 'yes' or 'no'.

Picture postcards

Picture postcards are useful for sorting activities with younger pupils. Make sets of category labels, enough for one set per group, such as: Local area, UK, Europe, Distant Places; or seaside, transport, buildings, people. Put a variety of postcards in sorting bags and give one bag to each group. Pupils take turns to draw out a card and put it in the appropriate category, explaining briefly their reasons for the choice.

If the cards have been used, the reverse side will also contain information which pupils can use, such as the postmark, stamp and message. This can become a game if they work in pairs or small groups and give clues from the information so that others can work out the source of the card.

You could also cut up old postcards to create jigsaws. Pupils should then reassemble them using the clues from the picture. Cut the cards up into different size and shape pieces to differentiate the activity for appropriate levels of ability.

Photo | Kathy Alcock and John Collar.

Developing key geography skills through having fun

Back-to-back: Using geographical vocabulary and maps

In groups of three, give each pupil a label – A, B or C – and a pencil or washable pen. Pupils A and B must sit back-to-back and not look over their shoulder. Pupil C needs blank paper. Give pupils A and B a photocopied or laminated map each that you have prepared earlier at an appropriate scale. (Laminating the maps and using washable pens means you can use the same resource many times.) Pupil B decides on a route to get from one place to another on the map, and marks this on their copy. Pupil B then gives instructions to pupil A so that they are able to replicate the route on their map. Pupil A can ask questions to help them. Pupil C remains silent but makes written comments on what is happening. After a pre-determined time period, the drawing stops and the two routes are compared. Pupil C reports back on what was successful or not during the activity. Using this information, the activity is repeated, with roles rotated and a different route selected, until all three pupils have completed each part.

This could be used as an assessment strategy. The pupils will have fun and learn – so will you. Younger pupils can engage in this activity providing the map you give them is appropriate. Do ensure the pupils think about what they have learnt and the knowledge and understanding they have used, perhaps as a plenary session.

Sing a song

Sing a song with a geographical theme. You might make up your own songs to familiar tunes, for example 'I am the weatherman' to the tune of 'I am the music man'. You could also download songs: try *www.learninggamesforkids.com*, or *www.singup.org*, which is free to join and has over 60 geography-related songs about the world.

Hold it up!

Create 'story sticks' (Figure 4) to help pupils explain and retell geographical processes. For younger pupils teachers will need to make this resource themselves. Older pupils can make these themselves by researching, for example, 'The story of a banana from tree to tummy' or 'The journey of the River Rhine from source to mouth'. They select five or six stages in the story which are presented visually and mounted on

Figure 4 | Story sticks. **Photo** | Stephen Scoffham.

canes or pencils. Groups of pupils use these prompts to retell the process in an imaginative way. You will be amazed how this can release pupils to excel when they can hide behind a role and present knowledge and understanding orally and creatively. Another use for this type of resource is as a 'put in the right order' activity. This makes better use of time than colouring, cutting out or sticking in books which is so often seen in classrooms and is not good geography, even though the learning that it is promoting may be.

Find a furry friend to help!

Puppets and toys are also useful in helping pupils to display their understanding. Pupils can hide behind the character, and if they get it wrong it is the puppet not them! Role play can also help pupils escape from the fear of making mistakes. They can retell familiar stories, or create their own, using appropriate geographical vocabulary, and recount journeys and experiences undertaken. Barnaby Bear has many a story to tell, and indeed, so will the toys belonging to your pupils.

Having fun learning in sand and water

Early years pupils can have great fun in the sandpit creating landscapes – tunnels, mountains, bridges, settlements. While engaging in water play they are learning about how water moves, carries things, transports and deposits. In the role-play area they engage in real-life activity given the right environment for learning. Talk to the pupils as they play, show them pictures, play with them, let them ask you questions, listen to them. You will learn as much about what they know and understand by just being there. This should be seen as a vital part of your role as a teacher and not left to the supporting adults.

Maths in mind

Mental maths starters should be set in a real-life context. Try this idea: A bus leaves Canterbury bus station with 23 people on board. At Asda it picks up four more. Outside the College, five get off and two get on. Once it reaches the Park and Ride ten get off and five get on. The bus travels on the A2 towards Dover. It stops at the Woolage turn to pick up one more passenger. How many people are now on the bus?

This idea can be developed in numerous ways. You can use a map together with the mental maths, find the route taken, ask questions, or suggest enquiries. Pupils can take turns in preparing the challenges.

Trails as treasures for teachers

One of the features of geography lessons is that they can easily provide a context for learning in a number of other subject areas as well. A trail around the local area or a visit to a contrasting locality could involve the following:

- writing words to describe your feelings about a place which develops into a poem, letter or piece of descriptive writing;
- noting or recording sounds which can lead to making music that evokes the character of the locality;
- investigating change within the buildings in a community can be linked to historical enquiry;
- field sketches can be drawn and annotated to cover a range of themes.

Picture this: virtual visits

You can use geography resources such as teaching packs, photographs and video clips for other curriculum areas. For example, use a picture showing life in an Indian city as the context for a story. You begin the story then divide pupils into groups and they take turns to continue to make up the story using the characters, buildings and features portrayed in the picture. For recording of evidence purposes the story telling can be taped.

Problem solving

Problem solving can lead to disaffected children being stimulated to learn and discover for themselves. I witnessed an example of this in a school in Kent. The teacher began the lesson by saying: 'You have a problem to solve'. This was clearly the first time this approach had been used in this way. Without exception the pupils sat up higher in their seats and looked engaged. I recorded the exchanges that followed, some of which are given here ('pupil' refers to different pupils):

Pupil: 'What's the problem?'
Teacher: 'The village needs a new bypass.'
Pupil: 'How do you know?'
Teacher: 'Well what do you think?'
Pupils began to discuss quietly amongst themselves.
Teacher: 'OK. You spend a couple of minutes thinking about that.'
After a few minutes the consensus was in agreement with the statement but they decided they needed some evidence to prove they were right. They also went on to decide what other information they needed in order to solve the problem.

What followed was one of the 'magic moments' of my career in education as I witnessed one of the best geography lessons I had seen. Maps and aerial photographs were found, the internet was searched, pupils went to ask questions of others in the school, telephone calls were made, faxes and e-mails sent, plans for visits and further investigations were made. I returned to the school several weeks later and the pupils couldn't wait to tell me what they were doing 'in geography' now. Magic!

Lesson planning

Motivation through choice

All too often, differentiation is not apparent within geography lessons and when it does occur it generally means a different level of difficulty in terms of what is recorded. Differentiation may be by task, by text, by interest, by ability, by choice. In taking account of differences, pupils themselves may be able to select an appropriate activity to motivate them to progress their learning. Alternatively, teachers may need to guide and direct choice in order to address the gaps in knowledge and understanding as well as issues relating to learning styles. Having a range of possibilities on offer allows for this to occur. Here are two examples:

Option 1: Reading the landscape

Use either the view from the window, or a large photograph (printed, or displayed on the IWB) – for example, of an area which is due to be developed in some way or a distant locality view.

Ask the pupils to select from the five activities listed below. They should do one (or more if they wish) but not all of them.

Task
- ▥ Generate a list of questions
- ▥ Create a list of words or phrases
- ▥ Describe the scene in words or pictures

- ▥ Explain the activity within the picture
- ▥ Create a survey based on the scene

Follow-up activity
- ▥ Devise a quiz for others to complete
- ▥ Compose a rap, song or poem
- ▥ Create a collage from photographs, drawings and descriptions
- ▥ Act out the activity as 'playlets'
- ▥ Undertake the survey and present results in a variety of ways

Photo | Paula Richardson.

Option 2: Create a travel guide for the teacher

The aim is to make a class book or resource pack which relates to significant places around the world. Research by Wiegand (2006) suggests that seven-year-olds can generally name seven or eight countries; by the time they reach eleven they are able to name around fifteen. Western Europe and large countries like the USA and Australia are usually well known but many children have very little awareness of the developing world. With support they can develop their knowledge quite quickly.

Tell the class you want to go on holiday, spending a few days in several different places. (The range will depend on the pupils. It may be within your local area, county or region, the country, or be worldwide.) You will plot the route but need their help in order to plan your journey, visiting interesting places. Ask them to create a double-page spread of interactive activities and information about a place in your chosen area they have visited or know well. Give them some guidance as to suitable material without limiting the scope of their creativity. A brief class discussion before beginning the task could ascertain that they may include maps, pictures, letters in envelopes written from the place, lift-the-flap activities, quizzes, games, pictures of artefacts, information panels, websites and so on. This activity could be linked to ICT depending on the resources available and age and ICT competency of the pupils (and teacher).

Using ready-made schemes of work

Many schools use published schemes of work to support their geography teaching. These provide a valuable framework but there are often advantages to personalising the materials to make them more applicable to your own situation. If you are responsible for leading INSET, clearly this is a message which should be passed on to colleagues along with the benefits of using personal experiences, enthusiasm and themes which are of particular interest to them as teachers. This is likely to lead to a higher degree of engagement.

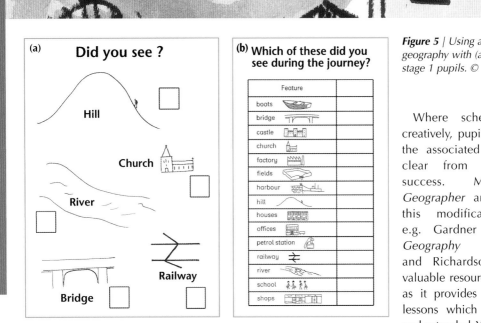

Figure 5 | *Using a journey to promote geography with (a) EYFS and (b) key stage 1 pupils. © Kathy Alcock.*

Where schemes are used creatively, pupils are engaged in the associated activities, as is clear from Barnaby Bear's success. Many *Primary Geographer* articles exemplify this modification approach, e.g. Gardner *et al.* (2007). *Geography Plus* (Owens and Richardson, 2011) is a valuable resource in this respect, as it provides a framework for lessons which can be adapted and extended. You might also find *The Early Years Handbook* (de Bóo, 2004) stimulates cross-curricular thinking. Here are some suggestions:

▥ Pack a case or rucksack with the clothes and items you would take if you were visiting an island, a contrasting locality by the sea or a mountain environment, or going on a round-the-world trip. Discuss with your pupils what you have selected.

▥ Give pupils a map of the area you are studying and ask them to suggest what they would need to take with them if going on holiday there, using only the evidence from the map. This is an excellent way of assessing pupils' ability to read and use maps in a meaningful context.

▥ Listen to and make music related to different themes. Alternatively, you could devise a worldwide music quiz, in which children try to guess which country different musical extracts come from (Kelly, 2009).

▥ Record clips from travel and other appropriate TV programmes and show them to pupils without the sound track: the challenge for pupils is to create their own accompanying commentary.

▥ You might also like to show the class some video extracts. The BBC series *Planet Earth*, for example, has some breathtaking footage of wildlife in extreme environments – deserts, glaciers, oceans, rivers, caves, high mountains, jungles, forests and polar regions. Support material for using video in teaching is available from Film Education (*www.filmeducation.org*).

Journeys and visits

Fieldwork and first-hand outdoors experiences are an important component of geographical education. For many of us, it was precisely these practical adventures in learning which fired our enthusiasm for the subject. The academic geographer, Peter Gould, decided to become a geographer while birdwatching on the cliffs of Devon as an adolescent; I committed myself to a future career in geography teaching when involved in a frightening, wet, climb down Gordale Scar in the Malham area of Yorkshire. Sadly, residential fieldwork is not possible for many pupils today. However, you can compensate to some extent by using journeys to

Figure 7 | *Teaching how to play. Work by Y1 pupils.*

Stuck in the Mud

How to play Stuck in the Mud

1) Choose 4 players to be the chasers.

2) Everyone runs around. The chasers wait for a minute.

3) If the chasers catch you then you have to stand still. You have to stand in a star shape.

4) To be back in the game someone has to crawl under the persons legs who is stuck.

5) You are free to play until a whistle has blown at the end of the game. Keep a look out for your friends who are " stuck in the mud "

This was made up by Charlie Cole

support and develop geographical activities. Here are some suggestions:

- When taking pupils on a journey (whatever the curriculum subject) ask them to look at the map and follow the route beforehand, then to complete an 'I have seen' checksheet as they go along (Figure 5). This could become part of your school policy.
- When visits are planned, encourage the staff involved to include some geographical games such as 'I spy to the north/south/east/west ...'. For younger pupils this may need simplifying to in front/behind/above/below.
- During fieldwork ensure you include activities which relate to people as well as places. One idea is to ask pupils to survey what people are doing or carrying as they walk past. Prior to the visit get pupils to create their own categories such as walking, communicating, riding, listening, using a mobile phone, walking a dog, etc.

Holidays

Holidays and out-of-school excursions are vastly under-used resources. Create a school 'holiday pack' of ideas for pupils to undertake when going away on holiday. Figure 6 lists suggestions for making the most of these valuable, first-hand experiences of other localities.

Learning about distant places

Engaging pupils with the wider world to create balance and understanding is essential if we are to help them to become global citizens. This area is developed more fully in Chapters 16 and 21, but here is one idea which was used successfully.

Year 1 pupils wanted to know about a project which our church was supporting to help children in a region of Northern Ghana who have severe eye problems. I had agreed to show a video and share my knowledge of the area and the project. During the discussion, I asked the pupils what games they liked to play and what games they thought the children in Lingbinsi would want to play once they could see again. They made some suggestions and together we decided it would be good if they could send information to the children in Lingbinsi about the games they liked to play. Figure 7 shows an example of what the

Photo | *Paula Richardson.*

Figure 6 | Holiday geography. After Alcock, 2001.

Pupil activities for undertaking in the classroom before, during, or after a holiday

▪ Using a map at an appropriate scale find the place of origin of cards or letters you receive.

▪ Display a map showing the route to the holiday destination and the itinerary if visiting more than one place.

▪ Plan the detail of the journey – the stops, meal breaks, where and when fuel might be needed, overnight stops.

▪ Search for information about the places to be visited while on holiday.

▪ Make a list of questions to find the answers to while you are away.

▪ Write a letter or send an e-mail request for information from the local Tourist Information office.

▪ Compile a display showing what life is like in the place visited.

▪ Run a question and answer session in class for other pupils to ask questions about the place visited.

▪ Find the cost of buying several different products from a local shop on holiday and compare these with buying the same or similar items from a local shop at home.

Activities adults could help children undertake while on holiday

▪ Send a postcard to the class with a picture which shows some significant landmark, feature or aspect of life in the place you are staying. Use stamps of different values if possible.

▪ Find out what is grown or produced in the local area. Are there any regional or local specialities?

▪ Eat a meal made from locally-produced products or cooked in a traditional way for the area, e.g. Cornish pasty, Spanish paella, Italian pizza, French cheese, Devon cream tea, Scottish shortbread, Bakewell Tart.

▪ Buy an article using local currency if appropriate. For young children, unused to dealing with money themselves, holidays are often a good time to introduce this idea.

▪ Devise a list of products which can be bought in most towns in Britain and abroad, for example, one litre of milk, a loaf of bread, six eggs, a bottle of fizzy drink, one kilo of tomatoes, four oranges, one ice cream. Find the cost of these things in a shop in your holiday destination. Convert the prices into pounds sterling if appropriate.

▪ Discover how many different forms of transport are used in the place visited.

▪ Take a journey, even if only short, on local public transport.

▪ Visit and make notes about a place of interest which can be used in a talk to the rest of the class.

▪ Collect information about the area from, for example, the local Tourist Information office.

▪ Try to discover the meaning and origin of local place names.

▪ Discover how the place you are visiting is changing. What are the current issues affecting the lives of local people?

▪ If possible, read a local newspaper to discover some things which are similar to and different from the place where you live. Consider, for example, the sports played, the goods for sale in shops, and the entertainment available.

▪ Draw pictures, write notes or make a sketch map of what you can see from where you are staying, to show what it is really like to people who have never been there.

▪ Take photographs of people and places which you can talk about back at school.

▪ Talk to people who live or work in the area to find out what they like or dislike about living in that place and about the work they do. How are their lives changing?

▪ Look for signs and symbols and discover what they mean.

▪ Make sketches of interesting buildings and label them to help you to remember what they were really like.

▪ Make a list of the names of the people who you meet during your holiday and the jobs they do.

▪ Collect artefacts such as coins, stamps, tickets, leaflets, carrier bags and wrapping paper, local produce, leaves and flowers, shells and stones. Make sure you note where you found/got them and do not take away anything from conservation areas.

▪ Find a quiet place and write down all the words which come into your head as you look around. Do the same in a noisy place.

▪ If staying in a foreign country, learn a few words or phrases in the local language, e.g. good morning, thank you, please, my name is.

▪ Find out if any famous people came from the area where you are staying.

Activities for pupils to undertake on the journey to their holiday destination

▪ Make animals from pipe cleaners.

▪ Make up games using car registration plates. For example, find words which use the letters in the same order, or devise sums which involve adding or multiplying the numerals together.

▪ Complete an 'I have seen ...' tick sheet with words or pictures of things you see out of the window.

▪ Make surveys for about five minutes of, for example, colours of cars, types of vehicles, shapes passed, number of traffic lights.

▪ Play games such as 'I'm thinking of ... (see page 53)

▪ Go through the alphabet thinking of objects or names beginning with each letter in turn.

pupils produced. They laminated them and sent them together with crayons and small toys which they thought the children might enjoy. In return, the school received photographs and information from the Ghanaian teachers about what their pupils liked to do, to eat and games they played in their village. The UK pupils had their vision widened and positive images were created.

Note

Many of the suggestions and ideas in this chapter involve activity and experiences which will not lead to anything being recorded in the traditional way in geography books or folders. This should not prevent you from using them. Be creative about the way you record the evidence. Use audio and video recording techniques and take photographs. Use technology to support what you believe in and be able to justify your practice by demonstrating improved knowledge and understanding from the pupils.

References and further reading

Alcock, K. (2001) 'Distance learning', *Primary Geographer*, 44, pp. 32-3.

de Bóo, M. (2004) *The Early Years Handbook*. Sheffield: The Curriculum Partnership.

Gardner, D., Gardner, P. and Price, J. (2007) 'Chembakolli isn't India', *Primary Geographer*, 62, pp. 25-28.

Gardner, H. (1983) *Frames of Mind*. New York: Basic Books.

Gardner, H. (2000) *Intelligence Reframed: Multiple intelligences for the 21st century*. New York: Basic Books.

Gilbert, I. (2002) *Essential Motivation in the Classroom*. London: Falmer.

Kelly, A. (2009) 'Sounds geographical', *Primary Geographer*, 68, pp. 34-36.

Kirchberg, G. (2000) 'Changes in youth: no changes in teaching geography? Aspects of a neglected problem in the didactics of geography', *International Research in Geographical and Environmental Education*, 9, 1, p. 5.

Owens, P. and Richardson, P. (eds) (2011) *Geography Plus: A primary toolkit for creative teaching and learning*. Sheffield: Geographical Association.

Wiegand, P. (2006) *Learning and Teaching with Maps*. London: Routledge.

Websites with geographical games

Countries and capitals *www.kidsgeo.com/geography-games*

Geographical Association Worldwise Quiz *www.geography.org.uk/getinvolved/worldwise*

Learning games *www.learninggamesforkids.com/geography_games.html*

Maps *http://mapzone.ordnancesurvey.co.uk*

Puzzles *http://puzzlemaker.discoveryeducation.com*

Volcanoes *http://volcano.oregonstate.edu/kids*

World development *www.globalgang.org.uk*

World map *www.oxfam.org.uk/education*

See also the think piece on 'Using Games in Geography' on the Geographical Association website *www.geography.org.uk/gtip/thinkpieces*

Blow wind blow

Photo / Kathy Alcock and John Collar.

Young children making sense of the world

The Early Years Foundation Stage (EYFS) applies to children aged between three and five years in a variety of settings such as nurseries, playgroups and schools. In these important early years, children are forming values and attitudes that will colour their perception of the world around them and predispose them to learning about it. This is a crucial period in which educators need to ply their craft appropriately if they are to lay secure foundations for future development. One of the main aims of the EYFS framework is to make children aware of their place in the world and help them to make sense of it. As a result geography is at the very heart of early learning, encompassing as it does aspects of social, physical and cultural worlds that are necessary for meaningful understanding of our surroundings.

This chapter outlines the principles, provision and processes that facilitate the learning and teaching of geography in the early years. The EYFS framework is organised into six areas of learning. While we recognise that geography is subsumed under the area entitled 'Knowledge and Understanding of the World', we use the term 'geography' throughout this chapter for two reasons. First, geography can be found in all of the six areas of learning, and second, practitioners need to know what experiences and skills are essentially geographical within all areas of the curriculum in order to promote a balanced approach to geographical learning.

Principles underpinning early geographical learning experiences

A principle is an important underlying assumption or belief that shapes the way we act. The Geographical Association has identified three core principles that underpin all learning in the Early Years Foundation Stage, namely:

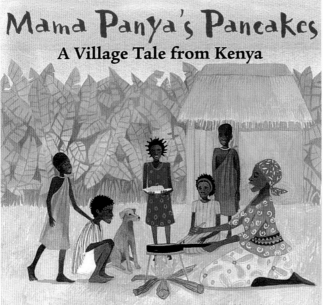

Mama Panya's Pancakes
A Village Tale from Kenya

written by Mary and Rich Chamberlin   *illustrated by* Julia Cairns

Illustration | *Mama Panya's Pancakes. Cover reproduced by courtesy of Barefoot Books. Illustration © Julia Cairns.*

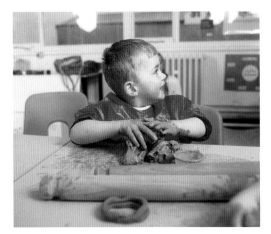

Photo | *Kathy Alcock and John Collar.*

■ Young children learn best through self-initiated and supported play.

■ Links should be made between the 'areas of learning' to reflect a holistic approach in the education of young children.

■ Young children learn best when they feel valued, secure and are able to build positive relationships with peers and other adults.

(Geographical Association, 2003).

Research findings strongly suggest that young children learn best in situations that promote self-initiated and self-directed activities, in other words, play (Wood and Attfield, 2005). Young children need time to freely explore the world around them and try out a range of responses in order to investigate, discover, reflect on and evaluate a range of learning experiences. First-hand experience and sensory interaction are vital components in play, as is appropriate intervention to reinforce, extend or challenge newly emerging concepts. The skill of the practitioner lies in the provision of stimulating and appropriate materials, resources and contexts and the ability to intervene at the optimum moment for learning. This skill is necessary for both child-initiated and supported play.

Play is a rich and varied activity that knows no subject boundaries, but rather encompasses a range of different learning categories in which common and specific skills will need to be learnt and practised. Skills are often subject transferable. For example, the enquiry skills used by geographers are also appropriate tools for many other areas of learning. We believe that it is beneficial to children's learning that the value of skills acquisition and their role in learning is flagged up by practitioners. Thus one key part of early geographical learning is to teach essential skills in holistic learning contexts, thereby enabling children to reflect on what they have done and how they have done it.

Young children are best able to make sense of their place in the world when:

■ They are inspired to think about their own place in the world, their values, and their rights and responsibilities to other people and the environment and given opportunities to actively participate;

■ Their wealth of knowledge, under-standings and feelings about people and places are drawn on by practitioners;

■ They are supported and encouraged to construct their own meanings about people and places;

■ They are encouraged positively to identify with other people and places

■ Practitioners recognise that children's sense of identity is rooted in the places where they live and play;

■ Their home areas, families and communities are valued; and

■ They actively experience a range of high quality, stimulating environments.

We recognise the specialised skills that parents and practitioners have that allow them to intervene sensitively and appropriately, as partners in children's learning.

The best practitioners impart the message that the child is valued for who he or she is and what she or he already knows. Children who feel valued in this way are more confident and will be more inclined to try new and different things and more willing to share their findings with others. We can, and should, model the value that we place on the lives and backgrounds of others. As recent research by Siraj-Blatchford *et al.* (2008) has shown, Early Years practitioners are powerful role models for the young children in their care.

Figure 1 | *Key ideas underpinning the Geographical Association's position statement on EYFS geography.* *Source* | *Geographical Association, 2003.*

Geography starts when we begin to value our place, and that of others, in the world and acknowledge the importance of our actions within it. The approaches that we believe underpin this process are outlined in Figure 1.

The importance of allowing children to participate actively in real learning contexts has been shown by Hart (1997). In a ground-breaking study, he argued that children's concern for the environment was born out of their affective unmediated contact with it and that the best outcomes were achieved when children's opinions were genuinely valued by adults. Indeed, it seems that even very young children are capable of making and enacting decisions about their environment with appropriate support. This of course stresses the value of first-hand experience in the outdoors. It is a requirement of the EYFS that children have regular and structured outdoor experiences and desirable that the outdoors is used whenever appropriate to stimulate and facilitate geographical learning. Outdoor provision should include a range of stimulating materials and settings in which pupils are encouraged to actively enquire, reflect and participate in desired change. Such learning is all the more valuable, because the pupils' role within it renders it meaningful and relevant. Catling (2003) rightly questions the lack of voice that young children often have within our society and calls for this to be corrected.

Photo | Paula Owens.

Children's early experiences of place may vary enormously but they all bring some awareness and understanding of geographical concepts to early learning contexts. Research by Blades and Spencer (1987, cited in Matthews, 1992) has shown that children as young as three were able to use simple maps in a rudimentary way, while Spencer and Darvizeh (1981, cited in Matthews, 1992) demonstrated that children of this age were capable of recalling routes travelled just once, using given photographs. The practitioner can build on this burgeoning understanding by actively teaching relevant skills inherent in observation, enquiry, communication, reflection and evaluation.

It is also important, when building on children's knowledge, to take opportunities to reinforce positive concepts and challenge negative ones. In fact the early years are the best time to challenge stereotypical thinking. As Scoffham and Potter (2007) observe, children's attitudes become entrenched as they get older and are harder to change. For this reason it is important that children have access to positive images of other peoples and cultures in global and local contexts. These images may be gleaned through a range of resources and first-hand experiences. Appropriate examples include:

- Experiencing the story *Mama Panya's Pancakes* (Chamberlin and Chamberlin, 2005), coupled with the opportunity to make and eat some (delicious) pancakes.
- A visit from a parent who may show artefacts and talk about their culture and beliefs.
- An email link with a school or institution from another country in which photographs and/or drawings can be exchanged.

While geographers tend to draw out similarities and differences between our own and other cultures and places, with very young children it is more fruitful to dwell on aspects of similarity. As practitioners, we have a duty to encourage tolerance, understanding, responsibility and respect, with a view to developing global citizens who will have the confidence, knowledge and skills to act fairly, capably and equitably in the world they will inherit. These attitudes for learning need to be started early.

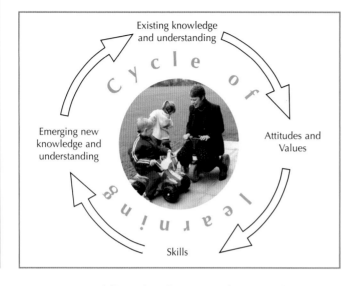

Existing knowledge and understanding

Cycle of learning

Emerging new knowledge and understanding

Attitudes and Values

Skills

Figure 2 | *The cycle of learning.*
Source | *Geographical Association, 2003.*
Photo | *Kathy Alcock and John Collar.*

The process of learning

We have already stated our belief that play is central to young children's learning. The Geographical Association (2003) sets out a model for learning that has play at the core (Figure 2). The model suggests that learning can be seen as a cycle that uses children's present levels of knowledge, understanding, skills and attitudes as a starting point.

We see the model as a flexible planning tool. A cycle of learning may be of different lengths, ranging from a single activity to a sequence undertaken over several weeks or more. We also recognise that within this process there is a constant cycle of learning that reflects the enquiry process (see Chapter 7), as new knowledge becomes existing knowledge and the process starts again. In addition, children need to revisit stages in the cycle in order to consolidate what they have learned. So while it may be possible to progress through the stages in a linear fashion such a progression is likely to lead to shallow learning that lacks meaningful roots. The rationale for this model is as follows:

1. Why start with prior knowledge and understanding?

All teachers are aware of the importance of establishing what their pupils already know, understand and can do before embarking on new learning. This helps to ensure that, whether activities are pupil-initiated or teacher-led, the work that you plan is at a suitable level and pupils have a cognitive framework into which the new learning can be accommodated.

2. Why is it important to develop attitudes as a base for new learning?

The EYFS is organised around four key principles: a unique child, positive relationships, enabling environments, and learning and development. These principles contribute to the Every Child Matters (DfES, 2003) objectives; they also embody attitudes and values which include:

▮ Giving children freedom to use their senses and be physically active and exuberant in both built and natural environments; developing curiosity, awe and wonder

▮ Stimulating children's enquiry about the world through explorations, investigations and questions; developing a sense of responsibility for the environment and their actions within it

▮ Developing children's respect for self and others; appreciating and valuing differences so that everyone feels included and understood, whatever their personality, abilities, ethnic background and culture.

In establishing the values base for new learning, take into account the ethos of the school, available provision, and the example of teachers and other role models. You also need to make the most of opportunities as they arise, whether identified by a colleague or stemming from pupils' current interests and ideas. For example, take your pupils on a walk to observe the changes in autumn, giving them the opportunity to play in the leaves and select some to take back to school.

Figure 3 | Opportunities for geographical experiences can be found in all aspects of the EYFS.

Opportunities can be found here...

Knowledge and understanding of the world (KUW)
Use a range of first-hand experiences to:
- Explore a range of real and created environments – school grounds, local facilities, model farm
- Observe similarities and differences in environmental and social contexts – compare our home to a place in a story
- Record the world around us in a variety of ways – models, maps, sounds, pictures
- Develop enquiry skills – develop curiosity through asking questions, make predictions, make informed choices, model research techniques using non-fiction books, and the internet

Personal, social and emotional development (PSE)
- Develop positive attitudes towards, and a respect for, people, places and cultures
- Embrace ethnic and cultural diversity through positive images – displays, stories, pictures, non-fiction texts, visits and visitors
- Show awe and wonder in response to places and events in the environment – rainbows, waterfalls, mountains, sunsets, waves, skyscrapers, bridges, places of worship
- Become curious about the world around them – Where do rivers begin and end? Where does rain come from? Why does it get dark?

There...

Physical development (PD)
- Enjoy and take part in physical challenges – follow routes, climb up/down hills, up/down climbing frame, negotiate obstacles
- Use relevant vocabulary – movement, direction, distance, location, speed
- Use spaces around them – control physical movements (forward/backward, left/right, up/down), find personal space in which to work, play or sit
- Take part in a range of activities in places outdoors – dig and plant, experience weather, visit wildlife area/other place, and indoors – use small world toys to create new or improve existing small worlds and environments; role play travel agents, garden centre staff, airport staff, weather reporters

Creative development (CD)
- Explore environments using all their senses – street, playground, supermarket, station, park, countryside, beach
- Explore resources from a variety of cultures and climates – artefacts, pictures, music, foods, clothing, poetry, story
- Employ natural materials creatively – clay, straw, wool, wood, shells, sand, twigs, leaves, water
- Appreciate the creativity of others' religions and cultures through visits, festivals, architecture, dance
- Use natural events as a stimulus for creative responses – waves, wind, rain, thunder

Holistic View of Learning

And everywhere...

Communication, language and literacy (CLL)
- Look at, and listen to, stories, non-fiction or rhymes about weather, places, people, cultures, journeys
- Make and read signs and symbols – label places (quiet area, messy area), label features in the room, look at symbols and signs in the environment, make personal pictorial representations, become familiar with other symbolic languages (e.g. Braille)
- Use a range of vocabulary to communicate knowledge and understanding of the world – naming, describing, positional vocabulary
- Talk about the world for a variety of purposes – discuss likes and dislikes, plan a journey, give instructions for a route to follow, describe pictures/features, investigate/enquire/ask questions about the environment
- Communicate own views and listen to those of others – Where shall we put the bird table?

Problem solving, reasoning and numeracy (PSRN)
- Observe, recognise and sort number, patterns and symbols in a range of environments – shapes in buildings, brick patterns, sorting and making symbols for outdoor play area
- Measure, order and record the world around us – distances in footsteps, pebbles and rocks by size, weight, types of transport
- Use positional vocabulary – on, in, under, next to, near, far away, through
- Use and give a range of directions – using control technology, e.g. roamer to programme left, right, forwards, backwards

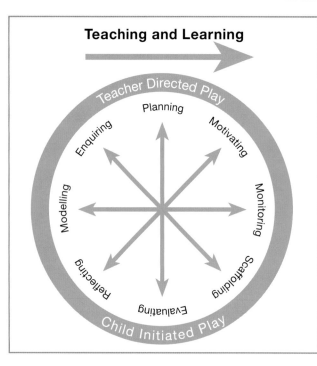

Teaching and Learning

Teacher Directed Play

Planning

Enquiring

Motivating

Modelling

Monitoring

Reflecting

Scaffolding

Evaluating

Child Initiated Play

Figure 4 | Enablers for learning.

3. Why skills next?

Investigating the world using a multi-sensory approach, developing an enquiring mind, making connections and exploring varied modes of communication are key elements in the EYFS framework. If children are to accommodate new learning they need to refine and develop new skills. In working towards the overall goal of making sense of their place in the world, they will be learning to input information about the world (asking questions, observing, recording, etc.) and learning to output information about the world (communication).

Try to develop awareness of skills and how they are used (metacognition) through teaching, practising, sharing and valuing. For example, a pupil making a painting as a means of exploring different colours and shapes of leaves is also encouraged to talk about the painting – colours chosen, why and how it was painted.

4. Why put new and emerging knowledge at the end of the cycle?

The EYFS aims to:

▦ Develop knowledge and understanding about places and peoples, near and far.

▦ Provide a range of positive experiences in varied and challenging environments.

We believe that children acquire new knowledge as a result of motivation and skills acquisition. Recognising new learning, and having existing/uncertain knowledge challenged in supportive ways are important elements in this process.

The teacher's role will be to challenge existing knowledge, to reinforce and to extend knowledge as appropriate. This must go together with applying knowledge. For example, ask the pupil 'If you were making a book on autumn what might you include and what materials might you use?'

Geographical learning in the EYFS framework

The way in which geographical experiences can be developed in all of the six areas of learning in the EYFS framework is shown in Figure 3. Recognising what 'counts' as geography will not only help practitioners, it will also ease pupils in their transition from one stage to the next.

While it is important to plan for pupil-initiated and teacher-directed activities, ideally these two modes of experience should mesh seamlessly into a unified learning process. We have identified eight key enablers for learning (Figure 4), that describe different approaches a practitioner might take to intercept periods of pupil-initiated and teacher-directed play. In practice there is no ideal

Photo | Kathy Alcock and John Collar.

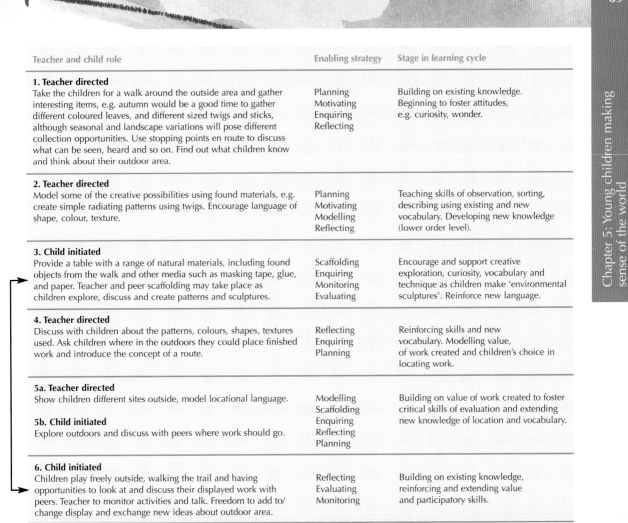

Teacher and child role	Enabling strategy	Stage in learning cycle
1. Teacher directed Take the children for a walk around the outside area and gather interesting items, e.g. autumn would be a good time to gather different coloured leaves, and different sized twigs and sticks, although seasonal and landscape variations will pose different collection opportunities. Use stopping points en route to discuss what can be seen, heard and so on. Find out what children know and think about their outdoor area.	Planning Motivating Enquiring Reflecting	Building on existing knowledge. Beginning to foster attitudes, e.g. curiosity, wonder.
2. Teacher directed Model some of the creative possibilities using found materials, e.g. create simple radiating patterns using twigs. Encourage language of shape, colour, texture.	Planning Motivating Modelling Reflecting	Teaching skills of observation, sorting, describing using existing and new vocabulary. Developing new knowledge (lower order level).
3. Child initiated Provide a table with a range of natural materials, including found objects from the walk and other media such as masking tape, glue, and paper. Teacher and peer scaffolding may take place as children explore, discuss and create patterns and sculptures.	Scaffolding Enquiring Monitoring Evaluating	Encourage and support creative exploration, curiosity, vocabulary and technique as children make 'environmental sculptures'. Reinforce new language.
4. Teacher directed Discuss with children about the patterns, colours, shapes, textures used. Ask children where in the outdoors they could place finished work and introduce the concept of a route.	Reflecting Enquiring Planning	Reinforcing skills and new vocabulary. Modelling value, of work created and children's choice in locating work.
5a. Teacher directed Show children different sites outside, model locational language. **5b. Child initiated** Explore outdoors and discuss with peers where work should go.	Modelling Scaffolding Enquiring Reflecting Planning	Building on value of work created to foster critical skills of evaluation and extending new knowledge of location and vocabulary.
6. Child initiated Children play freely outside, walking the trail and having opportunities to look at and discuss their displayed work with peers. Teacher to monitor activities and talk. Freedom to add to/change display and exchange new ideas about outdoor area.	Reflecting Evaluating Monitoring	Building on existing knowledge, reinforcing and extending value and participatory skills.
7. Teacher directed Discuss the outcomes of the trail. Encourage children to say how/why the trail has improved their environment.	Reflection Evaluation	Emerging new knowledge and understanding and values.

Figure 5 | *Cycle of learning: Creating a sculpture trail.*

Photo | *Paula Owens.*

prescribed order or combination in which enablers might be utilised. Rather we see them as flexible and sensitive tools in a vibrant learning environment. The subsequent examples illustrate how they might be used and demonstrate their wider relevance.

Cycle of learning: example 1
Evaluating and developing the outdoor area by creating a sculpture trail

We have chosen this as our first example of a cycle of learning because it utilises first-hand experience of the outdoors, builds on prior knowledge and encourages pupil participation.

Teacher and child role	Enabling strategy	Stage in learning cycle
1. Teacher directed Gather all the waste generated in the nursery/reception classroom over the course of a single day. Next day, with children, look at the waste (health and safety regulations important here) and consider the implications for what happens to it/ where it goes/possible impact on environment.	Planning Motivating Reflecting	Building on existing knowledge. Beginning to foster attitudes.
2. Teacher directed With maximum child involvement consider what needs to be done to change home corner area so that it becomes a 'waste management' area, encouraging recycling, reusing and repairing of waste from the home.	Planning Scaffolding Enquiring Reflecting	Using design-and-make skills to create waste management area Developing new knowledge (lower order).
3. Child-initiated 'Free' play in home waste management area. Children talk and play out some ideas generated during the planning and making phase. Peer scaffolding may be taking place here with the teacher acting as an observer	Modelling Enquiring Monitoring Evaluating	Using recently gained new knowledge. Using skills of sorting. Fostering attitudes and values.
4. Teacher directed Circle time discussion to gain children's ideas about what they have been doing in the waste management area, how they feel about it, whether any changes are needed, does it 'work', roles generated.	Reflecting Evaluating Planning	Reinforcing skills, values, knowledge and understanding (key concepts).
5a. Teacher directed Teacher role plays with children in the home corner, modelling roles/questions/activities. **5b. Child-initiated** Child role plays and teacher monitors whether play has changed as a result of circle time discussion.	Modelling Scaffolding Monitoring Evaluating Planning	Building on existing knowledge. Extending skills and understanding of key concepts (higher order).
6. Teacher directed Discuss and evaluate the use of the waste management area over the last week(s) and consider why it is important and relate to real life and waste centres.	Evaluating Assessing Planning	Emerging new knowledge and understanding and values.

Figure 6 | *Cycle of learning: Waste management.*

Overall aims of the sequence of activities

To develop skills of observation, communication and evaluation and enable the acquisition of relevant vocabulary and, as a result, to encourage critical decision making in the design of part of the outdoor area.

Learning objectives

- Develop enquiry and investigation skills (KUW)
- Develop co-operation and decision-making skills (PSE)
- Acquire a range of relevant vocabulary (CLL)
- Express responses to outdoor settings in a range of media (CD)
- Plan a simple route (KUW)
- Be able to take action to improve the environment (KUW/PSE)
- Express views about aspects of the environment (KUW/ CLL)

This activity (Figure 5) could take place at different times of the year using different found and gathered materials.

Cycle of learning: example 2
Using the home corner area as an example of waste management in the home

We have chosen this as our second example because there is encouragement from the government for citizenship and sustainable development to be integrated into learning at all levels of education. We believe that geographical learning provides an excellent context for these cross-curricular themes and that their emphasis on positive action has the potential to lead to some really purposeful and deep learning.

Key geographical concepts	
Sense of place	What is this place like?
Similarity and difference	How is it like your kitchen? How is it different to your kitchen at home?
Location and spatial pattern	Where are the waste bins? Are they easy to get to?
Change and continuity	Is there anything you would like to change in our area? What would you like to keep the same?
Cause and effect	Why did we change our home corner area? What difference has it made? If we didn't sort all our rubbish like this what would happen to it?
Appreciation	How does this help us look after our place?
Roles, responsibility and participation	Who decided to change our home corner area? Why did we decide to do it? Do any of you do this at home?

Figure 7 | *Developing key geographical concepts.*

Overall aims of the sequence of activities

To involve pupils in redesigning the home corner area in order to promote ideas about recycling and the reuse of materials as necessary for waste reduction, thus developing the knowledge, understanding and skills for them to take positive action to improve the environment.

Learning objectives
▒ Develop enquiry and investigation skills (KUW)
▒ Understand what a home is like – inputs and outputs (KUW)
▒ Understand the effects human activity can have on places (positive and negative) (KUW)
▒ Be able to sort materials into categories – recycle, reuse and repair (KUW/PSRN)
▒ Be able to take action to improve the environment (KUW/PSE)
▒ Plan out and then make the waste management area in home corner (CD/PSRN)
▒ Be able to reuse materials creatively (CD)
▒ Use vocabulary related to home and waste management (CLL)
▒ Ask and respond to questions about place (adaptation of home corner) (KUW/CLL)
▒ Talk about the world they are 'manipulating' using increasingly complex sentences (CLL)
▒ Understand symbols for recycling/reusing/repairing – standard and ones generated by themselves (CLL)

Photo | *Kathy Alcock and John Collar.*

Resources
▒ Usual home-corner kitchen items, e.g. sink, cooker, washing machine
▒ Waste area – different bins labelled for recycling packaging, reusing packaging and recycling food waste with one bin for anything that cannot be recycled, repaired or reused
▒ Posters/symbols to put around the area in appropriate places

Activities
Figure 6 sets out a sequence of activities which may take place over a week or more. As well as indicating the relationship between learning that is teacher-led and that which is child-initiated, it also shows which enabling strategies can be used (see Figure 4) and which stage in the learning cycle each activity relates to (see Figure 2).

Photo | *Kathy Alcock and John Collar.*

The teacher's role

These two examples of developing a sculpture trail and a waste management project show how the teacher's role shifts from directing and leading tasks to observing and monitoring pupil-initiated activity and back again. The enabling strategies used at any point will depend on the stage of learning.

In the waste management project the teacher draws on pupils' existing knowledge, using it to help them think in a way that they may not have considered before. They all know that we throw rubbish away during the school day, but they may not have thought about the amount we dispose of and the effect this is having on the environment. The discussion and activity aims to stimulate the pupils' interest in what is to follow. Depending on how the pupils respond, the teacher will adapt the loose plans for the next activity to take account of general and individual needs. For example, some pupils may need to develop subject-specific vocabulary, others may have misconceptions about the names and types of materials involved.

As far as planning is concerned the teacher's role will clearly shift from week to week. At the start of a project there needs to be an overall plan that sets out some clear learning objectives and indicates the range of activities that might take place, including a possible sequence. It is also important to relate the work to the six areas of learning in the Foundation Stage curriculum, identifying the resources required and the points at which pupils' learning can be monitored (for example, through recorded observations that have a clear focus). Short-term planning is also needed, on a day-to-day and weekly basis, which takes account of observations and evaluation of the pupils' activity and learning. In any learning experience pupils will be operating at a number of different stages in terms of their development, skills, knowledge and understanding.

In the examples cited in this chapter it is not necessary to plan different activities to match pupils' abilities. The activities are open-ended and it is possible for each pupil to act out roles, interact with others and use vocabulary that is appropriate for their level of understanding. The key role of the practitioner, therefore, will be to differentiate through intervention and scaffolding – varying the types of questions asked of each pupil, and making suggestions for further play based on careful observation of the previous activity.

Using targeted intervention to scaffold learning means that assessment has a critical part to play in the learning process. It also requires a certain level of knowledge on the part of the practitioner – i.e. the knowledge to be able to recognise what is taking place, to link it with frameworks for knowledge, understanding and attitudes, and therefore to identify what to do or say next that will best support each pupil.

One way of prompting pupils and helping to direct their thoughts is by asking appropriate questions. This approach is particularly compatible with geography which makes extensive use of enquiry questions to structure learning. Figure 7 identifies some key geographical concepts and shows how they can be developed. Further advice on asking questions is given throughout this handbook (see index).

Conclusion

The teaching and learning of very young children can be likened to a wheel that is forever turning, albeit at different speeds, and which rotates through periods of pupil-initiated and teacher-directed play. Although these periods will be planned for, it is essential that the settings chosen for EYFS geographical studies are flexible enough to allow for unexpected opportunities and demands as they arise. For example, a pupil may return after a holiday and bring in postcards and objects that prompt curiosity in the class, or an unusual weather event may provoke a raft of questions.

Good provision for learning in the EYFS will also involve a range of indoor and outdoor settings, a variety of resources and a clear underpinning ethic. Young children need to be exposed to a range of experiences that encourage curiosity, invite physical and sensory exploration, and provide opportunities for them to evaluate and change their environment. Current practice shows that when given adequate support, even very young children can think sustainably and make responsible decisions about their surroundings (Knight, 2009; Martin and Owens, 2008). Personal involvement is one of the best ways of developing values and is a powerful motivator for learning. Geography, because it taps into a range of skills and different ways of thinking, is uniquely placed to develop this. When children begin to value themselves and others and make meaningful connections about their actions within physical and social spheres both near and far, then they truly begin to make sense of the world.

References and further reading

de Bóo, M. (2004) *The Early Years Handbook: Support for practitioners in the foundation stage.* Sheffield: Curriculum Partnership.

Catling, S. (2003) 'Curriculum contested: primary geography and social justice', *Geography*, 88, 3, pp. 164-210.

Catling, S. (2006) 'What do five-year-olds know of the world? – Geographical understanding and play in young children's early learning', *Geography*, 91, 1, pp. 55-74.

Chamberlin, M. and Chamberlin, R. (2005) *Mama Panya's Pancakes.* Bath: Barefoot Books.

DCFS (2008) *The Statutory Framework for the Early Years Foundation Stage.* Nottingham: DCSF.

DCSF (2008) *Practice Guidance for the Early Years Foundation Stage.* Nottingham: DCSF.

DfES (2004) *Every Child Matters: Change for children in schools.* London: DfES.

Geographical Association (2003) *Making Connections: Geography in the Foundation Stage. A position statement from the Geographical Association.* Sheffield: Geographical Association.

Hart, R. (1997) *Children's Participation: The theory and practice of involving young citizens in community development and environmental care.* London: UNICEF/Earthscan.

Knight, S. (2009) *Forest Schools and Outdoor Learning in the Early Years.* London: Sage.

Martin, F. and Owens, P. (2008) *Caring for our World: A practical guide to sustainable development for 4-8 year olds.* Sheffield: Geographical Association.

Mathew, M. H. (1992) *Making Sense of Place: Children's understanding of large-scale environments.* Hemel Hempstead: Harvester Wheatsheaf.

Palmer, J. and Birch, J. (2004) *Geography in the Early Years.* London: Routledge Falmer.

Scoffham, S. and Potter, C. (2007) 'Please Miss, why are they so poor?', *Primary Geographer*, 62, pp. 5-7.

Siraj-Blatchford, I., Sylva, K., Taggart, B., Sammons, P. and Melhuish, E. (2008) 'Towards the transformation of early childhood practice', *The Cambridge Journal of Education*, 38, 1, pp. 23–36.

Wood, E. and Attfield, J. (2005) *Play, Learning and the Early Childhood Curriculum.* London: Sage.

PASSPORT

I look like this

Photo | Kathy Alcock and John Collar.

CHAPTER COVERAGE:
CONCEPTS • CROSS-CURRICULAR LINKS • GOOD PRACTICE
• PLANNING • PROGRESSION • QUESTIONS • TRANSITION

Understanding and developing primary geography

'[Geography] is learning about the world and the environment.'
[10 year old]

'[Geography] is education about map work and learning how our world is getting destroyed, and understanding how big the world is.'
[10 year old]

What is geography?

Geography is part and parcel of our personal survival kit. It is a way of looking at the world that focuses our learning on what places and the environment are like, why they are important to us, how they are changing and how they might develop in the future. To make sense of the features and layout of our immediate and the wider world, we map it, both to see where things are and to help us understand how it is organised. Recognising spatial patterns helps us to understand the variety of natural and human processes at work in the environment. It also enables us to plan ahead, whether to devise routes for travel or to reorganise parts of the locality.

But such knowledge and understanding are only one part of geographical awareness. Of equal importance is how we feel about different places. Places have meaning for us; they are where we are, not just where we reside or go to school, to play or to work, but where we feel 'at home' or 'out of place'. We relate to places, and this relationship is a key element of our personal identity.

We also have a wider concern for the world around us. We have a clearer understanding today about how we are affecting the environment than ever before. In our concern to improve our own lives and the lives of others, we have begun to realise that using resources wisely, managing the natural environment and repairing inadvertent damage is essential for our future. Geography encompasses all of this. The idea of the global citizen who realises the interplay and interdependence of the local and the wider world and who argues for responsible action in day-to-day life lies at its heart.

Traditionally geography has been defined as 'describing the Earth'. For each of us, today, geography:

- helps us to know where we are and know what is there, giving us a sense of location;
- develops our understanding of the environment, the natural world, modified landscapes and the social environment;
- provides a vocabulary to describe the features of the environment and the processes that shape it;
- enables us to understand the spatial layout and organisation of the world about us and recognise the spatial distributions, patterns and relationships in the environment;
- takes forward our understanding and appreciation of places, of their importance to us, of their impact on us and of how we can manage and develop them;
- introduces us to the nature, role and value of maps in 'seeing', understanding, interpreting and valuing the world, from the local to the global;
- help us to recognise how changes to places and the environment happen and affect us, both as a result of natural processes and through human activity;

Attitudes and values	Knowledge, concepts and understanding
The aims of geography in primary education are to:	The aims of geography in primary education are to:
■ Stimulate and develop children's interest in their own surroundings and in the variety of natural, modified and social environments and conditions around the Earth ■ Engage children's sense of wonder at the beauty and variety of the world ■ Inspire in children an awareness of their own place in the world ■ Develop in children informed concern about human impact on the quality of the environment and places in order to enhance their sense of responsibility for the care of the Earth and its peoples in the future	■ Enable children to extend their knowledge about the features, nature and character of their immediate surroundings and more distant environments, to support a sense of what it means to live in one place rather than another and as the basis for a framework of place knowledge ■ Develop children's appreciation of links and connections and their understanding of social and natural processes in creating and changing patterns and relationships in different landscapes and human activities ■ Build children's competence in using enquiry skills and analysing and communicating geographical information

Figure 1 | *Aims for geography in the curriculum. Adapted from Catling, 1998, and updated in line with government guidance.*

■ develops our sense of the value of sustainability, and of our stewardship of our world, at local and global scales;

■ helps us to recognise and value our interdependence with other people in our own area and the wider world and to appreciate the diversity evident in the world among peoples and environments.

Inevitably, then, primary geography teaching is concerned with knowing about and understanding the Earth, with developing the skills to do this well, and with fostering attitudes and values that enhance people's lives, places and the environment. All of this is natural for younger children, who are curious about their own and the wider world, who want to explore and investigate people, places and the environment, who wish to develop and enhance the skills to do so, and who enjoy and value the variety they see about them and have concerns for fairness and their future.

Including geography in the curriculum

The importance and value of geographical learning was recognised in the debate leading towards the introduction of the national curriculum in the 1980s. As a result geography was one of the subjects included when the national curriculum was introduced through the Education Reform Act of 1989. The first national curriculum geography programmes of study and attainment targets were introduced in 1991, followed by revisions in 1995 and 1999. From 1996 onwards a separate curriculum, for the Early Years Foundation Stage (EYFS) was also developed for younger children. This included a number of areas of learning one of which, 'knowledge and understanding of the world', relates directly to geography. As a result geography, in one context or another, has been a required component of the school experience of all 3-14 year-old children since 2000.

It is worth noting, then, that the period of formal geographical learning extends for eight years during nursery and primary school, with only three more years at secondary level (though a sizeable minority of pupils take geography for another four years). This gives early years and primary school teachers considerable opportunities to enhance pupils' geographical learning. Useful support for planning and resourcing classroom units of work at this level can be found in *The Early Years Handbook* (de Bóo, 2004), *Practice Guidance for The Early Years Foundation Stage* (DfES, 2007) and the Geographical Association's *Geography Plus* series (Owens and Richardson, 2011).

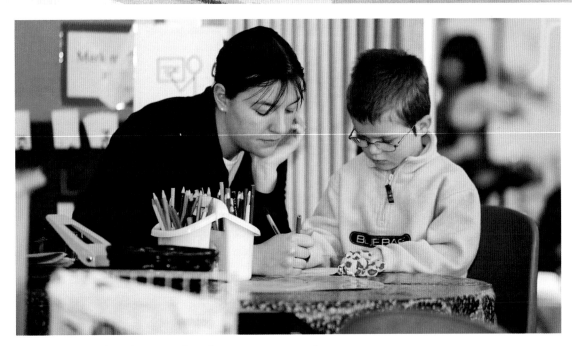

Photo | *Shaun Flannery.*

The focus of primary geography

Three key elements stand at the heart of geography in the early years and primary curriculum:
1. an understanding of places;
2. an understanding of the natural and social (or human) environment; and
3. an understanding of spatial organisation.

These different elements interact with each other and are underpinned by a fourth component – geographical skills and study methods. Without the gathering, examination and evaluation of data there can be no understanding of the interactions between place, environment and spatial organisation.

These elements also provide the basis for the aims for primary geography set out in Figure 1. They emphasise the importance of undertaking rigorous geographical investigations and enquiries. They also indicate clearly that geography is not only about being informed about and having an understanding of the world; it is also about fostering particular values and attitudes to the ways we treat our place, our planet and our fellow human beings.

Understanding places

The study of places is concerned with what places are like, how they came to be as they are, how we use them, how they might change and what we feel about and think of them. Developing the idea of place is not simply about exploring one place – our own – but involves comparing a number of places, from within the UK and across the world. For younger pupils the focus is on small areas which they can examine in detail. Through their studies, particularly of their own places, pupils will begin to develop their sense of place and personal identity. In addition, they will start constructing cognitive or mental maps of the locality, country, Europe and the world as a basic locational framework to which to relate other places they encounter throughout life.

Understanding natural and social environments

We cannot look at places without looking at their environment. The word environment is frequently used simply to refer to the natural world but for geographers it has a wider meaning. As well as looking at natural features such as rivers, mountains, seas and coasts, geographers seek to understand the physical processes that created them. It is also important to recognise that human activity has modified the environment to a considerable extent. For example, farming, industry and settlements now cover much of the natural habitat and landscape of the UK. Examining social forces is another aspect of geographical work. People have an impact on places through work and leisure activities. What they think about the environment – their perceptions and feelings – affect the decisions that they take. Geography seeks to examine why we might want to preserve natural environments or revive derelict sites and how we might use natural resources more sparingly and sustainably. Inevitably, this will involve studying controversial issues and recognising and weighing up different viewpoints. Pupils will also need to explore their own attitudes and values, considering where they stand on some issues and looking at what they might do to bring about improvements. Essential to this is the recognition that people do not always do things in the same way in different parts of the world. Culture plays a role. Where you live, what access you have to resources, how you are treated, and what your society values will all play a part in how you respond. Fundamentally, geography examines the interplay within and between the social, modified and natural environments to help children learn how to contribute to their own community and to the world at large.

Photo | Tina Horler.

Understanding geographical space

To understand our environment we need to understand its spatial organisation. Knowing where something is, either in relation to other things or on an abstract grid, is a key geographical idea. This is why maps are so important. Modern photographic and computer technologies use satellite-based global positioning systems (GPS) to pinpoint just about anywhere on the Earth's surface. By mapping locations and features geographers can identify distribution patterns which provide clues about the character of different places. As well as identifying land use patterns in cities, towns and agricultural areas, space satellites provide information about weather patterns as they develop and move and so help us to make predictions. In all these ways, spatial and temporal information about the environment helps us to understand how the world works.

Using methods of study in geography

Pupils need to learn how to read, interpret, use and make maps, not least as a life skill but also as a key tool in appreciating the nature of the environment and the processes that shape it. At its heart geography is about the world 'out there'; it does not exist without a wide variety of information gathered from the environment. This can only be obtained by going outside. Fieldwork provides the raw data, the observations, the sampling, the measurements, the photographs, the sketch maps and the conversations that provide the basis for geographical understanding.

Photo *| John Halocha.*

Pupils need a clear sense of purpose and the capacity to ask focused geographical questions if they are to use techniques well and know when the evidence is useful. Thus, at the core of environmental observation and data gathering is effective enquiry. For example:

- What is it?
- Where is it?
- What is it like?
- How did it come to be like this?
- How is it changing?
- How might it change and what are the alternative possibilities?
- What impact is change having or might it have?
- What different viewpoints and opinions are there, and what do I think and feel about this?
- What, realistically, might, could or should be done next?
- What do I think, feel and/or do?
- How does it compare to other similar or different examples?

To use and respond to such questions does not just require gathering information at first-hand; it will often be essential to use secondary sources as well. Maps, photographs, drawings, charts, tables and diagrams are some of the resources available. But however the information is collected it will need evaluation. As well as describing what environments and places are like, geography also involves making considered judgements about current processes and causes and indicating what might happen next based on the balance of probabilities. Furthermore, geography also looks at what it might be best to do and, thus, how the environment and places might be managed, now and in the future.

Developing primary geography

The early learning goals and the national curriculum identify the range of geography to be studied (see latest guidance on official websites). To illustrate the connections between, the continuity within, and the potential for progression across the varied elements of pupils' geographical experience in the Early Years Foundation Stage and key stages 1 and 2, Figure 2 outlines the geography requirements.

In the Early Years Foundation Stage children should be encouraged to develop their observational skills and to find out more about features in the school and the immediate area as part of their growing awareness of the world. They need to find out about people and physical features. Their observations and enquiries should be built around their personal experience and they should be encouraged to express their own views and opinions. The information that they encounter about other peoples and places will form the basis for discussion and examination of the wider world beyond direct experience in the nursery and reception class. Learning an initial vocabulary about the environment is a key aspect of this experience.

In key stage 1, children's understanding will be developed through more structured investigations of the local area and a contrasting place in or beyond the UK. Learning about people and the way the environment is changing will continue to be important. Children will

Geographical elements	Early Years Foundation Stage	Key stage 1	Lower key stage 2	Upper key stage 2
Throughout their geographical studies, children should:				
Developing geographical curiosity, enquiry, language and skills	Show curiosity and interest in exploring their surroundings Ask questions Observe, identify and find out about features locally Use everyday words about features, places and positions	Ask geographical questions as they undertake geographical enquiries Observe and record evidence Undertake fieldwork Use and make plans and maps, at a range of scales, and use globes Use personal knowledge and selected primary and secondary sources, including online sources Communicate what they find out, beginning to use geographical vocabulary	Ask geographical questions and contribute to planning their geographical enquiries and learning Collect and record evidence Analyse evidence, draw conclusions and communicate findings, extending their use of geographical vocabulary Use fieldwork skills and methods Use globes, atlases, maps and plans at a range of scales Use personal knowledge and a range of primary and secondary sources, including online sources	Ask geographical questions and plan, undertake and evaluate geographical enquiries and learning Collect, record and analyse evidence, draw conclusions and communicate findings using geographical language Identify and explain different viewpoints Use appropriate fieldwork techniques and instruments Use globes, atlases, maps and plans at a variety of scales Use personal knowledge and a variety of primary and secondary sources, including selecting online sources to aid their enquiries Investigate, analyse and process data on local and global issues using ICT
Developing understanding about people, cultures, places and locations	Explore and investigate places using all their senses, as appropriate Identify various features in their environment Begin to know about their own and other cultures Explore the idea of belonging to groups and communities Begin to compare and contrast different features and changes in their immediate area	Find out about the physical and human features of their own locality Know the location in the UK of their own locality and be aware of where other places are in the world Find out how their locality has changed over time Explore how their own and others' ways of life change with location and time Use the internet to explore distant and contrasting places Compare their own with another place	Know the locations of significant places in UK, Europe and the wider world Describe what places are like and where they are Investigate how and why neighbourhoods and communities change Describe how and why places are similar to and different from each other	Appreciate that communities and neighbourhoods and the people living in them are diverse, changing and interconnected Consider how people can live and work together to benefit communities Explain why places and communities have much in common and but are also diverse, and make comparisons between them
Developing understanding of spatial locations, patterns and connections locally and worldwide	Identify and look closely at some patterns in their environment	Note links between their own locality and elsewhere, in the UK and beyond Make observations about where features are located and why they might be there	Identify patterns in communities, places and environments Appreciate relationships between physical, built and economic and social environments Understand that people, places and environments are connected, and how	Understand a variety of geographical processes that cause change in the physical and human world in different places Recognise how human patterns are influenced by human and physical processes Know about factors affecting weather and climate Recognise how places fit within a wider geographical context and are interdependent
Developing understanding of environmental impact and sustainability	Express views about places they like and dislike	Find out about significant environmental issues and events, and express views on them Participate in decision-making activities relating to improving the local environment or community Recognise the difference between what is fair and unfair in the ways people use and look after the environment	Consider issues affecting, and the impact of people's actions on, other people, places and the environment Become aware of how the different ways people live around the world can have consequences for the environment and for others' lives, from local to global scales	Address issues of place and environmental concern through decision-making activities and actions Recognise how decisions about places and environments can affect the quality and future of people's lives, and identify ways to become involved Know why it is important to manage environments sustainably, now and in the future, and about ways to manage them Distinguish fact and opinion in matters about people, places and environmental issues

The geographical context: aspects of children's geographical learning to develop throughout the EYFS and across their primary schooling	▪ Children should develop a secure understanding of how and why places develop, how they may be sustained and how they might change in the future. ▪ During the EYFS and the primary school geography curriculum children should investigate people and cultures, communities, places and environments at local, national and global scales. ▪ The range of geographical topics and themes that children might study includes their own community and locality; cultures and communities in localities in other parts of the UK and the world; sustainability; resource access, such as to water, food and energy; economic inequalities; weather and climate change; and landscapes. ▪ Through these studies children should develop informed perspectives on local, national and global issues and their impact on people, communities, places and environments. Such studies should include topical matters and examples. These should engage with challenging and controversial topics and themes, helping children at all ages to learn ways to study and deal with these and consider their own views. ▪ During their geographical studies across the EYFS and primary schooling, children should use fieldwork, first-hand experience, and primary and secondary sources, including ICT, in their enquiries and investigations. ▪ Children should apply key skills and develop literacy, numeracy and ICT skills in their geographical studies during the EYFS and primary schooling. ▪ Across the EYFS and primary schooling there should be an appropriate balance of geography subject teaching and learning and of studies in which other curriculum subjects and areas are appropriately linked with geography.

Figure 2 | *Geography in the EYFS and developing across key stages 1 and 2. See latest guidance on official websites.*

Photo | *Tina Horler.*

also develop their awareness of the world beyond the local area using atlases and maps to find out about places. In observing the environment pupils should consider ways to look after and to improve it. This will develop their sense of environmental care and initiate an early understanding of sustainability. In undertaking these studies, younger pupils will also begin to think about why some parts of the environment change and others do not, and about the locations of different features and activities they see. Pupils should be encouraged to use and extend their growing geographical vocabulary as they explain their ideas.

Figure 3 | *Progression in geographical enquiry from the EYFS to year 6.*

Foundation Stage	Years 1 & 2	Years 3 & 4	Years 5 & 6
Talk about observations of features in the immediate environment and in photographs	Make observations about features and activities in the local environment and in secondary sources	Give reasons for some observations about places and the environment from direct experience and secondary sources	Explain reasons for making observations about places and the environment from direct experience and secondary sources
Answer questions about features	Respond to questions about places and environmental topics	Respond to geographical questions, for instance, why might we find shops grouped together in towns?	Respond to geographical questions, for example, about the relationship within river processes
Ask questions about what they see around and in pictures to gain information	Ask questions about places and environmental topics	Ask geographical questions, such as why are there more vehicles using this street?	Suggest suitable geographical questions for investigation, such as, Where would a new shop best be situated?
Talk about how they find out information	Discuss ways to carry out an enquiry	Offer own ideas for planning the enquiry, e.g. for a fieldwork investigation	Plan a geographical enquiry, for instance, about a particular locality
Sometimes collect and record observations and information	Collect and record evidence	Collect and record evidence, for example through a survey	Collect, sift and record appropriate evidence
Talk about what they have observed about the place or environment	Use evidence to describe what there is or what happens in a place or environment	Begin to analyse evidence and draw conclusions	Analyse and evaluate evidence to draw conclusions about the topic of and questions in the enquiry
Talk about what they think about the place or environment	Express views on features in the environment	Identify their own views about geographical topics Begin to recognise that others hold views about places and the environment	Identify and explain the various viewpoints held by different people about places and the environment. Begin to appreciate the arguments put forward for viewpoints and that different people may hold opposing views sincerely
Extend vocabulary to describe features and activities in places and the environment	Extend vocabulary to describe features and activities in places and the environment Begin to use appropriate geographical vocabulary	Extend further their use of appropriate geographical vocabulary	Extend further their use of appropriate geographical vocabulary, including the use of more technical terms
Talk about what they have seen and found out	Communicate findings in different ways	Communicate findings as if to an audience and appropriate to the task	Communicate findings in ways appropriate to the topic of the enquiry and as if to an audience
Talk about what they liked or did not like about finding out	Discuss what they have learnt from the enquiry and if they liked doing it	Evaluate the outcome(s) of enquiries and investigations and what they have learnt about undertaking an enquiry	Evaluate and reflect upon the outcome(s) of the enquiries and investigations, to consider both the skills, knowledge and understanding that they have gained and what has been learnt about undertaking an enquiry that can be applied in their next geographical enquiry

In key stage 2, these burgeoning ideas are taken further. Children's ability to initiate and organise enquiries grows as they begin to gain a deeper understanding of geographical questions. Examining localities, now perhaps at the scale of the school's catchment area, in the UK, Europe or elsewhere in the world, provides a basis for comparisons. Looking at specific aspects of the human and physical environment should develop ideas about settlements and water, and their roles in people's lives. This is an opportunity to examine the location and distribution of features and events and look at patterns in physical and human environments, as well as the processes which shape them, such

Figure 4 | *An outline of possible progression in geographical studies from EYFS to year 6 (see also Catling and Willy, 2009).*

Encountering Geography: The Early Years Foundation Stage

Pupils should:

Observe and find out about features and activities in the nursery/school and local streets;

Talk about what they like and dislike about their immediate environment;

Use pictures and discussion to develop awareness of peoples, environments and places;

Talk about the lives of other people;

Play with environmental toys, and listen to stories about what people do in a variety of places and environments.

Geographical Awareness: Years 1 & 2

Pupils should:

Describe features and activities in the local area and other environments

Use enquiry questions and a variety of sources to find out about localities near and far;

Examine people's lives in places, and their cultures;

Look at similarities and differences between places;

Express views about places and environmental matters;

Observe that environments change and find out how they can be looked after.

Geographical Engagement: Years 3 & 4

Pupils should:

Contribute to planning their geographical enquiries and how they can carry them out;

Examine the location of features and activities and patterns they create;

Consider how some changes in places and the environment are caused, and look at the impact on people's lives;

Consider the links between where people live and what they do;

Look at what settlements are like, using a locality as one example among others;

Study how people are affected by and can affect the environment;

Consider how people can improve the environment.

Geographical Involvement: Years 5 & 6

Pupils should:

Plan, undertake and share enquiries using a variety of resources;

Analyse ways in which human and natural processes create and shape localities and aspects of the environment, such as rivers or coasts, and affect locations and geographic patterns;

Compare how places are changing, and consider the effects of change;

Explain the importance of the interdependence of peoples and places;

Study how decisions affect places and environmental issues, and appreciate the reasons why different people hold different views on issues;

Identify and justify ways in which they can be involved in sustaining environments.

Geographical skills

Geographical skills are to be threaded through all years. Children need to develop experience and skills that support their development of:

- the use of photographs of all sorts - elevation, oblique and vertical - and at a range of scales;

- the use of maps of all sorts and at a range of scales, from playmat maps and large scale plans to atlas and wall maps;

- the use of various secondary sources including information books and texts of all sorts, the visual media, and ICT (e.g. CDs, websites);

- the development of vocabulary, from everyday words and phrases to geographical terms;

- the use of fieldwork, to draw on the key geographical primary source.

as settlements and communities; rivers or coasts; weather and climate; and related social and economic issues. Children will discover how people affect and manage the environment, damaging, sustaining or improving it through the decisions they make. Through their encounters and studies of places and environments around the world, children will build up their locational knowledge. Building on their descriptions, children will develop their analytic and evaluative skills and use increasingly precise geographical vocabulary.

This outline indicates a potential progression from the nursery to the end of the primary school. It involves moving from the local outwards in increasing depth from the earliest years. From asking rather general and, indeed, random questions about places and the environment, pupils build up a sense of effective geographical questions and, with good guidance, become more selective and thorough in their enquiries. Figure 3 illustrates such a progression in the development of geographical enquiry from the EYFS to the end of key stage 2. This involves using increasingly precise geographical vocabulary, as well as moving from specific examples to more abstract ideas and concepts. Over time, pupils extend their information base, and can better make comparisons and identify possible ways to improve the environment and consider

By the end of key stage 2 most children should be able to:

■ give examples of ways in which physical, social and economic features and processes affect people's lives, places and environments;

■ give reasons for some of the shared and diverse characteristics found between lives, communities, places and environments around the world;

■ outline how and why communities, places and environments develop, how they may change in the future, and how they are interdependent;

■ appreciate, explain and take actions to care for the environment and live sustainably now and for the future, and recognise that these can be contested;

■ locate on maps from local to world scales places related to their own experience and interests and important places in the news;

■ use and respond to questions while undertaking geographical enquiries, using skills such as fieldwork and resources such as the web, maps and a range of data sources.

Figure 5 | *Expectations for achievement in geography by the end of year 6. Adapted from Catling and Willy, 2009.*

reasonably how they might act to do so. Figure 4 presents one way in which this progression in geographical learning could be structured. It outlines the way in which the focus of geographical studies might evolve from the EYFS to the last two years of key stage 2. It also provides a basis for identifying the emerging geographical understanding which most primary pupils should have when they move on to secondary school and to study geography at key stage 3. This is outlined in Figure 5, as a summative statement for pupils' geographical learning in primary education.

Interconnectedness in geography teaching

No aspect of geography can really be taught in isolation. In planning geography teaching, it is important to consider geographical methods at the same time as geographical content. When pupils study their locality, for example, they will talk about what people do there and what the place means to them, examine different physical features and decide on suitable enquiry questions and the mapwork and fieldwork skills they will employ. The working group that devised the original national curriculum always envisaged that schools would integrate skills, places and themes in their geographical studies (DES/WO, 1990). This interrelationship can be expressed visually using a cube to represent the curriculum (Figure 6). One of the advantages of this model is that it provides a unifying framework. At the same time it is flexible enough to match different physical environments and a range of planning strategies.

It is also important to recognise that geography makes strong links with other curriculum areas (Rowley and Cooper, 2009). The study of water, soils and rocks in science, for instance, is integral to an appreciation of how rivers shape the landscape. Equally, recording the lie of the land in art or representing the seashore in music provides another dimension to geographical investigations. More than any other subject, geography serves to bridge and unify different curriculum areas (Figure 7). You can use these overlaps to your advantage when it comes to finding time for geography in an over-crowded timetable.

Moving primary geography forward

Since the introduction of the national curriculum in 1989, the quality of geography teaching in the early and primary years has steadily improved. By early 2000 geography teaching was at least 'satisfactory' in more than 90% of primary schools and 'good' or better in 47% (Catling *et al.*, 2007; Ofsted, 2006, 2008). Pupils' progress and achievement, however, lagged behind and was only 'good' or better in 36% of schools. Compared to English, maths and science these figures are not strong; but they represent considerable progress since the late 1980s, when geography teaching was generally in a very poor state (DES/WO, 1989).

If we examine the nature of the 'good' and better geography teaching, a number of characteristics emerge (Catling *et al.*, 2007; Ofsted, 2008; Catling and Willy, 2009). One is that

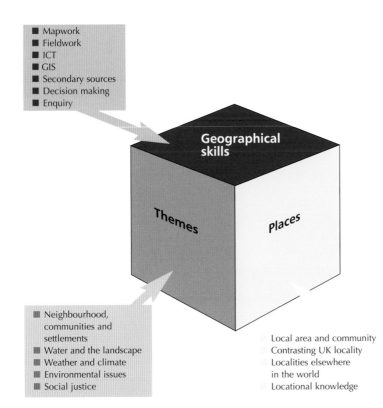

- Mapwork
- Fieldwork
- ICT
- GIS
- Secondary sources
- Decision making
- Enquiry

Geographical skills

Themes

Places

- Neighbourhood, communities and settlements
- Water and the landscape
- Weather and climate
- Environmental issues
- Social justice

Local area and community
Contrasting UK locality
Localities elsewhere
in the world
Locational knowledge

Figure 6 | *Geographical studies involve combining skills, places and themes.*

pupils find the geography they are studying stimulating and engaging, and can relate it to their own experience. Another is that children respond well to teachers who convey confidence in their geographical understanding and can support pupils' learning with well-focused guidance. Such teachers tend to:

- be clear about the geographical intentions of units of work and lessons;
- use a variety of creative and engaging teaching methods and activities;
- differentiate the tasks while ensuring suitable challenge;
- make use of appropriate vocabulary;
- employ demanding questioning techniques;
- involve the pupils in debate;
- support work with effective resources; and
- use formative assessment proactively to respond to pupils' needs in lessons.

Rather than being isolated, effective geography lessons link to long- and medium-term planning for geography in the school. From EYFS to the end of key stage 2 the units of study show a clear structure and progression, with teachers building on the work of their colleagues so that progression in experience and learning can occur. In such schools, a fair and reasonable amount of

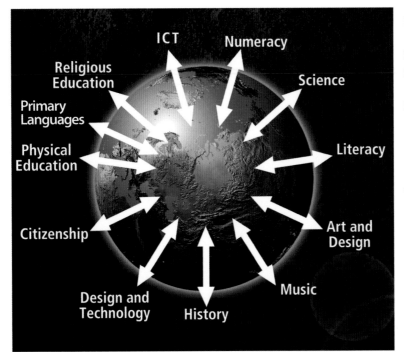

Figure 7 | *Exploring many different curriculum areas through geography.*
Source | *Geographical Association, 2003.*

time (in relation to other subjects) is given to geography and pupils can undertake independent research and follow up personal interests and lines of enquiry. Geography lessons are also, in part, linked to topical occurrences and issues.

Good practice involves encouraging pupils to relate and synthesise information, to analyse and explain their findings, and to evaluate and indicate possible solutions to problems in places and the environment. They also need to look for similarities and contrasts in what they study. This occurs in a school which values geography, as it does other subjects in the curriculum; looks for the appropriate links between subjects and makes good use of them; and ensures that suitable resources are available for pupils to use. It also occurs in schools where the senior management supports the geography subject leader in monitoring and developing geography across the staff. Such schools are not dependent on a single good teacher of geography; the quality and consistency of pupils' geographical learning is the result of a whole-school commitment to enabling pupils to do well in their learning.

It is a matter of some concern that at present less than half of nursery and primary schools meet these standards. Yet there is the foundation in current geography teaching on which to build. Almost all primary schools have schemes of work that include geography, and very many nursery schools and other early years settings have devised activities in the local environment for even their youngest children. Fieldwork is reasonably evident, though it is not always easy to organise, or frequently organised (Ofsted, 2008; Catling, 2010). When it does happen, it is clear that pupils are strongly stimulated in their geographical learning. Much use has been made of locality packs to support the study of places in other parts of the world, and enquiries into the school grounds and local issues are an excellent means of studying environmental sustainability. However, much geography teaching in primary schools lacks challenge and stimulus (Ofsted, 2008), with an emphasis on descriptive activities rather than analysis and explanation. There seems to be an inappropriate use of commercial worksheets to demonstrate that geography has been taught, instead of the pupils really engaging in looking at real places, environments and events, drawing on the news and topical concerns.

There are two main needs. First, teachers should raise their expectations of pupils in their geographical learning. Second, teachers need the confidence to provide stimulating, imaginative and effective curriculum planning and classroom teaching, underpinned by focused and appropriate formative and summative assessment. We need to widen our approaches to geography teaching, and draw on a more contentious range of topics – to move beyond descriptive reports to analysis, explanation and evaluation. There are links here with the development of active geographical citizens.

Developing analysis, explanation and evaluation

Observing and describing places accurately provides a vital foundation for the development of geographical learning and understanding. However, pupils need to move beyond the initial gathering of information in order to appreciate different viewpoints, make judgements and put forward proposals for improvements. The best learning occurs when pupils are encouraged and challenged to offer their own explanations for phenomena they have observed or identified. In these situations they begin to develop the key concepts which stand at the heart of geography – location, pattern and process – and apply some of the principles and ideas which are unique to geography. If we wish to promote higher order skills of this kind it needs to be featured in our planning. Figure 8 illustrates some ways in which the skills being

Skills	Examples with a geographical focus
Information-processing skills	Observing in the environment the feature/scene in a photograph Identifying features on maps using pictogram and abstract symbols Reading the landscape/urbanscape of an area through a synthesis of the symbols on a map Reading information from graphs and charts showing, e.g. traffic data, rainfall, temperature Reading information from thematic maps showing, e.g. building and land use, the distribution of shops, etc. Reading cross-sections showing, e.g. river-bed depth
Reasoning skills	Drawing sketch maps to show, e.g. the key features of an area, the distribution of specific features such as houses Drawing diagrams to show, e.g. the sequence and relationship in river and coastal processes Drawing a series of pictures to show, e.g. changes in an area over time Using a set of photographs, e.g. of different sorts of scenes, sort them into urban/rural, view/detail, particular features
Enquiry skills	Examining maps, photographs, sketches, diagrams and charts to generate questions, e.g. about an environmental issue Selecting appropriate graphical resources from which to gather information, e.g. for a locality study, including maps and photographs Making drawings and sketches to show the equipment and processes used in an investigation, e.g. of river processes Drawing maps, pictures or diagrams to show, e.g. a prediction of the possible outcome of an investigation into wind direction and sheltered areas in the school grounds
Creative thinking skills	Creating models and drawings to show, e.g. how a new development might look in the local area on a piece of derelict land Given various resources, creating, e.g. a particular type of home or shop in the home corner Making a poster to show, e.g. ways to tackle an environmental problem, such as litter disposal Create a story-board sequence to show, e.g. the day in the life of a child in a particular community Using a map as a basis, create a wall painting, e.g. of how an area might have looked in an earlier period
Evaluation skills	From a range of published visual sources create a collage of helpful and unhelpful visual images, e.g. of the way places are shown in various travel brochures Use graphics to show what is felt about, e.g. a particular environmental concern, such as 'smiley' or 'dismayed' faces Draw cartoons to show, e.g. views about a decision in a role play related to change in a community Create a visual set of criteria, e.g. to use to judge the 'pollution', cleanliness and care for a street or park

Figure 8 | *Some examples of geographical approaches for developing creativity and thinking skills.* **Source** | *Catling, 2002, p. 7.*

promoted across the primary curriculum can be developed in geographical studies.

Widening awareness of the world

It is crucial that pupils of all ages explore both their known world and the world beyond their experience. The local area is a vital part of geographical study as it grounds pupils in their direct experience. However, geography also involves developing an understanding of more distant people and places and forming an informed appreciation of the planet on which we live. This means that in their work on geographical themes and localities pupils need to encounter places at a range of scales. This needs to be planned for, using carefully selected examples as well as incidental and topical events as they occur in the news and even from the pupils' and your own direct experience.

Widening pupils' sense of the world also involves moving beyond the comfortable to examining some of the problems and difficulties that affect people, places and environments. This may involve local change and developments about which people feel strongly, or problems that people face in other, less-well-off parts of the world. On a local level, a study of the school playground might lead to proposals to make it a more varied, attractive and stimulating place. On a global level, finding out about the causes and impact of poverty on people's lives in another part of the world may cause children to reconsider, and perhaps modify, the way they live their own lives. Figure 9 illustrates a number of such possible topics.

Active learning for geographical understanding

Geography studies the world as it is today. It is based on what happens in the world directly around us and further afield. We can keep abreast of what is happening locally through our use of personal information, through what we hear from friends, from the local press and radio

Figure 9 | *Some possible topics for geography units of study in the early years and primary geography curriculum. Adapted from Catling, 2003.*

Geography topic	Focus of study
Exploring the school environment	To consider who the school is for, and how and why it is used in this way; school as friendly or fearful; inclusion/exclusion, dark corners, open spaces, crowds and quiet areas, signs and symbols; designing the school space as place; school as a community. Examine the features, spatial layout, use of school building and grounds; look at activities undertaken in school, why, where; consider benefits and problems in the way schools are laid out, structured, regulated; access, impact of features, layout; examine issues in school and how they relate to the nature of the place, such as peer and adult relationships, access to space, environmental quality, change; ideal school layouts, functions, organisation; proposals for improvement.
Playground and play area space (in and/or out of school)	To examine the use of playground space, included and excluded children, changing use of space; who uses the playground, multiple uses and users of the playground; places in the playground in the mind; creating playground landscapes; fair uses of space, timing; rules for space, activity and relationships; playground traditions; changing playgrounds.
Limits to mobility (in and/or out of school)	To understand the environment experienced by those with mobility difficulties, young, old, disabled, parents of toddlers; feelings of exclusion; inhibitors to movement and access; approaches to improvement; quality review of the environment.
My locality	To explore the local area through children's eyes and experience; what they value; places used and avoided, reasons why; variations between children; what to improve or set aside for children, how to leave it; use of local facilities and services; concerns and hopes for the future; what other and younger children might want of the area; proposals for the future.
Taking care in the local area	To work with a local group to care for, improve and manage an area; contact with local environment groups, why conservation and environment groups do what they do, people's attitudes to and concerns for the environment, why act; examining how children and adults are involved in environmental management and sustainability in other places nationally and globally; work on a particular environmental activity; examining the outcomes and consequences of actions.
Water for people	To investigate water as a fundamental human need; ways to access water, water use, water control, excessive and limited water access/use; people's experience of water access, variations in access, attitudes to water plenty and scarcity; water as a source for agriculture, industry, energy, leisure, environmental quality, household activities, sanitation; water in the community; sources of water; control of water; water aid, community development and aid, personal responses to water need and use; water in the future.
The impact of poverty: far and near	To explore the nature and impact of poverty in different contexts around the world; local poverty issues, poverty in different parts of the world; the effects and impact of poverty; causes of poverty, how poverty is maintained and exploited; views of poverty; attitudes to and feelings about people in poverty; poverty and its impact on the environment; ways to tackle poverty; aid and poverty; who benefits from poverty; creating and overcoming poverty.
Getting into place	To study particular localities in non-UK areas of the world; children's lives in communities and neighbourhoods; the questions to ask, the resources to use; how do different people use places, why these variations exist; what are people's views of, interests in, attitudes to, concerns for, hopes about the future of their locality; local features, facilities and amenities; the impact of change; local features.
A fairer world	To investigate the issues of fair trade and work; study of a particular product from source to home, e.g. bananas, trainers; employment, work practices; who is involved, their contribution, benefits, losses; trade control, who wins/loses; consumer choices, place of purchase; being a consumer, making choices; commitment to fair trade; attitudes to and use of income, expenditure, personal practices, willingness to change.
Future world	To consider and propose how the local area and other places and environments might become; how we would prefer them to be; personal and group ideas for the future for ourselves, the local community, for others and globally; examining the role of values, attitudes and preferences in thinking about the future; possible impacts of ways the world locally and globally might change and be; alternative scenarios, positive and of concern; the role of and difference between prediction and proposal; how we might change one particular aspect of our home area and of another place.

Photo | *Paula Richardson.*

and television and through fieldwork. We are aware of what is happening in other parts of the world through similar media reports. To these we can add the increasing use of the internet as a source of local and distant knowledge. Geography teaching not only needs to focus on the world about us as it is now, but it needs to recognise that the study of the day-to-day world requires an active approach rather than the passive study of predigested information. It also involves critical examination, not unquestioning acceptance. Children want to relate geography to their own lives and the issues that affect them (Martin, 2006; Catling and Willy, 2009).

Pupils are enthused by tasks that provide challenge, use their experience, draw on their understanding, have practical dimensions and involve them actively. Such activities should reinforce and extend their understanding, through new contexts and examples as much as through new ideas and content. There should be variety in the tasks used and they should challenge pupils' thinking, however incrementally.

Geography develops positive appreciation of places and the environment. As such it links strongly to aspects of citizenship education, for example, through understanding the planning that underpins decision-making and promoting global awareness. The overlap between citizenship and geography is explored in greater detail in Chapter 21. What is important to note at this point is that there are good opportunities for cross-curricular working.

Resourcing geography teaching

Geography is a resource-rich and resource-needy subject. Focusing as it does on the world today, it is essential that the materials we use are up-to-date. Commercial publications provide information about other places but they date very quickly; indeed they begin to date the moment they appear. This makes more immediate resources, such as the news reports on radio and television, newspapers and the internet, all the more important. Pupils need to recognise the limitations of such current, almost ephemeral, material. It may be inaccurate, selective and even contain bias or prejudice, depending on the source. These same concerns need to be kept in mind when selecting published materials for schools, whether CDs, textbooks, information books, photo packs, or video/DVD programmes.

Some resources can be created in school, and many can be obtained very cheaply or free; however some resources must be bought, and such investments can be expensive. It is very important, therefore, that proper, annually updated, budgeting takes place in school. Essential resources include Ordnance Survey maps, atlases, reference books, CDs, an annual subscription to the Geographical Association to receive *Primary Geographer* and access to GA online material.

Connecting with key stage 3 geography

Early years and primary geography provides pupils not just with an introduction to geography but with a variety of opportunities to develop their geographical awareness, knowledge, understanding, skills and values. Geography is part of their primary experience for between six and eight years. As pupils move into key stage 3, they will work with teachers whose specialism, or one of whose teaching subjects, is geography. There are clear overlaps between the key stage 2 and key stage 3 geography requirements. For example, many of the primary geography themes, as well as enquiry and skills (see Figure 2) are further developed in the secondary phase. More specific examples of geographical development include increasing the scale at which pupils study places and regions, from the national to the global; extending studies of water and land/coastscapes into work on geomorphological processes; deepening investigations into settlement and environmental issues; looking more extensively at sustainable development; and making greater use of Ordnance Survey maps and GIS (QCA, 2007).

There are a number of ways in which primary schools can support pupils as they move into key stage 3. These include termly meetings between geography subject leaders to share ideas about topics and teaching methods. This will help secondary geography teachers to recognise the importance of the geographical work undertaken in primary schools, and encourage primary teachers to acknowledge the opportunities for pupils to develop their geographical learning in the initial years of secondary education.

Conclusion

We are curious about our world, however far we travel in and over it. We are fascinated by its variety, its physical environment, the people who inhabit it, what they do, their cultures and what we make of each other. Geography explores what the world is like, what happens in it, the impact we have upon it, how we can limit the damage we do to it and, indeed, how we can help to make the world a better place. It is a moral imperative that we pass the world to the next generation in as good or better condition than we inherited it and that we equip them to undertake the task of creating a world as fit or better to live in, with less damage and potential harm to resolve than we inherited. In summary, we can say that geography in the nursery and primary school should:

- use and develop pupils' natural curiosity about the world around them, near and far;
- explore and develop pupils' geographical ideas and skills so that they can explore and investigate places and the environment more effectively;
- encourage pupils to learn through fieldwork experiences and activities;
- examine and clarify pupils' existing experience and awareness of places and environments;
- develop pupils' existing knowledge and understanding of their own and other places and environments;
- develop pupils' spatial awareness from a local towards a global scale;
- help pupils recognise their interdependence with the rest of the world;
- enable pupils to understand how places can be sustained and how people can live within their ecological means, both now and in the future;
- build positive attitudes towards other peoples;
- help pupils build a global perspective from their local perspective and feed a global appreciation into their sense of the local;
- enable pupils to value diversity in peoples, cultures, places and environments;
- combat ignorance and bias to avoid pupils developing stereotypes and prejudice, and raise awareness of the partiality of our understanding of people and places, such that we may always intend to overcome it;

▥ foster in pupils the desire to act responsibly themselves and in working with others in order to minimise damage and enhance improvement to wherever they are on the planet, for the good of that area, and for the good of the wider world.

The vital role of geography in the early years and primary curriculum is to support and enable the development of informed, concerned and responsible members of the local and global community, whose sense of wonder, interest in and fascination with the world about them leads to active engagement in sustaining and improving people's lives in their own places, other environments and across the wider world.

References

de Bóo, M. (2004) *The Early Years Handbook*. Sheffield: Curriculum Partnership.

Catling, S. (1998) 'Geography in the national curriculum and beyond' in Carter, R. (ed) *Handbook of Primary Geography*. Sheffield: Geographical Association.

Catling, S. (2002) 'Thinking geographically', *Primary Geographer*, 47, pp. 7-9.

Catling, S. (2003) 'Curriculum contested: primary geography and social justice', *Geography*, 88, 3, pp. 164-210.

Catling, S. (2010) 'Organising and managing learning outside the classroom', in Arthur, J. and Grainger, T. (eds) *Learning to Teach in the Primary School*. London: Routledge.

Catling, S. and Willy, T. (2009) *Teaching Primary Geography*. Exeter: Learning Matters.

Catling, S., Bowles, R., Halocha, J., Martin, F. and Rawlinson, S. (2007) 'The state of geography in English primary schools', *Geography*, 92, 2, pp. 118-136.

DCSF/QCDA (2010) *The National Curriculum Primary Handbook*. Coventry: QCDA. Available at *www.curriculum.qcda.gov.uk/new-primary-curriculum/index.aspx*.

DES/WO (1990) *Geography for Ages 5 to 16*. London: DES/WO.

DfEE/QCA (1999) *The National Curriculum: Handbook for primary teachers in England*. London: DfEE/QCA.

DfES (2007) *Practice Guidance for the Early Years Foundation Stage*. Annesley, Nottingham: DfES.

Martin, F. (2006) *Teaching Geography in Primary Schools*. Cambridge: Chris Kington Publishing.

Ofsted (2006) *The Annual Report of Her Majesty's Chief Inspector of Schools 2005/06*. London: The Stationery Office. Available at *www.ofsted.gov.uk/publications (last accessed 25 June 2010)*.

Ofsted (2008) *Geography in Schools: Changing practice*. Available at *www.ofsted.gov.uk/publications (last accessed 25 June 2010)*.

Owens, P. and Richardson, P. (eds) (2011) *Geography Plus: A primary toolkit for creative teaching and learning*. Sheffield: Geographical Association.

QCA (2007) *Geography: Programme of Study for Key Stage 3 and attainment target*. Available at *www.qcda.org.uk/curriculum/geography (last accessed 25 June 2010)*.

Rowley, C. and Cooper, H. (eds) (2009) *Cross-Curricular Approaches to Teaching and Learning*. London: Sage.

Websites

Geographical Association *www.geography.org.uk*

Ofsted *www.ofsted.gov.uk*

Standards website *www.standards.dcsf.gov.uk*

Geography Teaching Today *www.geographyteachingtoday.org.uk*

Section 2

Geographical skills

Chapter

7. Enquiries and investigations

8. Mapwork skills

9. Using photographs, sketches and diagrams

10 Fieldwork and outdoor learning

11. Geography and language development

12. Geography and ICT

Pupils' work /
St Matthew's
Primary School.

What is London like? Busy!

CHAPTER COVERAGE:
ENQUIRIES • ENVIRONMENT • ISSUES • PROGRESSION • QUESTIONS

Enquiries and investigations

'Enquire, investigate and explore ... all have something in common – they are all approaches to learning in which children are active rather than passive. Children are actively involved in the creation of personal and shared meanings about the world, rather than being passive recipients of knowledge that has been created or selected by the teacher.' (Martin, 2006.)

Learning and enquiry

Would you be surprised if, during an interview, you were asked how you think children learn? It is not an easy question. The most direct response I ever received was 'Somewhere between when I tell them and when they want to!'. What response would you give? And how does your notion of learning relate to your school's curriculum policies? This may sound like an uncomfortable grilling but these are very important questions.

Over the years teachers have come to recognise that the enquiry approach is a powerful strategy for promoting pupils' learning. Research suggests that meaningful learning occurs when investigations are directed by challenging questions and lead to solutions and/or reasoned viewpoints. Key questions help to guide this process, serving to signpost the paths that lead to understanding. Such an approach can help pupils to manage their own learning, handle issues objectively and use skills with a clear purpose.

The national curriculum has always emphasised the enquiry approach. It also highlights creativity and thinking skills. Active learning is encouraged as children undertake enquiries using various methods, media and sources including fieldwork. In geographical and other related studies children should investigate the world around them from the local to the global. The aim of such studies is to fire children's curiosity and imagination.

Theoretical background

The enquiry approach has a strong theoretical base. As Roberts (2003) points out, many educationalists follow Vygotsky in arguing that knowledge is not transmitted directly from teacher to pupil; rather pupils learn about the world by actively making sense of it for themselves. Vygotsky focused especially on the difference between what children can do on their own and what they can do with support from others. He called this the 'zone of proximal development'.

Vygotsky's work and the notion of the zone of proximal development has implications for geographical enquiries. It challenges the notion of totally independent work, reminds us that pupils will need teacher support when they are working with new ideas, and suggests that enquiries should not be beyond what they can achieve at the time (their zones of proximal development). In practice this means that pupils will need assistance from the teacher both

The main characteristics of key questions are that they:

- are an immensely powerful way of planning a curriculum with structure;
- unlock the door to learning about key ideas and processes;
- give direction and structure to a topic, emphasising what pupils are investigating and why;
- are the driving force behind enquiry learning;
- demand enquiry, require investigation and beg more questions;
- may be awareness raising, descriptive, explanatory, speculative, moral/value based or reflective;
- should be shared with pupils;
- provide professional development for teachers generating them;
- stimulate skills development to enable them to be investigated.

Figure 1 | *Key questions.*

when they are planning their enquiries and when they are conducting and analysing their investigations.

Asking questions

Educationalists have classified the questions posed in the classroom into many different types. As far as geography is concerned, the effectiveness of an enquiry will depend upon the teacher's understanding of key questions and general questioning skills. You might pause to ask yourself the following questions:

- How often are my questions posed clearly and succinctly?
- What proportion of my questions are open and closed?
- Do I deliberately arrange my questions in a logical sequence?
- How am I encouraging pupils to ask their own geographical questions?

It is well worth having a serious word with oneself, and with colleagues, about the use of questions in the classroom and their associated contribution to pupils' learning.

Remember too that asking questions is not restricted to cognitive matters only. Questions that are carefully and sensitively posed can also be effective for exploring the affective domain. Attitudes, beliefs and values are a vital ingredient of geographical studies and the subject offers many opportunities for considering the viewpoints of pupils and of other groups and individuals.

Key questions

Effective geographical enquiry depends initially upon the quality of the key questions posed for the learning experience. There have been many attempts to devise a definitive set of questions for geography. Storm (1989) suggested five basic questions which could be applied in any circumstances:

- What is this place like?
- Why is this place as it is?
- How is this place connected to other places?
- How is this place changing?
- What would it feel like to live in this place?

Notice that, above all, these questions beg more questions and require further investigation before an answer can be attempted.

The characteristics of key, or leading, questions are listed in Figure 1. The origin of key questions must obviously lie in the intended learning outcomes (objectives) of your curriculum and, for most teachers, these will be related to the programme of study for each key stage. Key questions unlock the door to learning about the concepts implicit in the programme of study statements for places and themes. Key questions also stimulate the development of the skills needed for the enquiry.

The best key questions will involve pupils in conducting a sustained enquiry and

Stage 1a	Awareness raising
Stage 1b	Generating enabling questions
Stage 2	Collecting and recording information
Stage 3	Processing the gathered information
Stage 4	Drawing conclusions from the processed data
Stage 5	Sharing the learning and affective outcomes
Stage 6	Evaluation by all concerned

Figure 2 | A framework for managing a focused geographical enquiry.

synthesising information. For example, you might ask them what life is like for the people who live in a specific village as opposed to those who live elsewhere. This question has real scope, unlike one asking how many people live in that village. The latter question can be tackled relatively easily using reference skills and leads to a closed and definite answer. In fact it is subsumed by the first question. To consolidate your thinking, compare the investigative potential of these two questions:

1. When did the Romans occupy England?

2. How do we know the Romans occupied England?

Generally, questions which begin with 'how' and 'why' are more conducive to geographical enquiry than those that begin with 'what' and 'when'.

Progression in enquiry

The precise wording of a key question can be significant. For instance, 'Why are there differences in land use in our local area?' encourages a higher level of geographical thinking and analysis than the question 'How is land used in our area?'. You will need to be aware of progression in geographical enquiry. As you plan your work, you should consider the following parameters:

■ the enquiry focus

■ the degree of pupil involvement in planning

■ the range of viewpoints considered in issues

■ the nature of the skills needed for the investigation

■ the range and type of resources.

Add the progression in key questions and you have an excellent tool for monitoring this component of the curriculum through the key stage(s).

oto | John Halocha.

Focused geographical enquiry

There is an important distinction between a focused enquiry route (Figure 2) and general enquiry which can permeate the curriculum. In Figure 2, notice how Stage 1a is an orientation phase when pupils relate their previous experiences and existing knowledge to the chosen enquiry. This is followed by a focusing phase (Stage 1b) when initiative-taking begins in earnest and a range of enabling questions is raised as the enquiry process gets started.

Stages 2, 3 and 4 mark the information phase and should be the time of intense and purposeful geographical activity. Factual statements and generalisations emerge during Stage 4 as pupils attempt to answer the key question. Interpersonal skills are practised during the important Stage 5, the outcome of which can influence the responses during Stage 6 when feelings are revealed, including self-evaluation. These last two stages represent the reflective phase. Such a structured and substantial piece of work could be part of topic work or make up the bulk of the study unit.

A well-organised, well-resourced and sharply focused geographical enquiry makes serious learning great fun for your pupils whether you are working in the classroom, school grounds or off-site. Procedural skills are practised as the enquiry process moves into action with

To Upper
Clatford &
Anna Valley

St Peter's
Church

To Andover

Royal Oak
PH

Clatford
Primary School

Shop

Club

area of buildings

buildings mentioned
in text

The Clatford
Arms PH

Garage

N

0   200
metres

To Longstock
& Stocksbridge

Figure 3 | *The local area of Clatford CE Primary School, Goodworth Clatford.*

individuals and learning teams engaging in activity-based tasks. You know it makes sense!

General enquiry

Unlike focused enquiry, a strategy of general enquiry should permeate the geography in your school. Posing challenging and open questions encourages the investigative and higher modes of thinking in the classroom. However there is a caveat: beware of over-dependence upon this approach; it can become a predictable recipe and restrict the variety of teaching and learning strategies used by the teacher. As one pupil reportedly advised a newcomer to the class: 'Don't look at anything in the room or she'll ask you a searching question about it!'. Many pupils pick up a great deal through direct teacher transmission; how you relate your knowledge and experience can be decisive.

Local traffic problems (upper key stage 2)

Background

Local issues lend themselves admirably to the enquiry approach as they are real and immediate. With this in mind, Clatford CE Primary School, near Andover in Hampshire, decided to investigate with year 6 the traffic problems created in the school's vicinity (Figure 3) by the arrival and departure of pupils. This issue related to the pupils' own school and was one in which they were likely to be personally involved – promising ingredients for a learning experience. Of course, this issue is not unique to the school and its village, Goodworth Clatford.

Approximately 12 hours of curriculum time were allocated to the topic and links with mathematics, ICT and English were recognised and established. Opportunities to revise, practise and learn geographical skills were identified and teacher enthusiasm was channelled into the enquiry process.

Four key questions emerged from discussion of the learning objectives and formed the framework for the enquiry.

Question 1: Why are journeys made?

Question 2: Where do our pupils come from and how do they get to school?

Question 3: What effect does our coming to and leaving school have upon the village?

Question 4: What can we do to ease or solve any problems that may be caused?

Why are journeys made?

The topic opened with a discussion about journeys, including movements on the Earth's

RESULTS OF QUESTIONNAIRE; GETTING TO SCHOOL

A total of 117 questionnaires was returned, representing 73% of the current number on roll. There were responses from all six teaching groups and the relatively large sample can be regarded as representative.
The following data was obtained

ORIGINS OF PUPILS COMING TO SCHOOL

Anna Valley	33%	Andover	26%
Upper Clatford	20%	Local village	19%
Chilbolton	1.5%	Longstock	0.5%

MODE OF TRAVEL TO ATTEND SCHOOL

Car 94%   Walk 5%   Bicycle 1%

DIRECTION OF ARRIVAL BY CAR

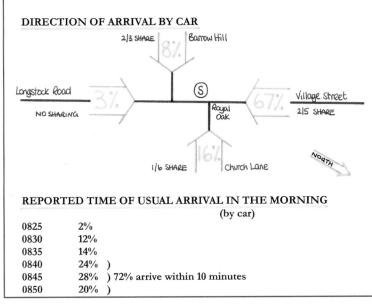

REPORTED TIME OF USUAL ARRIVAL IN THE MORNING
(by car)

0825	2%
0830	12%
0835	14%
0840	24%)
0845	28%) 72% arrive within 10 minutes
0850	20%)

Figure 4 | Results of questionnaire on 'getting to school'.

surface, spanning journeys within and beyond the classroom and within and beyond the home: helicopters passing over the school from nearby Middle Wallop; moles tunnelling under the school's playing field; clouds moving across the sky making shadows over the landscape; the River Anton flowing through the village; earwigs moving when a log is disturbed; getting to school and back home again. A matrix logging scale of journeys against, on, under and above the Earth's surface stimulates pupils to think geographically.

Reasons for such movements were discussed through questioning and many pupils began to grasp the following generalisations about journeys. They:

■ are made for a reason and have a purpose;
■ can be of different lengths;
■ take place at different times;
■ use varying modes;
■ can have peaks or rush-hours;
■ can occur on, above or below the Earth's surface.

It was decided not to include the key idea that routes, for various reasons, often deviate from the most direct path, with main routes tending to be more direct than minor ones.

Where do our pupils come from and how do they get to school?

Following the exploratory session, pupils mapped their journeys from home to obtain groceries, clothing and medical care, one map being produced for each service. The journey to school was then the focus of investigation and the second key question stimulated the crucial enabling questions of 'What do we need to know?' and 'How do we find out?'. A simple questionnaire was proposed to obtain the raw data: origin of journey and route followed; mode of transport; possible sharing of transport; and approximate time of arrival at school in the morning. Pupils soon realised the need for a simple format and agreed to

Figure 5 | *Logging the traffic outside the school.*
Photo | *Tina Horler.*

observe anonymity by just recording the year group on the returns. In addition to ticking boxes, one section of the questionnaire invited parents/guardians to state their own feelings about taking and collecting youngsters from school (it also informed parents of the work being carried out by year 6). The questionnaires were distributed to all year groups with great anticipation and returns were grabbed avidly for processing.

The total number of returns represented almost three-quarters of the pupils and from such a representative sample it was possible to produce a summary which involved mathematical as well as drawing and design skills (Figure 4). One important finding was that seven out of ten pupils usually arrived at school during the ten minutes before the bell.

With at least nine out of ten arriving by car and two out of every three coming along Village Street from the north, this led naturally to a closer look at things in the vicinity of the school gate.

Weather	rain	dry	dry/cold	dry
Day and date	Tu 4/3	We 5/3	Th 6/3	Fr 7/3
Total no. of vehicles logged	259	225	339	223
No. coming from Anna Valley direction	114	85	92	101
No. coming from Longstock direction	100	65	195	70
No. coming down Church Lane	45	75	52	52
No. using Royal Oak car park	22	20	48	30
No. parked in road outside school	64	65	111	84
No. parked in Church Lane	0	7	0	1
% of cars arriving after 0835 hours	83	94	84	70
% of cars parked more than five minutes in road	3	11	2	2

Figure 6 | *Results of fieldwork investigation into traffic near Clatford CE Primary School.*

Cars parked across driveways of private houses, leaving the occupants unable to leave their property while the car was there. Many of these cars were left unattended for several minutes, some up to 10 minutes.

71 Longstock Road has had its garden spoilt with wheel marks where people have pulled in to the side to pass other cars.

People do U-turns at the T-junction.

People park on the zig zag lines.

Cars are parked outside the old people's bungalows for up to 10 minutes when parents take their children on to the playground and then stand and watch them play. This leads to other cars having to park even further up the village, thus increasing congestion.

During the period from 0830 to 0855, the road is reduced to single line traffic. When the buses arrive to take children to Stockbridge, there is a virtual standstill, as the road is totally blocked.

During this period mentioned, there can be as many as 19 cars per minute passing or parking.

One car was left unattended with its engine running.

One car was left unattended on the road with two small children inside.

Parents chat while their cars are parked on the highway which is obviously congested.

At no time was the Royal Oak car park full.

Figure 7 | *Pupils' observations of traffic problems at Clatford CE Primary School*

Now came the time to organise a traffic count with a clear purpose in mind and to establish the real scale of the scene. The pupils measured the widths of the roads near the school and calculated the amount of land available for vehicles in the parking area opposite the entrance at the Royal Oak (the landlord offers this facility at dropping and collecting times). The average width and length of a car was also calculated. In addition pupils devised their own recording sheet for logging the arrival and departure of cars and organised coverage of the study area on four consecutive mornings in early March from 0815 to 0850 hours (Figure 5). It was raining the first morning!

Figure 6 presents data collected by pupils on the four mornings. They also reported events and human behaviour during the survey mornings (Figure 7). Pupils witnessed several examples of dangerous

Movements Compared

On class 6 maps showing journeys from home to buy groceries, clothes and for medical care, people travel in different directions, although they are moving for the same purpose. They have different destinations.

Although we travel for the same purpose to Clatford School, we don't go to different destinations. Instead we all converge on one place, although we may come from different directions.

This pattern of movement will lead to traffic congestion.

Looking at traffic movement outside Clatford School.

Traffic coming from Longstock has been found to be greater than that of Anna Valley / Upper Clatford in our traffic survey. However we have found out that most people coming to school come from Anna Valley / Upper Clatford, so we can only assume that the majority of traffic coming from Longstock passes school for a different reason than to drop off children there. This reason might be that they are coming along the Longstock Road and Barrow Hill, turning right and driving into Andover. However this does make the traffic congestion outside Clatford School even though they do not park there. The busiest time is from 8:35 to 8:55.

The busiest day is a Thursday, when 14 cars pass the school per minute. We think that Thursday is the busiest day because it is market day in Andover. On Thursday 339 cars passed or stopped outside the school.
Unfortunately most people park outside the school rather than in the Royal Oak car park. Because of laziness people do not park in the Royal Oak. They could park on Church Lane, but not on the corner because drivers cannot see round the corner of Longstock Road.

As I have said, I think that it would be a good idea to put a policeman on duty between 8:35 and 8:55 at the T-junction outside school. We also could have a no-stopping-for-more-than-3-minutes rule on the road outside the school. The policeman would ensure this. It would be helpful to have 2 mirrors at the junction were Church Lane meets the Longstock Road and the road from Anna Valley / Upper Clatford, so that drivers could see round the corner.

Figure 8 | Traffic survey by Laura May, year 6, Clatford CE Primary School near Andover.

driving, illegal parking, lack of thought for local residents, lack of thought for other parents, a small example of gridlock, a relatively high density of traffic and the peaking of traffic.

What effect does our coming to and leaving school have upon the village?

The key issue had now emerged and most of the pupils were part of it! One youngster deduced that the problem must be worse at the end of the school day when the infants depart at 1520 hours and Y3-6 come out ten minutes later. 'At least other people are not coming home from work at the same time' said another. Most pupils grasped the fact that all the traffic arriving and departing in such a short time had a clear impact on the school's immediate locality. It was decided that next year's class could build upon these investigations and take a close look at the traffic situation in the afternoon, as well as checking if the current situation had improved or worsened. The latter was a perfect prompt for the final key question.

What can we do to ease or solve any problems?

The last key question contributed to the reflective phase of the enquiry. Several residents had complained about traffic chaos in the mornings, how their drives were blocked and their own journey to work hindered. The Parish Council had debated the matter and contacted the County Highway Authority who stated that while there had been no reported accidents at or near the T-junction, they would agree to mark white lines around the junction. Suggestions for alleviating the traffic problem included imposing a 20mph speed limit near the school, encouraging more pupils to cycle to school, raising awareness of the problem regularly in school newsletters and improving the provision of bus transport.

It was a salutary experience for the pupils to realise that problems of this kind cannot be solved in a trice and that some changes in drivers' behaviour would go far towards mitigating the effects upon the village. The last word comes from Laura May (Figure 8).

Photo | *Paula Richardson.*

Improving the environment (key stage 1/lower key stage 2)

There are many different opportunities for developing geographical enquiries and investigations with children. You can embark on these studies with the youngest children and develop them with increasing depth throughout the primary years. As the previous example illustrates, the immediacy and relevance of local issues motivates children and captures their imagination. Here are some more examples which show how good practice often features in practical investigations.

In one suburban school reception class, children found out more about the school surroundings (Goldingay, 2006). They began by selecting different materials and equipment from a box containing crayons, paper, string, sticky tape, magnifying glasses, binoculars, digital cameras and so forth. Over a period of half an hour they explored the grounds recording and responding to their environment in different ways. This activity allowed these very young children to investigate their surroundings and begin to connect with the outside world. It also provided the basis for further work. The children were surprised by the amount of rubbish and litter they discovered in the school garden. After a discussion they decided to put up signs such as 'please pick up your rubbish' and 'please look after our pond'. This activity worked well because pupils were able to develop a sense of ownership and ask questions. In terms of curriculum planning it related directly to the enquiry question, 'How can we improve our local area?'

In another school, a year 3 class decided to find out more about the development of the harbour area where there were plans to build a giant superstore (Ofsted, 2008). Before embarking on their investigations pupils spent some time finding out about map symbols and learning to read maps so they could record their findings. They then made a site visit. Going out on a study visit enabled pupils to gain a real sense of place. They stopped at intervals along the way to discuss different aspects of the harbour development. This led to some passionate discussions about the effectiveness of seasonal car parks which are often empty in winter and tend to suffer from litter and vandalism. At the site pupils conducted a traffic survey to see what impact the development might have on the local road network. They also gained a greater appreciation of the area and interviewed each other about the effect of proposals. On returning to the class the children took part in a public enquiry activity. They worked in groups to explore different viewpoints and articulated their ideas with great enthusiasm. These strong feelings provided the basis for extending the work and opportunities to engage the local council planning officers and representatives from the development company.

Figure 9 | *Children surveying the traffic outside their school.*
Photo | *Jane Phillips, Hallam Primary School, Sheffield.*

Postscript

This chapter has attempted to analyse a fundamental element of the geography national curriculum in a nutshell and to amplify it through exemplars. Like effective INSET, has it provoked thought, challenged you professionally and sown the seeds of change in pedagogical attitudes and behaviour?

Clearly, geographical enquiry is a teaching methodology, part of the teacher's toolbox, and is a professional skill that needs to be developed in tandem with the crucial ability to think geographically. As one of the Ofsted annual reports declares: 'Enquiry skills are best developed when addressing a real problem… The best enquiries build cumulatively on pupils' previous learning and explore the issues in ever increasing depth' (Ofsted, 2002, p. 7).

References and further reading

Buckley, A. (2007) 'Power to the pupils!', *Primary Geographer*, 64, pp.16-17.

Goldingay, S. (2006) 'Bringing geography to life', *Primary Geographer*, 61, pp. 16-17.

Martin, F. (2006) *Geography in Primary Schools: Learning to live in the world.* Cambridge: Chris Kington Publishing.

Ofsted (2003) *Geography in Primary Schools: Ofsted subject reports series 2001/02.* London: Ofsted.

Ofsted (2008) *Geography in Schools: Changing practice.* London: Ofsted.

Roberts, M. (2003) *Learning through Enquiry.* Sheffield: Geographical Association.

Storm, M. (1989) 'The five basic questions for primary geography', *Primary Geographer*, 2, pp. 4-5.

Pupils' Work | *Cold Ash Stream by Rachael Hall, Y5/6 Parsons Down Junior School.*

Mapwork skills

to | Paula
hardson.

The need to record, revisit and pass on information to others is of fundamental importance to all our lives, and one of the most effective ways of achieving all these things is by making and using maps. Maps and plans are simple, clear and decisive means of communication. A classroom plan provides a view of something that children can see in its entirety. It also shows how the space in a room is used and organised. A plan of the whole school uses the same techniques but involves abstract thought because it is not possible to see the complete internal arrangement of the building except by mapping or map-based modelling.

Why are mapwork skills so important?

Once a plan is created then distributions, locations, associations of areas, links and communications, routes and resources are revealed. It is easy to see why mapping is held to be the most powerful mechanism of geographical enquiry. It has improved our lives in immeasurable ways but it can also be seen to have encouraged activities which radically affect and exploit the environment. Whichever way one looks at it, map skills are key skills for the modern world.

How do I start?

The suggestions in this chapter recognise the tremendous scope of mapwork based activities. However many teachers may find themselves constrained by lack of time and curriculum pressures. The ideas and activities suggested keep this in mind. While teachers will need to make a selection to suit their own circumstances, this choice needs to be made on a foundation of background knowledge, planning and objectives.

Objectives are best seen through outcomes. Pupils will want to be able to describe where they are, to record information in their local environment, and to be able to plan routes and journeys. With growing experience they should be able to use these skills in understanding other locations in the UK. Finally, in a media- and travel-based culture, familiarity with European and world maps is essential for having views on the wider social and environmental issues which daily fill the news.

Mapwork is enhanced by an exciting range of resources, from aerial photos and satellite images to worldwide internet links and interactive computer programmes. Increasingly adults use modern technology as a regular part of daily life, to buy travel tickets, plan routes, and check locations and weather. Children should appreciate that knowing where you are, knowing how your locality relates to the wider area and knowing how it is linked to other places, are desirable life skills.

What map resources should I have?

The following list gives an idea of the resources you might want to consider. As a general rule, acquire the resource in each category that is easiest to get hold of and is most likely to be used regularly because it's actually useful!

1. Basic plan of the classroom: let pupils of all ages make their own plans of the classroom. The older ones should do this to scale with some accuracy. However, there are times when a basic, accurate, copiable blank outline, which you have prepared yourself, will be useful.

2. A school plan: if any building work has been done recently then your school may well have an accurate scale plan. If not you may have to make your own.

3. Local street plans.

4. Ordnance Survey maps: the Explorer maps at a scale of 1:25,000 now cover the whole UK mainland and contain a wealth of detail including open access land and leisure activities. A set of six will be useful for class group activities.

5. UK maps: a UK wallmap should be displayed somewhere in the classroom for instant, regular reference. Road atlases at 3 or 4 miles to the inch (a lesson in itself here) can also be sourced very cheaply.

6. Europe base map: these can be obtained from the internet but also appear in books.

7. World base map: these are easy to obtain as above.

8. Atlases: pupils should have access to a set of up-to-date atlases. Remember that you will need a balance of physical maps, political and thematic maps.

9. Globes: A traditional globe on a stand is always useful. Make sure that the printing and colours are of good quality. There is a range of inflatable globes up to sizes as big as the pupils which can really excite their imaginations.

10. Satellite images: are now widely available and can inspire a variety of lessons. For instance, images showing the UK at night can stimulate discussion on how light pollution is now blotting out the stars in urban locations.

11. Informal local maps: Collect all the local leisure maps you can from Tourist Information Centres, libraries and leisure outlets, or make your own (Figure 1). See if you can find a postcard with a picture map of the attractions in your area. Town trails and leaflets describing walks are especially useful as they are often supplemented with pictures and explanations. These maps tend to be 'informal' in that they emphasise key features at the expense of accurate distance and scale. There are excellent discussions to be had about this.

12. Transport route maps: Bus and train timetables contain route diagrams showing communication networks, e.g. there is a map of the entire network in the all-UK railway timetable.

13. Historical maps: investigate appropriate websites; you could also try the archive room at your nearest main library.

14. Aerial photographs: these are widely available on the internet. Google Earth is one of many sources.

15. Photopacks: sets of photographs that portray themes such as 'coasts and mountains' or world locations are widely available; but can be expensive.

16. Overhead transparencies: one of the best ways of generating a large map for a wall display is to project an outline onto the wall using an OHP. Adjust the position of the projector to obtain the magnification you require and copy the shape.

Figure 1 | *Creative co-ordinate game: children draw numbers and letters out of a hat to identify a co-ordinate square, then make the appropriate animal noise.*

What do I need to know to read a map?

Most households have an atlas of one kind or another. Even so, many adults find using a map a demanding and a complex task. If children are to develop confidence with maps they need constant practice in using and making maps and plans in real situations. Equally, time on task, the age of the learner and the complexity of the material are all crucial factors in learning.

Maps, like all methods of communication, have their own rules. In teaching map conventions it is best to start with maps of the immediate locality. Pupils will be familiar with this area and they will be able to make constant comparisons between what they know and what is on the printed sheet. All the items in the following list will, at some stage, be new and possibly confusing to pupils. Try to present each idea carefully using a mixture of direct teaching, practical work and discussion:

1. Location grids: Grids were first pioneered in Roman times by Ptolemy to enable places and features to be located on maps. The simplest is the alpha-numeric grid which uses letters to describe vertical columns and numbers for the horizontal rows. This gives a simple letter/number description for each square on the grid and is commonly used for street plans. Ordnance Survey maps use a more sophisticated system of four- or six-figure co-ordinates to locate features within a square. Set realistic goals for pupils before worrying about complex co-ordinates. Children should be able to locate themselves on school and local plans and use alpha-numeric grids with confidence (see Figure 1). Use real situations like the many 'You are here' visitor boards in most town centres to develop the work.

2. Plan view: All formal maps show features in plan view (as though seen from directly above). Plan views are much less of a problem to children nowadays as images of the Earth from space on television are common. However, in making their own plans younger children especially need help with viewing 3-D objects from above and translating them into plan view. A set of photographs showing oblique and overhead views of common objects will help children appreciate the differences. You could make your own set of digital photographs.

3. Colour, words and lines: Maps are a highly efficient way of using colour, words and lines to create an almost instantaneous mental picture of an area. Colours are immensely useful and pupils should explore the different ways in which they are used to show countries, height above sea-level or the different types of road. There is no standard system and the only thing that cartographers seem to agree on is to use blue for the sea.

The way that words are written is also significant. The size and boldness of the type usually indicates the size and importance of the settlement. The Ordnance Survey uses Gothic script for historic sites. Other words such as 'Pennines' may be overlayed because they refer to an area rather than one specific point.

Lines provide the linkages across maps and describe the routes of roads, railways, rivers and boundaries. Larger scale maps may also show tracks, footpaths, and lines of power cables. A system of grid lines is often added for reference, sometimes drawn in blue. Pupils need to appreciate that some lines depict features that exist on the ground while others exist only on the map.

4. Symbols and numbers: Symbols allow information to be displayed in a concise way and reduce the need for labels which may be confused with place names. The majority of formal published maps have a key explaining the meaning of the symbols that they use. On thematic maps, symbols may have statistical significance and be crucial for interpreting data.

Numbers on maps may provide information about roads, heights of hills and distances between places. Here too colour is used for slightly different types of information. Most pupils enjoy working with symbols as they are often tiny pictures or stylised outline shapes (Figure 2). You need to encourage them to make keys of their own symbols, make collections of symbols and learn how to consult and interpret a map key.

5. Scale: Maps 'shrink' the real world to make it fit onto a piece of paper. Maps which show large areas have to shrink the world much more than maps which show small areas. The amount by which the map has shrunk reality (the scale) is indicated by the representative fraction. For example, a representative fraction of 1:1000 means that one centimetre on the map represents 1000 centimetres on the ground. Maps of this scale will show the outline shapes of individual houses and gardens. By contrast, a map which is drawn to 1:120,000,000 (the scale used in many world maps) will show very little detail indeed. Children need time to appreciate the difference between large- and small-scale maps. You can practice by drawing plans of familiar objects, starting with a scale of 1:1 and then reducing the scale for larger objects. When it comes to measuring distances on maps encourage children to use a ruler and the scale bar which usually appears with the key. When it comes to calculating distances that involve twists and bends, such as the distance by road to different places in the local area, a piece of string will be helpful to get around the corners.

6. Compass direction: Since the sixteenth century it has been the convention to orientate maps to the north. Children need to be very secure with their ideas of 'left' and 'right' before embarking on more complicated compass directions. North and south take precedence over east and west in describing intermediate points such as NE and SW. Giving instructions using compass points is not easy especially if you are facing south and therefore moving 'down' a map. If the four cardinal points of the compass are on display

Figure 2 | *Investigating spaces in school.*
Source: Scoffham et al., 1995.

Spaces in school

1. Draw the correct symbols in each area of the school plan.

learning resources

cleaning

study area

activity area

offices

cooking

2. Imagine you are in Class 3 of this school. Look at each part of the building in turn and decide how useful it is to you. Colour the chart below using the following key:

KEY
essential to me ....red
useful to me ....yellow
not needed by me ....blue

3. Show your results on a pie chart. Put in the red first, then the yellow, then the blue.

Start your pie chart here.

AREA	essential to me	useful to me	not needed by me
hall			
staff-room			
head teacher's room			
secretary's room			
class 1			
class 2			
class 3			
class 4			
class 5			
kitchen			
caretaker's room			
library			
boys' toilet			
girls' toilet			
corridors			
playground			

4. Colour the school plan using the same code.

5. On a separate piece of paper redesign the school leaving out all the areas that are not essential to you.

in the classroom then maps can be orientated with the true direction. Pupils of all ages need to discuss direction to put their thoughts into words and explanations. It is important with younger pupils to establish a directional and relational vocabulary such as 'beneath', 'near', 'distant', 'steep', 'high', 'over there', 'above', 'straight on', 'up', 'down', 'back', and confidence with 'go left or right'. Pupils of all ages should be able to describe route instructions in words. Small-scale group activity in the immediate area contrasted with the routes taken by explorers or by characters in a story can develop this work.

What is a sensible sequence of teaching and learning?

Hopefully you are already beginning to establish your own set of priorities for developing and promoting map skills. However, it's useful to have an overview of the way learning generally develops in this area. Figure 3 outlines some of the key stages. It must be stressed that this is a developmental framework rather than a year-by-year syllabus. Each row indicates a desirable development of understanding and accomplishment. If you are working with pupils who are proficient in the skills in the middle of the sequences, then you should introduce them to more complicated skills. However the early parts of the sequence should also be revisited to assess their underlying competence, fill in gaps and to see if any misconceptions have arisen.

When teaching map skills you need to set the pupils challenges which involve the use of maps and plans. In this way they will come to appreciate that maps are a natural and absorbing part of everyday life. Here are some simple enquiry questions which will help to prompt discussion:

Primary Geography Handbook

Figure 3 | *A sequence of mapwork skills and activities.*

	MAKING A START			MAKING PROGRESS		A SENSE OF ACHIEVEMENT	
1 KNOWING WHERE YOU ARE (LOCATION)	Where am I in the room? Location of objects	What parts of the room do I use? Positions on a class plan	Where can these things be? Location on a school plan (with grid)	How can I describe where I live? Using a local street plan (with grid)	How can I describe my local area? Using an OS map (discuss grid)	How can I describe where in the UK I live? Using a UK map (use grid)	How can I describe where the UK is in the world? Using a world map (with grid)
2 MAKING AND USING MAPS AND PLANS (PERSPECTIVE)	What can we tell from a drawing? Drawing objects	What is a plan? Drawing a plan view	How can I show places on a plan? Plans from models and layouts	How do I get to School? Mental maps	Are there reasons for the way places are arranged? Recording information on a school plan	What can I tell from an aerial photograph? Comparing local plans, OS maps and aerial photos and historic maps	How can maps help people understand my views? Using world and country maps and satellite images to locate and convey information
3 SYMBOLS, LINES AND COLOUR (CONVENTIONS)	How do things group together? Giving general classifications to sets of objects	What can you tell from a symbol? Using symbols	Can I make effective symbols? Creating symbols	Where are the busiest places in school? Adding colour, lines and symbols to a school plan	What landmarks might help me remember a school trip? Using an OS map to plan a school trip	How might the weather affect my day? Weather maps	How does my way of life affect other parts of the world? Atlas thematic maps
4 DISTANCE (SCALE)	How far is it? Using distance vocabulary	Where are they? Using positional vocabulary	What journeys can I make? Route instructions	What are the effects of different scales? Drawing to scale	How does scale affect a plan? Using a scaled school plan	How are different maps of the same area useful? Maps at different scales	What's special about the UK? Scale of continents and oceans
5 ROUTES AND JOURNEYS (DIRECTION)	What is a route? Defining a route	How can I use right and left? Directional vocabulary	What journeys can I make? Routes with direction and distance	How useful are compass-point directions? Using compass points	From which direction do most children travel to school? Routes on OS and UK maps	What is the best way to explore the local area? Writing a local trail	How can I find my way? Orientation
6 USING ATLASES AND GLOBES	What are globes and maps? Describing maps and globes	How do maps show land and sea? Distinguishing land and sea	Why are maps and pictures useful? Relating maps and pictures	Where are these events happening? Locating major world features	How good am I at using an atlas? Using index and contents	Do I live in a region? UK atlas maps	Are European countries the same? Use world atlas maps
7 THINKING SKILLS	Naming locations	Classifying areas	Identifying associations	Describing resources	Comparing systems	Analysing change	Generalising interactions

■ 'How can I help a visitor to find my classroom?'

■ 'Which is the quickest way from my house to school?'

■ 'Which is the safest way?'

■ 'Why might the two routes not be the same?'

■ 'Would I enjoy a holiday on the Isle of Arran or the Isle of Wight?'

■ 'What would be similar and what different about the two experiences?'

Remember, the idea is not to be ever pressing on into new and unknown territory. Map skills need to be used constantly and practised. Remember too that children – and adults – will need to apply the whole sequence of skills if they are transposed to a new situation. When staying at a field study centre, for example, everybody (both pupils and adults) will need to go back to the beginning to establish their sense of location, direction and place. The point of teaching map skills is to make this an efficient and intuitive reaction; a crucial ability in a society where travel and mobility are at a premium.

Finally, keep in mind that children do not always progress in lockstep; within the sequences pupils will be at different stages of understanding. Telling right from left is a good example. There will be pupils in top juniors who are unsure while others happily made and used the distinction years before. To sum up, don't take anything for granted, don't limit the opportunities you offer pupils, and do use all the skills in real-life, practical, enquiry situations as much as possible.

Here are some suggestions for these practical activities. Each one appears in Figure 3 listed alongside the relevant idea in the skills sequence.

Practical activities

Knowing where you are (Location)

1a. *Where am I in the room?* Help pupils to develop a vocabulary which enables them to describe where they are by reference to other people and fixed objects. Collect useful words and display them for reference during a group discussion.

1b. *What parts of the room do I use?* Discuss the different areas in the classroom such as a reading area or an activity area. Colour a class plan to show these areas. What space is left? Is it possible to give it a description too? Could there be a better arrangement?

1c. *Where can these things be?* Make a 'Treasure Hunt' around the school. Give pairs of pupils a school plan with numbered locations. On a separate sheet or set of cards are puzzle descriptions of an object or feature at each location for pupils to identify ('What is made of wood and can be sat on?'). After the hunt add a simple grid to the plan and work at identifying the puzzle locations by using grid references.

1d. *How can I describe where I live?* Draw concentric circles on a local street plan with the school at the centre. Extract information from each ring. Are any particular buildings indicated? Are there open spaces, footpaths or railway lines? Where do the children live? Collect the different terms for road such as street, avenue or close. Are there reasons for using these different words? Overlay a grid to locate features.

1e. *How can I describe my local area?* Use the local OS Explorer map to decide what might be the extent of your local area. Then work in groups to extract all the information possible about what is in the area. It should range from churches and telephone boxes to

Pupils' work | Y4, Abbey Primary School, Leicester.

car parks and nature reserves. Discuss the OS grid at a level appropriate to the group.

1f. *How can I describe where I live in the UK?* Use both physical and political maps to describe the location of the school in relation to the rest of the UK using specific features from both sorts of maps. If the maps have grids, are they the same? How useful is a grid reference in writing a detailed location description?

1g. *Where is the UK in the world?* Write a description of where the UK is on a globe or world map using at least five different location features and a grid reference.

Making and using maps and plans (Perspective)

2a. *What can we tell from a drawing?* Pupils draw familiar objects and also draw round items such as their hands. Discuss the ways in which drawings differ from the real thing. Why is it useful to have drawings? When you draw around objects why are some results more recognisable (a hand) than others (a matchbox)?

2b. *What is a plan?* Help pupils to make a model of a real or imaginary room in a box. Draw around the model furniture, cut out the outlines and make plans of the room.

2c. *How can I show places on a plan?* Make picture maps of a story, or the school grounds or an imaginary village or island. The pictures should be linked by roads, rivers or paths. Use a coloured background to give an idea of town, country or water.

2d. *How do I get to school?* Draw a route map of the journey to school showing landmarks and features including turnings and crossroads. With so many pupils now reaching school by car, try to encourage them to make notes to describe their journey as they are actually travelling.

2e. *Are there reasons for the way places are arranged?* Colour-code rooms and areas on a school plan to show places used for learning, places for administration and places for health and welfare (including play). Are there reasons for the way the school is planned? Could it be arranged in a better way?

2f. *What can I tell from an aerial photograph?* Which local plan or map best compares with a particular aerial photograph? Why are maps necessary at all?

2g. *How can maps help people understand my ideas?* Write a short report, including maps, about a world issue, such as the great distances much of our food is transported.

Symbols, lines and colour (Conventions)

3a. *How do things group together?* What is a forest, river, cliff or mountain? Assemble photographs which children can sort into sets.

3b. *What can you tell from a symbol?* Make symbols for the different areas of the classroom or the different rooms in the school. What sort of things do you have to think about to make a simple symbol for a place?

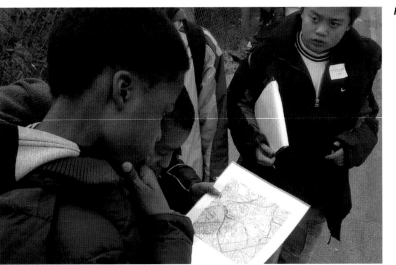

Photo | *Gemma Kent.*

3c. *Can I make effective symbols?* Create and add symbols to a school plan to indicate key places and activities around school. Select the most effective ones to create a useful school plan for visitors.

3d. *Where are the busiest places in school?* Put the pupils in pairs, give them a school plan and coloured markers and ask them to plot all the journeys they make to different parts of the school during a day. Where are the busiest places? If pupils from a class at the other end of the school make similar journeys, do the busy places remain the same? Can the congestion at busy places be relieved?

3e. *What landmarks might help me remember a school trip?* Working from an OS map, encourage children to create a landmark-spotting trail of the route you intend to take on a class trip. Were all the features spotted or did some turn out to be much more prominent than others?

3f. *How might the weather affect my day?* Discuss how weather maps provide snapshots of constantly changing weather conditions. How can you read the signs and symbols to gain clues about how the weather pattern might develop?

3g. *How does my way of life affect other parts of the world?* Use thematic atlas maps to identify global links.

Distance (Scale)

4a. *How far is it?* Make up a game, perhaps in teams. 'Fetch something from the most distant part of the room', 'Which is the nearest pencil to you?', and 'Put a shoe in the middle of the room'. Children might make up their own in groups or pairs.

4b. *Where are they?* Draw something in the middle of the room, something as far away as possible, something in between. Try the same exercise outside.

4c. *What journeys can I make?* How many different journeys from the room can be made going through only one door? How many if you go through two doors? How many through three? Which is the longest and shortest journey for each of these? How do they compare between one another? If possible plot the routes on a school plan.

4d. *What are the effects of different scales?* Draw a building or a face on squared paper of different sizes. Provide 1cm squares, 2cm squares and 4cm squares. If necessary the pupils can draw their own grids. Which was the most useful size on which to draw the object? Why?

Photo | *John Halocha.*

4e. *How does scale affect a plan?* Provide three sizes of squared paper with squares of 1cm, 2cm and 4cm. If 1cm equals a metre draw a plan of the classroom. Do the same on paper with 2cm equalling a metre and then 4cm equalling a metre. Which is the best scale for the class plan and why? How would you express the scale in numbers?

4f. *How are different maps of the same area useful?* Compare an OS map, a street plan and a tourist or other specialist map of your local area. Create a map of information for your pupils.

4g. *What's special about the UK?* Compare the UK with a country in each of the continents outside Europe.

Routes and journeys (Direction)

5a. *What is a route?* Ask pupils to walk the most direct way from their seat to the door. Can they describe it? What would the longest way be? How could you record these routes?

5b. *How can I use right and left?* Ask pupils to list the things they can do just with their left and then right hands. Then try to describe routes around the room using left and right direction instructions. Some pupils may find it useful to hold a 'l' and 'r' card in each hand as they go.

5c. *How many different journeys from the room can be made going left through one classroom door?* How many going right? Compare and plot on a school plan.

5d. *How useful are compass-point directions?* Pupils use and make up and follow routes around school using N, S, E, W.

5e. *From which direction do most children travel to school?* Using a local map or plan plot the addresses of class members. From which general direction do the majority of children come?

5f. *What's the best way to explore the local area?* Devise a local area trail.

5g. *How can I find my way?* Find the nearest open space or patch of countryside. Work in groups each with an adult. On a map showing just the perimeter of the area plot the paths to be found and useful landmarks.

Using atlases and globes

6a. *What are globes and maps?* As a whole group look at a globe and a large wall map and make a class list of all the words that pupils associate with each. Try to agree on a definition of a globe and a map perhaps as a puzzle to take home to try on an adult.

6b. *How do maps show land and sea?* Discuss land and water on various maps. Help pupils to make simple imaginary maps of their own, including some water.

6c. *Why are maps and pictures useful?* Use a large physical map of the world and a pack of pictures of world landscapes. Use clues to decide where the picture might have been taken.

6d. *Where are these events happening?* Make a class list of world places and events known to the pupils and then locate them on globes and atlas maps.

Photo /
Paula Owens.

6e. *How good am I at using an atlas?* Select one word for every letter of the alphabet from an atlas index. Is each a country, a place to live, or a feature? In which continent is it located?

6f. *What region do I live in?* Look at regional maps of the UK. How has the extent of your local region been decided upon? Is your local area typical of the regional character?

6g. *Are European countries all the same?* Use physical and climate maps of Europe to explore the range of landscapes and weather.

Maps and ICT

Electronic and digital mapping is now part of most people's lives. Satnav systems in cars and easy internet access to street plans are commonly used for daily journeys or to find locations for holidays, events, business or travel. Local areas may be searched for different categories such as schools, shops, places of worship, leisure facilities or visitor information offices and the resulting maps and plans printed off. Google Maps and the Ordnance Survey are now in the basic toolkit of most internet users. They offer many free mapping resources and services which may be used in classroom projects.

At a basic level, the Ordnance Survey Get-a-map service will provide a free Landranger map of a particular location and, similarly, Google Maps will provide targeted street plans with alternative views including aerial photographs and actual photographs from the local area. These organisations also offer educational packages to develop mapwork skills.

The Ordnance Survey's Mapzone site has many downloadable resources with suggestions for teaching a wide range of skills, from map symbols to grid references, scale, relief and measuring distance. There is also a Map Builder package to customise UK and world maps. Google has its own site, Google UK Schools, providing classroom ideas for the primary years. These include lesson plans for various projects including 'Exploring your area': children identify their school area using maps, satellite views and Google Earth and investigate a range of local features such as railway lines, parks, shops and rivers. They can add information and images to the maps.

The Multimap website offers straightforward street plans of specific locations, but these may be modified to appear as an OS map, an aerial photo or a bird's eye view which shows streets and individual houses at an oblique angle. All these images may be printed.

Other sites, especially local ones, can be found simply by searching the internet. For instance Kent County Council has an excellent 'Explore Kent' website which shows all public rights of way in the county, down to details of gates, stiles and bus stops. Children should be encouraged to use all these sites as a normal part of conducting local or distant investigations. They accept internet use as part of everyday life; but the power of maps to provide and record information, at their fingertips, will excite and enthuse them!

Using maps to develop learning and thinking skills

Maps have the power to turn the abstract ideas, which we form in our heads, into visual reality. Only a handful of people will ever actually see the UK complete from space. Even fewer can expect to see the whole world in one go except as a map. Maps and plans have a potential for radically extending our understanding by portraying the layout and organisation of the school, revealing the network of roads in a town or region or showing the distribution of natural vegetation such as forests and grasslands. Maps contextualise information within defined spatial boundaries, allowing us to make comparisons, formulate plans and develop generalisations. The identification and analysis of patterns, processes and relationships stands at the heart of geography. The way that mapwork can help to promote attitudes and values is equally important. Pupils need to develop both local and global perspectives, and appreciate the sequence of change that links the past to the future. As their understanding deepens, so their values will mature.

Figure 4 puts in sequence these three aspects of mapping – the personal, the practical and the potential – describing a variation in emphasis at certain ages. It is built up of simple assessment statements derived from and referenced to the ideas and activities in Figure 3. In Figure 4 the activities are re-worded to give a profile of what an individual pupil might have achieved. This can be used for self-assessment or as a handy list for a teacher to take stock of progress. The two tables together show how a mapwork skill can be described, taught as a geographical enquiry and, finally, assessed in terms of how effective it has become as part of a child's life skills.

The personal reaction to place is about direct experience, visual reaction and attachment. The child is at the centre of their world and feels that others see things exactly as they do. It is an exciting time when children's sensitivity to their surroundings is combined with an emerging appreciation that places can be described and organised.

The practical application of mapwork skills is about understanding and explaining the environment. It relates to the growing sense of confidence in children that they have a measure of power and control over where they go and what they do. It is about awareness and action and the development of ideas and strategies.

The potential use of maps links to assessing and explaining the patterns, processes and relationships in the world; it is about values and attitudes, the local and the global, the sequence of changes from past to present and into the future. It is about thinking globally and acting locally.

Figure 4 | *How children relate to maps.*

PERSONAL INFORMATION	PRACTICAL APPLICATIONS	SEEING POTENTIAL
1a. I can describe where I am in the room.	1c. I can use a school plan.	1g. I can describe where the UK is in the world.
1b. I can describe the different areas of the room.	1d. I can describe where I live.	2f. I can compare maps and photos.
2a. I can talk about what a drawing shows.	1e. I can use a map of my local area.	2g. I can use maps to communicate my ideas.
2b. I can explain what a plan is.	1f. I can use a map of the UK.	3f. I can understand a weather map.
2c. I can record information on a plan.	2e. I can interpret information on a school plan.	3g. I can use maps about themes and issues.
2d. I can describe my journey to school.	3c. I can make symbols for my own sketch maps.	4f. I can select maps at different scales.
3a. I can group things into sets.	3d. I can add colour and lines to maps.	4g. I appreciate the scale of continents and oceans.
3b. I can describe what a symbol might mean.	3e. I can extract information from an OS map.	5f. I can help others to explore the local area.
4a. I can describe how far away things are.	4d. I can describe how scale changes maps.	5g. I can use clues, maps and equipment to locate where I am.
4b. I can describe where things are.	4e. I can use a scaled school plan.	6f. I can describe the region I live in.
4c/5c. I can describe a short journey.	5d. I can use compass points for directions.	6g. I can describe some similarities and differences between European countries.
5a. I can plan a short route.	5e. I can plot routes on maps and plans.	
5b. I can use directions like 'left' and 'right'.	6b. I can explain the special uses of colours on maps.	
6a. I can describe what a globe or a map is.	6c. I can compare maps and pictures.	
	6d. I can use an atlas to locate places.	
	6e. I can use the index and contents of an atlas.	

What does research tell us?

Developing mapping skills with young children has both attractions and significant hurdles. Research suggests that children may not appreciate aspects of scale, distance and direction until the later years of primary school. However, the visual nature of the medium means that maps and plans are suitable for expressing and exploring ideas from the earliest years onwards.

Palmer and Birch (2004) describe how children around the age of five tend to draw pictures in which known places are linked in some way (topological maps) but which show few other map characteristics. By contrast, by the time they are ten, children are likely to produce much more accurate and detailed maps which involve abstract ideas of scale, direction and symbolic representation (Euclidean maps). Palmer and Birch conclude that no child is too young to be

Pupils' work | Abbey Primary School, Leicester.

introduced to maps. Interestingly, the ability to orientate a map seems to be a key step in developing competence in map work and should be worked at from the earliest years. The years between six and eight are particularly crucial in moving children from the impressionistic use of maps to more abstract understanding and most children will happily work with the idea of routes and symbols even before then.

Although there is considerable debate about how best to introduce maps to young children, the importance of environmental experience is widely acknowledged. Catling (1998) reports how teaching young children mapwork in the context of the local area can radically improve their knowledge of local features and develop their confidence to the point where they are willing to recognise the extent and limitations of their knowledge. Structured talk and conversation also appear to have a crucial role. Large (2004) investigated whether young pupils who travelled to school by car were less aware of the landmarks and other features than their walking counterparts. What she discovered was the crucial importance of parental involvement – those who talked with an adult about their journey scored highest, regardless of their mode of transport.

Children naturally want to engage with maps from the earliest age. The crucial question is how best to develop their understanding. Wiegand (2006) provides a very useful and authoritative account of different theories of cartographic understanding, from which he concludes that no single approach is sufficient to explain children's learning (p. 25). The value of diverse approaches was also affirmed by a small-scale study into different ways of teaching about the UK map (Scoffham and Whyte, 2009). There is potential here for your own action research. If you keep a record of the maps that children draw and the context in which they were generated it will develop into a valuable archive for future research. It might also shed light on whether there is any observable difference in mapwork skills between girls and boys. There are many questions to investigate.

Conclusion

Give pupils as much exposure as possible to maps of all kinds. Set little problems of orientation in real situations and constantly encourage pupils to draw picture maps of their own location, landmarks, journeys and of those in stories. It is vital for pupils constantly to work on the school site and in the local area so that they can locate, relate and record the places, features and resources familiar to them.

Remember also not to take any aspect of the interpretation of maps, plans, globes or atlases for granted. Seek instead to involve pupils in discussion and encourage them to put their thoughts into words and sentences. Listen carefully for partial understanding and misconceptions. It may take children considerable time, for instance, fully to grasp the hierarchy that underpins the components of an address. The relationship between villages, towns, cities, regions, countries and continents is not immediately obvious. Furthermore, as Wiegand (1998) has found, the ability to sketch a broadly accurate representation of the continents is present in only ten percent of upper juniors. So don't expect too much and try to provide contexts that link mapwork to other ideas such as environmental issues.

Finally, you need to help pupils to establish a clear vision about the usefulness of map skills as key skills for life. Today's children – tomorrow's adults – need the practical ability to locate and orientate themselves. They should be able to convey spatial information to other people in a succinct and accurate way. They also need to know how to extract information from maps so that they can describe and interpret world processes and events and the context in which they occur.

References and further reading

Catling, S. (1998) 'Children as mapmakers' in Scoffham, S. (ed) *Primary Sources: Research findings in primary geography.* Sheffield: Geographical Association.

Catling, S. (2004) 'Environmental mapping', *Primary Geographer*, 53, pp. 4-6.

Large, J. (2004) 'Watch how you go', *Primary Geographer*, 53, pp. 26-27.

North, W. (2009) 'Creating digital maps with primary pupils', *Primary Geographer*, 70, p. 32.

Owens, P. (2008) 'My walks: walk on the child side', *Primary Geographer*, 67 pp. 25-28.

Palmer, J. and Birch, J. (2004) *Geography in the Early Years* (second edition). London: Routledge.

Plester, B., Richards, J., Shevelan, C., Blades, M. and Spencer, C. (2003) 'Hunt from above', *Primary Geographer*, 51, pp. 20-21.

Potter, C. and Scoffham, S. (2006) 'Emotional maps', *Primary Geographer*, 60, pp. 20-21.

Schmeinck, D. (2007) 'Making a case for maps: the importance of spatial understanding in geography', *Primary Geographer*, 63, pp. 36-38.

Scoffham, S. and Whyte, T. (2009) 'My UK map', *Primary Geographer*, 69, pp. 24-25.

Wiegand, P. and Dickinson, J. (1996) 'Draw me a map of the British Isles!', *Primary Geographer*, 25, pp. 20-21.

Wiegand, P. (1998) 'Understanding the world map' in Scoffham, S. (ed) *Primary Sources: Research findings in primary geography.* Sheffield: Geographical Association.

Wiegand, P. (2006) *Learning and Teaching with Maps.* London: Routledge.

Whittle, J. (2006) 'Journey sticks and affective mapping', *Primary Geographer*, 59, pp. 11-13.

Websites

Cassini maps *www.cassinimaps.co.uk*

Google Earth *www.earth.google.com*

Multimap *www.multimap.com*

Ordnance Survey children's site *http://mapzone.ordnancesurvey.co.uk*

Ordnance Survey maps *www.ordnancesurvey.co.uk/oswebsite/getamap*

Quikmaps *http://quikmaps.com*

Soft Teach Educational (Local Studies) *www.soft-teach.co.uk*

Streetmap *www.streetmap.co.uk*

Worldmapper *www.worldmapper.org*

Geographical Association overview of globes and atlases
www.geography.org.uk/download/GA_EYPGlobesandAtlases.pdf

See also the think piece 'Making and using maps' on the Geographical Association website
www.geography.org.uk/gtip/thinkpieces

Aerial Photographs

Geography

Land Use

Blu-tac a centimetre grid transparency over an aerial photo of the Brenchley and Paddock Wood area.

Use the ordnance survey map of the same area and write down the co-ordinates of these locations.

Transport (orange on Ordnance survey maps).
Gedges Hill. _J 18,J18_
Pixot Hill. _H7 & H8_
Pearson's Green Road. _M10, M11_
Castle Hill. _Q 12, Q13_

Industry & farming (red on Ordnance Survey maps).
Widmore Farm. _P9, P10_
Gedges Farm. _P17, P16_
Goshen Farm. _P5, P6_
Moatlands Farm. _S10, S11_

Recreation and open space (green on Ordnance Survey maps).
Market Heath. _B14, C14_
Brenchley Village Bowling Green. _E14, E15_
Great Wood. _J6_

Residential (grey on Oranance Survey maps).
...........house. _D9_
The Police house. _E13_

Service Areas (black on Ordnance Survey maps).
Brenchley Church. _C8_

CHAPTER COVERAGE:
FIELDWORK • FUTURES • ICT • LOCAL AREA • MAPWORK • PHOTOGRAPHS

Using photographs, sketches and diagrams

Visualise this! A young child is constructing a complex model from boxes, tubes and copious amounts of glue. When a visitor asks 'What are you making?' he replies matter-of-factly, 'I don't know, I haven't seen it yet!'. This gives delightful insight into a child's thinking. The boy needs to see what he is making. He isn't able to visualise the outcome.

There is a lesson here for geography teaching. We spend a lot of our time trying to describe settlements, landscapes, patterns, processes and other aspects of the world but do we actually succeed? Part of the problem is that geographical language uses 'ordinary' words such as river, town, mountain or storm. When we use these terms we tend to assume that children can create, in their own mind, images similar to ours; that they share our visualisation or understanding. But are we sure this is so? What does a child 'see' when we talk, for example, of the 'currents in the river'? Using visual resources, either first-hand through fieldwork, or through pictorial and photographic images, can help a child really see the geography.

What is graphicacy?

Children increasingly make sense of their world through visual images which, for young children, provide more information than text. The skill of interpreting pictorial forms of spatial information is known as graphicacy. It is an essential form of communication, a life skill which has been described as the 'fourth ace in the pack' alongside, and arguably as important as, literacy, numeracy and oracy (Balchin and Coleman, 1965). Graphicacy is a form of visual literacy which can be compared with print literacy in that both employ similar processes: identifying, decoding and interpreting symbols. Furthermore, both print and images depend on prediction, observation, supposition and narrative skills. In developing their graphicacy skills pupils will need to use signs, symbols, diagrams and photographs (including aerial photographs). They will also use maps, atlases and globes and make maps of their own (see Chapter 8).

Understanding pictures and photographs

As adults we consciously or subconsciously interpret spatial information in pictures – holiday brochures, newspapers, estate agents' windows – gathering information about shape or form, scale, size and distance, as well as aesthetics. So illustrations are a powerful tool in geography teaching, and essential for learning about localities and processes.

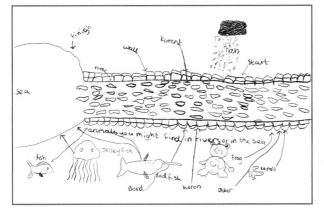

Pupils' work | *But teacher said there were currants in the river!*

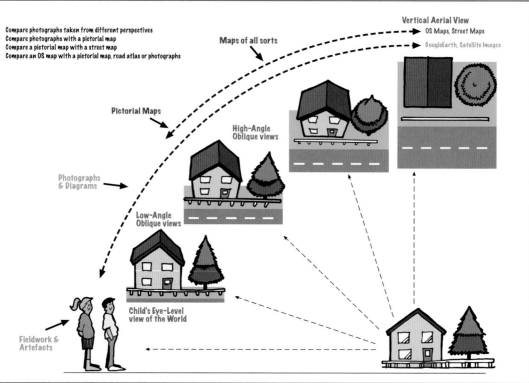

Maps of all sorts

Vertical Aerial View
OS Maps, Street Maps
GoogleEarth, Satellite Images

Compare photographs taken from different perspectives
Compare photographs with a pictorial map
Compare a pictorial map with a street map
Compare an OS map with a pictorial map, road atlas or photographs

Pictorial Maps

High-Angle
Oblique views

Photographs
& Diagrams

Low-Angle
Oblique views

Child's Eye-Level
view of the World

Fieldwork &
Artefacts

Figure 1 |
The range of graphicacy resources that pupils should experience provides a form of progression.

We tend to assume that pictures are easy to understand, and take it for granted that children see what we see. But this is not so. The skill of looking at, understanding and interpreting pictures has to be taught through planned, directed study. Research tells us that young children see a picture not as a whole but as a series of unconnected details selected at random. Reception pupils focus first on big things, things they know, recognise and can name, then size and colour become important. By year 2 pupils focus on lots of detail, especially foreground detail, including things relatively unimportant to the understanding of the photograph, and not necessarily the main essence of the picture. By year 4 they tend to concentrate on the main essence and associated objects. Detail is less important to them than getting basic understanding of the picture, whereas by year 6 pupils get a grasp of the whole picture and are able to generalise (Mackintosh, 1998).

Using photographs

There are a number of strategies and techniques which will help younger pupils to 'see' the content of a picture or photograph. To begin with you can encourage them to:

▥ develop the specific vocabulary for identifying different features by describing, discussing and labelling photographs;

▥ give the picture a title, to help generalise the 'whole';

▥ see all of the picture: look at the foreground, the middle ground and the background, the right and the left, using appropriate positional language, e.g. near to, next to, far from;

▥ place labels with specific vocabulary (which you have provided) around pictures as appropriate;

to | *Kate Russell.*

- label or annotate a black and white photocopy, referring to the coloured picture;
- label a 'field sketch' or line drawing of the photograph that you have provided (later the children will make their own).

Once you have helped pupils to 'see' photographs, they need to be helped to gather information from them, to 'read' them. This requires them to look closely, to focus on relevant detail, to categorise and compare. Encourage and help pupils to:

- sort geographical pictures into sets: e.g. river/not river, local/not local, like/don't like, and explain their sorting. Postcards often provide a good range of images for this activity;
- sequence collections of photographs: e.g. sequence pictures from a story, put a series of photos of local shops in order, sequence the landmarks seen on a recent walk, order photos of a river from source to mouth;
- join or overlap successive photographs (of townscape or landscape) into a panorama: e.g. a set of photographs taken from the top of a tall building or hill (to do this, take a series of photos with about 25% overlap, as you turn round on the spot);
- match pictures: e.g. same building taken from different perspectives or elevations, same view taken in different weather/seasons, and explain. This can sometimes be resourced with postcards;
- appreciate size, scale and distance, e.g. talk about how big, near or far the elements are;
- handle increasingly complex or unfamiliar photographs, encouraging both comparison and generalisation;
- make a 'field sketch' or line drawing of a photograph, identifying key elements, buildings, landscape features: e.g. by tracing (use a plastic pocket) or freehand;
- label, annotate, colour elements of a field sketch to indicate reading of photograph: e.g. identify different types of land use such as agricultural, industrial, residential;
- take their own geographical photographs, to use in practical activities;
- use the internet to access and exchange photographs.

Interpreting photographs

The information pupils gain from photographs is influenced by their past experience, geographical vocabulary, their imagination, preconceived ideas and stereotypes. These often need challenging. You can help pupils to interpret photographs by organising questions into categories. Here are some suggestions which you could apply to the photo overleaf:

- Observation and description (Makes children interrogate the picture)
  What can you see? What is it like in this place?
- Interpretation, explanation and classification (Requires children to locate learning in their own conceptual framework)
  What are they doing? Why are they doing it outside?
- Comparison (Requires application of learning to a new situation)
  Do people do this, or something similar, in your local area?
- Evaluation (Requires children to make judgements, express opinions and evaluate information)
  Would you like to do this? Would you like to live there?

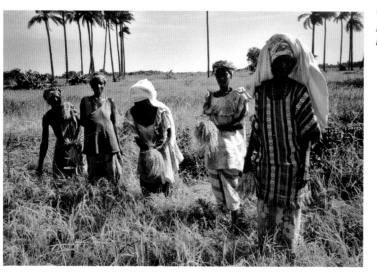

Women harvesting rice near Mandinari, The Gambia.
Photo | *Margaret Mackintosh.*

▥ Extrapolation (Requires children to extend their understanding to determine implications or consequences of natural processes or human actions)
Could this be done more easily? What would happen if they had machinery?

Chambers (1996) gives a slightly different, but equally useful, sequence of open questions providing progression:

▥ Concrete	What can you see?
▥ Descriptive	What are they doing?
▥ Speculative	Why are they working in a group?
▥ Reasoning	Why are they doing it by hand instead of using machinery?
▥ Evaluative	Is this the 'best' way for these people to do this work?
▥ Problem solving	How could their work be made easier or more efficient?

Be creative in your use of photographs, use tried and tested activities and develop your own. The teacher's notes in most resource packs provide many ideas for appropriate activities. These include: labelling, titling, making friends, describing, sequencing, 'good' and 'bad' adjectives, speech or thought bubbles (what is s/he saying/thinking?), questioning, cropping/masking, 'outside the picture', freeze frame, matching sets, drawing photographs, alternative views, comparisons. Whichever you choose, think about the purpose of the activity. Is it helping pupils to see, to read or to interpret the photographs? What graphicacy skills and geography are they learning?

Ultimately, pupils need to appreciate that because geography explores people's attitudes and values some questions simply do not have a 'right' answer. Indeed, the photographer and the people being photographed will probably have different interpretations of what is happening even though they are both there at the time. Pupils will also discover that because you may not know the answer you will join in the enquiry or discussion with them. Encouraging pupils to work in pairs or small groups to explore and compare their own ideas (and use the vocabulary) can be productive since each pupils' 'reading' or understanding of a picture is different, influenced by their own attitudes, perceptions and previous experience.

What do you need to do?

1. Identify appropriate internet sources and make a collection of geographical photographs for use throughout the school. These could be thematic general views (urban and rural views,

landscapes, townscapes, human and physical features); settlement (homes, occupations, buildings, journeys, transport); environment (aesthetics, issues, changes); weather (types and effects); water in the environment (rivers, sea, lakes, reservoirs, canals). Good sources include websites, newspapers and old calendars. So too are key stage 1 big books and photopacks focusing on UK, European and other localities. Try to include aerial as well as ground-level views and images showing different weather conditions and seasons. Pictures of issues and changes are also likely to be particularly valuable. Geography is not just about describing places, it also involves finding out about the forces that are influencing and affecting them at a deeper level.

2. Train children to use – to see, to read, to interpret and to question and challenge – pictorial resources.

3. Develop strategies for progression and differentiation in the use of illustrations. In addition to using a range of pictorial resources from different perspectives, use enquiry and issue-based questions with photopacks. Another option is to devise a sequence of questions aimed at developing pupils' conceptual understanding (see Chapter 7).

Pictorial maps

Pictorial maps, using the term 'maps' loosely, often provide a delightful and useful transition between photographs and conventional maps of places. They help children make and understand the link between the horizontal and vertical view of the environment around them.

There is considerable variety of pictorial map. Some are artistic interpretations of oblique aerial photographs. Some are simplifications that include 3-D drawings of key buildings and landmarks but codify surrounding land-use with colour. One note of caution - Wiegand (2000) discussed the use of picture atlases and, alongside showing their value, emphasised how important it is to check what children understand the pictures to show. He illustrated this by reporting how children interpreted a picture of a red car, placed near Birmingham on a map of Great Britain. 'That's where there are a lot of cars, it's a traffic jam', 'It's a car park', 'That's where you buy cars, it's a garage' or even 'They just like red cars at that place'. Very few identified the map-maker's intention of 'It's a place where cars are made'.

Others are conventional vertical views, with road networks embellished with 3-D drawings of buildings. This format starts with playmats (with distorted scale), but it is also available as attractive commercial maps.

Many places now display pictorial maps in prominent positions on 'You are here' notice boards and there are abundant tourist brochures with attractive pictorial maps and diagrams. Experience suggests that children enjoy using these. They help their understanding so that negative attitudes to maps don't develop.

This progression of pictorial resources – eye-level, oblique and vertical photographs and postcards, pictorial maps of all sorts and conventional maps, atlases and globes – should not be used in isolation to teach graphicacy skills or mapwork. Their use should be integrated into geographical work as a tool, in a similar way that a dictionary is used in literacy – as a tool that communicates meaning about processes, patterns and places (see Figure 1).

Aerial photographs

As adults we do not often use aerial photographs, although satellite images and Google Earth have helped to revive our interest.

Oblique and vertical aerial photographs have different characteristics. In oblique photographs features are easier to identify, but there is distortion because the foreground detail is larger than the background. In vertical photographs shapes, sizes and patterns are easier to identify, and since there is no distortion the outlines can be traced and compared directly with a map.

Children have a ground-level view of the world. Understanding maps – the geographer's main tool – requires an understanding of a vertical view of the world. This is a big conceptual leap which pupils need help to make. Aerial photographs provide a link between the real world which children see and the abstract world of the cartographer. The photograph has the merit of showing what is actually there, not just the things the map maker has selected to include. The progression from ground level to low angle, high angle and vertical perspective helps children make the transition. You can illustrate this by starting with young children's experiences of toys and models and progressing to familiar environments such as the school and local streets before looking at unfamiliar places.

Figure 2 | *Progression in perspective using toys and models. Can pupils sort the photographs into sets of different perspectives and then work out which way the photographer was facing?*
Photos | *Margaret Mackintosh.*

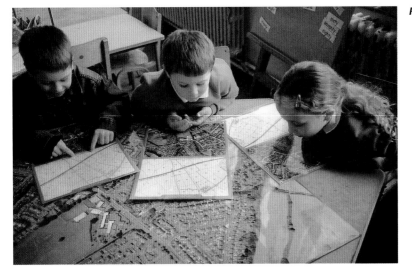

Photo | *Margaret Mackintosh.*

Toys and models

Take photographs from different perspectives and have multiple copies printed for pupils to sort and match (see Figure 2).

Take oblique and vertical aerial photographs of different arrangements (e.g. of train set, Lego models) for pupils to reconstruct, using the photograph as a pictorial layout diagram or map.

Real environments: school, school grounds, area around school

Identify human and physical features including buildings (landmarks) and routeways; recognise plan shapes, colour, texture, tone and pattern.

- Label an outline drawing of a photograph.
- Add detail to an incomplete fieldsketch.
- Make a sketch map of part of a photograph.
- Recognise different land uses.
- Trace a vertical photograph to make a map.
- Select and add detail to the map.
- Match a photograph to a real map, orientating appropriately.
- Identify relative and actual position, compass direction, scale and distance.
- Identify the time of day or year when the photograph was taken.

Plester *et al.* (2003) have shown that the youngest pupils can benefit from using aerial photographs. In the school environment they can recognise the correspondence between a photograph and the landscape. Using a photograph rather like a map they can identify features, locate themselves and locate places. Using a photograph like a treasure map they can locate treasure!

Unfamiliar environments

Undertake similar activities to above, extending learning to new situations, especially settlements, rivers, environmental changes and issues. Map patterns made by features (e.g. town buildings, road networks, rivers, fields), and patterns of land use; compare with own area, identifying similarities and differences; compare vertical and oblique views.

Satellite images

Identify features and patterns e.g. settlement, transport, rivers, coastline, land use; link with vertical, oblique and ground level photographs including those available through the 'street view' camera icons on Google Earth; describe routes; link with maps and globes.

What do you need to do?

1. Collect website addresses for vertical and oblique aerial photographs, e.g. of classroom equipment (furniture, toys and models); the school (some taken from nearby tall buildings, if possible); the school grounds (possibly taken from the school roof – close-up oblique); the local area; other localities.
2. Collect postcards, calendars and books showing oblique aerial views – there are some excellent ones available such as *The Earth from the Air* (Arthus-Bertrand and Brown, 2005).
3. Identify and use appropriate clips from television programmes that show aerial or satellite imagery, such as programmes on world journeys and natural history.
4. Encourage pupils to use Google Earth and the internet to access and share appropriate images, perhaps through a PowerPoint presentation.

Signs, symbols and logos

In adult life we gather spatial information from road signs, locational and directional signs at airports and other public places and spaces, many of which include internationally accepted symbols. We also discover the location of significant buildings, including specific shops, railway stations, National Trust properties and so forth, by identifying logos, both in the real world and on maps. And, of course, we gather information from weather forecast maps by interpreting symbols.

There are many practical ways in which pupils can learn about signs in your school. To begin with they can look for examples of signs, symbols and logos that are already in use. For example, there will be directions to the Head's office, and signs on the toilet doors. You might also encourage pupils to:

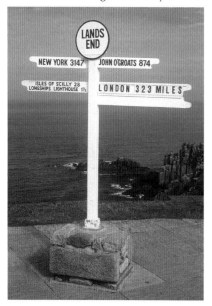

■ Erect signposts or symbol-posts around school, the pupils inventing the symbols, indicating direction and distance to, for example, the library;

■ Erect a playground signpost or symbol-post, indicating direction and distance to nearby landmarks (e.g. the town centre, the secondary school), to nearby towns and villages, and to more distant localities (e.g. London, Edinburgh, New York), providing opportunities to incorporate compass and mapwork;

■ Devise symbols to indicate the location of equipment in the nursery or reception class – link these with symbols for pupils to place on a model or plan of the classroom;

Photo | *The Land's End & John O'Groats Company.*

- Put appropriate symbols on various spaces and places in and around school - link these with a plan of the school;
- Place 'traffic' signs at key points to encourage safe movement in and around school: older pupils, identifying a movement problem in school, might like to study and 'solve' it with the use of signs and symbols;
- Create their own weather forecast symbols and charts, collect newspaper weather charts, and watch television weather forecasts.

Diagrams

In adult life we interpret diagrams showing spatial information when we use a car maintenance manual or a dressmaking pattern, assemble flat-pack furniture, wire up electrical equipment, plan a new kitchen or study diagrams in textbooks or newspapers. These are all two-dimensional representations of three-dimensional structures, requiring the ability to interpret perspective.

Children need to be taught to 'see' and 'read' diagrams in much the same way as they need to be taught to 'see' and 'read' photographs. Developing the skill to understand two-dimensional representation of three-dimensional structures starts with toys. Among other things you could encourage pupils to make toys from assembly diagrams (e.g. Lego, Meccano and Airfix), and create models from diagrams (e.g. with boxes or wooden bricks). As well as

developing geographical skills this work will provide many cross-curricular opportunities in technology, maths and science. You might also encourage children to:

- record 'landscapes' made in the sand tray;
- make drawings/diagrams to record the layout of play situations (e.g. the home corner set out as a café, a travel agents, a shop);
- represent familiar objects such as building blocks, perhaps constructed to represent local buildings, in both side and plan view;
- add labels to postcards and photographs to identify and highlight key features.

One type of diagram which has a unique role in geography is the field sketch. Field sketches attempt to summarise aspects of an urban or rural landscape using hand-drawn outlines and supporting notes, e.g. different areas in a school playground or the course of a river in a mountain environment. Making a field sketch depends not so much on artistic ability as ability to generalise and identify key features in a

Photo | *Paula Richardson.*

Figure 3 | *Practise identifying key features on field sketches from photographs.*
Photo | *Margaret Mackintosh.*

real world setting. You can practise making field sketches in the classroom working from photographs before taking pupils outside (Figure 3).

Developing a sense of place

Everyone sees and experiences a place differently. Is one person 'right' and another 'wrong'? Of course not. We all have different angles and view-points. People are increasingly aware of this nowadays and recognise the validity of mult-iple perspectives. In the same way we need to remember that each pupil will interpret photographs and perceive places differently, depending on their own experiences, opportunities and interests, and those of their family. They will compare the view with places they know, and make judgements. It follows that in building up your own photograph collection you should try to assemble as wide a range of images as possible. Include the backstreets as well as the town centre. Photograph bad points as well as good things, not just key features. There will be lots of possible responses to these images – a different one from each pupil – and they are all right. Value each pupils' perceptions and ideas.

You also need to encourage pupils to think about places as social spaces or areas where people go about their daily lives, getting to know different districts, streets and buildings as they pursue their various interests and opportunities. Everyone has a different set of social interactions which contributes to their individual sense of place. These interactions will influence how children interpret photographic images of places as they use their geographical imaginations. Ask pupils 'What is this place like for you, your family, other people?' and expect a wide range of valid responses.

Remember too that when they look at photographs children interpret visual images as text. They will be using the images to tell themselves a story with all the distortion and bias this involves. To help your pupils to appreciate that photographs are taken with a purpose or point of view ask questions like 'Who has chosen these views?', 'How do they make you feel?', 'What message is given?', and 'Do the photographs tell the whole story about the place or event?'.

Four photographs of Phear Park, Exmouth, telling different individual tales, but together making a bigger story.
Photos | *Margaret Mackintosh.*

It is important to help pupils to appreciate how hard it is to communicate what a place is really like. If they appreciate this in their own locality and in culturally familiar 'western' environments they will be better placed to understand the limitations of the images in photopacks of culturally unfamiliar distant localities. Ask pupils to make a PowerPoint presentation about their local area. How will they decide which photographs to include, for example which type of housing, which shops? How will other people interpret them? Discuss whether a photopack can ever tell the whole story about a place.

You can illustrate the way that visual images select and distort information in this simple classroom activity which also works well in INSET sessions. Ask pupils to bring photographs to school from local or national newspapers of a major geographical event such as an earthquake, volcanic eruption, flooding, wind farm proposal, dwindling fish stocks or deforestation. Add photographs which you have collected yourself of other major news items which have happened in the same time span. Mount each one on A3 paper and arrange them on desks around the room. Use the photographs as 'text' to tell a story. When pupils have looked at all the pictures ask questions like:

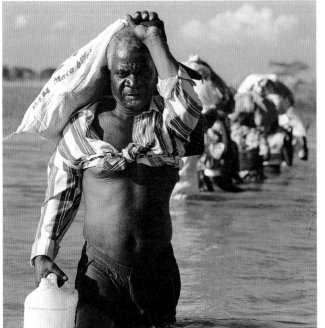

- ▥ What is it about?
- ▥ Are all the photographs about it? (to eliminate non-exemplars)
- ▥ What is the place like?
- ▥ Who is involved?
- ▥ What would you like to ask them?
- ▥ What do the people think about it?
- ▥ What did it feel like for them?
- ▥ What is the story? (Sequence the photographs, e.g. before, during and after)
- ▥ Why did it happen?
- ▥ Could it happen again?
- ▥ What is the future?
- ▥ What do you feel about it?

These questions were used with photographs of flooding in Mozambique, but could easily be adapted to other topics.

Photo | *Per-Anders Pettersson/UNEP/Still Pictures.*

Arctic perennial sea ice has been decreasing at a rate of 9% per decade. The first image uses data from 1979; the second from 2003. **Photos** | *NASA.*

Thinking about the future

Change is a key concept in geography. As well as changes which happen on a daily, seasonal or longer time span, change also involves anticipating different possible futures. Young children can be introduced to the idea of change by using Jeannie Baker's delightful picture book *Belonging* (Baker, 2004). Each page shows the view through a window onto a city street. A series of gradual changes transform the scene from a desolate concrete jungle to a thriving habitat, illustrating how we all depend on the soil.

Discuss with pupils the view from their own bedroom or school window – changes, alternatives, their likes and dislikes. Consider what might happen in the future – next year, in five, ten, twenty-five, a hundred years' time. This will help them to understand not only how change happens, but also how they can influence change to some extent. This work links very well with children's strong concerns for the environment. Experience suggests that they respond well to this because, as with the work on geographical imaginations, there isn't just one right answer. The pupils' different opinions can be valued and discussed. Children see their world as it is now. Helping them to visualise the future is vital if they are to appreciate how important it is that intelligent decisions are made in the present (Hicks, 2002).

Understanding geography depends on visual images. Children can see geography through fieldwork, film and video, photographs, diagrams and maps of all sorts. They usually see their world at ground level, in close-up – the small picture: each image is like a piece in a jigsaw.

They also need to use oblique and vertical aerial photographs to see their world from above and from a distance – the big picture. This helps them to make sense of their immediate surroundings, and localities further afield, to see how each individual jigsaw piece fits and contributes to the whole picture.

Historical, geographical and social understanding link together through exploring places in the past, present and future. You may find it helpful to think of these three dimensions as a continuum and as a context for developing children's graphicacy skills.

Useful resources

- Newspaper photographs
- Television news clips
- Postcards, including oblique and aerial images
- Calendar photographs
- Photographs of your local area, from ground and elevated levels – keep old photographs to identify change
- The internet; especially the Geographical Association online gallery for GA members

References and further reading

Arthus-Bertrand, Y. and Brown, L.R. (2005) *The Earth from the Air*. London: Thames and Hudson.

Baker, J. (2004) *Belonging*. London: Walker Books.

Balchin, W. and Coleman, A. (1965) 'Graphicacy should be the fourth ace in the pack', *Times Educational Supplement*, 5 November.

Chambers, B. (1996) 'Step by step', *Junior Focus*, April, pp.2-4.

Eyre, G. (2010) 'Photos in global learning', *Primary Geographer*, 71, pp. 20-21.

Halocha, J. (2008) 'Progressing through pictures', *Primary Geographer*, 65, pp. 24-26.

Hicks, D. (2002) *Lessons for the Future: The missing dimension in education*. Oxford: Trafford.

Mackintosh, M. (1998) 'Learning from photographs' in Scoffham, S. (ed) *Primary Sources: Research findings in primary geography*. Sheffield: Geographical Association.

Mackintosh, M. (2008) 'The process of progress', *Primary Geographer*, 65, pp. 5-14.

Plester, B., Richards, J., Shevelan, C., Blades, M. and Spencer, C. (2003) 'Hunt from above', *Primary Geographer*, 51, pp. 20-1.

Wiegand, P. (2000) 'cARTography', *Primary Geographer*, 42, pp. 16-17.

Websites

Geograph (images of every grid square in Britain) *www.geograph.org.uk*

Geographical Association online gallery (GA members) *www.geography.org.uk/resources/photogallery*

Google Earth *www.earth.google.com*

Ordnance Survey mapzone *http://mapzone.ordnancesurvey.co.uk*

Weather forecasts *www.bbc.co.uk/weather*

Photo | Paula Richardson.

Fieldwork and outdoor learning

The buildings, streets and environment around your school are a valuable learning resource. Whatever their age, children can undertake a great variety of activities outside the classroom. This work stimulates their curiosity, promotes creative engagement and leads them to value their locality. It is also linked to raising standards and achievement. This chapter outlines ways of developing local fieldwork and gives practical advice about how to organise visits. There is also important safety advice for subject leaders and recommendations about where to go for further information relating to out-of-school activities.

Fieldwork is using an outdoor experience to provide an environment to test out ideas and hypotheses, and to help pupils to extend their understanding of the world around them. However, as teachers, we know it is more than that. It is allowing our pupils to see for themselves and experience things as they are in the real world: to hear traffic noise, see the rainbow and feel the wind is all part of the magic of 'going out'. Exposure to television, advertising and other media has extended children's awareness of other places and environments, but they may nevertheless remain uncritical, unobservant and unchallenged. Even well-travelled pupils often make little use of either observation skills or the experiences they have of their own locality.

Fieldwork or out-of-classroom experiences offer you the opportunity, through a structured pathway, to help pupils to become observant, to develop the skills of recording, analysis and deduction and, it is hoped, to develop enquiring minds. Over a hundred years ago the great geographical educationalist Sir Archibald Geikie made the important link between research enquiry using observation and recording in the field, and good practice in the primary classroom. In the 1960s the Plowden Report (Central Advisory Council for Education, 1967, p. 231) reaffirmed that teachers' willingness to 'exploit their localities as teaching laboratories' is an essential part of developing pupils' geographical knowledge. Recent Ofsted reports continue to stress this message. For example, the *Learning Outside the Classroom report* (Ofsted, 2008) declared emphatically that learning outside the classroom helps to make subjects 'more vivid and interesting' (p. 7) and can 'contribute significantly to raising standards and improving pupils' personal, social and emotional development' (p. 5).

As adults we know that it is 'the doing' which can help us to reach a fuller understanding of things; for children this need 'to do' is even greater. Fieldwork gives them real practical opportunities to see, hear, feel and understand for themselves. This practical experience can use a range of environments such as the interior and exterior of the school itself, local streets and buildings or more distant localities including places visited during residential field visits.

How can I plan and organise fieldwork experiences?

Out-of-classroom experiences can provide stimulating support for any topic, serving either as an introduction to a topic, to enhance work in progress or to pull threads together at the end.

Street Survey

- Write down the name of the street and put the date of your survey:-

| | street | | date |

- Put a cross in a suitable place on each line:-

Quiet	——————————	Noisy
Tidy	——————————	Untidy
Interesting	——————————	Boring
Colourful	——————————	Drab
Well-kept	——————————	Neglected
Like	——————————	Dislike

- Does the street furniture blend in well with the street?

    Yes —————————— No

- Is the traffic moving freely?

    Yes —————————— No

- Are there any parked vehicles?   Yes [   ]   No [   ]

- Are they causing danger to people?

    Yes —————————— No

- Can people walk about freely?

    Yes —————————— No

- In this box draw the thing that you find most interesting:-

Figure 1 | A sample questionnaire for use in an urban area.

Sometimes it is really important for you to take the pupils outside without doing too much preparation and to ask them to look with fresh eyes at a place or an activity. Questions such as 'What is happening?', 'What is this place like?', 'What do you think about this?' will often elicit spontaneous and interesting responses. These kinds of conversations and discussions will help to give pupils moments of awe and wonder and excite their curiosity and thinking. At other times it will be important to ensure that pupils have an activity to complete or to practise a specific skill such as sketching or map reading. The most important thing, however, is that you consider a variety of approaches for your work outdoors. In the early years pupils will need many experiences of 'seeing it' for themselves, and the local area is excellent for looking at places, people, jobs and services. Even at this young age pupils should also be taken further afield on occasion, for example to the seaside, the countryside/a big town so that they can experience the unknown and the unfamiliar.

Introducing pupils to a variety of places will help to challenge their understanding and their perceptions and open their eyes to the nature of different places. Remember that older pupils may repeatedly visit the same locality in their fieldwork over time so it is important to ensure that there is progression in terms of activities, analysis and intended learning outcomes to keep the study of the same area fresh and interesting. When you organise geography fieldwork you also need to strike a balance with other curriculum areas. History, art, maths, English and other subject areas will all overlap in place studies. It makes sense to develop these links but you also need to have clear geographical objectives otherwise the focus of what you are doing will become blurred and the geographical work may become too diluted to be useful.

When they undertake fieldwork pupils can work in a variety of groupings, with a partner, in a small group, as a whole class, or even with pupils of other ages and abilities from the rest of the school. All too often when pupils are taken outdoors they end up as slaves filling in worksheets. Try to avoid this and encourage them to observe, sketch and think about what they are seeing. Pupils also need to reflect on what they observe and appreciate that when it comes to the environment there are very few situations where it is possible to be definite about what is 'right' and 'wrong'.

Digital cameras, video cameras, hand-held GIS equipment and mobile phones are an excellent way of recording what pupils see. They can help to record not only what is observed on the visit itself, but more importantly, those changes which occur over time and are sometimes hard to capture in other ways. All the information collected can be archived in school and used as a baseline for investigations in subsequent visits as well as providing a range of material for class PowerPoint presentations.

Fieldwork provides many opportunities for pupils to investigate things for themselves as a homework activity, and bring their findings into school for discussion and analysis. Data collection is another valuable activity for pupils to do at home. The questionnaire in Figure 1 is an excellent example which can be completed from outside their houses. Alternatively, if each pupil asked two people to complete the questionnaire as a homework exercise the class would quickly assemble a significant data set. The pupils could then analyse the results and draw conclusions using a prepared database on the computer. Not only does work of this kind represent good practice, but you can collect first hand data without even having to organise a visit!

Which places can I use for fieldwork?

One way of structuring fieldwork is to start with the pupils' immediate surroundings and gradually broaden into less familiar territory as they become more confident with each area and better at conducting their enquiries and investigations. However, it is important that pupils have the opportunity to experience different locations throughout their school years so that very young children, for example, are not simply confined to the school grounds but are also given experiences in places further away. A simple 'nested hierarchy' of fieldwork areas is shown in Figure 2, and the different potential of each area is examined in detail in the paragraphs which follow.

School grounds and the school buildings

The school buildings and surrounding grounds provide an initial stimulus for observing, recording and enjoying work outside the classroom. They also provide a useful context in which to practise sketching, estimating and evaluating aspects of the environment. This means that when pupils are further afield time is not wasted in learning how to perform these skills; they can be put to use directly, and related to the work in hand.

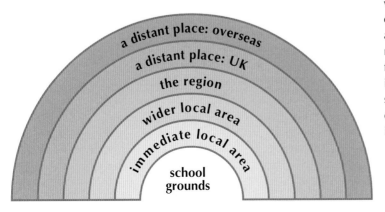

Figure 2 | *Broadening fieldwork horizons.*

Urban

Investigation of local shops/shopping parades/corner shops.

Comparison of buildings/designs/materials.

Assessment of litter problems, recycling issues.

Environmental walks to assess quality of the environment using an index.

Investigation of the impact of traffic in the area – How is parking/speeding controlled? Is it effective?

Visit to a building site – monitor progress.

Identify and collect logos/signs – do patterns emerge in the provision of services?

Map the land use of the area using a key.

Map routes to school/pupils' houses.

Design/locate a leisure centre.

Rural

Complete a seasonal walk (each term to record changes).

Investigate the village/local services provided.

What is the effect of any closures, e.g. local shops?

Map the land use of the area using a key.

Identify/visit areas of change, e.g. a new building under construction, a road/bridge development.

Examine housing types/styles/ages.

Map where pupils live – routes to school or town.

Interview residents – What is good about living in the area? What are the drawbacks? What changes would they like to see?

Walk to assess environmental quality of the area using an index.

Investigate traffic problems.

Figure 3 | *Lines of enquiry for urban and rural fieldwork.*

Activities in the school grounds could include:

- finding different kinds of building materials;
- 'dating' the area on a map – Which parts are older/ newer?
- using map keys;
- finding pleasant/boring/ warmest/coldest spots around the grounds;
- making up directions/routes round the site;
- sketching the views from the site;
- doing an environmental audit of the site;
- improving/changing the site;
- identifying the impact of seasonal/time changes on the site.

Immediate local area

The potential of the local area will vary enormously from school to school, but some of the following themes will be suitable for investigation:

- Streets, roads, buildings
- Local shops
- Recreation, park areas
- Woodlands, fields
- Water features
- Transport links – car parks, traffic
- Local viewpoints
- Industrial estates
- Pupils' home areas
- New developments, e.g. building sites
- Service provision in the area

Photo | *Tina Horler.*

The local area has the benefit of being accessible and can therefore be visited frequently, cheaply and for a variety of reasons (Figure 3). Individuals and groups can revisit to check evidence and observe changes over time. However it is important that out-of-classroom geography activities are not seen to be restricted to the study of the local area on foot, while other curriculum areas, such as history, involve more exciting visits by coach to castles, famous houses and open-air sites!

Visits to more distant places in the region, the rest of the UK and overseas

Travel to places away from the immediate vicinity of the school provides a number of benefits and experiences for pupils. They begin to see their own area in a wider context and can identify the inter-relationships which exist between them. They may see some contrasting environments and be able to compare how things change from place to place. The journey itself will also be part of the experience. It is quite possible that some of the pupils will never have been on a train journey before. Finance and school organisation have a major part to play in determining how often visits of this type can take place. However, it is very important to allow pupils to have these experiences to broaden their horizons in both the curriculum and the social sense.

One way of setting up visits further afield is to make links with another school and offer a series of return visits. The potential educational value is huge and the project can be very attractive financially. For example, if each school hosts its visitors for the day, the only outgoings would be transport costs to the school. Many primary schools are also taking longer residential visits to a centre either in Britain or overseas, often in France. These can be very exciting experiences for pupils and the personal and social benefits for those who go away from home are immense, even on a short stay. It is also possible to have just a one-night stay which could be suitable for younger pupils and which can still be very rewarding and exciting but without the greater financial commitment of a longer visit.

What guidelines should I follow?

In order to plan effectively for fieldwork and other out-of-school visits it is important that a policy or set of guidelines is established and used by all staff when planning off-site visits. By establishing links to the curriculum this will ensure that fieldwork or visits become part of the learning process rather than an optional extra which happens at the end of term. These guidelines will need to incorporate LA/Governor guidelines which already exist and have been approved by the governing body of the individual school.

Figure 4 offers some ideas that might be included in the policy. Each might only be a sentence or so, thus ensuring that the document as a whole is concise and helpful to those who use it. The *Fieldwork File* resources (May and Richardson, 2005) provide guidance on all aspects of fieldwork safety.

A policy document might consider:

1. The importance of working outdoors
2. The aims and objectives of fieldwork
3. How visits can support and enhance different areas of the curriculum
4. Suggestions for locations and possible activities/ideas for progression
5. Assessment opportunities
6. List of fieldwork equipment/where equipment is stored in school

A list of resources such as:

1. LA guidelines/country code/health and safety guidelines
2. Templates of letters to parents/adult helpers/booking guidance
3. Chart for completing a site risk analysis
4. Medical forms
5. Mini-bus information

Figure 4 | *Towards a school fieldwork policy.*

How can I plan a visit?

Visits beyond the school grounds must always be planned with great care and with close attention to health and safety issues. The following checklist highlights the essential elements but detailed guidance will be available from your LA or local geography champion to help you through the process of organising a visit. Refer also to the list of resources, including websites, at the end of this chapter; these will guide you through the planning and organisation of fieldwork and outdoor activities.

The following is a possible checklist for planning fieldwork visits:	
1	Permission from headteacher	☐
2	Choice of location – aims, objectives, dates	☐
3	Refer to school/LA documents, insurance, costings, etc.	☐
4	Book visit/transport, check timings	☐
5	Fill in required forms/letters to parents, medical forms	☐
6	Do site visit and risk assessment	☐
7	Prepare pupils – activities, clothing, equipment	☐
8	Brief staff and adult helpers	☐
9	Keep good accounts of monies collected	☐
10	On the day: leave lists of participants at school, know emergency procedures, brief staff, organise equipment and who is responsible for bringing it back	☐
11	Follow up: letters of thanks, payments, classwork, evaluate visit and note any changes to be made	☐

Risk assessment and child protection issues

One vital element of preparing for an outdoor activity is visiting the site beforehand to carry out an audit: assess risks, identify safety issues and collect up-to-date information. For example, you will need to find out about parking, toilets and wet weather alternatives. Figure 5 provides guidelines which you might like to follow. Once you have completed the sheets you can file them as a resource when you return to school and update them as needed.

There are a number of stages to carrying out a risk assessment which ideally should be done not too long before the visit takes place.

A risk assessment should be undertaken for each new site that you use and updated for places you have visited previously (Figure 6). This is a valuable exercise that helps to identify issues which might create problems and helps you to decide if the area is relatively safe to visit. As well as recording possible hazards you can evaluate them on a scale from one to five, with five providing an unacceptable risk.

A risk assessment is not merely a paperwork exercise. It also needs to be shared with the pupils and helpers so that they too are aware of potential dangers. One way of doing this is to ask the pupils to identify what they believe are the main risks before they go on a visit. For example, one class that was about to visit the Pennines decided that the chief dangers they faced were (a) getting lost (b) falling over (c) falling into water. Their recommendations included staying in a group with a grown up, wearing walking boots with a good grip and taking special care near the edges of rivers, lakes and streams.

Figure 5 | *Outdoor learning record sheet.*

Location:

Address:

Tel: email:

Date visited: Year group:

Number of pupils: Topic links:

Number of adults:

Education facilities

Education officer

Educational resources/worksheets

Teacher's notes/guidebooks

Handling materials

Loans

Video/tape commentaries

Talks/activities

Practical details

Cost involved

Journey time

Parking facilities

Lunch room

Education room

Toilets

Shop

Aims of visit

On-site activities and organisation
(Attach any useful material)

Risk Assessment completed   Yes/No
(Attach assessment)

Overall risk comment

Follow-up work

Evaluation/comments

RISK ASSESSMENT QUESTIONS

Place:
Date of assessment:
Name of person making the assessment:

1. What are the hazards which could occur here?
   (Narrow pavements, many people, steep banks, deep water, slippery grass, hidden bends, etc.)

2. What could happen as a result of a particular hazard?
   (Pupils pushed off pavement, difficult to cross the road, slip and fall, not be able to see the view.)

3. What is your evaluation of the situation? Is the place safe to use?
   (Cross the road further down, use the pavements which are wider, use the pedestrian crossing at X, give clear instructions at point Y to remind pupils to take care, put staff in correct positions, use X Street as an example rather than Y Street.)

4. Date and sign the assessment details.

Add any further information
(Where will the first aid kit be? Emergency telephone numbers. If there is an accident who will deal with it?)

5. Review
   When will a review of the location be needed?

Pupils' work | Shelley Primary School, Horsham.
Photos | Helen Martin.

Figure 6 | *Stages to consider in a risk assessment exercise.*

Falling over wearing walking boots with grip, keep to the path and walk sensibly, don't mess about near the edge

falling in don't go near the edge, walk carefuly, take care, dontmess abovt, don't run off,

Any helpers who have significant access to pupils during the field trip will need to give their consent to a Criminal Records Bureau check. This is now a standard procedure and your LA or governing body will have a system in place. Be sensitive in the way you explain what needs to be done. After all, it is for the benefit of the helpers themselves and will give peace of mind to parents whose children may be in their care. You also need to see that any adults who accompany the pupils are aware of the code of behaviour expected of them in relation to the pupils in their care. And most important of all, make quite sure they know what the visit is about and what you want the pupils to learn from it. A short briefing paper for helpers would be useful.

How can I ensure progression in outdoor learning?

The local area is relatively accessible and cheap for outdoor work and pupils may find that they visit it several times during their primary school years. This can result in the area, or certain features of it, being overused. For example, a pupil might be asked to study the local shopping area several times over, often using similar activities. For this reason liaison between staff who teach different year groups and key stages is crucial. Figure 7 gives an example of how a study of a local shopping centre can progress from a simple analysis of the area (for lower primary) to a more in-depth exercise (for upper primary). This approach takes account of pupils' increasing maturity and understanding in various ways, such as:

■ A move from closed to more open questions

■ An increase in problem-solving or decision-making activities

■ A movement from one to several variables

■ A move towards collaborative work and more independent learning.

One of the striking aspects of outdoor work is that it can be tailored to meet the varying needs of individual

A shopping parade – lower primary age

1   On your base map, write in the types of shop, or colour them in and make a key in the margin.

2   What is the use of the floor above most of the shops?

3   Which types of shops are missing from here?

4   Is parking easy?

5   How many parking spaces are there?

6   How long do cars tend to stay here?

7   Why is this?

8   Where do you think the shoppers come from?

9   What can you do here besides shop? (telephone, recycling banks, postbox, etc.)

A shopping parade – upper primary age

One of the shops is empty. You have decided to rent it and open a …

1   You need to decide what service or shop is needed here. How will you do this? Question shoppers? How many? Look at other shopping possibilities in the area? What is the market for your service/shop?

2   You have to decide on a window display, signs, layout, uniforms, opening hours.

3   Plan for your staffing – write an advert for staff (look at examples in local newspapers). Think about costs and rates of pay.

4   Plan your opening date. How and where will you advertise it? Local paper? Local radio? Free gifts?

5   How will you make sure your shop/service survives?

Figure 7 | *Progression through outdoor learning in the same location.*

pupils within a group. Teachers often find that some pupils are able to investigate the environment and analyse evidence to quite a high level even though their skills of reading and writing are relatively poor. It is important to offer these pupils a range of ways in which to record their findings so that their geographical attainment is not masked by their ability to read or write. You may find that asking them to record evidence using a tape recorder, digital camera or by choosing a scribe within the group can help the geographical understanding to shine through. It is also important to see that you challenge pupils who are more able than average. One way of doing this it to pose further questions, speculate on different 'what if' scenarios, and invite independent research back in the library or using the internet. Fieldwork provides the evidence for what exists in the environment at that precise moment and so it is important for all the participants to analyse the findings, discuss the reasons for the answers and think about how things might look in the future. All pupils can then participate by making a contribution to the final presentation of their work.

Are activity sheets useful?

While it is important to allow pupils to observe and use all their senses without too much distraction from worksheets, there will always be times when a structured approach will be helpful. It may well be that some pointers to stimulate questions/identify features/observations may be more appropriate at certain times on a sheet which then can be recycled and used again, rather than a sheet for writing on. The following are some simple rules for making an activity as useful as possible. The best test for a successful activity sheet is to ask yourself if you would enjoy/be able to do it yourself!

1. The sheet should always be clear and well laid out.
2. The text should not be too crowded or contain too many tasks or directions on the same page.
3. There should be a variety of activities, including an open-ended one if possible.
4. Questions which begin with How? Why? Which? Where? tend to produce better answers than those which begin Do? Does?
5. Answers should require a variety of styles of response: draw, estimate, decide, underline, count, and so on.
6. Vocabulary should be straightforward.
7. Pupils should be encouraged to use their senses whenever appropriate and safe: hear, see, smell, feel, taste.
8. Pupils should be asked for their views and give reasons for the things they like/dislike.
9. Cover survey sheets with plastic and get pupils to mark their answers with drywipe pens so the sheets can be re-used.

Resources for fieldwork

It is important to build up resources for local fieldwork, not least to help and inspire other colleagues. The resources should be centrally located and it is helpful to have several copies of the most useful items. It is also essential to keep adding to the bank of items with, for example, photographs of changes in the area, and newspaper cuttings.

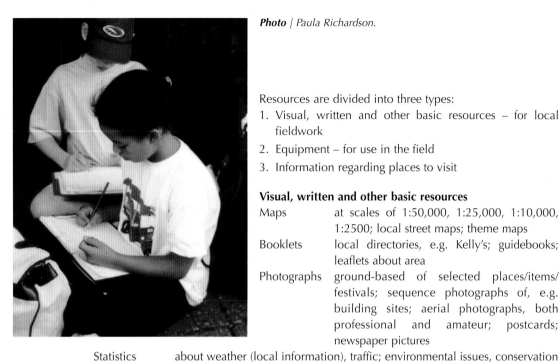

Photo | *Paula Richardson.*

Resources are divided into three types:
1. Visual, written and other basic resources – for local fieldwork
2. Equipment – for use in the field
3. Information regarding places to visit

Visual, written and other basic resources

Maps	at scales of 1:50,000, 1:25,000, 1:10,000, 1:2500; local street maps; theme maps
Booklets	local directories, e.g. Kelly's; guidebooks; leaflets about area
Photographs	ground-based of selected places/items/festivals; sequence photographs of, e.g. building sites; aerial photographs, both professional and amateur; postcards; newspaper pictures
Statistics	about weather (local information), traffic; environmental issues, conservation in local area. The last three, plus local Census data, are often available through local Borough/Council departments
Audio tapes	local people talking about changes/living in the area
Newspapers	cuttings about a variety of local issues
Previous work	data collected on previous fieldwork visits as evidence of change – and for making comparisons
Artefacts	relating to local geology/industry/local history

Equipment

Key stage 1
- clipboards
- tape measure
- magnifying glasses
- metre rulers
- non-standard measures, e.g. foot
- stop-watch/clock
- compass
- rock hardness testing equipment
- thermometer
- large-scale base maps
- plans, e.g. school, shopping area
- simple soil testing kit
- simple hand-held anemometer
- wind sock
- rain gauge
- soil profiles in jars

Key stage 2 – as for key stage 1 plus:
- recognition cards for trees, etc.
- quadrats
- soil augers
- water pollution testing kit
- maps (1:50,000 and 1:25,000)
- noise meter
- wind gauge
- more sophisticated soil testing kit (to include chemicals)
- cloud identification charts
- clinometer

At both key stages you should use appropriate ICT equipment, e.g. digital cameras, mobile phones and electronic measuring devices.

Photo | *John Halocha.*

Activities

Out-of-classroom activities should take advantage of the chance pupils have to see, measure, identify and reason out things for themselves. Fieldwork is an opportunity to focus attention on a small area and develop the skills of recall, thinking and prediction as well as techniques of sketching, map reading, measuring, and so on. It is also important to help pupils to look at the detail as well as the big picture, for example, looking at how the brickwork of a house is constructed and then working out how to show this on a sketch. You can help pupils to achieve excellent field sketches by asking them to label features which are hard to draw, thus reminding them that artistic merit is not the main function of a field sketch!

The two activities below suggest some ideas for using the local area in a creative way with pupils.

Picture activities

1. Take pictures of specific places in the immediate area, e.g. church, set of traffic lights, shops, memorials. On a large, possibly hand-drawn, map of the area displayed in the classroom, ask the pupils to locate the photographs correctly. Ask them to check these on their way to and from school and discuss their findings the next day.

2. Take a series of photographs in the area or in school, and cut them in half. Ask pupils to sketch in what is missing or complete a simpler activity such as matching them up. Again ask them to check when they are outside. The checking is important as it involves pupils in decision-making aspects of the activity.

What is our place like?

Tell the pupils they are responsible for planning a short walk for some visitors round their local area. They will have to choose the most interesting places to show them in a given amount of time. The pupils will need to discuss what makes their area interesting/special/memorable. If you decide that the visitors come from abroad it will provide an opportunity for pupils to decide what characterises their area and makes it different from elsewhere.

Walk the pupils round with a view to deciding which places/views/buildings will be best to include. The outcome might be a guided tour, a brochure, or perhaps a PowerPoint presentation.

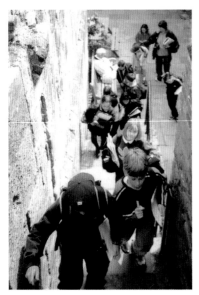

Photo | Paula Richardson.

If you can organise some visitors to undertake the tour, pupils will have a chance to develop their social skills as well as their geographical ones! Evaluating the project is also important: What went well? What didn't go so well? What would we change?

Conclusion

Fieldwork and other out of classroom activities offer opportunities for interesting and innovative teaching and learning: they bring a real and practical dimension to our pupils' geographical experience. The argument for fieldwork has also been dramatically strengthened in the past few years by neurological studies of the brain. We learn best, it seems, from rich multi-sensory environments that provide a range of messages and meanings. Immediate feedback is also highly desirable (Goswami, 2008). Fieldwork provides both of these things. It is a vital part of the arsenal of teaching strategies available to teachers and thus a key technique for promoting geographical learning.

Fieldwork allows pupils to see what is really happening rather than what is supposed to happen. A quiet street may become a busy thoroughfare for traffic in the rush hour as drivers try to bypass a bottleneck of traffic further back in their journey. It is the personal observations and investigations which can help pupils to understand how and why their environment is a constantly changing place. We should remember that for many pupils a fieldwork visit may be one of the most exciting and memorable events of their lives. When did we last give our pupils a fieldwork experience to remember?

References and further reading

Austin, R. (ed) *Letting the Outside In: Developing teaching and learning beyond the early years classroom.* Stoke-on-Trent: Trentham.

Central Advisory Council for Education (1967) *Children and their Primary Schools* ('the Plowden Report'). London: HMSO.

DfES (2006) *Learning Outside the Classroom Manifesto.* Nottingham: DfES.

Goswami, U. (2008) 'Principles of learning, implications for teaching: a cognitive neuroscience perspective', *Journal of Philosophy of Education*, 42, 3-4.

Haynes, S. (2007) 'The foundations of fieldwork', *Primary Geographer*, 63, pp. 18-19.

May, S. and Richardson, P. (2006) *Fieldwork File: For the primary years.* Sheffield: Geographical Association.

Ofsted (2004) *Outdoor Education: Aspects of good practice.* London: Ofsted.

Ofsted (2008) *Learning Outside the Classroom.* London: Ofsted.

Owens, P. (2007) 'Why fieldwork matters to every child', *Primary Geographer*, 63, pp. 12-14.

Websites

Adventure activity licensing *www.hse.gov.uk/aala*

Health and Safety Executive *www.hse.gov.uk/schooltrips/index.htm*

Geography Teaching Today *www.geographyteachingtoday.org.uk/fieldwork*

Learning Outside the Classroom *www.lotc.org.uk*

See also *Primary Geographer*, 59, Spring 2006, which focuses on outdoor learning; and the think piece 'Fieldwork at KS1&KS2' on the Geographical Association website *www.geography.org.uk/gtip/thinkpieces*.

Shells lay motionless on the beach like jewels on a golden carpet.

Eels swim in the vast cold sea.

Algae clings to pieces of drift wood.

Seaweed tangles around your feet as you step into the water.

Herring gulls perch on the grassy cliff spying on the local fishermen.

Oceans roar as they crash into the shore.

Rockpools, full of life waiting to be explored.

Every day the tide delivers a parcel of surprises for visitors to investigate.

CHAPTER COVERAGE:
CONCEPTS • ENQUIRIES • CPD/INSET • LITERACY/STORIES
• MISCONCEPTIONS • PROGRESSION • VOCABULARY

Geography and language development

O nce upon a time, a master and one of his most useful and well-regarded servants began to have a deep discussion about their importance to one another. Each felt they were more important to the other. Fortunately, they were sensible enough to see that this kind of argument could have gone on for ever without either being deemed to have won it. So, being basically faithful allies in spite of their difference in status, they simply had to agree that they were mutually indispensable.

Over the last few decades many similar discussions have taken place between teachers with curriculum responsibility for English and for geography as they have tried to make sense of the relationship between their respective subjects in planning for the primary phase. Practitioners have made considerable efforts to tease out these links and to understand in some depth how these two different subjects can enrich each other. They are to be congratulated for their efforts; it must have given many teachers both the confidence and the experience to move the curriculum towards cross-curricular collaboration and to develop the creative activities which have always been a feature of the best primary practice. As we enter a new phase in education which encourages us to reaffirm curricular 'breadth and balance' it seems likely that creativity, in both teaching and learning, will continue to be at the forefront of our efforts.

This chapter begins from the premise that, however much we have been encouraged to see literacy as the supreme priority, English and geography should not be viewed as master and servant, but as mutually supportive elements in a holistic approach to children's learning. It aims to show how geography lessons, while still pursuing specific geographical objectives, can also be part of the solution in raising literacy standards rather than yet another demand on hard-pressed teachers. Geographers investigate our world, local and global, by asking questions, discussing issues and solutions and presenting findings. The ability to listen to others' views and to communicate in speaking and writing is essential to good geographical work. At the same time, by providing varied, stimulating and relevant learning experiences for pupils, geography offers some of the richest and most relevant contexts through which these essential literacy skills can take root and flourish.

Where is geography on the curriculum map?

Geographers are well known for their anxiety about defining the position of their subject in the curriculum and justifying its continued existence to others who may ask them some taxing questions. Is it an arts subject or a science subject? Is it social science or economics? Why does local geography fieldwork sometimes become enmeshed with history? Are we actually studying maths when we undertake a litter or traffic survey? Why is some of the information we need in studying the landscape really geological, biological or technological?

Geography is about **places** and the relationship we **humans**, as the Earth's most influential inhabitants, have with them. At the heart of geography is the simple idea that all places are 'distinctive' or different from one another. The reasons for this distinctiveness can be traced to the fact that every place has a unique set of **physical** (natural) and **human** (manufactured) **features**, which are not found in exactly the same combination in any other place. Description and comparison of **places** and their characteristic features, using the **skills** of geographical enquiry, are the starting point for most geographical studies whether at a high academic level or in an infant classroom. Explanation of the similarities and differences between places demands an understanding of **processes** within the physical and human domains and leads us towards recognition of **patterns**, which help us to generalise our conceptions of the planet. Geography also offers flexibility. It can start from the study of a particular place, or set out to study a particular process, or begin from a theme or issue in the environment.

Figure 1 | *A working definition of geography.*

Eminent geographers have made sense of these questions by visualising geography as a bridge which links the arts subjects and the sciences, or even as the bridge of a ship from which the whole curriculum can be surveyed and navigated! They often describe geography as an 'integrative discipline', one which uses knowledge from many subjects and brings ideas together to develop a multifaceted understanding of our world. Figure 1 provides a working definition of geography. The terms highlighted in bold are those central to understanding the subject.

What can the content of geography contribute to literacy development?

Understanding that geography is a flexible subject that occupies a focal position on the curriculum map helps us to see why it can offer such an breadth of opportunity for literacy and language development. When studying geography, we need not only to use technical and scientific language to explain places, features and processes, but also to employ descriptive, evaluative, aesthetic and emotive language in expressing personal responses to places or issues. Units of work which set out to explore issues about the quality of an environment, for example, demand that we combine scientific explanation about the causes and consequences of environmental damage with evaluative and possibly even emotional responses regarding its impact on people. Such work also promotes information-seeking skills from non-fiction texts or the internet and may encourage the use of stories, myths and fables and poems. It inspires writing in all these genres too. Most importantly, geographical studies provoke us to employ these different aspects of literacy work together, and in doing so bring the distinctive elements of the different genres into sharper focus.

When the national curriculum was first introduced, school geography and literacy work benefited hugely from a surge of activity in the production of new pupils' information books, geographical stories as well as poems, photopacks, audio, video, and CD resources. The increasing use of the internet and email contacts between schools around the world has opened up further exciting arenas for using and exploring language in geography lessons and geography through literacy.

The introduction of the National Languages Strategy can be seen as a further such opportunity. For example, simple issues such as describing where we live, how we get to school, distances, directions and modes of transport, can all be profitably combined with map work and provide a context for developing basic conversational French, German or Spanish as well as English (Lewis, 2008). Thus geographical work has the potential to support pupils' progress in language and literacy development. This goes far beyond the very important, though rather limited, requirements of the national curriculum and its supporting directives.

How does the process of geographical enquiry link to literacy development?

While understanding the relevance of *what* geographers study is important to considering geography's relationship to language work, so, too, is the knowledge of *how* geographers work. The current documentation and advisory materials all tell us that even the simplest geographical activities for young children should be pursued through geographical questions and investigations. This 'enquiry approach' is central to all geographical work and is well exemplified in both published schemes of work and in medium term planning frameworks, which are often structured around 'key questions'. The enquiring process begins when pupils are motivated to ask pertinent questions about their surroundings. Finding the answers to these questions involves setting up an investigation within which they begin to comprehend, process and present information in the form of description, explanation, hypothesis and evaluation. So not only will they speak, listen, read and write about geography, but the very processes of thinking, of developing new concepts, of refining ideas and of testing them out on others to confirm understanding are heavily language dependent. In essence the approach which is advocated mimics the professional geographical research process at a level accessible to young children. It also ensures that good primary school geography relies on first-hand experience of the outdoor environment (see Chapter 10).

This strong emphasis on fieldwork experience has transformed the way that geography is taught in many primary schools. Also, outdoor work has always been regarded as a powerful stimulus to self expression. The unsolicited response in Figure 2 was written at the computer late one evening at a County Durham residential centre by a pupil with limited family opportunities for travel or literary support. She had been taken, during a geography field visit, to see the spectacular waterfalls at High Force and Low Force for the first time. It is a committed, emotional response to the landscape, partly descriptive but with some embryonic explanation.

Yet it also contains elements of scientific comprehension, some newly-acquired specialist vocabulary, an element of story and a personal communication with her teacher. Within it there is ample evidence for those tracking her development

---

High Force

At first I felt frightened and worried then it started to grow on me. It was really fun I loved it but the power of the water is amazing. How a 11 year old boy survived is unbelieveable it is a miracle that he is alive today. The white spray is all over the place particularly over the plunge pool. What more can I say just it's fantastic. The height of the thing is high let me tell you. I'm only glad sir had a tight hold of me because I felt dizzy when Sarah took a picture. The force of the water is incredible the speed of the thing is fast it just zooms down. Thankyou sir for keeping a tight hold of me.

Low Force
Wynch bridge

Dirty water flowing down, the foam sticking to the rocks, the rocks at the side look like steps. The sound, sounds like when you run the tap but much louder. It was BRILLIANT
But some people find it scarey and are frightened but <u>not</u> me
p.s I also felt surprised because the last time I came it was much cleaner some people do not care what they throw into the water.

Figure 2 | *A personal response to two waterfalls by Paula Cook, Consett, County Durham.*

Key question	Concept	Language skills
What is it?	Naming and identifying	Developing new vocabulary as pupils encounter an increasing variety of physical, human and environmental features and processes. Stories, poems, information books and dictionaries are important sources of words and ideas for all age groups.
Where is it?	Locating places and features	Understanding and using prepositions of place (in, beside, behind, under, etc.) out of doors and on pictures. The description of relative locations leads to the use of specialised vocabulary of absolute location (compass points, grid references, latitude, longitude) on globes and maps.
What is it like?	Describing and comparing	Developing descriptive language from visual and other sensory stimuli, progressing through increasing clarity, improved vocabulary and attention to detail, and through the ability to describe and compare at an increasing range of scales. Acquiring and practising comparative and superlative adjectives and adverbs and noun hierarchies.
How did it come to to be like this?	Explaining	Sequencing an explanation or hypothesis. Weighing and ordering ideas to enhance meaning. Offering alternative explanations using the language of tentative reasoning. Drawing on an increasingly wide range of geographical factors in framing ideas using drafting and editing skills.
How is it changing and what might happen next?	Hypothesising and predicting	Using tentative language to predict, speculate and suggest hypotheses about places and the processes of change. This may include expressions of uncertainty, hope, anxiety, delight, anger, relief and persuasive language in relation to environmental issues. Oracy is highlighted in debate, drama and role play.
How do I feel about it?	Evaluating, expressing opinion and caring	Employing expressive language to convey opinions of, or evaluative, aesthetic emotional responses to places (e.g. landscape appreciation, conservation). Could involve prose, poetry, opinionated/journalistic writing or oral responses such as speech making.

Figure 3 | *How key questions in geography link to basic literacy skills.*

of parallel progress in language and geography, as well as some indication of her immediate literacy needs. Best of all, being directly inspired by nature, it is written with spirit, a quality so very difficult to achieve in a book-based lesson.

Developing language and literacy through the geographical enquiry process

A recurring theme in this handbook is the planning of geographical work through a sequence of geographical questions usually referred to as the 'key' questions. The question sequence shown in Figure 3 has been recommended in both statutory and advisory documents, and has been widely adopted by teachers as a powerful planning tool. It has theoretical roots in Bloom's taxonomy of educational objectives (Bloom, 1972) and helps to clarify the purposes of geographical study and to support the tracking of progression in learning.

As pupils move through this enquiry sequence learning develops from simple recognition and description towards explanation and hypothesis, being continually revisited in different projects and making increasing levels of demand on their thinking processes. It is worth noting that the final question in the sequence does not necessarily demand a higher level of thinking, for it demands an evaluative response, and this can be attempted even by the very youngest learner.

We can also envisage how progression occurs within the context of each question. For example, when young pupils who are looking at a river are asked a 'What is it like?' question, they will answer using simple known words such as 'the water bends' whereas more experienced pupils could offer 'the river's channel is meandering'. Similarly a 'Where is it?' question may at first elicit only simple place references such as 'over there' or even self-referenced ones like 'behind me'. But these responses might be expected to progress with teaching, from relative to absolute locations, as described in four- or six-figure grid references. The overall implication of these two ways of tracking progress is that pupils who are operating at differing national curriculum levels may be encouraged to take part in the same enquiry at the same time but, through the judicious intervention of a teacher who is aware of their capabilities, can progress their understanding at a pace which is appropriate for them. It is worth taking time, perhaps as an INSET activity, to trace in detail the relationship between the skills demanded in a geographical question sequence and those defined as indicative of achievement in the national curriculum level descriptions.

Engaging in enquiry with pupils does not, however, involve confronting them with a mechanical set of structured questions. It involves helping them to consider these types of questions, and framing them in ways which they find understandable. The general aim is to induct young pupils into the excitement of an enquiry which has relevance to their own lives, such as 'How can we make our local area safer?', so that they begin to ask their own questions and to research answers for themselves. By tracking the nature of their questions the teacher will again be able to trace progression.

Planning geography and literacy work

It is important when planning for geography and English in tandem to be clear about time allocation for the two subjects. A day's fieldwork and follow-up may consume a complete half-term's geography time, yet there may be several different aspects of geography which need to be addressed within that half term. So there may be a temptation to dismiss the fieldwork as being too time-consuming. However, if we can be more confident of saying precisely what language development is accruing from our work in the field, then opportunities are opened up for deeper, more rewarding, multi-purpose outdoor work.

An excellent way to begin any new geography topic is to elicit what the pupils already know and what they want or need to know. As well as defining starting points for the teacher, this approach involves pupils in framing statements and questions and, with the teacher's support, in refining and grouping them. As part of this process the teacher or more able pupils will model different ways of composing and writing and there will probably be opportunities to discuss the structure and punctuation of statements and

Planning for Progression

From:	To:
writing in geography	
■ single words and phrases;	■ longer sustained pieces of writing;
■ writing with a simple single focus (e.g. describing a street scene);	■ writing with several sub-sections (e.g. describing stages in a survey);
■ writing for a single audience (e.g. teacher).	■ writing for many different audiences (e.g. other pupils, local newspaper).
reading in geography	
■ text with low readability age;	■ text with high readability age;
■ text selected by the teacher;	■ text found and selected by pupils (e.g. on CD);
■ reading a text, all of which is relevant;	■ reading a text from which relevant information has to be extracted (e.g. entry in atlas);
■ texts from a single source (e.g. KS1/2 book).	■ texts from many different sources, possibly conflicting (e.g. brochures).
speaking and listening in geography	
■ short answers to closed questions (one response expected);	■ answers to open questions for which pupils explain their thinking;
■ discussion in class or small groups;	■ speaking aloud in front of a class in discussion or role-play;
■ listening to or giving a narrative account (e.g. story of a journey);	■ listening to or giving an analytical account (e.g. how the water cycle works);
■ listening to and using simple vocabulary.	■ listening to and using specialised geographical vocabulary.

Figure 4 | *Summary of the use of geography in language development.*

MOUNTAIN
A mountain is bigger than a hill. A mountain is rocky, and very high mountains have snow on the top. You have to climb up a mountain. The top is called the peak.

The Matterhorn |
Photo | *John Royle.*

questions viewed together. This work could well provide the focus for a literacy lesson, and can certainly be justified as such even though it may have a geographical purpose.

Figure 4, compiled as a result of a joint initiative involving the Geographical Association provides a neat way of outlining the progression of language skills through reading, writing and speaking in geography. It is evident from this that not only can progression be planned for both subjects together, but geography can play a huge role in literacy development. Teachers may consider using this framework as a tracking device to ensure that geographical work is indeed providing appropriate support for each main element of the literacy strategy.

Geographical vocabulary

Geography is frequently criticised for having an obscure, specialised vocabulary which is inaccessible to non-specialists. Primary teachers attending INSET courses are often particularly anxious about specific terms used in physical geography. So it is important to ask how much specialist vocabulary is appropriate to primary pupils' needs and how we should go about introducing it. There are many pupils who might become quickly excluded from understanding by just one or two unfamiliar words, and in this respect a non-specialist may be more sensitive to their plight than a 'geographer' who is liable to slip technical words into a conversation unwittingly. However, there are other pupils who revel in terminology, if only to impress, and it would be a pity to stifle this enthusiasm. Agreeing with colleagues a set of words to be developed within each topic is a profitable aspect of whole-school planning. The implications for some purposeful dictionary work are evident (ongoing word level work).

We have little knowledge of what understanding pupils come to school with, although all teachers have come across examples of pupils knowing the same words but attaching different meanings to them. Wiegand (1993) notes that urban pupils often think the term 'hill' (which is three dimensional) has the same meaning as 'slope' (which is two dimensional), perhaps because they rarely see entire hills not obscured by buildings. Devlin (1994) identified homonyms as a particular problem in geography. Most children attached the word 'peak' to a cap and might therefore visualise a mountain peak as a protrusion from the side rather than the summit. We can easily forestall such misunderstanding by mentioning a more usual meaning whenever we introduce a new term, e.g. 'The top of a mountain is called the "peak". Can you think of any other things that are called a peak?'

In introducing river terminology to pupils, teachers are surprised to find that new terms like 'tributary' are more easily absorbed that familiar words such as 'source', 'channel' and 'mouth' which have a double meaning. A 'channel' is where you find a favourite programme, a 'mouth' is very useful for eating and talking, and 'source' conjures up a very familiar red bottle! Similarly, in the north east of England a 'geyser' is a slang term for an old man so the vision of hot geysers spouting out of the ground conjures an interesting spectacle! We therefore need to think about how we can deliberately dismantle the known meaning of homographs and homonyms before building the new one.

All this will not only offset geographical misconceptions but offer a contextualised opportunity to teach about homonyms, homophones and homographs and to introduce some of the ways in which words are used colloquially in different geographical regions. For example, words such as 'stream', 'burn', 'beck', 'piddle' all refer to the same landscape feature but enrich and enliven our vocabulary. Pupils might also explore the cultural origins of regional dialect as part of their vocabulary acquisition work (Lewis, 2001).

It may also help if we are more specific about how we use particular terms. Using 'countryside' to refer to rural areas avoids confusion with 'country' in the sense of a state until pupils are mature enough to have the dual meaning of 'country' explained. Finally, giving simple derivations of terms is possible for older juniors – 'cumulus' is like 'accumulate', and 'tributary' is from the same root as 'contribute'.

Following on from the whole-school effort to agree suitable key vocabulary for topics, a good CPD activity would be to highlight homophones, homonyms, homographs and dialect words and those which have a variety of meanings. A shared approach will benefit both the geographical learning and the whole process of vocabulary acquisition. A fundamental need is for a more detailed understanding of pupils' geographical vocabulary development, something that could be achieved for your school by keeping a shared notebook of piecemeal evidence of pupils' understanding to inform your shared planning and practice. It also offers an excellent opportunity for final year or Masters students to explore an under-researched topic.

The language of location

Expressing position is a fundamental geographical skill. It begins with the gradual acquisition of place language and progresses towards sophisticated knowledge of mapping conventions and the ability to define absolute location.

Map reading itself has much to offer literacy skills. Skimming and scanning are necessary approaches to reading a map, offering a contrasting technique to sequential left-to-right reading, and so helping to develop awareness that in reading for information different approaches to text are needed. Also, young children need to understand that places and features such as mountains and even farmers' fields have names just as people do. Maps are therefore a tremendous resource for consolidating teaching about proper nouns and capital letters.

The skills involved in describing geographical location can also be developed through stories. For example, the progress of events in a story is sequenced in place as well as time and, if we encourage pupils to map the story, their comprehension and visualisation of spatial relationships can be assessed. Pupils' own story writing may be enhanced by encouraging them to invent settings and make imaginary maps, and this in turn can support their ability to visualise sequenced events. Resources such as the classic picture book *Rosie's Walk* (Hutchins, 2001), along with well-known fairy tales and poems, provide an excellent stimulus for this kind of work.

Using language to describe features and places

Retrieving information from pictures is another essential geographical skill with implications for language development. Here, experience shows that children pick out details relevant to their own immediate interest, such as animals, people, vehicles and other foreground details, rather than the surrounding landscape. We therefore need to develop strategies for directing their attention. One possibility is to cover part of the picture, arouse pupils' curiosity by asking them to guess what is there, and then reveal it only when their attention is fully focused. It is also important to teach the vocabulary that will enable them to say where things are, e.g. near part, far part, distance, foreground, background, left and right.

The ability to describe accurately is a general language skill which teachers constantly monitor as vocabulary grows. Outdoor work within geography can greatly enhance the skill of describing if it deliberately focuses on the full range of sensory stimuli in the environment. You can focus pupils' attention by asking questions such as 'Is it rough or smooth?', 'Does it have a smell?' and so on. Even when we are limited to secondary sources, studies of unfamiliar places, based on multimedia packs, can still invoke descriptive writing which involves empathising with the people who live there. For example, 'How do you think the inhabitants of Chembakolli feel when the monsoon breaks?'. Most teachers are well practised at taking children into a picture by using questions to help them to imagine sensory experience: typical questions include 'What do you think you could hear in this place?', 'Do you think you could feel the hot sun on your face?', 'What would happen here if the wind began to blow hard?' (see Chapter 9).

Activities where imaginary islands and countries with geographies, culture, laws and customs are invented by groups of pupils also give great scope for language development through descriptive invention from making lists of products to writing 'national poetry'. They are also excellent vehicles for assessing pupils' geographical understanding of the constituent features of different kinds of environment and offer huge scope for creativity across the curriculum (Figure 5). You might consider some or all of the following: What are the laws of your country?; What is your language like?; Do you use the Euro or some other currency? (maths); How does it work? Have you any famous artists, architects, musicians, engineers, scientists? What did they do that made them famous? See Chapters 15 and 16 for further ideas to extend this work towards the understanding of international relations and global citizenship.

Using story books and poetry

The use of picture story books in the Early Years Foundation Stage (EYFS) and key stages 1 and 2 geography is well documented. Among the most popular are Mairi Hedderwick's Katie Morag stories based on the island of Struay, a fictitious place inspired by the real Hebridean island of Coll. Coll is also the focus of an excellent geography picture pack, *Discover Coll* (Graham and Walker, 2003; see also Chapter 8) and the *Isle of Coll map* (Geographical Association, 2004a).

By the Sea

The lashing waves,
Crash against the cliffs
And eat them away,
Never sleeping night or day.
At night the moon glistens on the sea
And makes the fish silvery
Under the waves they dash
In and out
Arrows of swift light
On a summer day
Children play on the beach
Eat rock
And run along way
To reach the cool waves
To paddle, dip toes
Splash
They never think these same waves
Crash on cliffs, and eat rock too-
            Did you?

Figure 5 | Responding to a geographical experience with creative writing. **Photo** | Melanie Norman.

The Geographical Association has also recognised the value of teaching EYFS geography through fictional characters. It has produced a wide range of materials focused on Barnaby Bear, which include geographically-grounded literacy lesson activities. These publications include whole-class big books, annotated with respect to both subjects (Jackson, 1999-2003), and differentiated little books with geographical themes for guided reading groups (Lewis, 2000-2003). Another addition is *Barnaby's Local Area Album* (White, 2003) an information text in scrapbook format which acts as a model to support early descriptive and evaluative writing about your own local area.

For older pupils there are many texts which use powerful writing and illustrations to engage children in geographical issues. Good use can still be made of old favourites, such as *Rainforest* (Cowcher, 1990); and for older and more able children excellent descriptive passages may be taken from longer texts, including the landslide episode in *The Railway Children* (Nesbitt, 2007). The Primary Champions Ning ho (*http://geographychampions.ning.com*) contains details of up-to-date story books which are being continuously updated and reviewed by peers. Another useful source is the Tide~ website (*www.tidec.org*) which offers a good range of relevant geographical and environmental texts particularly useful for distance place and globalisation topics.

In my own experience, recalling a small landslide I once witnessed in the Scottish Highlands provided an engaging stimulus to explore geography with the aid of a few photographs. The landslide blocked the single track road and resulted in the local children

Site visits can stimulate language development, particularly if they involve an element of drama.
Photo | Paula Richardson.

arriving at school the next day on a rowing boat!

Creating a mystery element within a story is another useful device, as it stimulates questions and answers on the way. I once found (or said I did!) a bashed-up tin of baked beans in a Lakeland beck. The mystery of how it arrived there fuelled children's curiosity, stimulated geographical questions and enabled me to move on to teaching about a local flash flood which had swept away a campsite, the stock of a local shop and a man in his pyjamas. The man was saved only by the fact that there was a bend in the road down which the flood had coursed. The current, fastest on the outside of the bend, swept him against the wall of the shop, where he was rescued by the owner who was trying to hook up some of his disappearing stock! This true story then stimulated imaginary maps and offered a good opportunity to assess the children's understanding of the Lakeland landscape, mapping conventions and the ability to sequence events in space as well as time.

Making comparisons and offering explanations

In the progression from simple geographical description of a single place or feature to more complex comparisons, the need for comparative language arises. Geography gives pupils many opportunities to practise manipulating comparative forms such as 'smaller than', 'more industrialised than', 'not quite so cold as', and so forth. There will also be opportunities to introduce comparative hierarchies or word ladders like 'dwelling, hamlet, village, town, city, metropolis', or 'hill, mountain, range, chain and system'.

As pupils progress towards secondary level it becomes increasingly important for them to acquire the skills of logically sequenced explanation. By using varied approaches to classroom practice and providing frequent opportunities for spoken interaction and presentation you can enhance both primary geography and language work. Activities in which pupils propose changes to their environment and adopt the role of a planner or developer are rich examples of contexts in which pupils explain and justify their intentions and present ideas for class discussion. The judicious use of writing frames in geography can help pupils to move from these spoken explanations towards well-organised written sequences.

Adopting the enquiry approach implies a constructivist stance to learning geography, so we must be prepared for many early 'explanations' to be only partially tenable. It is vital for pupils to know that expressing uncertainty does not imply weakness in their understanding but is rather a recognition of the complexity of some geographical processes. Tentative language is a strong feature of all geographical explanation, even at high academic level, not only because of the range of variables that influence places, but also because there are still many gaps in our understanding of the world. So the subject offers great scope for hazarding explanations: 'It might be because the weather …','It could possibly make a difference to …', 'Maybe it will be washed away or …'. Realising that there are often several possible and equally tenable explanations offers great comfort to non-specialist teachers too. In a climate of true enquiry there is no place for an all-knowing expert. The teacher's role is simply to apply the tacit knowledge and sharper logic of adult experience to the exciting task of helping pupils gradually to refine their own geographical reasoning.

Enquiries into the way places are changing and evolving also offer great opportunities for self-expression as they invoke personal viewpoints and engage the emotions as well as the intellect. Pupils' own views may be presented through speech, drama, articles for class newspapers, letters, prose or poetry and will include opinion, persuasion, uncertainty, hope, anxiety, relief, anger and delight. The power of discussion in supporting concept development and refining understanding highlights oral language as an essential element of all environmental geography work.

A good example of how to study a local issue was when pupils from years 5 and 6 at Lumley Primary School, County Durham, working with education students from the University of Sunderland, undertook a land use survey of their village and identified four pieces of open land which might well come under pressure to be developed in the near future. In role as development and construction teams, they set about planning new land uses for these sites following a discussion to establish what their village most needed – a supermarket, light industrial units, a leisure centre and a drive-in McDonald's! Having surveyed the sites and agreed on which environmental features were worth preserving they drew detailed exterior and interior plans, manipulating a great variety of geographical variables from car parking space to noise pollution. A 'public meeting' (role play) followed in which plans were presented orally and debated for their merits or otherwise by pupils acting as politicians and NIMBYs. The heated argument which erupted from some proposals and the eloquence with which controversial issues, such as the removal of half the school field to accommodate the leisure facility, were debated, provided ample evidence of the power of a personally experienced geographical context in promoting oracy. Looking at this from the standpoint of geographical pedagogy, the activity was one in which a holistic experience of geography, incorporating skills (map reading and map construction), places (the immediate locality), themes (settlement, environmental quality), patterns (land use conflicts) and processes (environmental change), was experienced and enjoyed by all the participants.

Developing a library for geography

Of the many kinds of geographical stimulus mentioned in this chapter, books are arguably still the most important resource in most primary schools. In spite of the increasing use of appropriate internet sites, the maintenance of a library to support geography is still a priority for the subject leader. It should include as wide a collection as possible of children's fiction organised to support individual topics. This is best visualised as a shared task for the staff and a judicious co-ordinator can harness substantial progress for all by setting up a CPD activity in which colleagues are encouraged to identify and evaluate the school's existing materials in the light of the needs identified in the SEF.

Most schools will find that their existing stock abounds in picture story books with striking settings which support the acquisition of geographical vocabulary and present concepts in a form which is enjoyable for pupils. It is important to ensure, however, that the pleasure of stories is not compromised by an over-zealous teacher trying to extract the last grain of geography from the pictures! The secret of using stories well rests on enjoying them with the pupils in an atmosphere of relaxed anticipation, with no unwelcome geographical interruptions. After all, good stories bear much re-reading and this in itself is a powerful aid to consolidating the geographical language and ideas they contain. You can always return to particularly useful picture spreads if their content is vital to the lesson, and pupils can be invited to develop geographical ideas in a follow-up discussion which does not interrupt the story itself. These comments confirm the legitimacy of pursuing geographical as well as literary ends in the literacy lesson. If the purpose of literacy is to attach meaning to text then it may just as well be geographical meaning as any other.

Many poetry collections which schools already have in stock include poems with geographical potential. In addition to the CPD activity suggested above, a co-operative search (in-service time, perhaps) or a competition for older pupils to amass suitable examples, could be organised. A selection of poems relating to different aspects of geography could be word-processed in large print onto cards (a good job for adult helpers), illustrated by pupils and laminated for classroom use. Interactive whiteboards (IWBs) also offer the potential to add poems or individual verses to suitably blank areas (such as the sky or sea) of photographs. This might also encourage pupils to compose their own or class poems on screen!

The collection of information texts for geography is more problematic. Ideally, each unit of work requires a selection of books at different reading levels. To optimise their use they need to double as resources for teaching information skills, so they should all contain adequate contents pages and glossaries. Books which are to be used by pupils themselves have to be strongly bound. A good variety of styles of presentation – text and pictures, comic strips, speech bubbles – has more appeal to children, as do books, referred to as 'faction', where characters to whom the pupils can relate act as guides through the factual information. Question and answer formats are particularly helpful for geography since they reflect the enquiry idea. Vetting for outdated or stereotypical images, bias and prejudice needs to be carefully done, too. It is important to be aware that some modern environmental texts contain images, of whaling for example, which many pupils find distressing. What better way to raise this awareness than to ask colleagues to bring one book they would use and one they would not use to a CPD session for discussion?

For obvious commercial reasons, publishers have been unable to embrace the demand sparked off by the national curriculum for information about specific localities in other parts of the world. Instead, non-fiction, place-based series tend to concentrate on whole countries or continents. Such resources are invaluable sources of background material but are not adequate in themselves for detailed locality studies. A good source of support has come in the form of resources from organisations such as ActionAid, Oxfam, the Development Education Centres, and the Geographical Association itself (Figure 6). These have greatly aided the quest for materials detailed enough to foster empathetic understanding of other communities.

As your library expands, making colleagues aware that it can be used in both geography and language lessons will enhance its use. Where resources for foundation subjects are scarce there is a strong case for some deliberate co-operative planning in the buying of books between the language and geography co-ordinators. Another source of reading material in the classroom is display. Most geographical topics provide excellent inspiration for colourful assemblages of pupils' work and these are at their best as a resource for literacy development, where the pupils themselves have been actively involved in their planning and presentation.

Figure 6 | *Resourcing distant place studies at key stage 1: a picture map of Tocuaro.*
Source | *Geographical Association (2004b).*

Of particular value are interactive displays, which provide things to do as well as to look at. Participation can be invited by the use of bold captions based on geographical questions, changed periodically to refocus attention and renew interest. Finally, one should not forget the value of traditional geographical resources (globes, wall maps, atlases, aerial photographs and weather charts) as a stimulus for the development of geography and language skills.

Some suggested types of lesson

A number of suggestions are offered below, in which the session or topic time is deliberately organised to facilitate related geography and English language teaching. The list is not exhaustive but may spawn many other ideas of your own.

- A geography session leads into a creative writing follow-up such as writing a poem after fieldwork or writing a descriptive postcard from a distant locality.
- A literature experience is used to stimulate a geographical enquiry, e.g. a reading of *The Snail and the Whale* (Donaldson, 2003) leads into an exploration of the globe and the plotting on a world map of all the journeys and places visited.
- The literacy session is about reading for meaning but the context is part of the current geography topic and uses geography information texts.
- The geography written work is designed for a particular audience, e.g. after researching weather stories older pupils write stories about weather for younger ones or prepare a display for a parents evening.
- A speaking and listening activity compares different representations of St Lucia from published resources and internet sites.
- A geography topic concludes with the making of an information book about it, involving aspects of book production and page design (ICT), and preparing a contents list and glossary in language time.
- Groups of children are invited to invent a country and make a map of it. They consolidate 'features vocabulary' and learn about proper nouns while plotting imaginary towns, rivers and mountains. They also explore ideas about what a country is by inventing a national flag, currency and language, and by writing laws, inventing folk tales and traditional recipes, and composing imagined biographies of the country's most celebrated inhabitants.

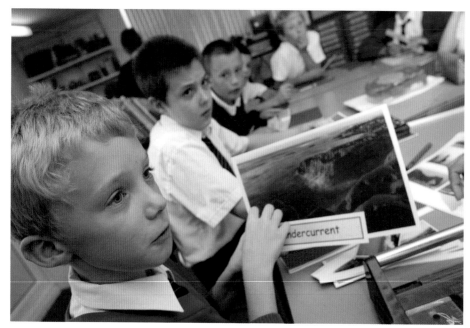

Photo |
Shaun Flannery.

Attractive as it might be for teachers with demanding timetables to make time economies by combining English and geography, this chapter is not about making space in an overcrowded curriculum. Nor is there any intention to represent geography as the sole vehicle for language development. Using language well is a vital life skill. It supports our understanding, brings alive our thoughts and gives expression to our beliefs. English not only shares a central place on the curriculum map with geography but also fundamental educational goals. Both subjects are strongly concerned with communication and seek to nurture our growing connections with fellow humans in other parts of the world. Geography provides a tremendous range of exciting real-world contexts in which pupils can be offered an inspiring range of language experiences. But equally, to give pupils the best possible experience of geography we need to use quality literary resources and offer pupils the fullest possible opportunity for self-expression in speech and writing within our lessons.

The Guest House   The Hotel

The holiday house is Made of wood. ✓
The holiday house has lots of different rooms. ✓

The hotel is made of brick. ✓
The hotel has lots of bedrooms. ✓

Pupils' work | *Courtesy of Greg Walker.*

References and further reading

Bloom, B. (ed) (1972) *Taxonomy of Educational Objectives: Handbook 1, cognitive domain*. London: Longman.

Cowcher, H. (1990) *Rainforest*. London: Corgi.

Devlin, M. (1994) 'Geographical vocabulary in the junior school', *Issues in Education*, 2, 1, pp. 26-30.

Donaldson, J. (2003) *The Snail and the Whale*. London: Macmillan.

Geographical Association (2004a) *Isle of Coll map*. Sheffield: Geographical Association.

Geographical Association (2004b) *Tocuaro map*. Sheffield: Geographical Association.

Graham, J. and Walker, G. (2003) *Discover Coll*. Coalville: Wildgoose Education.

Hutchins, P. (2001) *Rosie's Walk*. London: Red Fox.

Jackson, E. (2000-2003) *Barnaby Bear big books*. Sheffield: Geographical Association.

Lewis, L. (2000-2003) *Barnaby Bear little books*. Sheffield: Geographical Association.

Lewis, L. (2001) 'What's in a name?', *Primary Geographer*, 45, pp. 23-24.

Lewis, L. (2008) 'En route à l'ecole', *Child Education*, April 2008, p. 50.

Nesbitt, E. (2007) *The Railway Children*. London: Penguin.

White, K. (2003) *Barnaby Bear's Local Area Album*. Sheffield: Geographical Association.

Wiegand, P. (1993) *Children and Primary Geography*. London: Cassell.

Websites

Geographical Association *www.geography.org.uk*

National Languages Strategy *www.primarylanguages.org.uk*

Primary National Strategy *www.nationalstrategies.standards.dcsf.gov.uk/primary*

Tide~ *www.tidec.org*

See also *Primary Geographer*, 56, Spring 2005, which focuses on 'Talking Geography' and the think piece 'Geography and Literacy' on the Geographical Association website *www.geography.org.uk/gtip/thinkpieces*

CHAPTER COVERAGE:
DIFFERENTIATION • GOOD PRACTICE • ICT • INCLUSION/SEN • PHOTOGRAPHS • PLANNING

Geography and ICT

This chapter looks at the opportunities for, and some of the challenges of, using Information and Communication Technology (ICT) in primary geography, set in the context of the wider curriculum. It includes guidance on how to use ICT to help children learn about mountains. A range of websites are suggested; some of these are aimed at pupils, others are to help teachers in their planning and professional development.

The world of education is changing rapidly and over the last decade many primary schools have undergone huge transformations in terms of pedagogy, staff and physical appearance. Educational changes have been many, rapid and revolutionary; but none has been more dramatic than in ICT. To begin with, technology itself has advanced considerably. Computers are faster, sleeker and more affordable, and laptops and other portable equipment have liberated users from the tie of a central location – particularly important for fieldwork. School computers are now generally networked, enabling software and printers to be shared, and making it easier to save and retrieve pupils' work. Peripherals such as digital cameras, interactive or Smart boards, scanners and data projectors are in use in most primary schools. Software developments have brought about great improvements in the range and quality of programs available to pupils, including simplified versions of 'grown up' software suites. Many schools are now using free software and the immense growth of the internet, coupled with an increase in educational websites, has led to further innovation, including virtual learning environments and learning platforms, Web2 applications such as blogs, NINGs, Skype and social networking sites such as Facebook.

The government is strongly committed to raising standards in ICT in education, and major initiatives, often supplemented by local resources, have sought to make technological advances accessible to all primary pupils. This central and local investment has led to a huge increase in the quantity and quality of hardware in schools, including networks, computer suites and other peripherals. Most teachers have their own laptops, and there has been a concerted drive to improve teachers' ICT skills and their confidence in using ICT across the curriculum. The Action Plan for Geography, and the courses offered either face to face or online by the Geographical Association, are examples of initiatives that have helped teachers exploit the potential of this new equipment and software.

The 2008 Ofsted report on geography indicates progress since the 2002 report:
'The use of ICT in geography has grown with improvements in teachers' skills, better access to the internet and high-quality software. Digital projectors and interactive whiteboards have added positively to geography teaching in some schools. In particular, the use of geographical information systems is revolutionising and extending pupils' experiences in geography. Visual images from around the world bring immediacy to the learning. Satellite technology can bring landscapes to life. Data can be overlaid and used with interactive maps to interpret patterns and solve problems. Yet, while some schools are using these new opportunities very effectively, others are reluctant to take the risk or do not have the skills or resources to do so.' (Ofsted, 2008, p. 22.)

How ICT supports the geography curriculum

■ ICT has created new ways of exploring the world through maps. Maps can be interactive, and of variable scale. They are easily accessible and can be integrated into a variety of media

■ Multimedia software can help pupils to investigate geographical topics that would be too remote, too dangerous, or take too long, without ICT

■ The internet and email enable pupils to interact with peers and other communities, to access and research information, and to exchange details of weather, environment and culture. This brings otherwise inaccessible localities into the classroom, and can help to develop global citizenship and awareness of similarities, differences and diversity in world cultures

■ ICT can offer pupils opportunities to work in role, engaging with 'real time' situations which promote teamwork, citizenship and thinking skills. Mapping skills can be rehearsed in simulated environments before being used in the real environment.

Figure 1 | The contribution of ICT to teaching geography.

ICT in the curriculum

The first computers were introduced into primary schools in the early 1980s, and in 1990 ICT was included in the general teaching requirements of the national curriculum. Since then ICT has been steadily upgraded and its use promoted in all subject areas. ICT is thus seen as a generic skill which is essential for learning and life and which, more specifically, enables children to:

■ find and select information from digital and online sources, making judgements about accuracy and reliability

■ create, manipulate and process information using technology to capture and organise data, in order to investigate patterns and trends; explore options using models and simulations; and combine still and moving images, sounds and text to create multimedia products

■ collaborate, communicate and share information using connectivity to work with, and present to, people and audiences within and beyond the school

■ refine and improve their work, making full use of the nature and pliability of digital information to explore options and improve outcomes.

Key skills as far as geography and other related subjects are concerned include undertaking investigations and enquiries using methods, media and sources including GIS, databases and the internet. Breadth of learning stipulates that pupils should develop and extend local and global links through communications and collaboration tools such as email, video conferencing and podcasting. Skype enables pupils to talk to other children all over the world. In the guidance on curriculum progression there are many references to ICT tools, giving examples of new technologies.

In conclusion, primary geography provides a rich and purposeful curriculum context for pupils to develop their ICT capabilities. At the same time, the use of ICT considerably enhances geography. Teachers who plan for ICT in their units of study and who integrate it well, generally reap the benefits in terms of the quality and value of teaching and advances in pupil learning.

Using Flip Video.
Photo *| Kate Russell.*

ICT and geography

ICT offers great opportunities for pupils to research up to date, topical information, including photos and maps, and to present and communicate their work in new ways, using pictures, graphs, maps and even moving images and sound. The Flip Video camcorder is easy for primary pupils to use. As Becta puts it:

> ICT helps pupils learn in geography by providing access to large quantities of information on people, places and environments. It also provides the framework for analysing data to investigate patterns and relationships in a geographical context. Once pupils have made their findings, ICT can then help them organise, edit and present information in many different ways. (Becta/GA/RGS, 2009.)

Enhancing enquiry skills

Most geographical enquiry-based work can be purposefully enhanced with ICT (Figure 1). The use of databases, spreadsheets, data-logging equipment or the internet will certainly be an advantage where pupils are asking geographical questions, making observations, or recording and investigating data from fieldwork and secondary sources. These tools can also enhance the study of a local issue such as traffic and parking, investigations into shopping or leisure, the weather, or a local river study. Open-ended or generic software will help pupils organise the information they have collected, look for patterns and produce graphs. They can use digital photographs to illustrate their work.

Geographical enquiries invariably involve creating, using and interpreting maps. A wide range of maps can be found online (see websites such as Multimap, Streetmap, Google Maps, Bing maps and Get-a-map. Online digital mapping programs, for example Bing Maps, now incorporate Ordnance Survey (OS) mapping.) Specialised software and websites are also available to help pupils to generate maps, such as Quikmaps. Pupils can communicate the results of their enquiries in the form of text, pictures and graphs, with a word processing or presentation program. Using ICT-generated work alongside materials produced using other media can be effective: pupils could create a 'tourist guide' or an 'eyesores and treasures trail' of their local area, combining digital photographs with text. Many schools now have their own website, or virtual learning environment (VLE), where they publish information about the school; this is an opportunity for pupils to contribute material and information from their geographical enquiries. email enables pupils to enter into a dialogue with schools in other localities; they could research each other's localities, finding out what it is like to live there, exchanging photos and other resources. These reciprocal links are mutually beneficial – 'my here becomes

Photo |
Gemma Kent.

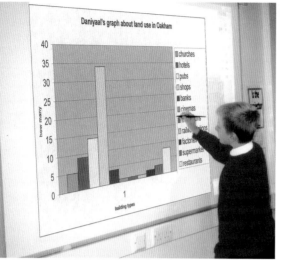

Photo | Kate Russell.

your there' – and may lead to exchange visits. Used responsibly, social networking sites can also aid enquiry – even Barnaby Bear has a Facebook page!

Developing geographical knowledge

The many traditional sources of information available to geographers have been greatly augmented by the rapid development of the internet and the use of email. The problem now is often one of 'information overload': pupils need to focus on selecting only relevant information and rejecting the rest. With the increase in internet use, CDs have declined in significance, although they are still a useful way of storing digital images. CDs which focus on geography topics, with videos, animations, sound and other information, are available, but like books they can soon date. A digital sound recorder with sound editing software such as Audacity (free to download from *http://audacity.download-latest.com*) is very useful for collecting interview material, e.g. conversations with visitors about their jobs or life in another locality, or for recording sounds during a 'sensory walk' in the local area. Even young pupils will be able to use the recording and playback functions.

Understanding patterns and relationships

As pupils develop their geographical understanding they need to learn how to recognise spatial patterns. A programmable toy, such as a floor turtle or Bee-Bot, can help illustrate the notion of direction, especially if it is programmed to move around a large floor map or maze. While many computer games have little to offer educationally, some do help develop spatial and other geographical skills – for example, games where players use an on-screen map, or have to develop a mental map or make decisions. Beware, however, of programs that promote stereotypes or reinforce bad practice. Databases, spreadsheets, some simulations and some websites can also help to provide an insight into geographical relationships such as weather patterns or causes and effects of water pollution. Multimap and Bing Maps, for example, have the facility for overlaying a see-through map on top of an aerial photograph of virtually anywhere in the UK. The UN's InfoNation displays child-friendly comparative data from all countries.

Providing images of places

Primary geography aims to develop pupils' knowledge and awareness of the culture and character of a variety of contrasting places. Pupils can use email and the internet to obtain photographs, video, sound and other first-hand data, and some published CDs complement textbooks and television programmes. Websites (see page 174) can be a rich source of excellent geographical images, and image hosting websites such as Flickr can be used to store and access photos.

Photo | *Kate Russell.*

Investigating the impact of ICT

Geography provides a natural focus for investigating and comparing the uses of ICT inside and outside school. For example, pupils can look at ways in which ICT influences communications, leisure and employment. They can also investigate how travel agents and the retail industry use ICT, and how satellites help to forecast the weather. One school visited an airport to investigate how ICT and control systems were used. The airport staff were very helpful and showed the pupils the check-in procedures, the seat allocation system, the luggage security scanners and many other ways in which ICT impacts on the operation of a modern airport. A visit to a local shopping centre is another option: pupils could locate and observe control and monitoring systems such as automatic doors, cash dispensers, bar-code readers and supermarket stock control systems. They might also investigate store loyalty cards and how the information they collect is used. Another topic could be the operation and impact of surveillance cameras, speed cameras and traffic and pedestrian crossing lights.

Planning

Curriculum planning is critical to ensure purposeful activities reflecting continuity and progression of skills and activities. For a coherent approach to using ICT in geography, staff should work together to plan meaningful learning experiences. This process should involve several people – the relevant class teachers as well as those responsible for ICT, geography and related areas of learning. The planning process should be cyclical, undertaken when geography activities change or you acquire new ICT resources.

Planning should start by reviewing geography themes and topics, identifying areas which will naturally be enhanced by ICT. Try to introduce new activities slowly. If the changes are manageable then they are more likely to be successful. Any gaps can be filled over a period of time – do not attempt to make too many changes at once. A good place to start the planning process is to review current practice, monitoring pupils' work and talking to teachers and pupils. The next step is to consider if you could make better use of ICT in your geography teaching. Among the issues to be addressed are access to hardware and software and staff confidence and expertise. If colleagues lack the appropriate skills and confidence, you need to plan for suitable training, either in school or through a centre-based course. If additional resources are required, you will need to ask the head teacher and governors to incorporate them into the School Development Plan (see Figure 2).

It is important to ensure that pupils experience a broad and balanced range of ICT activities over a key stage. These need to be carefully worked out with clear regard to progression and differentiation, and be properly resourced. A few well-planned activities are better than several ad hoc ones with unclear objectives. They also need to be written into both the geography and ICT schemes of work. Once the activities have been planned you need to refer to the relevant curriculum policy documents and national guidance, to show the links between the subjects. It is also valuable to review the activities after they have been undertaken and, if necessary, modify them in the light of experience. Figure 3 shows some of the ways in which ICT can support good practice.

Figure 2 | *ICT resources checklist – does your school have these ICT tools?*

Although the quantity and quality of ICT equipment in primary schools has improved, there is an ongoing need to replace ageing equipment and improve pupil access to up-to-date ICT resources. As well as computers, these include programmable toys (Roamer and Bee-Bot), digital sound recorders, cameras, scanners, fax machines, data-logging equipment, automatic weather stations, internet and CDs. Does your school have these ICT tools? These are the resources you could reasonably expect to have access to:

Hardware and peripherals

■ Computer system (with CD drive) with internet access and a printer in each classroom, preferably linked to the school network (if there is one)
■ Many schools prefer computer suites for whole-class teaching, but this will depend on your accommodation; some schools find a trolley of laptops a more flexible option
■ An email address (one for each teacher and each class as a minimum)
■ A data projector, preferably linked to a laptop, for displaying presentations, digital slideshows, and a range of sources including websites
■ Interactive whiteboard or Smart board
■ Scanner
■ Digital cameras (still and video)
■ Digital sound recorders
■ Programmable toy(s) – there are several to choose from
■ Data-logging equipment and/or automatic weather station and appropriate software
■ A portable storage device ('pen drive' or portable hard drive)

Software

Generic software suitable for the age of your pupils; your ICT subject leader in conjunction with the LA or school ICT procurement team will probably decide which generic software you use, but applications should include:

■ Word processing
■ Desktop publishing
■ Presentation software
■ Graphics or drawing software, including a facility to edit digital photographs
■ Sound editing software
■ Database (or graphing software for very young pupils)
■ Spreadsheet
■ Internet browser
■ Email

Geography-specific software

■ Mapping software. My World is suitable for very young pupils
■ Websites such as Quikmaps, Bing maps and Google maps which enable users to add information (routes, photos, icons) to the online maps
■ Simulations or adventures which involve 'mental maps'
■ CDs of images and information about places, including encyclopaedias and atlases

Towards the future

Laptops, personal digital assistants (PDAs) or Netbooks for teachers and pupils

■ A school website, VLE or learning platform (geography can contribute to a local area study)
■ Video conferencing including Skype
■ Digital video camera – Flip Video
■ Global positioning systems (GPS)
■ iPhones
■ An email address per pupil
■ WiFi networked laptops which can be used in different classrooms

Catering for differentiation

All pupils, whatever their ability, benefit from ICT's potential to encourage motivation, develop skills and improve access to the curriculum. For pupils with mild learning difficulties, especially those in mainstream schools, your starting point should be to create activities for individualised learning using familiar equipment. However, pupils with moderate or severe learning difficulties may benefit from a range of specialised equipment, including voice recognition systems and software that reads text out loud. There are also several subject-specific learning programs which offer activities for a range of individual needs. Encourage more able pupils to use either a wider range of software or more of the functions of a particular program. They can also take more responsibility for their own work, including deciding on the most appropriate tools for a task.

General guidelines

1. Include some ICT-generated work, preferably by pupils, in your geography displays.
2. Set high standards of presentation and research in your own work to model what you expect of pupils.
3. Use a digital camera to develop digital locality photopacks, or store your photos on an appropriate website. Once they have been created the images can be used flexibly: in texts, printed out or displayed through a data projector using appropriate software.
4. Build up ICT resources alongside other topic resources (e.g. datafiles, a library of maps and images, a list of websites to support the study of particular themes and places). It is worth taking time to 'file' these resources in an organised way so that they can be retrieved easily for future use.
5. Celebrate pupils' geographical work with a wider audience by contributing to the school website or VLE. Particularly appropriate will be work about the local area, which will be of value to other schools too.
6. Keep your ICT skills up to date and pass them on to your pupils – but also be open to being helped by pupils!
7. Reinvent the slideshow, using images from a digital camera, scanned images or pictures saved from websites. MovieMaker is on most computers and PhotoStory 3 can be downloaded free from the Microsoft website.
8. Electronic communications greatly enhance school linking (with another school in this country or elsewhere in the world), but be aware that not all schools will be as well resourced as yours!

Working with pupils

1. Allow pupils to draft, redraft and edit work for final presentation at the computer – do not use a computer as an electronic typewriter to re-type handwritten work.

2. Aim for each pupil in your class to use ICT in at least two significant geography activities during the year, but preferably in each unit that they study.
3. Create the structure of a database, spreadsheet or base map in advance so that pupils can enter the appropriate information and analyse the results or add it to a base map.
4. Remember that some ICT activities are better suited to individual or collaborative work, especially word processing, and can initially be time consuming. However, this is compensated by the higher standard of work that results.
5. Encourage more able pupils to extend their work through additional research and independent learning.
6. Data handling is usually a group (or even whole class) activity as pupils take it in turns to collect and enter data and then analyse it. Lower ability pupils may work better with support from their peers.

Resources

- Many websites and CDs are good sources of information for you as well as your pupils.
- Ensure ICT equipment (especially printers, which are a common source of angst) is in working order and that classrooms have access to the appropriate software and disks.
- Ensure computers are on suitable furniture and that the screen is at an appropriate height for children. There should also be sufficient space around the computer for working space and for books. Health and safety considerations should be taken very seriously, especially those relating to E-safety; follow your school or local authority guidance very carefully.

Figure 3 | *Suggestions to support good practice.*

Photo | *Paula Richardson.*

Using ICT to learn about mountains

There are many opportunities for incorporating ICT into a unit of work on mountains. Pupils could use maps and images from the internet as part of their research and produce climate graphs using a database or spreadsheet. They might also prepare a PowerPoint presentation or a movie or devise a web page to communicate their findings to the rest of the school.

Useful websites

To make it easier to access these sites, you will find this section on the GA website at *www.geography.org.uk/primaryhandbook*; you can click on each url to access the sites.

Everest
There are many Everest sites commemorating the 50th anniversary of its conquest (2003).
Scholastic Publications *http://teacher.scholastic.com/activities/Hillary*
Unlocking the Archives *www.unlockingthearchives.rgs.org/themes/everest*

Himalayas
Mogens Larsen has been trekking in the Himalayas, India and Nepal. The photos you see on this site are all from these treks *www.himalayas.dk*
Nepal (from Jeroen Neele photo gallery) *www.home.zonnet.nl/jneele/argentina/index.htm*
Nepal and the Himalayas on the web *www.vic.com/nepal/related.html*

Mountain Regions
Global Eye Focus on Mountains *www.globaleye.org.uk/primary/focuson* (this is one of a series from Worldaware's Global Eye with features on Everest and Machu Picchu in the Peruvian Andes. Mountain Factfile might help the children to get going!) Iceland *www.sln.org.uk/geography/SLNgeography@Iceland.htm*
Mountain Nature *www.mountainnature.com*
Mountain Voices *www.mountainvoices.org* (interviews with 300 people who live in mountain and highland regions round the world)
Peakware World Mountain Encyclopaedia *www.peakware.com*
Peru (Paddington Bear) *http://primary.naace.co.uk/paddington/index.htm*
Rocky Mountains, Canada *www.canadianrockies.net*
Snowdonia National Park *www.eryri-npa.co.uk*
The Austrian and Swiss Alps *http://alps.virtualave.net*
Tiki the Penguin visits Peru *http://tiki.oneworld.net/peru/peru_home.html*
Virtual Montana *http://194.81.33.34/virtualmontana* (this site, the result of collaboration between several groups including Liverpool Hope University College and the Field Studies Council, is particularly good for the French Alps, Banat Mountains in Romania, and Snowdonia in North Wales).

Websites come and go; some change their addresses and it can be frustrating to get an error message saying a website has not been found. These web addresses are given in good faith at the time of writing; they are among the most useful and most flexible and mostly come from well-regarded and well-known sources. A good search engine like Google will help you find others, but searching the internet can be a time-consuming process. I recommend giving pupils a few sites to look at for specific purposes in a lesson otherwise they may waste time searching and not have enough time for research! The ones below are just a small selection of numerous ones which can be used.

Global
Action Aid *www.actionaid.org.uk*
Christian Aid *www.christianaid.org.uk/respources/games*
Global Eye *www.globaleye.org.uk*
On the Line (Oxfam) *www.oxfam.org.uk/coolplanet/ontheline/index.html*
One World *http://uk.oneworld.net*
Oxfam for Schools *www.oxfam.org.uk/education*
PLAN ed *www.plan-ed.org*
Save the Children *www.savethechildren.org*
Tide~ global learning *www.tidegloballearning.net*
UN *www.cyberschoolbus.un.org* (includes 'Country at a Glance' and 'InfoNation')
UNICEF *www.unicef.org*
Vision Aid *www.vao.org.uk*
Water Aid *www.wateraid.org*
World Info Zone *www.worldinfozone.com*
World Vision *www.worldvision.org.uk/*

Guidance, advice and resources

Everyday geographies (Wendy North's blog) *http://primarygeogblog.blogspot.com*
Geographical Association *www.geography.org.uk* (join one of the Association's NINGS for different interest groups to keep you in touch with like-minded colleagues; e.g. the Geography Champions NING *http://geographychampions.ning.com*)
Geography Teaching Today *www.geographyteachingtoday.org.uk*
ICTOPUS *www.ictopus.org.uk* (ICT online primary user support).
NAACE *www.naace.co.uk* (professional association for those working in educational ICT).
Ofsted *www.ofsted.gov.uk*
Primary Geography Pages *http://homepage.ntlworld.com/anthony.pickford2*
Primary Resources *www.primaryresources.co.uk/geography*
Teachernet *www.teachernet.gov.uk/teachingandlearning/subjects/ict/bectadocs/prim*
Teaching Ideas *www.teachingideas.co.uk/geography/contents.htm*
Tom Barrett's blog *www.classroom20.com*

Images

BBC The Day/Week in Pictures *http://news.bbc.co.uk/* and search for the Day/Week in Pictures
Bing maps *www.bing.com/maps* (high quality aerial imagery)
Earth from the Air *www.earthfromtheair.com*
Earth Cam *www.earthcam.com* (links to live web cams around the world)
Free Foto *www.freefoto.com* (great for UK)
Geograph *www.geograph.org.uk* (an interactive project aiming to cover every grid square of the UK, which you and your pupils could join in with!)
Geography Photos (Ian Murray) *www.geographyphotos.com*
Google Earth *http://earth.google.co.uk*
Images of England (English Heritage) *www.imagesofengland.org.uk*
Images of the World *www.imagesoftheworld.org*
Jeroen Neele Visiting the World *www.home.zonnet.nl/jneele/argentina/index.htm*
Picture Search *www.picsearch.com*
Window on our World *www.sln.org.uk/wow*

LA sites

CLEO *www.cleo.net.uk* (Cumbria, Lancashire)
Hertfordshire *www.thegrid.org.uk/learning/geography*
Kent *www.kenttrustweb.org.uk/kentict/kentict_subjects_geo_index.cfm*
London Grid for Learning *http://cms.lgfl.net/web/lgfl/geography*
Shropshire *www.shropshire.gov.uk/curriculum.nsf*
South West Grid for Learning *www.swgfl.org.uk*
Staffordshire *www.sln.org.uk/geography* (geography teachers' forum:
http://learningnet.co.uk/geoforum)
Wakefield *www.gowilder.org.uk/geog*

Maps

Bing Maps *www.bing.com/maps*
Get-a-map (OS) *www.ordnancesurvey.co.uk/oswebsite/getamap*
Google Maps *http://maps.google.co.uk*
Mapping our World *www.oxfam.org.uk/education/resources/mapping_our_world*
Multimap *www.multimap.com* (for maps and aerial photos)
Old-Maps *www.old-maps.co.uk*
Ordnance Survey MapZone *http://mapzone.ordnancesurvey.co.uk*
Ordnance Survey *www.ordnancesurvey.co.uk*
Outline maps *www.eduplace.com/ss/maps*
Quikmaps *http://quikmaps.com*
Streetmap *www.streetmap.co.uk*
World Atlas *www.worldatlas.com*

Weather and climate

BBC weather site *http://news.bbc.co.uk/weather*
Cool Kids For A Cool Climate *www.coolkidsforacoolclimate.com*
MetLink *www.metlink.org*
Met Office *www.meto.gov.uk*
Weather at Keele *http://pangaea.esci.keele.ac.uk/weather*
Weather for Schools *www.weatherforschools.me.uk*
WorldClimate *www.worldclimate.com*
Yahoo *http://weather.yahoo.com*

School websites

There are many exemplary school websites which are well-designed, feature pupils' work and have interesting information, including photos and maps of their localities. It is difficult to single out specific sites, for fear of insulting the others. However, the following are sufficiently well-established and offer support and guidance to a much wider audience than the local one, so warrant inclusion here:

- Coxhoe Primary School *http://durham.schooljotter.com/coxhoe*
- Snaith Primary School *http://home.freeuk.net/elloughton13/index.htm* (especially for sections on Seaside, Water, Paris, India)
- Perton First School *www.perton-first.staffs.sch.uk* (especially for the travels of Barnaby Bear)
- Woodlands Junior School *www.woodlands-junior.kent.sch.uk/index.html*

Who can help me?

ICT is essentially a practical tool, requiring a 'hands-on' approach. While we hope this chapter may have given you some ideas and a context for development, you may still be left wondering 'Yes, but how?' Figure 4 suggests some other sources of help.

1. The ICT co-ordinator in your school (he/she will be delighted if you take an interest in ICT!)
2. LA advisers (ICT and geography) and your local ICT centre.
3. The Geographical Association Annual Conference (this is held around Easter and includes an exhibition of new materials as well as ICT workshops).
4. Regional conferences on primary geography.
5. *Primary Geographer*, the termly magazine published by the Geographical Association.
6. Educational shows and exhibitions, especially the BETT Show (in January), the Education Show (in March) and GA Annual Conference (at Easter).
7. Publications and support materials from The British Educational Communications and Technology Agency (Becta) (details on their website *www.becta.org.uk*).
8. Local support in your school cluster (liaison between secondary schools and primary schools is important – ensure ICT is on the agenda).
9. NAACE (*www.naace.co.uk*) is the professional association for those concerned with advancing education through ICT.
10. National guidance, policy and curriculum strategy documents, all available on the internet, along with examples of pupils' work.
11. The Primary Strategy has produced guidance for integrating ICT in geography.
12. *Technically Geography: Lessons combining geography and ICT* (Bowden and Copeland, 2004) lessons based on the QCA geography and ICT schemes of work.
13. Get inspiration from the Online CPD courses from the GA on *www.geographyteachingtoday.org.uk/online-cpd/course/primary-geography-and-ict* and GA primary CPD pages *www.geography.org.uk/cpdevents/onlinecpd*
14. The GA's ICT Working Group welcomes interested primary practitioners to join them, details at *www.geography.org.uk/aboutus/committeesworkinggroups/ictwg*; or join in with discussions in their group on the GA NING *http://geographical.ning.com/group/ictwg*, or meet them at the Annual Conference!

Figure 4 | *Sources of help on using ICT in geography teaching.*

References and further reading

Becta/GA/RGS-IBG (2009) *ICT in Primary Geography: A pupil's entitlement at key stages 1 and 2.* Available at *http://schools.becta.org.uk* (last accessed 29 June 2010).

Becta (2003) *Using web-based resources in primary geography.* Available at *http://foi.becta.org.uk* (last accessed 29 June 2010).

Bowden, D. and Copeland, P. (2004) *Technically Geography: Lessons combining geography and ICT for Y1/2.* Sheffield: Geographical Association.

Bowden, D. and Copeland, P. (2004) *Technically Geography: Lessons combining geography and ICT for Y3/4.* Sheffield: Geographical Association.

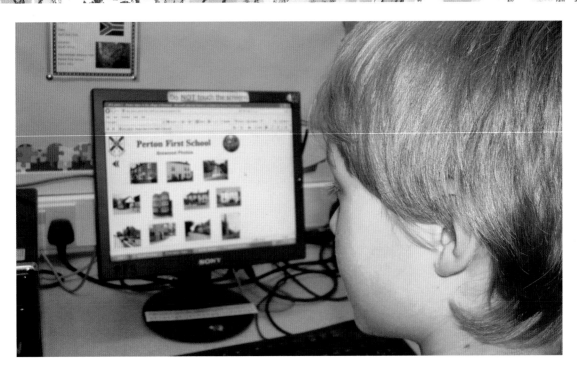

Photo | *Kate Russell.*

Bowden, D. and Copeland, P. (2005) *Technically Geography: Lessons combining geography and ICT for Y5/6*. Sheffield: Geographical Association.

Geographical Association (termly) *Primary Geographer*. Sheffield: Geographical Association.

Loveless, A. (2007) 'Preparing to teach with ICT: subject knowledge, Didaktik and improvisation', *The Curriculum Journal*, 18, 4, pp. 509-522.

Ofsted (2008) *Geography in Schools: Changing practice*. Available at *www.ofsted.gov.uk* (last accessed 29 June 2010).

Rodgers, A. and Streluk, A. (2002) *Primary ICT Handbook: Geography*. Cheltenham: Nelson Thornes.

Postscript

ICT should make an active rather than a passive contribution to learning, and as such it is possibly one of the most difficult aspects of the curriculum to organise and manage. It is also expensive, in terms of both resources and the time required for training and management. Because ICT itself is constantly changing, teachers sometimes feel threatened by it. The fact that pupils may have greater expertise and confidence in using computers than their teachers does not help. However, ICT is exciting and motivating and nearly every pupil will take to it with enthusiasm, irrespective of their age and ability. Finally, and most importantly, the fact is that ICT has enormous potential for enhancing and supporting geography teaching. Provided you start in a manageable way, and follow the guidelines set out here and in the many other support publications now available, your chances of success are high. Good luck!

People and places

Chapter

13. Using the school locality

14. Contrasting localities

15. The wider world

16. The global dimension

Our local area

Photo | Stephen Scoffham.

CHAPTER COVERAGE:
CITIZENSHIP • CROSS-CURRICULAR LINKS • ENQUIRIES • ENVIRONMENT • FIELDWORK • HISTORY • LOCAL AREA • PLANNING

Using the school locality

The school locality is a rich resource for geographical enquiry. It is highly accessible for fieldwork, can be studied in a great variety of ways and helps pupils to develop their sense of place. The school and its surrounding area provide a meaningful context for developing geographical skills and studying places and cross-curricular themes. Its potential for practical, first-hand work, building on existing knowledge and experiences, gives pupils of all abilities the opportunity to develop their confidence and achieve success both in school and in adult life.

By exploring the underpinning geographical principles and adopting good practice strategies for geographical teaching and learning in this area, teachers will become increasingly confident in evaluating and making more effective use of the school locality.

Defining the locality

The term 'locality' has a specific meaning in geography. At key stage 1 it refers to the school's immediate vicinity – the school buildings, grounds and nearby streets. At key stage 2 it covers a larger area, usually including the district where the majority of pupils live. It is helpful to think of the locality as three separate areas: the school buildings, the school grounds, and the surrounding area (see

Figure 1 |
The locality is best thought of as three separate areas.

Figure 1). More distant features – hills, church towers, factories – can be included if they contribute to the character of the area. You need to decide as a school on appropriate boundaries for your studies.

The importance of allowing children to explore their environment and learn from practical first-hand experience is recognised in the EYFS framework (DCSF, 2008). All six areas of learning provide opportunities for developing geographical understanding, but 'knowledge and understanding of the world' is especially relevant to local area work (see Chapter 2). At key stage 1 pupils study the links between their own locality and other places in the UK and beyond. At key stage 2 they study their own locality; a contrasting locality in the UK; and a locality in a different country. In the process they build their understanding of how:

(a) the present has been shaped by the past

(b) places develop and can be sustained in the future

(c) identities develop

(d) people, places and communities are connected at a range of scales.

The enquiry approach

Structuring geographical learning around the enquiry process (see Chapter 7) enables effective investigational work to be undertaken in the immediate environment. Teachers and pupils should identify a place, theme or issue to explore and then consider appropriate questions to structure their investigation. Pupils will then be involved in planning, collecting, analysing, evaluating and hypothesising. Ideally, the enquiry should focus on a real issue: for instance, 'Why is there a problem with litter in the playground?' or 'Where shall we site a new litter bin?'. The school grounds and local streets can be used as a focus for learning about the environment through the acquisition of knowledge, learning through the environment as a resource for study, and learning for the environment to consider issues, values and attitudes.

Learning outside the classroom is an integral part of the curriculum, offering opportunities for both independent learning and for co-operation with others; pupils will respond to these forms of learning in different ways. With infants, such work is best done little and often. Short periods of 10-30 minutes outside are best – although with younger pupils it can take more time to get them ready to go out than they actually spend working outside! Careful timing, allowing pupils to complete observations without getting bored, is essential. Unfortunately such work is always weather dependent and you need to learn to make the most of every possible learning opportunity. Remember that you can use the winter as well as the summer months. Pupils are used to going out in the playground in all temperatures – it is often the teachers who complain of the cold!

Planning

Any work outside the classroom demands careful planning and preparation. If more than one adult is available, and the activity has been explained beforehand, it will be possible to work outside with a whole class. However, with younger pupils especially, the ideal arrangement is a small group with a dedicated adult. A number of small groups can cover different aspects of the study in a controlled learning context, which allows individuals to exploit their own interests, with each group returning to the classroom when their tasks are complete. Careful preparation of helpers will help to ensure that all pupils are supervised, but will also allow them some independence. Ensure that all pupils know exactly what they are doing, have chosen a suitable resource or activity, can operate any necessary equipment and are physically comfortable. When pupils return to the classroom they must know where and how to store their findings, and be given time to share their findings with others. For advice on risk assessments and child protection issues, see Chapter 10, pages 140-143.

If you are well organised you will be more confident and better prepared to take advantage of any spontaneous opportunities which will inevitably arise when working outside and which frequently provide the high points of a study. All outdoor work must, of course, follow your school and LA policies. Conducting an appraisal of your locality will also form an essential part of your planning. As teachers we are often guilty of failing to explore the school grounds and

1. What are the key geographical features in your local area? Make an inventory of particular aspects of your locality such as:
   - different areas in the classroom, school buildings and grounds
   - viewing points for map and compass work
   - the layout of the site
   - local journeys and routes
   - physical features such as hills and streams
   - changes and new developments
   - local issues and concerns.
   Display your findings on a large master base plan of your district. Remember to update this on a regular basis so that you can see how your locality changes over a period of time. Consider if pupils would identify the same features.

2. What types of equipment are needed for local area fieldwork? You need clipboards, collecting and measuring equipment, and field study boxes, which any member of staff can use with their pupils. They should contain everything pupils will need to work outside successfully; small, self-sealing, plastic boxes are ideal.

3. Do you have an emergency fieldwork survival kit? This should allow you to stay outside no matter what! It might include everything from a pencil sharpener to a plaster or spare clothing.

4. Have you considered issues to do with safety and inclusion? Is there a school policy defining organisational procedures and requirements? Do you offer safety advice to colleagues? Are you able to cater for pupils of different abilities (see Chapter 24)?

5. How could effective use be made of other adults? Do you involve other adults in in-service training? Is there a training programme for new helpers? Are teaching assistants involved?

6. What vocabulary can be developed and how? Look at activities planned in the school grounds at both key stages. Make lists of key directional and place related vocabulary. Is there increased sophistication of language and vocabulary developed through fieldwork and active learning outside the classroom?

7. What resources do you need? Do you have access to recent as well as older photographs of your school building and local area? Are there any plans, maps and memorabilia? Do you have large-scale Ordnance Survey maps and aerial photographs of the school and its surroundings? Have these been used to devise an A4 simple base plan of your school and grounds that everyone can use?

8. Which parts of the curriculum can you cover in your local area work? Make copies of the programmes of study and ask colleagues to highlight appropriate sections at both key stages. Are you covering these effectively? If you are using prepared schemes of work, check that you are making the most of the opportunities for local area work.

9. Is there scope for developing geographical skills and cross-curricular links? Consider if you could make better links to literacy, numeracy, citizenship and ICT as you explore your locality.

10. How does your local area work help to develop a sense of place? Can you identify an issue or enquiry question to explore with colleagues? How can they plan to ensure active learning throughout the school? What are the opportunities for assessment? What records do you want to keep?

11. How will you assess acceptable risk and ensure that safeguarding procedures have been followed?

Figure 2 | *Questions to consider as you conduct an appraisal of your locality.*

locality on foot ourselves; the result is that we know less about them than our pupils do! If possible try to identify a school in-service training day when you can clarify your approach to local area work. Figure 2 provides a checklist of questions to consider.

Using the school and its grounds

Pupils learn best when activities revolve around their own interests and concerns. Younger pupils are particularly curious about their own sphere of operations – the building and grounds of their school – and primary school practitioners have long recognised the value of the school and its immediate environment to their pupils' geographical learning. In their reports, HMIs have consistently identified the value of work carried out within the immediate locality of the school, where practical field-work observations can most easily take place.

Within the school grounds, investigations can involve simple map-making, early observations 'in the field' and talking to people about their way of life and the world of work. Pupils can also be introduced to the interrelationships between human and physical processes. Their developing environmental awareness can be harnessed by encouraging them to take responsibility for their school environment. In this way the three key dimensions of primary school geography – place, space and the environment – can all be developed to provide pupils with memorable, vivid, active and relevant outdoor learning experiences.

A litter monster made by young children. The mouth provides a slit for rubbish to be put in. **Photo** /Stephen Scoffham.

Using the school grounds

Using a small area within easy walking distance has many advantages. It is a small-scale, relatively safe environment to which short visits can be fitted easily into school sessions. As well as being easily accessible, the school grounds also provide a safe environment from which to study the immediate locality, e.g. to undertake observational drawings of shops or houses across the road. All schools will have some distinctive features, inside and out, which are worthy of study. Using the school grounds enables pupils and teachers to explore micro changes in their environment and respond to any immediate changes that may occur, e.g. the arrival of workmen on the school site or flooding after heavy rain.

The following activities will help you to develop a greater geographical understanding of the school and its grounds. Some of them can be built into your curriculum plans for geography, others might provide the focus for an in-service training day. Such activities also provide an opportunity to convince others of the benefits of first-hand experiences and practical work.

1. Sensing

One of the most meaningful types of local environmental work for younger pupils is through using their senses: identifying what they can see, hear, smell and feel. The fifth sense of taste, for obvious reasons, is best avoided! Observation – learning to look carefully – is an important geographical and cross-curricular skill to learn and develop. Here are some ideas you might like to try:

- Spotting shapes and features
- Identifying likes and dislikes
- Brainstorming and composing word pictures
- Drawing a memory picture or mental map
- Going on a sensory walk
- Blindfold activities, requiring pupils to feel and use language to describe and identify features in the school grounds. (Their sense of smell might also be used to help them identify where they are.)

2. I-spy

Organise simple five-minute activities such as 'I-spy' around key vocabulary associated with the school building and grounds. Using a word bank, dictionary or alphabet display – particularly important when helping pupils to gain access to secondary sources – you can focus on features associated with particular letters or sounds through the use of an index. If you set up a database to store the data you have collected, it could become a starting point or a reference point for pupils involved in future local enquiries.

3. Listening and hearing

Sounds and noises make a significant contribution to the quality of the environment. Some sounds, like bird song and running water, have a peaceful quality; others can be disturbing, irritating or even frightening. What sounds can the pupils hear? Do the sounds differ from place to place? Can they record the sounds they hear and explain what they are?

4. Making rubbings

Give younger pupils the opportunity to record their findings in a variety of ways. Have you tried allowing them to make rubbings using large sheets of paper and chubby wax crayons? Try rubbing various features and then locating the rubbings on a large base plan, marking their correct positions.

5. Field sketches

Making sketches is one of the best ways of getting pupils to engage with their surroundings. Younger pupils find it hard to record whole scenes but will quickly gain confidence if directed to small details such as a door handle, an individual plant, or a small section of wall. Encourage them to add a title and make simple notes of the features they think are important.

6. Numbers walk

The school grounds can be used for practical work such as simple collecting, counting and measuring exercises, e.g. counting or plotting the position of doors, windows, drainpipes, covers, grates, steps and flags; or in a weather topic to read a thermometer, measure rainfall, observe cloud formations and movement, calculate wind speed and direction or even to take a closer look at soil.

7. Boundaries and barriers

Boundaries and barriers are a common feature of any school environment. Pupils will be familiar with the rules which affect them but may never have considered the reasons why they are there. Security, safety and organisation are usually involved in one way or another. Make a survey of boundaries and barriers around your school. Why are they there? Are they physical or do they depend on the interpretation of notices and signs? Why do we need them?

8. Weather watch

The weather affects everyone – particularly children. The school grounds provide a real context in which pupils can experience this phenomenon and make first-hand investigations and observations, such as:

- When do pupils need to wear a coat outside? Why?
- Why does the school roof leak?
- Why do some window frames need to be re-painted or replaced?
- What is the weather like today?
- How does it change?
- What seasonal differences occur?

9. Building materials

Take a close look at the building materials used in your school. What are they? Where did they come from? Why were they chosen for that part of the building? Use sensory activities to help pupils explore the textures, pattern, size and shapes of the materials. Set up a display table showing different examples.

10. Photographs

Organise a short walk or route round the school building or grounds linking different points of interest. Get the pupils to take photographs of key features. Encourage each pupil in the group to select one item to record (not their friends!) and display the pictures with captions round a map or plan in a later lesson.

11. Looking up, down and between

Learning to 'look down' is vital to the development of the plan view concept and mapwork skills. You might organise a walk with stopping places where pupils can record what they see when they look down on the ground and up in the sky. Can they sketch what they see? Extend the work by looking for views through archways or between walls and buildings. If the pupils draw and cut out the pattern of roofs and chimneys against the sky you will be able to set up a wall display showing local silhouettes.

12. Direction games

The playground can be a useful space for directional games. You might use giant directional arrows to reinforce key vocabulary such as up, down, eye-level, forwards, backwards, right and left, overground and underground. A simple base plan of the playground can be used for activities and trails. Pupils could consider which parts of the school grounds are natural/built/green. What sort of habitats have been created in this place? Which creatures live there and why?

13. Compass points

Use the playground and school grounds to give pupils first-hand experience of compass points. What can they see to the north, south, east and west? Get them to record their findings in words or pictures. Use a local map and atlas to find out what lies further away in each direction. Which direction would they need to take to reach the Sahara Desert or the United States for example? See if they can plan a route round the grounds involving compass directions and 90° turns. This will be useful practice for orienteering work at some later stage and could be reinforced by using a programmable toy or toys.

14. Surveying

You can use the school building and grounds to help pupils to develop simple survey techniques and learn to plot symbols on a base plan. For example, a simple land use survey could be carried out using a colour code system. Why do pupils think certain activities take place in particular locations? Are there better alternatives? Can you use the school building and grounds for practising questionnaire and interview techniques? For sampling specific locations for intensive small-scale study, use a PE hoop to delimit a sample area and focus the pupils' attention on a particular area for study.

Photo | Tina Horler.

15. Mapping

Mapping is a unique geographical skill, and every opportunity should be taken to practise and develop it. In the school building and grounds you have the most accessible and meaningful learning context for mapping skills. Using a familiar environment helps pupils relate their direct experiences to map making. Simple orienteering skills can be developed, based on trails using pictures or symbols as clues, or by following string to collect objects. Maps can also be used to follow and record routes and to identify locations, features and positions.

16. Ordnance Survey maps

Where possible you should use large-scale Ordnance Survey (OS) maps of your school building and grounds from an early stage. They are an excellent teaching resource and pupils often enjoy looking at them to spot information and find out more about their locality. Use OS maps to help you devise maps of the area, which pupils can use in their fieldwork activities. You can also enlarge selected areas for wall displays. Simply make an OHP transparency of the relevant section, project the image on a sheet of clean paper pinned to the wall and draw round the outline. You can vary the magnification by moving the projector backwards and forwards.

17. Aerial photographs

Aerial photographs are an excellent source of information about your locality and a useful way of complementing maps and plans. Research shows that children as young as three years old can make sense of aerial photographs of a familiar area. Older children can use the photographs to identify features (start with the school and their own house), trace routes between places and find out about changes and developments in their local area.

18. Eyeballing

Eyeballing combines observational and recording skills. Select a particular part of the school building or grounds and give pupils a photograph to focus their observations.

Can they go to the spot and make an observational drawing of a specific feature, e.g. a door or window?

Can they copy examples of writing in their environment?

Can they make a field sketch or conduct a census to answer a key question?

Can they find any date-stones or other clues which give historical information?

What can they see from different viewing points?

Can they add information to base plans or drawings to record where they have found the clues?

Photo | *John Halocha.*

19. Changes in your school

Most schools alter over the years. Some date from Victorian times, and may have undergone many modifications. Pupils enjoy being history detectives and seeking clues – e.g. foundation stones – that indicate the age of the original building, and identifying the changes that have been made. Give them a set of photographs and ask them to locate the features shown and mark them on a map. An extension would be to devise their own 'changes trail'.

20. Scavenger hunt

Explore the school grounds to find examples of pollution and other environmental problems. Think about the following questions to help you structure the work.

What items can they collect? (Use plastic bags as gloves.)

Where did they find their items?

Can they mark the locations on a base plan of the school?

What do the items tell you about your school grounds as a place?

Did other groups find similar or different things? Why do you think that is?

Can you find out more about the items you collected by talking to others?

21. Environmental quality

You can explore pupils' environmental concerns by asking them questions such as:

What do you think about the local environment? Are there any places which you think could be improved and who might make the changes? Once they have conducted their appraisal pupils can be encouraged to identify a project and set out to make the improvements themselves. Locating routes for new pathways, working out the plan for a wildlife area or designing extra play equipment are the kinds of projects which motivate pupils and harness a range of cross-curricular skills.

Using local streets and buildings

Local streets and buildings are an invaluable teaching resource and you should take every opportunity to develop outdoor work. The benefits are immense in terms of pupil motivation, providing meaningful learning experiences and illustrating ideas in practical ways. There is plenty of evidence to support this claim. In a survey of almost 2000 adolescents, four out of five said that knowing more about local buildings and places made them better behaved, and nine out of ten remembered more from outdoor work than class lessons (CABE, 2010). Our increasing understanding of the functioning of the brain also indicates the value of multi-sensory approaches to education (Goswami and Bryant, 2007). Ofsted offers further evidence: enquiry-based fieldwork 'supports higher levels of achievement' (Ofsted, 2008a, p. 21) and sharpens and deepens pupils' understanding of geography (Ofsted, 2008b, p. 34).

Some suggestions for local area work, focusing on geography and related subjects, follow; opportunities for applying mapwork and ICT skills will be apparent throughout. The need for a large-scale (1:1250) map of the area and other resources such as aerial photographs should also be noted.

1. Landscapes

Consider the landscape in your area and the way that people have responded to it. You might begin by recording hills and slopes on a base map of the local area. Are there any areas, e.g. sports grounds, which are particularly flat? Are there any cliffs or beaches near your school? You might also consider local rocks and soils. Set up a display table showing interesting samples from local homes and gardens. Some of these materials may have been brought from other areas so you will begin to discover things about the surrounding region as well as your own locality as you embark on this work.

2. Weather

Pupils can record the direction and the force of the local wind, and the amount of rain in terms of the time it falls and the water it provides. Encourage pupils to find places around the school which are especially wet or dry. What causes these variations in micro-climate? Are there any places in the immediate environment which tend to flood in heavy rain? Do back-copies of local newspapers carry reports of unusual weather and its effects on local people?

3. Houses and homes

You might begin a study of houses and homes by identifying different building materials, e.g. tiles, bricks and timber. The way these materials are used and combined has a significant impact on the character of an area. Pupils can study front doors, windows, and the construction of the buildings, e.g. terraced, semi-detached or detached. They should be given information about the age of buildings so that they can be aware of the growth of their local area. Identifying any listed buildings and plotting them on a map is another way of revealing historical patterns. An alternative approach is to identify or visit current construction sites. This will show how your settlement is changing and developing. Thinking about the future is an important part of geography.

4. Shops

Visits to local shops lead naturally into an investigation of the goods available and questions about where they originate. There may be opportunities for making a visit to a local supermarket to find out how it is organised and the work that people do there. Try to consider the issues that lie beneath the surface. How much of the produce on sale comes from local sources? What impact do warehousing, transport and distribution have on the environment? How much do producers get paid and does the shop stock 'fair trade' goods?

5. Community facilities

Leisure and community centres provide places where people can meet and they add to the quality of local life. What facilities exist in your area and who do they cater for? Examples might include mother and toddler groups, youth centres and old people's homes. Most schools are also within walking distance of a church. If you can arrange a visit and talk to the vicar about their work it will add to the pupils' understanding of the area. What facilities do pupils think are missing? You might identify a suitable project and draw up a proposal to discuss more widely in the school and, perhaps, the local community.

Eco-Schools

It is a governmental aim that every English school should be a sustainable school by 2020. The international Eco-Schools award programme provides a framework for schools to follow.

It comprises nine key environmental topics:
- water
- biodiversity
- energy
- global perspectives
- healthy living
- litter
- school grounds
- transport
- waste.

Schools can apply for three levels of Eco-Schools award: Bronze, Silver and Green Flag. More information and guidance can be found at *www.eco-schools.org.uk*.

Figure 3 *| The nine key elements of the Eco-Schools Programme.*

6. Transport

Pupils can record the number of cars, lorries, bikes etc. passing their school or another location and make maps and diagrams of railways, tramlines, cycle routes and footpaths. Are there any problems such as traffic congestion which need to be addressed? Are the public transport facilities adequate and does traffic have a negative effect on people's lives? You could bring the work back to a child level by recording the journeys and methods of transport which the pupils use themselves. Are all these journeys necessary and could they be made by other means?

Caring for the environment

Encourage pupils to engage in practical projects such as caring for gardens and pets, using water, energy and other resources wisely, and recycling waste rather than just dumping it. Organisations such as Groundwork and CABE (Commission for Architecture and the Built Environment) may have current projects you can get involved with. Alternatively you might contact local planners and other professionals to talk with pupils about the environmental aspects of their work. The Eco-Schools award scheme (Figure 3) has proved a very effective framework for stimulating environmental work in many schools. Such activities also link directly to Community Cohesion, Sustainable Schools and other government directives (see Chapter 20 for further details).

Making a trail

Trails can be an excellent way of structuring local area work and serve to focus attention on specific themes or issues. You might devise a trail of your own (perhaps as an in-service activity) or get the pupils to make one themselves. Either way there are a number of issues to consider:
- Decide whether there will be a focus on a theme (e.g. changes) or a topic (e.g. transport), or if you want the pupils to select points of interest along the designed route
- Decide whether you will observe the surroundings continuously along the walk or stop at set sites to undertake a number of studies
- Decide exactly where you are going to cross roads and access any other safety hazards
- See if you can include interesting or unexpected elements, e.g. by selecting a route down paths and alleyways
- Do not make the route too long and decide whether you want to create a circular walk

Photo | *Paula Richardson.*

- Provide pupils with a map to work with
- Set up questions and activities that have a clear educational purpose
- Keep the text brief so that participants do not spend too long reading the script while they are outdoors
- Try to include a variety of recording techniques, e.g. recording information on a table, adding labels to a drawing, making sketches, drawing maps and so on
- Take photographs of different features along the route which can be studied in detail back at school

Conducting research

As they work as 'street detectives' and find out about their local area, pupils will need to use a range of sources. It is important to teach them how to conduct their research. You can help them by identifying suitable research questions and issues and discussing the approach they are going to adopt. Some of the options include:

- Searching the internet for books and pamphlets about the local area, e.g. town guides, civic society appraisals, historical guides
- Reading newsletters and reports, e.g. from the local council, local clubs, parish churches
- Meeting with local residents, who have key information about the area
- Looking at photographs and artwork of the local area, both historic and current
- Watching videos which indicate views on, and activity in, the area
- Visiting the local library, museum and records office
- Contacting the local authority planning department to find out about new schemes and proposals
- Gathering information from the internet, e.g. from local websites
- Accessing Google Earth portraits of your area
- Studying maps, plans and aerial photographs
- Investigating local census returns
- Taking part in fieldwork outside the classroom

When pupils have completed their investigations it is helpful to save the resources they have collected as a digital library on CD. Future classes will then be able to access this for their research.

Recording findings

When the enquiry sessions have been completed it is important that pupils record the observations and information they have collected. Try to get them to collaborate and share ideas among themselves. Classroom discussions can help to raise questions and identify the issues that have emerged. Get pupils to draw their own maps and devise graphs, diagrams and graphical displays.

Here are some other ways of presenting findings:

- Design diagrams with annotations and labels
- Write a report summarising findings
- Create a mini pamphlet
- Write answers to prepared questions
- Write personal thoughts about key issues
- Make a PowerPoint presentation
- Design a postcard
- Design a map showing findings
- Print out digital photographs and write an explanation about each one
- Set up a display which includes sample items and display models

As they present their findings pupils will gain confidence in using and studying local maps. They should also be given opportunities to draw maps of their own. These might show important streets, compass directions, routes between places, specific sites and other geographical features. If you can provide a range of different maps of the local area – tourist maps, maps prepared by the council, bus maps and so forth – it will give pupils a range of examples to emulate as well as extra information about your locality.

Use Google Earth to find images of your local area.

Finding out about the local area is an important component of geographical work from the nursery through the primary and secondary school to GCSE, A-level and beyond. Blyth and Krause (1995) suggest that geography can be divided into two main components: 'Big geography' starts from distant places and considers the world as a whole space and environment at a national and continental scale; 'Little geography' fits within this framework and involves studies of particular places and their immediate surroundings. Pupils need to study both 'little' and 'big' geography

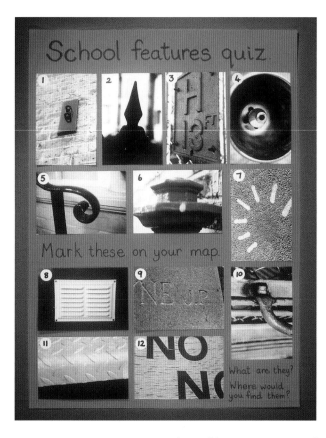

Photo | *Stephen Scoffham.*

at all ages. However, as they grow older and move through the curriculum their perspectives broaden and deepen. Contrary to popular belief children do not grow out of local area work as they get older. Rather they study it in a more sophisticated way. That is why learning about the locality is so important.

References and further reading

Blyth, A. and Krause, J. (1995) *Primary Geography: A developmental approach.* London: Hodder and Stoughton.

Bowles, R. (2004) 'Children's understanding of locality' in Catling, S. and Martin, F. (eds) *Researching Primary Geography.* London: Register of Research in Primary Geography.

CABE (2004) *Neighbourhood Journeys: Making the ordinary extraordinary.* London: Commission for Architecture and the Built Environment.

CABE (2007) *Our Street: Learning to see.* London: Commission for Architecture and the Built Environment.

CABE (2010) *Unforgettable Lessons: An introduction to engaging places.* London: Commission for Architecture and the Built Environment.

Catling, S. (2005) 'Children's personal geographies and the English primary school geography curriculum', *Children's Geographies,* 3, 3, pp. 325-344.

DCSF (2008) *Statutory Framework for the Early Years Foundation Stage.* Nottingham: DCSF.

Goswami, U. and Bryant, P. (2007) *Children's Cognitive Development and Learning (Primary Review Research Survey 2/1a).* Cambridge: University of Cambridge Faculty of Education.

Ofsted (2008a) *Learning Outside the Classroom.* London: Ofsted.

Ofsted (2008b) Geography in Schools: *Changing practice.* London: Ofsted.

QCDA (2010) National Curriculum. *www.qcda.gov.uk.*

Whittle, J. (2006) 'Journey sticks and affective mapping', *Primary Geographer,* 59, pp. 11-13.

Whyte, T. (2007) 'Personal geographies: children and their local environment' in Austin, R. (ed) *Letting the Outside In.* Stoke-on-Trent: Trentham.

Websites

Commission for Architecture and the Built Environment *www.cabe.org.uk*

Eco-Schools *www.ecoschools.org.uk*

Groundwork *www.groundwork.org.uk*

Learning Outside the Classroom *www.lotc.org.uk*

Mywalks http://*nuweb.northumbria.ac.uk/mywalks*

Mywalks and messy maps
www.geography.org.uk/cpdevents/onlinecpd/myplaceyourplaceourplace/mywalksandmessymaps

with contributions from Gemma Kent

CHAPTER COVERAGE:
EUROPE • FIELDWORK • MAPWORK • MISCONCEPTIONS • PHOTOGRAPHS • PLANNING

Contrasting localities

This chapter gives guidance about UK and other European localities schools might study as part of a balanced curriculum for key stages 1 and 2. Supporting resources and appropriate teaching strategies are considered and guidance given on planning and assessment.

> *Geography is about places. It is not just knowing about places themselves, but understanding the interdependence and connectivity of places ... This knowledge and understanding of other places, cultures and societies underpins sensitivity and tolerance and contributes to good citizenship.* (Bell, 2005)

Children live in a world that is full of relevant and significant places. These include not only their home and school environment, play areas and holiday destinations, but also places that they learn about from television programmes, films and books. Each place has its own 'character' which is determined not just by human and physical features and processes but also by our individual responses to them. Consequently, a central question for pupils to answer when studying any place, especially those they have not visited, is 'What would it feel like to live in this place?'. This question is relatively easy to answer when pupils are investigating their own environment but more complex when the place is further away and, therefore, unfamiliar to most or all of a class.

What is certain is that children are fascinated from an early age by places that are unfamiliar and distant. However, their ideas about these places may, understandably, involve inaccuracies and stereotypes. Place studies give teachers an opportunity to investigate and, through their teaching, challenge and modify pupils' initial ideas. Thus, before starting any place study it is important to explore pupils' existing knowledge and understanding. The results allow subsequent activities to proceed from the known to the unknown.

What ideas do young children have about unfamiliar places?

What notions do children who live in cities have about the nature of English villages? Before undertaking a study of a Surrey village, pupils in a year 4 class in an urban school were asked to complete a questionnaire about their ideas. These are some of the things they said:

- English villages are 'quite poor, not a rich place'.
- The people wear clothes that are 'torn because they don't have much money'.
- You might see 'girls wearing long black gowns and white aprons'.
- Work includes having 'to go into the forest to collect wood to light the fire with it' and being a 'shoe-shiner'.
- You would see 'pots where the food has been cooked' and hear some 'wild animals'.
- Life for people living in a village in England would be 'like African people they beg for food and water'.

In general, most pupils in this class saw villages as poor, impoverished and technologically backward places. Their ideas about village life were largely negative, historical and wildly inaccurate. The findings of a number of researchers indicate that most children tend to associate life in the developing world with primitive, hunter-gatherer images (Scoffham and Potter, 2007). It may well be that as children's ideas about distant places develop, they pass through a stage when they confront their deep-seated fears of an unknown, hostile world.

By contrast, the small number of pupils who actually had first-hand experience having been to an English village had much more accurate and positive impressions. One pupil, for example, recounted visiting his grandmother in a Somerset village, describing it as:

> *A place where there are shops, houses, not much traffic and with mostly old people but with some children. People work in a Somerfield supermarket and there is also a police station and the children there play football. The village is sometimes quiet and sometimes, not usually, noisy.*

As children make sense of the world, they rely on either direct experiences obtained through first-hand encounters, or indirect, second hand experiences. While direct experiences may be most influential and 'real' for children in informing their ideas and opinions about places, they are more regularly affected by indirect influences such as accounts of places visited by friends or family, through stories and, probably most significantly, television programmes.

Investigating pupils' existing ideas is simple and can be done in a number of ways. One approach is to gather evidence through writing, annotated drawings, word banks and word lists. Another option is simply to ask questions. This can be particularly revealing as it exposes children's existing knowledge and personal experiences as well as their opinions. With modification the following question set could be applied to any locality:

Photo | *Paula Richardson.*

- What is a village?
- Have you ever been to a village?
- Do you know anyone who lives in a village?
- What would you expect to see/hear/smell there?
- What kind of work do people do there?
- What do you think it is like to live in a village?
- How do you think village life is changing?
- What issues do you think will affect the village in the future?
- Would you like to live in a village? Why/why not?
- In what ways is the village similar to/different from our place?

Why study contrasting localities?

A balanced curriculum involves learning about places beyond the local area. At key stage 1, pupils should investigate links between their locality and other places in the UK and beyond. At key stage 2, they should study their own locality, a contrasting locality in the UK and a locality in another country. At both key stages pupils should learn how people, communities and places are connected and can be interdependent at a range of scales from the local to the global. (QCDA, 2010.)

You should select the localities you study according to the pupils' needs and school priorities; for example, community cohesion, or sustainable living. It is important that over the course of key stages 1 and 2 children study a broad range of locations. You should balance urban, suburban and rural studies from the UK, Europe and further afield (especially economically developing countries). Whichever places you choose, the scale of the study is important. With young children you might choose an area no larger than the school's vicinity, whereas with older pupils you might study a larger area. The important thing is that pupils should be able to make valid comparisons and contrasts with their own place.

Contrasting locality studies have a positive impact not only on pupils' geographical knowledge, but also on their personal development and well-being. This relates directly to the aims of *Every Child Matters*; for example, during fieldwork pupils learn how to be healthy and stay safe; during their enquiries they enjoy and achieve; and when investigating sustainable living they learn about economic well-being. These achievements, relating directly to Section 4 on Personal Development and Well-Being, can be recorded on the school SEF.

What can I do to support a locality study?

Most schools teach about distant places using resources from one of the following:

- A photopack produced by an educational publisher
- A school-produced locality pack
- TV programmes
- The internet
- CDs
- Story books
- A twinning arrangement with a school from a contrasting locality
- A residential school visit

Professionally-produced resources are widely used and have several advantages: they are conveniently available 'off the shelf', they are often written by professional authors, they tend to be well presented, and they are not too expensive to buy. However, you might decide to devise a resource pack of your own. The great advantage of doing this is that you can incorporate fieldwork into your teaching programme, providing an invaluable extra dimension to pupils' depth of understanding of a place that simply cannot be achieved in the classroom. You may also be able to develop cross-curricular links with history, citizenship and primary languages; possibly more.

How can a school produce its own resource pack?

A locality in the UK that contrasts with the children's own locality does not have to be very distant or very different. The majority of UK primary schools are probably no more than a short way away from a place that has characteristics that would allow children to find both differences and similarities with their own place. Moreover, the processes involved in producing a photo pack are largely similar for all localities. Here are some ideas to get you started.

First, select a place that is contrasting but easily accessible, to enable resources to be gathered easily and to allow fieldwork. Next carry out some research. A visit is essential but the internet may be useful in finding both written and pictorial information. If possible, make contact with a primary school in the place you have selected to see if you can establish links or gain extra information from local teachers. Additionally, you may be able to find a family who will co-operate in representing a 'typical' picture of everyday life.

The geography photopacks currently in use in your school will provide ideas for appropriate resources and teaching strategies but the most important task is to decide on suitable photographs. These will be more influential than anything else in informing pupils' ideas about the place and are likely to be the resource from which they will gain most enjoyment. If possible take your photographs on a bright day, preferably in the summer when the content of gardens, open spaces and so on is most interesting. You should also take more pictures than you intend to use and later select the twenty or so that provide a balanced and authentic perspective. While taking the photographs remember it is also possible to gather other valuable information and resources such as maps, old photographs and reports of current issues and events.

In general you should try to take photographs covering the following themes:
- physical characteristics, e.g. fields, hills, rivers, seashore, weather, rocks
- human characteristics including (depending upon the nature of the place) the variety of homes (cottages, flats, bungalows, terraces), types of shops, significant buildings (town halls, churches, police stations) etc.
- places where people work (factories, office blocks, farms)
- places for recreation (playgrounds, sports grounds, cinemas)
- environmental and planning issues to illustrate the concept of change and conflict.

Photos |
Bryan Ledgard.

It is important for people, preferably named people, to appear in some of the photographs as this gives an invaluable 'personal' link with the place that primary children find particularly appealing. Digital cameras make the job of taking a large number of photographs relatively cheap and easy. You can use a computer later to manipulate the size and content of the images you have chosen. Good quality colour reproduction is possible with modern colour printers. Enlarging the photographs to A3 size is helpful for infants, but A4 is suitable for juniors. Laminate the photographs to make them more durable.

Remember to take full advantage of the many free resources available online. Geograph *(www.geograph.org.uk)*, for example, has a photograph for every square kilometre of Great Britain and Ireland. Videos of many locations are also available on websites such as 'YouTube' although you need to vet them thoroughly before showing them to children. Many locations also have their own webcams.

Vertical aerial photographs, giving a unique overview of a place, are an invaluable resource. Aerial photographs taken across the UK are available from Getmapping *(www.getmapping.co.uk)* and Multimap *(www.multimap.com)*. Google Earth *(http://earth.google.co.uk)* is a fantastic resource, allowing pupils to view satellite images and switch to street views. Eye in the Sky *(www.tts-group.co.uk/eyeinthesky)* is another valuable source of aerial photographs and current and historical maps centred on a postcode of your choice.

A range of maps is essential for any place study. For places beyond the pupils' own locality small-scale maps allow them to locate the place (Where is this place?) and to consider the interconnectedness of places (How is this place connected to other places?). Larger scale maps encourage exploration of the place (What is this place like and why is it like it is?) and recognition of change in a place (How is this place changing?).

More detailed exploration of places is best served by OS 1:2500 maps (1cm represents 25m), available for rural areas, or 1:1250 (1cm represents 12.5m), available for urban areas. Such large-scale maps show small areas in great detail. The Ordnance Survey is an excellent source for a range of maps but the internet has sites that offer free maps such as Multimap and Streetmap (see above) and historical maps *(www.old-maps.co.uk)*. Additionally, ICT can be used to help children make their own maps. A good map-making programme is Local Studies *(www.soft-teach.co.uk)*. See Chapter 8 for further information.

You should also try to include case studies as these are very effective in helping younger pupils to explore, in context, the effect of change in a place, including environmental issues. Issues arise when there is conflict over how the land is used. Find out if there is an issue facing your chosen place. It might be a proposal for a new housing estate, the building of a superstore or a bypass, for example. Studying issues encourages not just an understanding of why change happens and how conflict arises ('How is this place changing?'), it also provides opportunities for pupils to consider their own and others' feelings about change ('What do I, and others, feel about this change?').

In posing and answering these questions you can meet teaching objectives within both the cognitive and affective domains. The cognitive domain is essentially concerned with knowledge and skills, while the affective domain is concerned with values and attitudes. Using issue-based case studies encourages 'confluent education': this links the cognitive and affective domains, helping pupils develop as both thinking and feeling individuals.

Why incorporate fieldwork into a UK locality study?

Fieldwork is essential for expanding and refining pupils' knowledge and understanding. As the Learning Outside the Classroom Manifesto (DfES, 2006 p.6) declares, 'it provides quality learning experiences in "real" situations [which] have the capacity to raise achievement across a range of subjects.' Depending on the nature of the place, activities might include sketching, land use and traffic surveys, map making, sensory descriptions of feelings, taking photographs, videos or sound recordings, and listing types of work done there. Pupils gain a much broader view from a direct study, and are also more likely to appreciate those intangibles that contribute to the 'personality' and character of a place. A feature common to all places is their dynamic, ever-changing nature, so it is important to build up additional resources that demonstrate change.

How can schools devise relevant locality studies?

Select a contrasting locality which will engage pupils. It could relate to an event like the FIFA World Cup; or it might link with a history study, such as Ancient Greece. If you have a link school you could study its locality, particularly if you are working towards the International School Award. If your school has a large immigrant population, this might provide the focus. The two examples below are supported by a range of published resources.

An island home

This unit links geography and literacy. The fictitious island of Struay featured in the Katie Morag stories (Hedderwick, 1997, 1998) is based on the real Scottish island of Coll. An authentic geographical enquiry needs photographs, but Coll's remote location has made this difficult, prompting the publication of several Coll resources. These include *Discover Coll: The Real Struay* photopack (Graham and Walker, 2003, see panel below) and *Isle of Coll map* (Thomas, 2004). Using these resources with the Katie Morag stories should expand the potential and range of the unit.

The Isle of Coll

Together with a colleague, I have compiled the contrasting UK photopack about Coll mentioned above. Physical geography features prominently on Coll so photographs were taken of hills, beaches, lakes and cliffs. The human dimension was represented by images of the school, various homes, shops and the island's only hotel.

In selecting the photographs compromises had to be made. There was no room, for example, for interesting events like the Coll summer show. Additionally, intangibles like the friendliness of the islanders, the peacefulness of the beaches, the strength of the wind and the sometimes unrelenting rain cannot be properly captured in words or pictures. Ultimately there can be no substitute for fieldwork.

Photo 1 | *A beach on the island.* **Photo** | *Douglas MacDowall. © Bluesky International.*
This photograph is of Feall Beach, typical of many around Coll. There is evidence of the tidal nature of the sea and there are sand dunes and cliffs in the distance. Beaches are common on Coll and even on a sunny day in early summer, there are no people here. A photograph such as this could allow key stage 1 pupils to talk about their own experiences of visits to the beach and to consider comparisons and contrasts.

Photo 2 | *Ben, Ellie and their father by some rock pools.*
Photo | *Douglas MacDowall. © Bluesky International.*
This photograph is of three members of a tourist family amongst the rock pools on Rubh' a' Bhinnein beach on Coll. It shows not just the physical characteristics of the coast, but most importantly visitors using and enjoying the place. Additionally, the children are finding out about sea creatures such as crabs and shrimp. The fact that the children are named provides a 'personal' dimension to a secondary source of information for pupils using the photograph.

Photo 3 | *Vertical aerial photograph of Arinagour.*
Photo | *Getmapping plc. © Bluesky International.*
This photograph, at a scale of 1:5000, shows the only settlement of any size on Coll, the village of Arinagour. Such photographs are a wonderful source of information about places. This image shows buildings, including piers as well as homes, a hotel, farm and school, and the physical characteristics of water and land. Additionally, it shows patterns in the land such as the varying depth of the sea, green fields and the rather barren, rocky land that covers much of the area. Used alongside a similar image of the pupils' own locality, fascinating opportunities are offered for comparison and contrast of both physical and human features.

Photo 4 | *Highland cattle.*
Photo | *Greg Walker. © Bluesky International.*
This appealing image shows the unfamiliar breed of highland cattle found on Coll. These cattle are ideally suited to the wet and windy climate with their double-thickness coats. They also have an environmental link with the island's vegetation, as they help distribute seeds from the plants as they graze.

The Royal Society for the Protection of Birds (RSPB) site in the south-west of Coll provides a case study of an environmental issue. This area is a breeding site for many birds, including the globally endangered corncrake, as well as the most suitable part of the island for farmers to grow crops. Corncrakes nest late and on the ground and when farmers cut their crops early in summer it disrupts breeding. A compromise over this conflict has been reached between the RSPB and the farmers who now cut later in the season and cut from the field centre outwards, allowing any birds still on the ground to escape. This example enables pupils to understand not only why the conflict existed on Coll but also to see that through communication between the two parties, and seeing the other's point of view, it has been possible to reach a compromise. Simultaneously, pupils have a context to understand important concepts of conservation and sustainability.

A contrasting UK locality – Llandudno

Two published packs offer quite different approaches to teaching Llandudno as a contrasting UK locality. *Llandudno: The study of a contrasting seaside locality* (Rowbottom, 2002) provides a wide range of maps and photographs with suggested teaching strategies, while *Storylink: Llandudno* (Dryden and Hare, 2001) combines fictional stories with factual case studies featuring real people from Llandudno. A problem with studying Llandudno arises, though, when fieldwork is required. There are two main solutions:

1. Adapt the questions to acknowledge that the study will be entirely classroom-based.
2. Apply the ideas to a closer locality, enabling fieldwork, and perhaps creating your own locality pack as part of the fieldwork.

For UK and other European place studies in key stage 1, a good starting point would be the excellent Barnaby Bear books and associated resources (Jackson, 2000-2003; Lewis, 2001-2003). This engaging bear has travelled to a range of places including Edinburgh, Norway, Brittany and Dublin. A strong case also exists for introducing Barnaby Bear into the EYFS curriculum, giving nursery and reception children an enjoyable introduction to unfamiliar places and an early opportunity to expand their knowledge and understanding of the world.

There are also opportunities for European studies in key stage 2. From a thematic perspective, a European example might provide an interesting river focus, and a study of different types of settlement, or an environmental issue, could be located in Europe. Up-to-date European locality resources appropriate for key stage 2 are not common; however, it is possible to devise resources for a European place study using school links, holidays, tourist information and the internet. If you do not have your own contacts the British Council (see page 203) will help put you in touch with an appropriate school.

> The teacher in one inner London school with an increasing Eastern European population decided to use *Roar, Bull, Roar!* (Fusek Peters *et al.*, 2006) as the basis for a contrasting study between Valašské Klobouky in the Czech Republic and the local area. Local residents spoke to the pupils about their first-hand experiences and pupils originally from the Czech Republic were able to share their expertise with their peers.

How can my school plan for progression and assessment?

When you plan work on contrasting localities it is important to focus on skills and concepts rather than content. Use the current government guidance, e.g. level descriptions, to ensure that your planning for the development and progression of geographical skills is conscious and deliberate. Remember that assessment is most effective where specific assessment tasks are an integral part of the normal sequence of lessons. This information should be used formatively to guide future teaching and learning. When assessing pupil achievement it is important to use a wide range of tasks. These could include written reports, map making, oral presentations, videos, role play and drama. The list is potentially endless!

What makes an effective conclusion to a study of contrasting UK and European localities?

Before completing the study you should find out how pupils' ideas have changed by asking them the same questions you used at the beginning. When this was done with the pupils in the inner city school described earlier it transpired that their ideas were much more accurate and authentic. The new ideas reflected knowledge and understanding gained from the resources and activities used in the village study, especially the visit. The pupils had greater confidence in showing their knowledge and understanding orally and in their writing and drawing. Additionally, they had a much more positive attitude towards life in the village and they valued what it had to offer those who lived there. Significantly, most pupils were now positive when asked if they would like to live in the village, and the influence of the field trip seems to have been the main factor in changing their attitudes.

When pupils are taught about localities in the UK and mainland Europe using a wide range of activities and resources, including fieldwork, they will be getting a real opportunity to refine their growing 'sense of place' and increase the depth of their feeling and thinking. Teachers should also be optimistic that they will be able to answer, with confidence and accuracy, that vital question: 'What would it feel like to live in this place?'.

References and resources

References

Bell, D. (2005) 'The value and importance of geography', *Primary Geographer*, 56, pp. 4-5.

DfES (2006) *Learning Outside the Classroom Manifesto*. Nottingham: DfES.

Fusek Peters, A., Fusek Peters, P. and Weckmann, A. (2006) *Roar, Bull, Roar!*. London: Frances Lincoln.

Scoffham, S. and Potter, C. (2007) 'Please Miss, why are they so poor?', *Primary Geographer*, 62, pp. 5-7.

Locality resources

Dryden, I. and Hare, R. (2001) *Storylink: Llandudno*. Sheffield: Geographical Association.

Graham, J. and Walker, G. (2003) *Discover Coll: The Real Struay*. Coalville: Wildgoose.

Hedderwick, M. (1997) *Katie Morag and the New Pier*. London: Red Fox.

Hedderwick, M. (1997) *Katie Morag and the Two Grandmothers*. London: Red Fox.

Hedderwick, M. (1998) *Katie Morag Delivers the Mail*. London: Red Fox.

Jackson, E. (2000, 2003) *Barnaby Bear big books*. Sheffield: Geographical Association.

Lewis, L. (2001, 2003) *Barnaby Bear little books*. Sheffield: Geographical Association.

Rowbottom, L. (2002) *Llandudno: The study of a contrasting seaside locality*. Coalville: Wildgoose.

Thomas, S. (2004) *Isle of Coll Map*. Sheffield: Geographical Association.

Contact information

The British Council *www.britishcouncil.org*

Websites

The GA website has an extensive online gallery of high-quality images of various localities available to GA members at *www.geography.org.uk/resources/photogallery*

We found out about rainforests

lovely
magical
wonderful
valuable
special
beautiful

STORYBOX
THE PARROT THAT TOLD THE TRUTH

VING THE
NFORESTS

Why do we have
DESERTS AND
RAINFORESTS

THE
GREAT GREEN FOREST
Paul Geraghty

Photo | Kathy Alcock and John Collar.

The wider world

1 Uses and develops their interest and natural curiosity about places.

2 Provides opportunities for them to explore ideas and skills.

3 Develops their existing knowledge and understanding of places, environments and cultures.

4 Helps them to examine and clarify their existing experience and awareness of places.

5 Develops spatial awareness towards a global scale.

6 Helps them to recognise their interdependence with the rest of the world.

7 Builds positive attitudes towards other people around the world.

8 Builds a global perspective that extends their present perspectives.

9 Helps them to value diversity in places, environments and cultures.

10 Combats ignorance, partiality and bias, thus helping to avoid stereotyping and the development of prejudice.

Figure 1 | *Ten good reasons for studying other places with young pupils.*

Photo | *Stephen Scoffham.*

Why study distant places?

Geography helps children to extend their world and to move towards a better, richer understanding of real places and people. Studying places beyond their local area provides great opportunities to capitalise on children's natural interest in, and curiosity about, people and places, and this alone can make it a very satisfying and enjoyable experience for both teachers and pupils. But there are many other good educational reasons for studying other places, including overseas, with young children, as Figure 1 identifies.

Research suggests that children often develop attitudes to other people and countries before they have appreciable knowledge of them. Without intervention, infants are liable to accept uncritically the bias and discrimination they see around them. Stories in the media of war, famine and disasters may distort their perceptions, as may stereotypes promoted in advertisements. The influence of family and, later, peer group pressure, may also confirm negative views.

Schools can help to redress this imbalance. Although there is no consensus on how children develop their ideas about the wider world, it is suggested that they become increasingly favourably disposed towards people of other lands as they move through the primary years. By the time they reach secondary school, stereotypes and misconceptions are much harder to shift. Finding about other places therefore needs to start early. But it is also important to recognise that such studies raise complex questions. Finding out about the wider world inevitably challenges us to clarify our own perceptions and the biases and prejudices which underpin them. Edward Said (1993), for example, has argued convincingly that colonialism still casts a considerable shadow over Western perspectives on the contemporary world. And as Picton (2008) observes, there can be no true ideas about a place; it may be more helpful to think rather in terms of multiple images. The challenge for teachers is to broaden children's perspectives. It is a challenge which has a central position in citizenship, social studies and geography education.[1]

[1]See also Chapter 1, pages 19-21.

How big should my 'distant locality' be?

When deciding which locality to study, it is important to choose a small area that children can compare and contrast with their own school locality and other localities they may have studied. It also needs to be manageable to understand and easy to relate to. A distant locality study is not, therefore, the study of an area as large as a country or region; rather, it is likely to be a village, part of a town or city, or perhaps a small island. However, in all locality studies, pupils need to become aware of how the locality they are studying exists within a broader context. When a distant locality is being studied, pupils need access to maps, globes and other sources to locate the position of the chosen locality within a country and continent, and to enable them to view it alongside their own home/school locality. At key stage 2 it will be relevant to include some locational knowledge.

It is also essential to have some background information about the country in which the locality is set so that you can discuss the main physical and human features (e.g. its climate and the location of its capital, major cities, rivers and mountain ranges) and how the chosen locality relates to, or is influenced by, these features. In addition, we should build on pupils' own experiences of different places and tap into the knowledge and experience of adults associated with the school. If you make an audit of the places where people associated with your school have lived you may find you can make use of their knowledge and experience.

How do I choose a 'distant' locality?

At key stage 1, children need to find out about the links between their locality and other places in the world; perhaps through a cross-curricular topic, such as 'food' or 'the seaside'. However, even at this early stage, geography subject leaders should encourage colleagues to include the study of an overseas locality in their planning, to widen pupils' perspectives and introduce them to other people and cultures. There are also opportunities for introducing knowledge and understanding of environmental change and sustainable development – all places are changing, and there are associated issues to consider. The availability of excellent resources for overseas studies at key stage 1 makes this an interesting and exciting option both for teachers and their pupils. The *Barnaby Bear* series of big books (Jackson, 2000-2003) and little books (Lewis, 2001-2003) are good examples.

When considering which locality to choose, it is valuable to consider the following questions:

Photo |
Elaine Jackson.

- What distinctive features does the locality have?
- How does the chosen locality provide a contrast with our locality?
- Do we want to visit the locality? If so, how/when?
- Could I use the local school as a host base?
- Will there be any opportunities for fieldwork?
- How appropriate is the locality for undertaking a geographical enquiry?
- Which localities are being studied at other key stages and years?
- What resources are available to sustain and develop the study?

Figure 2 | *Some advantages and disadvantages of sources of information for locality studies.*

Source	Main advantages	Main disadvantages
Artefacts	Interesting, 'real' evidence. Promotes discussion. Can enhance a display.	Insufficient on own. Can be difficult to 'extract' geography.
Account or talk by other adult, e.g. person from a distant place	Recent information and a good starting point. Interesting, particularly if combined with photographs, artefacts, etc.	Often little follow-up material available. Doesn't always focus on one distinct locality. Talk may not be pitched at right level or include sufficient geography.
Personal knowledge of the locality chosen	Your first-hand experience can bring the locality 'alive'. Photographs and artefacts from the locality can enhance the study.	You will need to prepare appropriate activities for the pupils to undertake. It takes time to put together.
Commercially-produced pack (usually includes photographs and some activities)	Can reduce planning time. Usually cheap as a relevant resource.	Often more material than is required, so need to be selective about which parts you use. Not always appropriate for key stage 1. Activities may not be geographically focused and lead to 'topic drift'.
Maps	Provide information about the location of places. Also good at showing details of physical features such as mountains and rivers.	Often difficult to access maps of specific places and regions. Internet maps are often aimed at an adult audience.
Video of a locality	Usually an interesting addition to a study. Whole class can view at one time.	Talk not always pitched at right level. Doesn't always focus on geography requirements. Difficult to find – often has a country or regional approach, not locality.
Photographs of a locality	Allows individual pupils/groups to 'see' the locality in some detail. If good quality, then can be very interesting. Easy to organise.	Selective and therefore may indicate bias and stereotyping. Not readily available for all localities. Tend to present a 'static' view.
Locality in the news	Interesting, topical, relevant. May have different accounts of the news of a locality, with some photographs.	Not always appropriate for key stage 1. Often insufficient detail for the study. May present an unbalanced view. Focuses on the unusual, rather than everyday life.
Book/story	Can be a good starting point. Can easily refer back. Usually high quality photographs. Useful for reference or as an additional source.	Few focus on a locality – usually a country or regional approach. Not always intended for key stage 1. Selective material, sometimes subject to bias/stereotyping in pictorial evidence. Usually an overview giving insufficient detail. Single copy in class unmanageable.

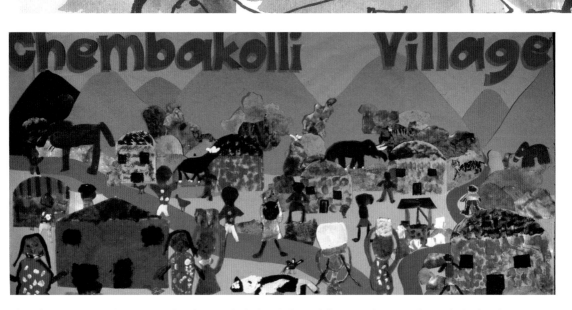

Photo /
Stephen
Scoffman.

- What potential is there to link the skills and themes of geography with the locality?
- Can I use my own experiences in the study?
- Have any children or adults in the school visited this place?
- Which localities am I, as the teacher, interested in?

At key stage 2, pupils need to learn about a different locality in another country, and many schools choose to focus on the economically developing world. As it is unlikely that your pupils will be able to visit an overseas locality, it is essential that you consider what secondary sources you have available before deciding on a locality to study. The ethnic composition of your school will also be significant. There is a wide range of resources available for locality study, some more useful than others. Figure 2 on page 207 sets out the main advantages and disadvantages of the different types of resource.

What about using TV programmes, DVDs and online video clips?

There is no doubt that television programmes, DVDs and online video can significantly increase interest in a place. The moving image is attractive and our pupils live in an age where it is pre-eminent. As more material become available we need to consider the following:

- Does it focus on a specific locality and aspects within it which are relevant to your studies? (It may not have been made with these in mind.)
- Does it have a positive commentary? (Children are not sophisticated viewers – the commentary needs to be exact, precise and true.)
- Does it show extremes or exceptions, highlighting the unusual or different? (Powerful images stay with you – the commentary is often forgotten.)
- Does it consider issues such as change and environmental problems? (Generalised descriptions of places can present a misleading portrait by, for example, only focusing on the positive or negative aspects of life in that place.)
- Are there suitable resources which can be used in follow-up sessions?

Children today are bombarded with images and information, but do not always have the skills to appraise them critically. Although you can introduce a topic with video material, it is often better used during the study. Either way, always view the material beforehand to check its suitability and so you know when to use the pause button.

How do I plan my study?

You need to be sure that over the key stage your planning involves work at a range of scales and in a range of contexts, including the UK, the European Union and the wider world. You also need to build in opportunities to develop ICT capability. Geography has immense potential for involving pupils in exciting and valuable ICT work: there are increasing numbers of useful secondary sources for information such as CDs, email, CDi, websites, and mapping packages, as well as open-ended software such as word processors and spreadsheets. These need to be included in your long-term planning to ensure appropriate coverage.

Some options to consider when planning are set out below:

■ Your school could 'adopt' a river, such as the Rhine or the Nile, stopping off at a number of settlements along the way. This approach would allow opportunities to develop much of the geography work in an integrated way.

■ Each locality chosen will have the potential to provide work about settlements. You may decide to look at a range of sizes and types of settlement over the key stage, comparing settlements in the UK, Europe or more distant locations.

■ Consider choosing a locality where weather data, particularly rainfall, is available or can be obtained. This can be compared with the worldwide weather data printed in some national newspapers, or from the TV news. Ideally the places chosen would be those with which the pupils are familiar, perhaps through news stories, holiday visits or their cultural background.

■ You may want to think about incorporating work on sustainability and change into your study.

■ Think also about cross-curricular opportunities. Primary languages, history and citizenship are obvious links.

■ Will your approach to planning mean that you will be able to capture the pupils' interest and imagination?

What should I consider when teaching about distant places?

The study must develop pupils' knowledge and understanding of places. The pupils need to be taught about the main physical and human features that give the locality its character; how the locality is linked with other places; and issues and problems that may affect it. These features will include, for example, rivers, landscape, hills, woods, weather, housing, land use, where people shop and what people do. At key stage 2 it will extend to how and why places change and the wider geographical context. It is easy to overlook some of the different elements of geography. The compass rose diagram, originally devised by Birmingham Development Education Centre, is an invaluable checklist for a balanced study (Figure 3).

One of the difficulties in studying distant places is the very real risk of presenting an inaccurate, biased or over-simplified picture. Geographers have an important role in providing opportunities to promote understanding, and in challenging ignorance and prejudice. A focus on a distinct locality, rather than a country or region, can help to avoid misleading generalisations which may be the basis of many prejudices. A locality study is a manageable size and so easier to comprehend. It can also be about real people with real lives, therefore

Natural
These are questions about the environment – energy, air, water, soil, living things, and their relationships to each other. These questions are about the 'built as well as the 'natural' environment.

Who decides?
These are questions about power: who makes choices and decides what is to happen, who benefits and loses as a result of these decisions and at what cost?

Economic
These are questions about money, trading, aid and ownership.

Social
These are questions about people: their relationships, traditions and culture, and the way they live. They include questions about how, for example, gender, race, disability, class and age affect social relationships.

Figure 3 | *The Development Compass Rose.*
Source | *Birmingham DEC, 1995.*

engaging pupils' interest. However, it is equally important to consider the locality within its country-wide context, otherwise pupils may have a distorted view of that country, assuming that it is all like the locality studied. This can be a particular problem if the resources that you are using focus on a single village in, for example, Africa or Asia.

Pupils need a broad, balanced picture, rather than a one-sided viewpoint, so consideration should be given to rich as well as poor, urban as well as rural, women as well as men. Beware of over-emphasis on poverty accompanied by simple and dogmatic explanations of the causes of poverty abroad. We must help our pupils to appreciate and value other cultures, ways of life and ideas. A distant place study should stress that spiritual values are more important than material values for millions of people in the poor – and in the rich – world.

Even before they reach school age, children will have attitudes, beliefs and values about other peoples and places. Some of these may be positive but others may be negative and critical. Indeed, we each have our own attitudes, beliefs and values about other peoples and places which we have not visited. Ideas and images come from a range of media sources such as television, articles in newspapers, holiday brochures, travel literature and films. Unfortunately these can, and usually do, present a very distorted view because of their selection for communication. They present unbalanced and incomplete images which may be reinforced within the home environment. Schools have a very important role in countering prejudice and racial discrimination and this is clearly reflected in the statement of values which underpin the national curriculum. Schools should ask themselves:

- Will our personal images of a place give the right messages to our pupils? For example, describing a place as 'primitive' or 'simple' is unhelpful and biased.
- Do we misinform because of our own ignorance of particular places, or because we use terms incorrectly? An example might be using the word 'country' to describe Africa.
- Do our texts in school describe some places as 'problem areas'? For whom are they said to be problematic? For example, in the Amazonian rainforests, the indigenous populations have lived there for centuries in equilibrium with their environment, but problems for these areas have come since the relatively recent settlement by Europeans.

It can be helpful to consider distant localities alongside your own locality. How would your locality appear to a visitor? What would you want a visitor to see? How would you present your locality to a visitor from abroad? You might also consider exploring visitors' ideas about other parts of our country – plenty of stereotypical images abound still. Consider also our traditions and culture in relation to how people from abroad might view them – Bonfire Night is an interesting one! Of course, all images have their limitations and in overcoming one set of stereotypes new ones may be created. However, by using a wide variety of images and providing plenty of opportunities to question and discuss them, it should be possible to build up a more rounded picture of life in a distant locality. The important thing is to be aware of these pitfalls so that we can make sure we do not fall into them and so that we can help pupils to develop an informed and balanced view of other people, places and cultures and the richness and diversity of our own heritage.

How do I study another place?

Pupils need to use a range of geographical skills and enquiry questions when they learn about a distant locality. The questions they need to ask are the same as when they study their own place:

- Where is this place?
- What is it like?
- Why is it like this?
- What is the landscape like?
- What goods and services are available?
- Where do people go to shop? What work do the adults do? How do people travel?
- What is it like to live there?
- What links does it have with other places?
- What is the weather like there?
- How is the place changing? How do the people feel about the changes?
- How is the locality similar to/different from our locality/other localities we have studied?
- How may this place change in the future?

How should I start my locality study?

Some options:

- Identify the locality on maps and globes. How would you get there? Consider various options – land, sea, flights, direct/following a particular route.
- Use a story from the country. What does it tell us about that country?
- Exchange ideas about what we know (or think we know!) about the country where the locality is situated. Discuss how we can find out about a country or place.
- Look at some photographs of the locality. Show a photograph with some of the picture hidden and ask what might be in the unseen part. Uncover the area and show the pupils the whole photograph. Are they surprised? As a whole class devise questions which will provide starting points to help them to find out more about the locality.

■ Show the pupils an artefact. Choose something which will capture the pupils' imagination. What is it? What is it used for? Who uses it? Where has it come from? What is it made from? What can it tell us about the place and people it belongs to?

If you start from the locality, remember that you will need to set the locality within its country, its continent and within the world, using maps and globes.

Can I design my own locality study?

Yes! Ideally, the chosen locality should be one which you have visited, or one that particularly interests you and for which you have collected plenty of relevant information and other materials. The information needs to be:

■ recent

■ accurate

■ relevant

■ interesting

■ unbiased.

If possible, collect information and resources relating to the following features/aspects of the chosen locality:

■ the location (include local maps)

■ landscape

■ weather (include local data if possible)

■ the people and their way of life

■ homes

■ work

■ access to services (water, for example)

■ transport

■ health

■ recent and current changes.

Figure 4 | *Jobs and schools provide good comparisons.* **Photos** | *Stephen Scoffham.*

You may also wish to collect information about other aspects of the locality such as religion, language, customs, food, the local school and leisure pursuits (Figure 4). Although these are not essential to meet curriculum requirements, your pupils are likely to ask you questions about all of these and more. The information needs to be collated in a way that enables pupils to gain access to it easily. If the locality cannot be viewed at first-hand by the pupils, then visual aids are vital. A range of clear photographs (prints or digital images on the IWB), showing the landscape, housing, the people and their lifestyles would be particularly helpful, as would a video, even an amateur one, to make the place 'come alive' for pupils.

What maps will I need for a locality study?

Suitable maps and plans of the locality are essential. If these are too detailed for younger pupils to use, you could draw simple outline maps to include only the information that is necessary, and in a form which relates to the level of the pupils' mapping skills. Your map should have a title, an indication of direction (perhaps an arrow pointing north) and a scale (even if only approximate). A simple key may also be included. Ideally a range of maps should be used for a locality study, including the following:

- Map of world – continent marked.
- Map of continent – country marked.
- Map of country – locality and significant features of country marked.
- Map of locality – main features marked.
- Plans of any important buildings (for example, named person's home, school, farm).

All small-scale maps involve some element of distortion (area, size, etc.) so it is essential to use a globe to identify the position of the locality in the world. To enhance the study, you could make a display of artefacts from the country, e.g. stamps, maps, food and products, coins, items of clothing, the national flag, a newspaper, stories, travel brochures and

Figure 5 | *Classroom display of artefacts.*
Photo | *Stephen Scoffham.*

Figure 6 | A Chinese New Year display, with children's 'Chinese writing'.
Photo | Paula Owens.

other pictures of the country. Even bus tickets, receipts and paper bags can be valuable sources of evidence which pupils can interrogate. Artwork from the locality, and recordings of local music are an excellent way of adding colour and atmosphere to the study (Figures 5 and 6). If the pupils can dress up in local costumes, eat some traditional food or say a few words in the local language such as 'good morning' and 'my name is ...' they are likely to engage even more whole-heartedly.

Should we link with our overseas locality?

There are obvious and very real benefits in making a direct link with a school overseas. Overseas links have the potential to develop in pupils a sympathetic and caring attitude towards other peoples and ways of life, as well as a sense of responsibility for the environment; they can also help to counteract prejudice. These claims are supported by research. Disney (2004) reports how a schools linking programme led children to develop much more diverse and informed images of India. A more recent study from Worcestershire (Pickering, 2007), indicates that pupils in schools with well-established school partnerships have much more positive images of Africa than those without partnerships. Finally, a survey conducted by Ipsos MORI on behalf of the Development Education Association (DEA, 2010) shows that learning about global issues nurtures outward-looking and socially responsible attitudes to issues as diverse as climate change, poverty, trade and world politics.

It is important to recognise that schools linking programmes may involve practical difficulties. For example, unless your partner school uses English there may be communication problems. Exchanging information via email and the internet has the advantage of being quick but is not always reliable, particularly in the economically developing world. However, there are also challenges on a deeper philosophical level. Disney (2004) observes that 'issues to do with power and social justice are never far from the surface where links between the UK and the poorer countries of the South are concerned' (p. 333). For this reason schools that incorporate their linking programmes into work on wider global issues appear to achieve better results: superficial studies run the risk of reinforcing prejudices and negative stereotypes. Perhaps even more fundamental in successful links is a long-term commitment to the project by teachers in both partner schools.

Although there is no general agreement about how children learn about the wider world and more research is needed into global schools partnerships, it seems that if pupils have a balanced teaching programme and are given access to appropriate information the results are likely to be beneficial. However we need to maintain a critical stance. Shah (2010) draws attention to the complexities of global power relationships and urges us to acknowledge that many of the key ideas which underpin global studies, such as 'development', are contested. Learning about other people and places also challenges us to reflect on our own lives and to articulate our values. We need to tread carefully as we negotiate this area of the curriculum.

References and further reading

Birmingham Development Education Centre (1995) *Development Compass Rose – A consultation pack.* Birmingham: DEC.

Development Education Association (2010) *The Impact of Global Learning on Public Attitudes and Behaviours Towards International Development and Sustainability.* London: DEA.

Disney, A. (2004) 'Children's images of a distant locality', *International Research in Geographical and Environmental Education*, 14, 4, pp. 330-335.

Disney, A. and Mapperley, J. (2007) 'Sustaining a school link', *Primary Geographer*, 62, pp. 16-18.

Halocha, J. (2007) 'Citizenship through school twinning', *Primary Geographer*, 62, pp. 36-38.

Holloway, S. and Valentine, G. (2002) 'Corked hats and Coronation Street' in Smith, M. (ed) *Aspects of Teaching Secondary Geography.* Oxford: Routledge.

Jackson, E. (2000, 2003) *Barnaby Bear big books.* Sheffield: Geographical Association.

Lewis, L. (2001, 2003) *Barnaby Bear little books.* Sheffield: Geographical Association.

Pickering, S. (2007) 'Learning in partnership', *Primary Geographer*, 62, pp. 13-15.

Picton, O. (2008) 'Teaching and learning about distant places: conceptualising diversity', *International Research in Geographical and Environmental Education*, 17, 3, pp. 227-249.

Said, E. (1993) *Culture and Imperialism.* London: Chatto and Windus.

Shah, H. (2010) 'Critical thinking in the context of global learning', *Primary Geographer*, 71, pp. 14-15.

See also *Primary Geographer*, 62, Spring 2007; the complete issue focuses on the global dimension and school partnerships.

Websites

British Council *www.britishcouncil.org.uk*

Oxfam *www.oxfam.org.uk/education/gc*

Teachers in Development Education *www.tidec.org*

Picture books about distant places

Aardema, V. (1986) *Bringing the Rain to Kapiti Plain.* London: Macmillan.

Browne, E. (1994) *Handa's Surprise.* London: Walker Books.

Chamberlin, M. and Chamberlin, R. (2005) *Mama Panya's Pancakes.* Bath: Barefoot Books.

Foreman, M. (2006) *Mia's Story.* London: Walker Books.

Heine, T. (2004) *Elephant Dance.* Bath: Barefoot Books.

Hoffman, M. (1995) *Grace and Family.* London: Francis Lincoln.

Krebs, L. (2003) *We All Went on Safari.* Bath: Barefoot Books.

Smith, J. (2003) *Lily's Garden of India.* Tunbridge Wells: TickTock Books.

Smith Milway, K. (2008) *One Hen.* London: A & C Black.

So, S. (2006) *Shanyi Goes to China.* London: Frances Lincoln.

See also the References and further reading for Chapter 16.

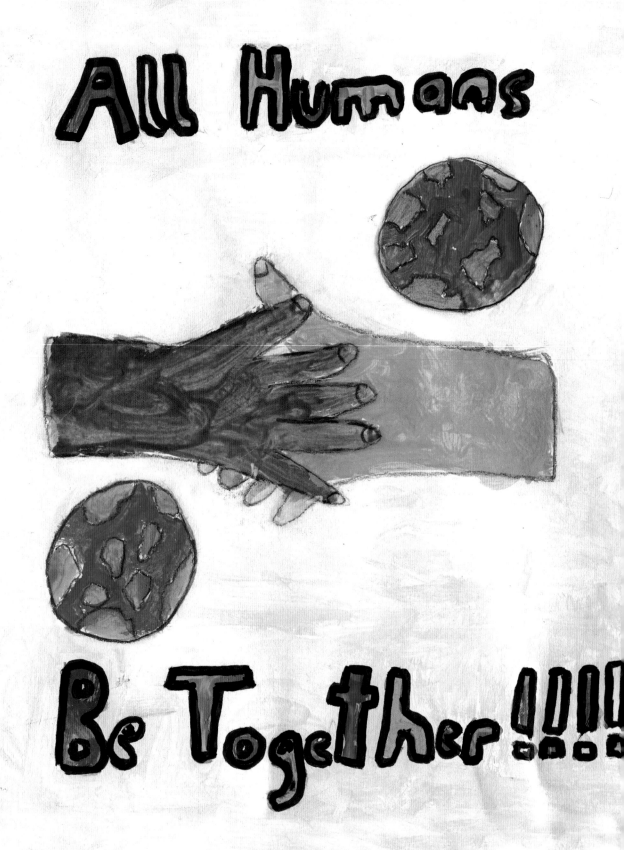

Pupils' work | Ferring Church of England Primary School, West Sussex.

The global dimension

'Only when the last tree has died and the last river been poisoned and the last fish been caught will we realise we cannot eat money'
(Cree proverb).

What is the global dimension?

This Native American proverb gets to the nub of the global dimension. It is in essence about social justice and living sustainably: how we choose to behave towards each other and towards Earth itself. In educational terms the global dimension can be applied to teaching and learning of any subject. However, it is inextricably linked with geography, not just because the words 'geography' and 'global' have an obvious connection, but because of the contribution that the global dimension can make to geography.

When geography is taught through the global dimension it has the capacity to promote meaningful spiritual, moral, social and cultural development. It also has the potential to encourage people to live more sustainably and gain a lasting curiosity, respect and concern for the planet. The global dimension is about developing critical thinking and gaining a better understanding of how the world works. It involves challenging racist, stereotyped and discriminatory views and promoting greater understanding and appreciation of different issues, places and people in the world. According to official guidance (DFID, 2005) there are eight key concepts underpinning the global dimension. These are:

■ **Global citizenship**
Gaining the knowledge, skills and understanding of concepts necessary to become informed, active, responsible citizens.

■ **Sustainable development**
Understanding the need to maintain and improve the quality of life now without damaging the planet for future generations.

■ **Social justice**
Understanding the importance of social justice as an element in both sustainable development and the improved welfare of people.

■ **Diversity**
Understanding and respecting differences and relating these to our common humanity.

■ **Values and perceptions**
Developing the ability to critically evaluate representations of global issues and an appreciation of the effect these have on people's attitudes and values.

■ **Interdependence**
Understanding how people, places, economies and environments are all inextricably inter-related and that choices and events have repercussion on a global scale.

■ **Conflict resolution**
Understanding the nature of conflicts, their impact on development and the importance of promoting harmony.

■ **Human rights**
Knowing about human rights, including the UN Convention on the Rights of the Child.

Photo | *Mary Young.*

These terms _____ ___ __ g___ ___al and are complex, so _____ r_____ ____ ____r thought. Regarding _____ __, ___ ____, e, Graves (2002, p.5) m____ ___ ___ ___ ____ t discussion, the term _ _____ ____ ____ ___ co-dependence; that ___ ___ ___ ___ ____l and able to make ___ ____ ___ ___ ___ _l pressures.' Clearly, ___ ____ ___ ___ is.

___ _____ __ __ ___ underlying the global _____ ___ ___ central to good education. They are at the heart of the curriculum, reflected in the aim that all young people should become responsible citizens who make a positive contribution to society. They underpin the thinking behind community cohesion, equality legislation, whole-school ethos, sustainable schools and the prevent agenda. The global dimension is also relevant across all areas of learning in both the EYFS and at key stages 1 and 2. The concept of interdependence, for example, can be illustrated in terms of inventions, languages, trade and communication through history and around the globe.

In order to translate these concepts into real-life classroom practice, it is helpful to consider (a) the knowledge and understanding, (b) the skills and (c) the values and attitudes that are required to enable pupils to understand the world around them and to make sense of their own place within it. Young and Commins (2002) present a framework which shows how to integrate global citizenship into the curriculum (Figure 1).

Knowledge and understanding about:
- Social justice and equity
- Diversity in all its forms
- Globalisation and interdependence
- Sustainable development
- Peace and conflict

Skills of:
- Critical thinking
- The ability to argue effectively
- The ability to see and to challenge injustice and inequalities
- Respecting people and things
- Co-operation and conflict resolution

Values and attitudes of:
- Having a sense of identity and self-esteem
- Empathy
- Commitment to social justice and equity
- Appreciation of diversity
- Concern for the environment and commitment to sustainable development
- Holding a belief that people can make a difference

Figure 1 | *Key elements of global citizenship.*

Why is the global dimension important?

It is important to teach about the global dimension:

... because we live in an interdependent world and we have responsibilities towards each other.

We are affected every day by geographical issues that highlight the interdependence of our world. Each day we make choices about where we go and how we get there. We choose what to read, listen to, or see on TV, and, perhaps, think about how much of it to believe. The decisions we make affect others across the globe. Buying fair trade goods that have been produced within an agreed ethical code has a direct bearing on the welfare of the producers. For instance, the Day Chocolate Company agreed to pay small-scale producers in co-operatives £100 extra per tonne for social welfare benefits. With fair trade goods there is also a minimum price ceiling so that, unlike in non-fair trade situations, producers do not find themselves subject to price fluctuations that can have a devastating effect on their lives. In all areas of consumerism we are having an impact on others on a daily basis:

■ When buying new clothes are we supporting sweat-shop labour where human rights are being violated?

■ Are we aware of the ethical operating practices of the pharmaceutical or fuel companies that we patronise?

■ Are we supporting local producers and initiatives?

■ Is our bank lending money to those making landmines?

Of course, you may well be acting unwittingly, but the information is available if you want it: try *Ethical Consumer,* or any of the journals listed at the end of this chapter. These are complex issues, and it will take time to do the research, but be assured, you are making an impact on someone, somewhere, whatever you do. Given the modern technology available to us in the UK, the excuse that we don't know what is going on is simply not plausible: if we are concerned about the impact we are having on other people and places, we need accurate information to inform our choices. Many young people acknowledge this: 78% of young people in a MORI poll conducted for the Development Education Association (DEA) believed that 'it is important that schools help pupils understand what people can do to make the world a better place' (DEA, 2008).

... because of the need to address the discrimination present in our society.

We surely all hold responsibility as educators and as human beings to address injustice in our society. The curriculum too enjoins us to challenge injustice, be committed to human rights and strive to live peaceably with others. In addition the amended Race Relations Act requires public authorities 'to take the lead in promoting equality of opportunity and good race relations, and preventing unlawful discrimination' (CRE, 2002). Vigilance against racism is especially important in areas of overwhelmingly white populations, where people sometimes wrongly assume there is no problem.

Although people from a minority ethnic background represent only 5% of the population in Britain today, black people are six times more likely than white people to be stopped and questioned by the police, and are disproportionately represented in the prison population.

Homophobia also needs addressing. Stonewall UK (2009) reports that nearly half of primary school teachers say that children, regardless of their sexual orientation, currently experience homophobic bullying of some sort in their schools. Similarly SCOPE (2010) reports that disabled people are four times more likely to be violently assaulted than non-disabled people.

... because we need to counter misinformation and stereotyped views about each other.

It is most important for children to learn about people and places with whom they are unfamiliar. As an illustration, here are two descriptions by pupils of countries they have never visited. Can you identify them?

Country A
There are no poor people
There are no black people
The policemen wear red and black uniforms
They eat frogs and snakes
(Source: Ballin, 2010, after Ritson, 1996)

Country B
They have very tall mountains
People who live there travel in big buses
They have beautiful coins
There are lots of industries

In fact both the descriptions are of the same country – England! The first list (A) was compiled by Kenyan children and the second (B) by Greek children. Both show how those who are unfamiliar with England can have very distorted perceptions. Could our views of other places be equally distorted? It is important for educators to be aware of potential misunderstandings, generalisations and assumptions. Without an understanding of the issues involved, such work can lead to stereotyping of individuals or whole nations and actually serve to promote mistrust and intolerance. As educators, we have a responsibility to ensure that pupils gain an accurate and fair image of different people and places. We can do this by presenting them with up-to-date, realistic information and by challenging views that are unfair and inaccurate.

... because there are so many inequalities in the world, which are caused by the way the world works.

One way of showing inequalities around the world involves comparing statistics for different places. For instance, on 11 September 2001 approximately 3000 people died in the USA as a result of a terrorist attack. Around the world on the same day approximately 2700 children died of measles, 6020 people died of diarrhoea and 24,000 people died of hunger (New Internationalist, 2001). This quiet carnage has continued each day since then but goes largely unreported, whereas the events in the USA rocked the world. How can this be if all human lives have the same intrinsic value? Or are we saying that they don't?

The other shocking point to be raised here is why, in this day and age with the technology that is available, are thousands of people dying from preventable causes? Answer: for reasons related to the unequal distribution of resources, unequal access to technology, and greed and self-interest on the part of those people in the world with power – the majority of whom live in the so-called developed world.

... because it is imperative that we live more sustainably.

Education for sustainability has long been addressed through geography teaching, for instance through studying land use conflicts and the abuse of natural resources around the globe. However, sustainable living is about more than the environment. It is about how we live and interact with others, and whether or not our everyday lives promote social justice. For example, we may think that slavery is a thing of the past but according to Anti-Slavery International there are at least 12 million people in 29 countries around the world today who are effectively working as slaves. This is clearly not sustainable.

Children can be introduced to sustainable living in many small but effective ways. Turning off the tap when we clean our teeth is one of them. Basing decisions to buy wooden products on whether or not they have come from a sustainable forest reserve is another. Recycling as much as possible is a third. Currently Britain only recycles 11% of its household waste whereas our Northern European neighbours recycle around four times this amount. We clearly have a long way to go in using resources more responsibly.

... because we can affect what happens in the future.

Professor David Hicks (Hicks and Holden, 2007) has established that young people are very interested in what sort of world they are likely to inherit. He suggests that it is important to encourage children to think about the kind of future they want and to help them move towards it. Certainly, an unpublished survey conducted by Oxfam Education showed that children of primary age are interested in global issues: fair trade, global warming and war were all mentioned. However, many also realised that they could make a difference through their personal actions, and suggested various ways of doing so, e.g. by learning more about the world, lobbying the council, wasting fewer resources or joining groups of like-minded people. We all have power to affect the future, and should take heart from the number of campaigns started by individuals or groups, which have championed particular causes and had a significant impact. If geography is about creating a sense of awe and wonder about the world, alongside that goes an opportunity for us to say what we think about its treatment in a variety of ways.

... because many schools have developed a link with another school.

Many schools and some ITE colleges in the UK have a link with, or arrange visits to, comparable institutions in another country – often a country in the 'developing' world. In order for these experiences to be mutually beneficial, it is of utmost importance that those involved in such linking are aware of the wider issues relating to this kind of relationship. For instance, are the expectations on each side equal and realistic? What are the perceptions of the schools/communities towards each other, and do these need to be challenged? What happens if the key link person moves schools? There can be many benefits all round to such exchanges, but only if issues like this are addressed.

... because global issues are of interest to pupils and can promote learning.

It is well established that active teaching methods such as role play, drama and simulation games which are integral to the global dimension are effective in promoting engagement and learning. In addition, research conducted by Ipsos MORI on behalf of the Development Education Association (DEA, 2010) shows that teaching about global issues is a powerful way of harnessing public support for international development, helps to build a more responsible society and encourages community cohesion. For example, learning about climate change either in or after school halves the percentage of the population who think that it is pointless to take preventative action. Furthermore, evidence from other surveys indicates that pupils feel it is important to learn about the lives of people in other parts of the world and believe they should spend more time learning about global issues in school.

Ten strategies to promote the global dimension in geography

So, if we feel that it is important to teach through the global dimension, the question to address is: How can we do that? Here are some ideas.

1. Give an all-round view of a place or country

When studying any place or a country, it is important to present an all-round view otherwise incorrect assumptions can be made or reinforced. As an example, look at the photo in Figure 2, taken in England. If this was the only photo you used to illustrate life in England to someone who had never been to the country before they would, understandably, get a rather distorted view of it. In order to avoid giving a one-dimensional picture, think in terms of opposites: urban-rural, traditional-modern, young-old, leisure-work, rich-poor, women-men. You really need a minimum of ten photos to give any sort of representative view. Try out this approach with a country you know well, then apply the same criteria when you put up a display on a country with which you are unfamiliar.

Figure 2 | *The epitomy of Englishness?*
Photo | *Mary Young.*

2. Don't generalise

It is nonsense to make sweeping generalisations about people, places or countries; yet it often seems to be done. For instance, take this recently overheard remark: 'Africans live in mud huts'. Well, yes, some people in some countries in the African continent do live in mud huts (which are often a very appropriate form of housing) but not every single person lives in one, in the same way that not every person in England lives in a stately home. Generalisation removes individuality and fuels stereotyping, but can be countered by presenting exceptions and focusing on particular individuals and instances.

3. Look for similarities before differences

When comparing people's lives around the world, focus first on how people across the world are similar rather than different. It is, of course, also important to acknowledge the differences between people and their lives. We are different colours, we have different experiences – but to look at similarities first is one way to stress our common humanity and to promote empathy. To find links, try this simple activity – it works equally well with pupils or in staff development sessions. Give each group a photograph of someone from a distant locality (see Figure 3). Ask them to find as many links or connections as they can between their lives and the life of the person in the photograph. It is helpful if you have some knowledge about the people's names and the places in the pictures, although this is not always possible. You may be surprised to find that it is always possible to make links, even if they are sometimes as tenuous as 'We all breath the same air'.

4. Compare like with like

Avoid asking questions which will inevitably lead to answers which present one place or country as superior to another. It is very difficult to compare a British city with a village in India without coming to the conclusion that in terms of apparent wealth, services, modern technology and access to health care the British city is 'better'. (Of course, if you use a different yardstick, e.g. living sustainably, looking after the elderly or cleanliness of the air, it may well be the village comes out on top.) However, if Delhi and Edinburgh are compared, there will be many similarities in terms of traffic, cafés, shopping areas and places of cultural and religious significance. With comparisons, stick either to rural or urban scenes.

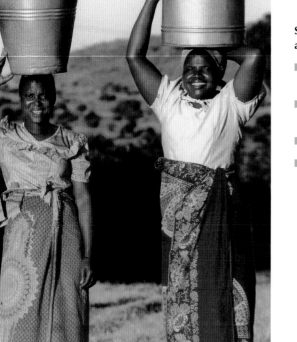

Figure 3 | *Two women collecting water near Lilongwe, Malawi, Central Africa.* **Photo** | *Mary Young.*

Some possible links between their lives and mine are:

■ They look pleased to be having their photo taken and I like having my picture taken too.

■ I have some material at home similar to that piece the woman on the right is wearing.

■ They look like friends, and I have friends.

■ There is a hill like that near my house.

5. Be prepared to challenge any discriminatory views that may arise

With all work exploring people and places, if you intend to promote equality and fairness it is essential that you are aware of, and can tackle, any prejudiced or discriminatory views that pupils may express. As an example, when students on a PGCE course were shown a photograph of life in a country town in Pakistan one of them commented 'They all look a bit primitive to me'. If such a comment is made, it is essential that you challenge it. To allow prejudiced comments to go unchallenged is in effect to condone them. Dealing with prejudicial remarks must be done sensitively, with an explanation given as to why the comment is unacceptable. You may choose to have a further quiet discussion with an individual after the session, but always let it be known that something unacceptable has occurred, in order to give a clear message to the whole class. Here are some ways in which prejudiced comments can be addressed:

■ Ask the speaker to explain what they meant or where their idea came from, then tackle it appropriately.

■ Ask the whole class if they think a particular comment is fair or not – and why. Discuss ways it could be re-phrased to make it fairer. A good test is to ask if the pupils would feel comfortable to make the comment in front of someone from that place or country.

■ Talk about the way some words, e.g. 'primitive' and 'tribal', carry negative connotations or can offend some people, so need to be avoided.

■ Encourage pupils to realise that something can be offensive to another person even if the person saying it didn't mean it to be – it is how the comment is received that is important.

■ Do a circle-time activity based on things that make us feel good and things that upset us. Link this to how we talk about and treat others.

If possible, avoid reacting crossly in telling the pupils a comment is unjust, or it may become something they purposefully repeat. For similar reasons always discuss why certain remarks are not acceptable.

6. Look for reasons and explanations

When looking at any problem or disaster anywhere in the world, encourage pupils to think about the underlying reasons rather than simply what has happened. World events may be complex, but their causes are very often to do with basic issues such as greed, unfairness, lack of sharing, and selfishness – basic concepts that children understand and often experience on a daily basis. Furthermore, don't be afraid of contentious issues. Geography is about the real world and we do children a disservice if we present them with a bland and cosy picture that they know to be untrue.

7. Think of solutions and not just problems

It is important when difficult issues arise in geography, for instance, the destruction of the Brazilian rainforest, that you enable the pupils to feel that they can do something positive about it. Leaving pupils feeling powerless can lead to them 'switching off' completely. Equally dangerous is to encourage pupils to think that simple solutions will fix things, e.g. 'The Brazilians should just stop cutting the trees down'. However, there are many things pupils could do if faced with this difficult situation. For instance, they could find out what is happening in the rainforest and why; read about the achievements of the rainforest campaigner Chico Mendes; or find out about how Fairtrade and other initiatives can help the indigenous people. You might encourage pupils to think about how to conserve places local to the school – a pond or an endangered wood – or set up an area of high biodiversity within the school grounds (perhaps Eco-Schools could help). As the environmental slogan puts it: 'Think globally, Act locally'.

8. Draw on the richness of the school and community

Often, there are pupils within the school whose experience and expertise can be drawn on in many ways, e.g. in teaching pupils another language, or in giving first-hand accounts of different places. Try to ensure such accounts do not reinforce negative stereotypes. Many children have multiple identities and heritages, have family in more than one country, speak several languages, are both Muslim and Welsh or feel both Tibetan and British, and so forth. Rather than overlooking this complexity, you should explore these issues and the diversity of the communities that make up the UK.

9. Find the right information and pictures to help you

There are many sources of up-to-date information and pictures to help you teach about the global dimension – just ensure you understand whose view is being presented! Development Education Centres have resources to help you, and there are many good websites and journals. Find time to keep abreast of current affairs – some radio and TV programmes, as well as newspapers, can be helpful in this respect. You could bookmark relevant news items and web addresses or save them as favourites, using thematic headings such as weather, landscapes, cities, transport and the environment, under different regions of the world.

10. Avoid being tokenistic

Sometimes schools see the global dimension of geography as enabling pupils to experience 'different cultures'. This work often includes a topic such as 'Food from round the world' or encouraging pupils to try on saris, or arranging a visit from African drummers. All of these things can work very well, but only if they are undertaken within the context of race equality, where issues of diversity have been explored by the teachers and pupils. Otherwise these activities may serve to reinforce stereotypes. For example, it is easy for white pupils – especially in mono-culturally-white areas – to explain that rice is eaten in India, while forgetting that they have it at home too! Missing this crucial link that brings us together across the world as human beings with many shared experiences means that the differences again prevail, and that stereotyped views and assumptions are not challenged. The same issues are true with the drummers, often billed as African (but from which country in that huge continent?). Without preliminary work and a commitment on the part of the school to promote the global dimension, pupils' comments about the 'exotic' costumes, the 'difficult' accents, the, 'Oh that's what they all do in Africa' go unnoticed, uninvestigated and unresolved.

Schools linking

More than 2000 schools in the UK have partnerships with schools in the majority ('developing') world; the One World Linking Association (*www.ukowla.org.uk*) can help you make connections. Such links are often a major stimulus for collecting information about your own locality, whether maps, text, sketches, photographs or numerical data, which can then be used in ICT presentations. They may also involve a strong cross-curricular dimension.

Whatever the link, global schools partnerships have the potential to lead to greater understanding of different cultures and can be a powerful way of finding out about children's lives, hopes and aspirations. However, they can also be tokenistic and promote inequality. Furthermore, the link may also highlight deep-seated cultural biases and preconceptions, many of which may be unconscious or only half acknowledged. Before embarking on a school link, therefore, it is important to consider some key questions to do with intercultural understanding, equality and social justice:

Promoting greater understanding and respect for different cultures
- How will you enable the children in each school to gain the sort of information about each other that will be likely to lead to greater understanding rather than to compounding of stereotypes?
- How will you avoid promoting attitudes of superiority or pity towards your link school in terms of how you deal with any differences of wealth, resources, or opportunity in different pupils' lives and in the details of their daily routines?
- How will you tackle dispelling any stereotypes the partner school pupils might have about this society, e.g. everyone is rich/there is no crime?

Issues to do with equality
- Will staff visits be reciprocal?
- What are the expectations of each school, and how will these be met?
- Will you fundraise for your link school? How will you balance the issues of helping your partner school financially or materially and seeing the two schools as equal?

■ How will you use the knowledge you gain from the professional experience, knowledge and perspectives of your colleagues/peers in your partner school? Similarly, what will they gain from you?

Issues to do with the exchange of information

■ Might there be any technical problems in exchanging information?

■ What effect would this have?

■ How could it be resolved?

■ Will the link be a whole-school commitment for both schools? If not, what will happen if the key staff member leaves the school?

The intention behind this chapter is to encourage you to think about the global dimension in your teaching. The issues may be challenging, but there are plenty of examples of good practice as to how geography and the global dimension are being linked. There are Development Education Centres in towns and cities around the UK; it is well worth checking if there is one near you. And remember, the global dimension is based on the premise that in order to teach about geography, or indeed anything at all, it is necessary to be anti-discriminatory, essential to be able to think critically, and important to be well-informed. What would be the point of education without these things?

References and further reading

Ballin, B. (2010) 'Making connections through school partnerships', *Primary Geographer*, 71, pp. 26-28.

CRE (2002) *Race Relations Act 2000*. Available at *www.equalityhumanrights.com*, (last accessed 18 March 2010).

Cree proverb. Available at *http://geocities.com/quotegarden/arbor.html*, (last accessed 18 March 2010).

DEA (2008) *Young People's Experiences of Global Learning*. London: Development Education Association.

DEA (2010) *The Impact of Global Learning on Public Attitudes and Behaviours Towards International Development and Sustainability*. London: Development Education Association.

DFID (2005) *Developing the Global Dimension in the School Curriculum*. Glasgow: DFID.

Garforth, H., Hopper, L., Lowe, B. and Robinson, L. (2006) *Growing Up Global*. Reading: Reading International Solidarity Centre.

Graves, J. (2002) 'Developing a global dimension in the curriculum', *The Curriculum Journal*, 13, 3, pp. 303-11.

Hicks, D. and Holden, C. (2007) 'Remembering the future: what do children think?', *Environmental Education Research*, 13, 4, pp. 501-512.

New Internationalist (2001) *Two Terrors*. November 2001. Available at *www.newint.org/issue340/facts.htm* (last accessed 30 June 2010).

QCA (2007) *The Global Dimension in Action: A curriculum planning guide for schools*. London: QCA.

SCOPE (2010) *Beating Disablism*. Available at *www.timetogetequal.org.uk*, (last accessed 18 March 2010).

Serf, J. (2010) 'Small and mighty: children's ideas about global learning', *Primary Geographer*, 71, pp. 8-10.

Stonewall UK (2009) *Homophobic Bullying in Britain's Schools: The teachers' report.* Available at *www.stonewall.org.uk/education_for_all*, accessed 18 March 2010.

Tide~ (2006) *Young Children and Global Citizenship.* Birmingham: Teachers in Development Education.

Young, M. and Commins, E. (2002) *Global Citizenship: The handbook for primary teaching.* Cambridge: Chris Kington Publishing.

Journals

Ethical Consumer magazine *www.ethicalconsumer.org*

New Internationalist *www.newint.magazine.co.uk*

Resurgence *www.resurgence.org*

Websites

Development Education Association *www.dea.org.uk*

Fairtrade Foundation *www.fairtrade.org.uk*

Global Dimension *www.globaldimension.org.uk*

Global Eye *www.globaleye.org.uk*

Global School Partnerships *www.dfid.gov.uk/globalschools*

One World Linking Association *www.ukowla.org.uk*

Oxfam Education *www.oxfam.org/coolplanet*

Sustainable Schools *www.teachernet.gov.uk/sustainableschools*

Teachers in Development Education *www.tidec.org*

UNICEF *www.unicef.org.uk*

World Development Movement *www.wdm.org.uk*

See also the think piece 'The Global Dimension at KS1&2' on the GA website *www.geography.org.uk/gtip/thinkpieces*, and *Primary Geographer*, 62, Spring 2007, which focused on the global dimension and school partnerships.

Section 4

Themes and topics

Chapter

17. Weather and climate

18. Rivers, coasts and the landscape

19. Settlement

20. Environmental geography

21. Citizenship and primary geography

Auntie Mabel flew her aeroplane in the pouring rain.

Hannah

Oliver W.

pouring

thunder

The water cycle

A cloud is millions of drops of water.

Clouds are blown by the wind.

Water evaporates from trees and plants.

Water runs into rivers.

Water is heated by the sun and evaporates from the sea.

Rivers flow into the sea.

computer

RM

Photo | Kathy Alcock and John Collar.

CHAPTER COVERAGE:
DISTANT PLACES • FIELDWORK • LITERACY/STORIES • LOCAL AREA
• MISCONCEPTIONS • PROGRESSION • SCHOOLS LINKING • VOCABULARY

Weather and climate

This chapter shows how observing and keeping regular weather records from the earliest years can enhance understanding of the impact of weather and different climates on both people and the environment.

The weather is very much part of 'Everyday geography'. It affects almost every aspect of our lives – clothes, food, buildings, the way we feel, what we see and hear, and so on. Daily variations in the weather provide material for greetings and small talk. The results of accurate observation and measurement are distilled and transmitted into our living rooms at regular intervals each day by weather forecasters, in language we can all understand.

A balanced curriculum should provide opportunities for pupils to undertake investigations and enquiries about the weather at all ages. Weather and climate make a particularly suitable topic for the later primary years but are also appropriate in the EYFS when children find out about the world around them. Any studies of places will involve learning about the local weather and its impact on people's lives. There are also opportunities to develop weather studies in the context of ICT. Indeed, the weather is an ideal cross-curricular topic, combining elements of English, mathematics, science and geography, and presenting opportunities in music, art, drama and other subjects.

There are five aspects to learning about the weather:
1. Observing and recording weather conditions and the effects of these on human activities.
2. Making weather instruments and recording data.
3. Observing seasonal patterns which make for differences in climate.
4. Finding out about weather conditions and patterns around the world.
5. Considering the causes and effects of unusual weather conditions.

Weather studies for key stage 1

The first question in class discussion time is often 'What is the weather like today?'. The answers can be used to prompt pupils to think about daily weather changes, as well as introducing them to an enquiry approach. You could start by focusing upon what a toy bear or other creature is, or should be wearing, to develop observation skills and to remind pupils that they too need to wear clothing which suits the weather. Making a daily weather diary is an ideal activity for encouraging pupils to observe, question and record, and to communicate ideas and

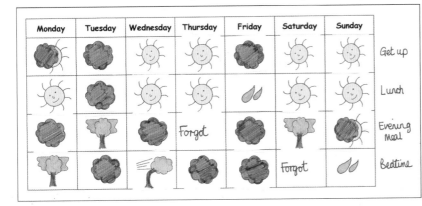

Pupils' work |
Claire McAlpine.

information. Personal diaries and stories are also valuable in helping pupils to select appropriate vocabulary to describe both the quality and quantity of sun, rain and wind. By year 1, pupils should be able to make practical measurements and use charts and graphs to note changes during the day, between days and also weeks, months and eventually years.

Observing and recording the weather on a regular basis from the earliest moments of a child's school life provides an important foundation for understanding hot and cold places. The use of secondary sources – pictures, stories and photographs – illustrates how such things as clothes and vegetation can provide clues to different conditions. Often, story-book pictures illustrate an environment as a whole, providing an opportunity to discuss the impact of the weather in different places. For example, *The Snail and the Whale* (Donaldson, 2003) and *A Balloon for Grandad* (Gray and Ray, 2002) portray different landscapes around the world, from green, well-watered Britain to tropical islands and rocky coasts.

Weather is one of those experiences you can focus upon as it happens. The pupils could take photographs of, for example, the pond frozen over, or an unwatered tub of flowers looking like a desert after a dry holiday, and attach them to their weather record for that day or week. You can use direct evidence of this kind when looking at other places, in particular places which contrast with the home locality. By the end of year 2, pupils should also be able to understand the difference between the seasons and how seasonal changes are reflected in the landscape. They also need to be able to relate consequences to causes and processes. For example, a flooded playground is the consequence of a heavy rainstorm. From observing and recording a local weather incident such as this, pupils could progress to looking at the water cycle.

Stories and pictures

Nursery rhymes, e.g. 'Incey Wincey Spider', 'Dr Foster', 'Rain rain go away', sayings, e.g. 'Red sky at night ...', and traditional stories, e.g. *The North Wind and the Sun* (Wildsmith, 2007) contain a wealth of inspiration for continuing discussions on the daily weather and what it feels like on different days and in different places. As well as considering the way daily weather affects the clothes we wear, pupils can look at what is happening to plants and trees. They could bring in fruits, leaves and flowers, noting how each season has distinctive colours, often related to temperature (e.g. red leaves are a reaction to cold, white blossoms appear as the temperature rises, an abundance of green reflects regular rainfall, yellows reflect harvest and dry grass). The variations from day to day and week to week can be used as starting points to develop a vocabulary and literary repertoire. Gradually, repetition and change will become apparent.

Photo | *Anna Grandfield.*

Year 1

Observing and talking about a familiar place on a regular basis emphasises the idea that weather changes from day to day. Once a class is settled, more systematic observation and ways of recording can be developed. Take specific

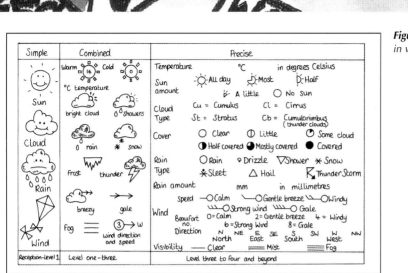

Figure 1 | *Progression in weather symbols.*

weather types, e.g. warm weather, cold weather, wet weather, windy and foggy weather. In the autumn term a late warm spell (Indian summer) can link with holidays past and to come. As the weather is changing, you might get the pupils to devise and use symbols (Figure 1). The symbols can be matched to pictures for each kind of weather. Have ready clothes suitable for dressing a cardboard figure or teddy for each season, to help emphasise that the weather influences what we wear. Pupils' understanding of changes in weather can be assessed by matching the clothes to the symbols at the end of the week.

Start using a thermometer by year 1 – there are specially large ones for infants. Look at the daily newspaper report to see if any other places had the same temperature. In Britain, the north cools down more quickly than the south in autumn, and spring temperatures are correspondingly later in rising. In winter the west is usually warmer than the east and vice versa in summer. These ideas can be developed by checking via e-mail with distant relatives if snowdrops, apple blossom or other flowers are blooming; looking at children in different climates and talking about the weather with other schools via fax or e-mail to send images and drawings; and deciding what to wear in hot and cold places (see Kindersley and Kindersley, 1995). Locate these places on a globe and relate them to the Poles and Equator.

As pupils become more secure in their number work they can begin to make measurements with more precision and ask questions about the element measured. Collect rain in a wide container, then measure it in a tall, narrow container – this maximises the smallest shower! Use consistent, non-standard measures, e.g. one jam jar per day. Decide which way the wind is blowing and use the playground compass or wind vane to name the direction from which the wind is coming (i.e. the opposite direction to which the arrow is pointing towards). Stand with backs to the wind and look at the way hair and clothes are blowing. Most winds are from the west or south-west so the most sheltered place in the playground will be on the east side. Shadows help – they point to the west in the early morning, to the north at midday, and to the east at home time. At first, use terms such as 'in front', 'behind' and so on to describe location, then casually introduce the four compass points. Practise location language to describe the wettest, driest, hottest and coldest places at school, locally, and in the world.

We experience the elements, such as sun and wind, with some or all of our senses and react to them in different ways: snow and frost are bright, cold and crunchy, and snow crystals make patterns. The following questions can be used to direct pupils' learning about the various elements:

Primary Geography Handbook

Photo | Stephen Scoffham.

Rain and snow

- Why do we protect ourselves (and plants and buildings) from rain and snow?
- What is waterproof, and what waterproof materials are there?
- What happens to rain after it has fallen? Compare trays of sand/soil, one covered with plastic to represent tarmac.
- What happens to puddles? Watch what happens to water in a saucer placed on a sunny window sill.
- Why are roofs often different shapes in wet/dry places? Look at sloping and flat roofs.

Wind

- In what ways is the wind useful? Can it push things - us, sails, boats, mills? Make a toy windmill.
- What does wind do to litter in the streets?
- In what ways is the wind harmful?

Sun and shelter

- What is shelter? Use a terrarium and a box model to consider the differences between greenhouses and ordinary houses.
- Why do we wear hats and sun cream?
- How do animals and plants adapt to the sun and heat?

Elements
breeze, clouds, fog, frost, gale, hail, ice, lightning, mist, rain, raindrops, snow, sun, thunder, wind.

Seasons
Summer: boiling, bright, calm, cloudless, downpours, drought, dry, fresh, hot, humid, light, pouring, shine, showers, storms, sunny, warm
Winter: chilly, cold, cool, crystals, dull, floods, foggy, freezing, frosty, gales, overcast, rainy, severe, snowy
Spring and *Autumn*: changeable, damp, dew, drizzling, frosty, gentle, mild, puddle, spell, spitting, splash, strong

Terms
anemometer, chart, diary, direction, gauge, heat, moisture, period, polar, rainfall, record, rose, season, shade, shelter, sock, symbol, temperate, temperature, thermometer, tropical, vane, weather, wind

Sayings
bitter wind, cats and dogs, crunchy snow, dawn, dusk, mackerel skies, mares tails, rainbow, squalls, thunderbolt

Year 2

In year 2 you might develop a seasonal topic each term – these lend themselves to cross-curricular work and can be revisited with increasing detail and complexity according to the development of the class. Figure 2 indicates the kind of vocabulary needed and possible by the end of year 2. A weather word book or weather word bank could be compiled using computer software.

Figure 2 | Weather vocabulary appropriate for the end of year 2.

Level	Rain	Temperature	Wind	Air pressure
1/2	Collect in wide bowls, measure in narrow, tall jars, one per day.	Thermometers should all be alcohol filled. Giant ones make reading easy and develop good recording habits.	Use home-made wind vanes showing four compass points, and wind speed indicators which give higher readings the stronger the wind.	
3	Collect in a straight-sided, level-bottomed jar with a scale in millimetres facing inwards. Record the reading in mm each day at the same time.	Maximum-minimum thermometers (from good hardware stores or garden centres) show temperature is an ongoing change.	Hand held anemometers and ventimeters (more robust) measure wind speed. The best of three readings should be recorded.	Use a sensitive home-made barometer with a scale graduated between high and low pressure.
4	Collect in a jar placed inside a cylinder sunk into the ground (the cylinder, e.g. tall coffee tin, acts as a shield for the rain collection jar). The rain is collected via a 12.5cm diameter funnel resting on the top of the jar and measured in a standard science measuring cylinder, as with official gauges.	Wet and dry bulb thermometers allow humidity to be measured – the more humid the air the more equal the readings, and the more uncomfortable the air! Cheap thermometers/hygrometers from garden centres give similar results.	Anemometers can be connected to a digital recorder for constant readings. Link wind speed readings, taken at the same time as other observations, to the eight points of the compass and the Beaufort Scale (Figure 4). Record on a wind rose.	Use an aneroid (banjo) barometer and link the readings to Radio 4 shipping forecasts. The concept of rising and falling pressure becomes interesting when considering storms at sea and the lines of equal pressure (isobars) shown on weather maps.
graph	Bar *Discontinuous data*	Line *Continuous data*	Circular *Directional data*	Line *Continuous data*

Figure 3 | *Progression in measuring techniques.*

By year 2 pupils can use home-made equipment to make more detailed and regular measurements of the weather to identify rain and temperature patterns (Figure 3). Plan to make reasonably accurate measurements of rain, temperature and wind for at least one week, three if possible, in more than one season.

It is helpful if there is a whole-school policy about the kind of weather symbols the pupils will use, and the progression of those symbols (see Figure 1). You also need to decide on progression in the use of measuring equipment. Finally, agree when detailed weather observations will take place and the audience for whom they will be useful.

Here are some suggestions for activities at this level:

- Link weather observations to weather poems or myths and legends (e.g. 'Persephone and the seasons' from Amery, 1999)
- Make picture maps to show the warmest, wettest and windiest parts of the school grounds
- Role play as weather forecasters
- Use different words to describe moisture, from dew, fog, mist, rainspots, showers, drizzle to downpours, storms and blizzards (thus making links between English and geography)
- Combine and extend weather symbols (see Figure 1)
- Use grid plans of the playground and neighbourhood to locate the best places for sun, shade and shelter, and refer to the four compass points
- Use fair tests to show evaporation from puddles or containers left outside
- Show how steam from a kettle condenses on to a cold surface
- Use two plants, watering one only, to show the importance of rain to growth
- Link wind with clouds – are all the clouds moving in the same direction as the wind (usually this is so)?
- Use a toy windmill to measure winds of different strengths
- Translate the Beaufort Scale into pictures (Figure 4). Pupils could make felt shapes from the pictures, then sew or glue them onto card as part of a display about the weather.

Primary Geography Handbook

Force No	Name	Wind Speed			Effect
		knots	kmph	mph	
0	Calm	0	0	0	Smoke rises straight up
1	Light air	1-3	1-5	1-3	Smoke drifts. Wind vane does not turn
2	Light breeze	4-6	6-11	4-7	Leaves rustle. Wind vane moves
3	Gentle breeze	7-10	12-19	8-12	All leaves move. Flags flutter
4	Moderate breeze	11-16	20-28	13-18	Small branches move. Litter blows
5	Fresh breeze	17-21	29-38	19-24	Waves on water. Small trees sway
6	Strong breeze	22-27	39-49	25-31	Large branches move. Wires whistle
7	Near gale	28-33	50-61	32-38	Trees bend. Umbrellas useless. Walking difficult
8	Gale	34-40	62-74	39-46	Branches break. Difficult to walk any distance
9	Severe gale	41-47	75-88	47-54	Tiles blown off. Fences down
10	Storm	48-55	89-102	55-63	Trees uprooted. Buildings damaged
11	Violent storm	56-63	103-117	64-70	Widespread damage (rare in UK)
12	Hurricane	64+	118+	71+	Devastation to everything (not in UK)

On weather maps a circle is shown with a line pointing in the direction from which the wind has blown. On the line are 'feathers' to show the strength. Half a feather = 1 and a full feather = 2. A gale = 4 feathers

Current UK weather reports give wind speed in miles per hour (mph) (where 1 knot is equivalent to 1.15 mph) or in names on the Beaufort Scale; wind measure scales are in mph, kmph or metres per second.

Figure 4 | *Beaufort Scale.*

Weather studies for key stage 2

Weather studies form a valuable component of geographical work at key stage 2. There are direct links between geographical enquiries and skills, the understanding of places, and work on patterns and processes. This involves learning outside the classroom and extends to understanding weather around the world.

Weather studies at key stage 2 will involve pupils in making more precise observations than at key stage 1 and lead them to analyse evidence and recognise patterns. Pupils can collect evidence in the school grounds, as part of a study of a contrasting locality, and by using their own recording equipment, digital cameras or other electronic media. What is important is that the evidence is integrated with the study of places and other themes such as environmental change.

In the context of locality studies, weather can be identified as an important contributor to the character of a locality and therefore as a characteristic to be used when comparing one place with another – in this place, rain falls mainly in daily thunderstorms throughout the year; in that place, droughts happen for months rather than weeks; and so on. In turn, these characteristics influence human activities and can, in the case of prolonged drought for instance, lead to profound changes.

Weather information about places around the world can be gathered from daily world reports in newspapers and used to help develop pupils' understanding of climate. Newspapers and other news media are also useful as sources of information about world events which may be directly or indirectly related to weather conditions. So, for example, a volcanic eruption or earthquake, while not being directly related to weather, raises questions concerning shelter and warmth for victims of the events. Similarly, pupils' appreciation of seasonal weather patterns could be fostered by asking them to think about what clothes an aid worker might take when visiting places where disasters have occurred.

An insight into the ways in which micro-climate may influence land use in a locality can be developed by considering the best place for a school garden, a wind turbine or solar panels. Further measurements of the amount of rain, sun and wind in different parts of the playground could lead to discussions about the siting of vineyards on south-facing slopes, or ski slopes on north-facing slopes.

Year 3/4
Record for three or four weeks, at the same time each day.
With a young, inexperienced class start with symbols.

Week beginning				Term				
		Mon	Tue	Wed	Thu	Fri	Sat	Sun
Temperature	°C 🌡 °F							
Rainfall								
Cloud cover								
Wind speed								
Direction								

Progress from pictogram graphs to linear
(temperature), bar (rainfall) and circular
(cloud and wind) graphs.

	M	T	W	T	F	S	S
Temperature (°C)							
Rainfall (mm)							

Begin gathering clues for wind speed
from a Beaufort Scale (see Figure 4).

Figure 5 | *Progression and differentiation in recording at key stage 2.*

Years 3 and 4

The lower junior pupil should be able to recognise that weather not only changes from day to day but also during each month and year. Combining more precise observations serves to show that sunshine does not always mean high temperatures and that rainy days can be mild – depending upon which way the wind is blowing. You can adapt the daily recording sheet (Figure 5) to take account of these variations as appropriate.

With weather data from around the world available in the daily papers, and on the internet (see below) you can devolve the responsibility for collecting data for several places to 'roving reporters'. In addition, pupils might discuss the different symbols that are used. Weather forecasting involves pupils in thinking about why people in different occupations need to predict the weather. Design technology can be used to make reasonably accurate measuring equipment and science can contribute towards understanding weather phenomena through simple experiments (see Chapter 12 for more ideas on the application of ICT).

Wind

Wind is air moving from one place to another; it brings heat and moisture from the place it has just left. Consequently winds are named after the direction from which they are travelling. The west wind usually brings cool, wet weather to the British Isles, picked up over the Atlantic, often in a series of low pressure systems. The north wind brings cold, clear or stormy conditions from the polar regions regardless of the time of year. Easterly winds bring snow, frost and fog in winter, coming as they do from a continent that is very much colder than our islands. In summer the position is reversed and east winds bring long spells of hot weather and even heat waves in July and August. Sometimes the British Isles are engulfed in warm, humid air – very welcome in winter, unpleasant in summer. This air has originated over the Tropics, in the region of the Azores. One of the reasons Britain's weather is so variable is that warm air from tropical regions is continually mixing with cold Arctic air in our latitudes.

KEY
☼: Sunny
☁ Cloudy
◊ Rain
☐ One day

Add the correct weather symbol each day to the pointer which shows from which direction the wind was blowing.

This record shows that rainy, cloudy days most often came with winds from the south and west.

Figure 6 | *Wind strength and direction (a) a wind rose, (b) a wind vane, and (c) a simple anemometer.*

In teaching about wind it is important to discuss how the source of wind affects its character. Support discussions about television and radio weather reports by looking at the globe to see where the air has originated. Use science experiments to help explain why land and water cool and warm up at different rates. Discover the wind direction by getting pupils to observe the action of dust, litter, leaves or tissue streamers in the playground and record the results on a wind rose (Figure 6). Use the UK map to mark on the wind directions in relation to your school. Do the winds cross land and sea? Could they have become drier before reaching you? Are winds from the west always wet?

Wind speed is a measure of the strength of the wind (see Figure 4). You could make several different wind measurers, such as a yoghurt pot anemometer (Figure 6), and refer to an official ventimeter (school supplies or ship's chandlers) or anemometers (school scientific suppliers) and adjust the scales so that all measurements relate (calibrate). Discuss how wind affects certain people, e.g. pilots, sea captains and athletes. Wind-generated electricity is a topic which has links with 'energy' in science, and raises environmental considerations in relation to siting wind farms in scenic areas.

Rain

Wind brings moisture, usually in the form of rain. Fog and dew may occur when warm humid air meets colder conditions, as when the ground has cooled during the night. Clouds are the result of the same process at higher levels – which is why the tops of mountains are often shrouded in

Total mm divided by number of days recorded or total for each of seven days divided by seven, then sum totals for each week and divide by the number of weeks, e.g. 4 weeks 0 monthly average.

Figure 7 | *Measuring and recording rain.*

Language	Description	Type and abbreviation		Height	Weather
Wispy, mares' tails, curls	High streaks fanning out ahead	Cirrus	Ci	High	Often more wind; usually storms after good weather
Sheet, layers, blanket	Blanket of low grey cloud which can reach the ground	Stratus	St	Low to high	Drizzle, fog which can become steady, wet, rain
Billowy, fluffy, heaps	White, flat-bottomed clouds which look like cotton wool	Cumulus	Cu	Low	Small – fair and sunny Large – showers
Dark, towers, castles	Large, dark clouds from ground to the highest level	Nimbostratus	Ns	Medium	Heavy rain or snow
Dark base, billowy towers	Marked, dark base which gets darker as rest of white cloud billows up to anvil shape	Cumulo-nimbus	Cb	Low to high	Very heavy showers with hail, thunder, lightning. Move away at speed

Figure 8 | Cloud characteristics.

mist, while valleys are clear and sunlit. Condensation on a glass of iced water illustrates the formation of dew and fog, and clouds can be created by blocking a glass jar containing hot water with an ice cube. The water vapour from rising, warm, moist air cools to form a cloud under the ice.

Rain falls when the droplets of condensed moisture are large and heavy enough to drop through the rising air beneath the cloud. They can be small (drizzle) or as large as hailstones. All the different forms of 'rain', including snow, are known as precipitation.

Measuring rain can be frustrating and disappointing – even when it rains heavily only a small amount will collect in a gauge (Figure 7). This is why the longer the observation period the more probable it is that significant data will be collected. Gauges can be positioned at contrasting sites round the school (such as under trees, at the foot of walls sheltered from rain-bearing westerly winds, in a puddle area, in a 'dry' area) and the results noted, together with possible explanations. You could extend the work by checking on the accuracy of national forecasts and putting up a display of photographs about droughts and floods at home and abroad.

Clouds

The appearance of clouds, and the patterns they make, are good indicators of weather to come and there is a rich vocabulary associated with their description (Figure 8). When recording cloud types and cloud cover it is important to look through the same window each day and to estimate the cover either as quarters or eighths (oktas). If you are learning about cloud types, choose a week when low pressure systems or 'unsettled weather' are forecast and make it an end-of-morning or afternoon game. Connect cloud observations with forecasting. Can pupils forecast the afternoon weather from the morning observations?

Ask questions:

■ What was the highest temperature you recorded?

■ When did this occur? Where?

■ What was the lowest temperature?

■ How much cloud cover was there?

■ What was the range of temperature?

Figure 9 | Measuring and recording temperature.

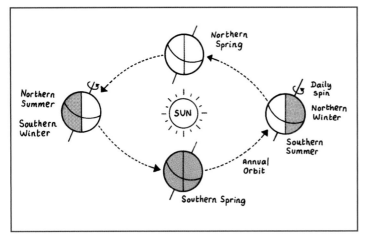

Figure 10 | *What causes the seasons? Demonstrate the movement of the Earth round the sun with a central light and small globe on its stand (this keeps the Earth's tilt).*

Temperature

When studying 'hot places' and 'cold places' it is important that pupils understand that temperature varies in these places both between day and night, and between seasons. For example, even in hot deserts the soaring heat of the daytime may be replaced with sub-zero temperatures by the end of the night, and polar regions are sometimes as hot by day in the summer months as places much nearer the Equator.

Some specialist thermometers record temperature variations over time. For example, maximum-minimum thermometers 'save' the lowest and highest temperatures (Figure 9) and are used regularly by gardeners to monitor changes between night and day temperatures. Using these thermometers will help pupils to understand why 'tender' plants from Mediterranean areas, such as geraniums and busy lizzies (Impatiens), have to be kept indoors until late May or June when all danger of night frost is past. The link between overnight temperatures and cloud cover can also be explored. Was there a blanket of cloud preventing the loss of warm air, or could the stars be seen? Is there a link between morning hoar frost or heavy dew and night-time weather?

Elements and terms
air masses, anticyclone, atmosphere, atmospheric pressure, cloud names, cold front, condensation, continental air, cyclone, depression, drought, evaporation, high pressure, humidity, insolation, isobar, isohyet, isoline, isotherm, knot, latitude, longitude, low pressure, maritime air, mass, maximum and minimum temperature, precipitation, prevailing wind, radiation, saturation, season, solstice, storm, storm tracks, sun hours, synoptic chart, tornado, tropics of Cancer and Capricorn, transpiration, tropical storm, tropical air, visibility, warm front, wind chill

Instruments and scales
Anemometer, aneroid barometer, Beaufort wind scale, maximum and minimum thermometer, ventimeter

Climates
Arid, equatorial, desert, maritime, Mediterranean, monsoon, mountain, polar, temperate, tropical

Figure 11 | *Vocabulary appropriate for the end of year 6.*

Years 5 and 6
Weather and climate

The conditions that prevail at a particular moment in a particular place make up its weather. The pattern of weather over a period of time is known as the climate. In general, the distance from the Equator is the key factor in determining climate, along with proximity to open water and the influence of the Earth's tilt and orbit (Figure 10). Upper juniors should be introduced to some of the different climates around the world, and make comparisons between their own locality and other places using appropriate geographical vocabulary (Figure 11). If pupils have regularly observed and recorded the weather earlier in their school careers they will be in a good position to undertake this work. A good school atlas will be an invaluable resource for extending the study and contains sample graphs for rainfall and temperature in representative locations around the world. By studying these, pupils can identify the hottest, wettest, coldest and driest months. You may also be able to obtain a satellite view of the world which shows the major areas of natural vegetation and discuss how these are related to climate conditions.

Pupils need to understand that climate statistics are based on average weather conditions. Use your own records to demonstrate average temperatures and rainfall for a week, or month

Figure 12 | *Sutton-on-Sea Primary School's weather web pages.*

if possible. You may also be able to gather information on precipitation and temperature for your region for a whole year (remember to archive on memory stick or CD). Daily newspapers provide weather data from around the world. Finding out about climate change from the internet could be a research exercise, either in class or for homework. Sometimes the hottest, wettest and other extreme readings are not obvious. Make a climate graph for your own locality, and if possible, for contrasting localities that you have studied. Use maths time to revise averages.

You might invite individual pupils to act as foreign correspondents, reporting back on weather conditions in their part of the world. This works particularly well if their locality or its region is prone to extreme conditions, such as tropical storms (hurricanes), monsoon flooding, severe snowfall or long drought. The reports could also refer to the lack of spring and autumn in tropical lands, and the twelve-hour day. In these areas, the seasons are identified by differences in the amount of rainfall rather than by fluctuations in temperature, and this – as the climate changes – has important implications for agriculture.

Microclimates

The way weather conditions vary around the school grounds has already been mentioned. Upper juniors can compare at least four sites and relate them to developments such as new seats, raised beds, animal hutches, solar panels or wind turbines. You may be able to broaden the study into the local area and consider possible sites for improvement projects, e.g. a sheltered corner where elderly people can rest, a greenhouse on allotments or a new bus shelter to keep out the wind and rain. The temperature, amount of sun, rainfall, and speed and direction of wind will all have significance. At this level, pupils should be taking accurate readings from instruments and encouraged to be as precise as possible. This will enable you to make comparisons with official and other automatic readings. Connect with school networks, e.g. Sutton-on-Sea Primary School's weather station web pages (Figure 12) are part of an online Montage Project, sponsored by the British Council, for schools around the world. This site has lots of weather-related data available, and it is possible to submit your own data which can be added to a larger weather databank.

Exchanging weather data

Some schools have set up interactive projects to exchange weather data. The GLOBE project alone has over a 1000 school links – mostly in the US but also in Europe and Japan, including over 300 primary schools in the UK. In addition, there are several internet sites which provide webcam pictures or transmit instant weather images.

Many current projects emphasise the core curriculum but incorporate geography in order to establish the significance of place in the worldwide pattern of weather and climate. This

Photo | *Tina Horler.*

means that the enquiry process becomes an important tool. For instance, pupils might ask the following questions when considering places for a holiday: How hot is it? Shall I need warm clothing for the evening? Is it likely to rain? Will the rain be heavy? Will it be windy? What games are played there? To answer these questions, pupils can visit a number of weather information sites such as BBC, CNN and Yahoo. Compare the information available from each – some are more comprehensive and child-friendly than others.

This chapter has emphasised ways of observing and recording the weather. When it comes to offering explanations for weather phenomena, primary school pupils often run into difficulties and end up giving confused and contradictory answers. In recent years there has been some fascinating research into children's ideas. One of the most comprehensive reviews is presented by Henriques (2000) whose findings are summarised in Figure 13. There are plenty of issues here which deserve further research. As a teacher it is important to realise that the best way to challenge misconceptions is through rigorous attention to detail when observing, recording and analysing weather data from the earliest age. Some misconceptions will, however, only be overcome as pupils mature.

Keeping records for the future

Weather studies in the primary school offer many opportunities for developing and using skills in recording and observation. In addition, they encourage pupils to think about the reasons behind some of the similarities and differences between areas around the world, and to empathise with those whose lives are dependent on or directly affected by weather conditions. Gathering weather data on its own could be an arid activity – geographers help to give life to the data. Both people and nature have learnt to survive in the hottest, coldest, wettest and driest places in the world – and all places in between. The climates which are found in these areas have in turn had no small part in developing the cultures created by people who live there. In order to be good global citizens and to understand the 'rules' of sustainability young children need to appreciate the inconstancy of the one medium, weather, which controls the source of the most constant human need – water.

By keeping and maintaining weather records over long periods pupils are part of a long and valuable tradition of weather watching that goes back at least as far as ancient Roman and Greek times. While the increased detail and accuracy of modern weather observation has obvious benefits for us all, even simple methods, such as those we use in our schools, still enable us to make useful predictions. And our records, which may span many years or decades, are things of value which in future years will provide a rich source of information about past patterns and changes.

Figure 13 | *Correcting common weather misconceptions. After Henriques, 2000.*

Weather phenomena	Children's misconceptions	Comment
Water cycle – Water evaporates from land and sea, the water vapour condenses to form clouds from which rain falls back to Earth, runs down slopes and flows into rivers and seas.	Children sometimes have an incomplete notion of the water cycle.	Children understand the concept of freezing before the more complex notions of evaporation and condensation.
Transpiration – Plants also contribute water to the atmosphere via transpiration.	Water only gets evaporated from the ocean or lakes.	Possible source: poor textbook, poster and media diagrams which only show evaporation from the ocean.
Clouds – Clouds are created when water vapour condenses onto dust or other particles in the air.	Clouds are made of smoke, cotton-wool and so forth. Clouds (and rain) are made by God. Clouds come from somewhere above the sky.	Some of these explanations are found in myths and legends.
Cloud types – A visible cloud is primarily tiny water droplets and/or tiny ice crystals; it is not water vapour.	Empty clouds are refilled by the sea.	Observe and discuss different cloud forms – cirrus, cumulus and stratus.
Wind – Winds are produced by the uneven heating of the Earth's surface.	Clouds block wind and slow it down. Low temperatures produce fast winds. Winds are caused by the spinning of the Earth.	All of these false associations can be disputed with observations in different seasons and referring to records.
Why clouds move – Clouds move when wind blows them.	Clouds move when we move. We walk and the clouds move with us.	Observe clouds move in the playground and local area.
Rain – Rain begins to fall when water drops in the cloud are too heavy to remain airborne.	Rain comes from holes in the cloud. Rain comes from clouds melting. Rain occurs when clouds are shaken. Rain occurs when clouds collide.	Demonstrate the effects of condensation using a fine net suspended over a kettle. Watch how the drops grow larger and eventually fall off.
Frost – Frost forms when water vapour comes into contact with very cold surfaces. The water vapour freezes directly instead of condensing into a liquid first.	Frost falls from the sky. Frost is frozen dew.	Use the minimum thermometer to measure night temperatutes. Discuss how freezers ice up when the door is left open!
Floods – Flooding occurs when there is more water than the ground or rivers can accommodate.	Flooding only occurs along rivers when the snow melts in the spring. Flooding only occurs after heavy rainfall.	Half truths; in towns the 'ground' can be blocked drains; in winter the ground can be frozen.
Droughts – Droughts occur when the normal rainfall fails to occur causing distress to plants and creatures.	Droughts only happen in deserts. Droughts are caused by God.	A drought is a disruption to an established pattern. Deserts are naturally arid and thus do not suffer from droughts.

Figure 14 |
Photographs to prompt children's views on climate change.
Photos | *Drax Power Station, Yorkshire: Bryan Ledgard.
All other images are licence free.*

Climate change and global warming

Global warming is an overall rise in the temperature of the earth, observable in the upper atmosphere, which has been noticeably increasing since the early 20th century. This temperature change has stimulated climate change around the world.

We know from evidence in ice cores, tree rings, sediments and rocks that there have been climate changes in the past. Britain has been variously a tropical swamp, a hot, barren desert with salt lakes, and – more than once – covered with ice. In the UK, the last ten thousand years are thought to be a warm spell between ice ages. But during this time human activity – clearing forest for agriculture, and burning wood, coal and oil to create energy for homes, transport and industry – has increasingly changed the natural world. These changes are taking place in every country and every continent and involve every section of society. As a result levels of carbon dioxide, water vapour, methane and nitrous oxide (the 'greenhouse gases') have increased, trapping solar radiation and leading to increasing temperatures around the world. In turn this has caused changes in the circulation of warm and cold air and ocean currents such as the Atlantic Gulf Stream and the Pacific El Niño. It has also led to more severe, and less predictable, weather. Belatedly, governments around the world are attempting to reduce greenhouse gas emissions and slow down climate change.

Children need to know about climate change and its impact on the global environment. However you should introduce this topic sensitively and recognise that it may upset some pupils. Consider solutions, as well as problems, so that children are not left feeling powerless. Good practice involves teaching in a spirit of optimism and emphasising the value of creative collaboration. One approach is to observe and collect weather data from your own locality and to gather information about other places from stories and news reports. Appreciating the wonder of the weather and the way that it changes will engage children emotionally. Remember, the weather is one of the child's first introductions to reality and it can connect them to other people and places. Your efforts to make a sustainable school and community will provide further ideas and illustrate the power of positive action. Keeping weather records from year to year will provide evidence of whether spring really is coming earlier each year. This might be one way to challenge climate change sceptics!

References and further reading

Ballin, B. (2008) 'www.climatechange.help', *Primary Geographer*, 67, pp. 34-35.

Bird, S. and Cooper, P. (2006) 'Microclimate enquiry and fieldwork', *Primary Geographer*, 59, pp. 26-27.

Heller, J., McManners, J. and Owens, P. (2006) 'Sustainability in action: leading by example on beating climate change', *Primary Geographer*, 61, pp. 28-29.

Henriques, L. (2000) 'Children's misconceptions about the weather: a review of the literature', available at *www.csulb.edu/~lhenriqu/NARST2000.htm* (accessed 10 March 2010).

Humphries, S. and Rowe, S. (2004) 'The garden: our laboratory', *Primary Geographer*, 55, pp. 4-7.

Kempster, E. and Witt, S. (2009) 'Make my future sustainable! Part 1: Children's ideas on climate change', *Primary Geographer*, 70, pp. 16-17.

Murray, D. (2006) 'CLIMATE: Serious conservation', *Primary Geographer*, 59, pp. 28-29.

Whitehouse, A. (2008) 'Weather around the world', *Primary Geographer*, 65, pp. 37-38.

Picture books

Aardema, V. and Vidal, B. (1992) *Bringing the Rain to Kapiti Plain*. London: Penguin.

Abholt, L. and Robins, A. (2008) *Eco-wolf and the Three Pigs*. London: Orchard Books.

Amery, H. (1999) *Usborne Greek Myths for Young Children*. London: Usborne Books.

Bradman, T. (2009) *Under the Weather: Stories about climate change*. London: Frances Lincoln.

Burningham, J. (1999) *Cloudland*. London: Random House.

Butterworth, N. (2003) *After the Storm*. London: Harper Collins.

Donaldson, J. (2003) *The Snail and the Whale*. London: Macmillan.

Gray, N. and Ray, J. (2002) *A Balloon for Grandad*. London: Orchard Books.

Kindersley, B. and Kindersley, A. (1995) *Children just like me*. London: Dorsley Kindersley/UNICEF.

Hickman, L. (2009) *Will Jellyfish Rule the World?* London: Puffin.

Hughes, S. (2002) *Alfie's Weather*. London: Red Fox.

Morch, R. and Hadow, P. (2007) *Who Will Save Us?* Newton Abbott: Rebecca Morch Publishing Ltd.

Wildsmith, B. (2007) *The North Wind and the Sun*. Oxford: OUP.

Websites

BBC weather *www.bbc.co.uk/news/weather*

CNN weather *www.cnn.com/weather*

GLOBE *www.globe.org.uk*

Meteorological Office *www.metoffice.gov.uk/climatechange/guide/effects/high-end.html*

UK Weather Cams *www.ukweathercams.co.uk*

Royal Meteorological Society *http://www.rmets.org/activities/schools/index.php*

Woodland Trust Climate Watch *www.naturedetectives.org.uk*

West Midlands Net *www.climatechange.wmnet.org.uk*

CHAPTER COVERAGE:
ENQUIRIES • FIELDWORK • GAMES/PLAY • LITERACY/STORIES • PROGRESSION • QUESTIONS • VOCABULARY

Rivers, coasts and the landscape

The delight all children have in playing by the water's edge provides an excellent starting point for teachers when planning work on physical geography. Remembering our own explorations as children can be a powerful planning tool for it is surely in our pupils' best interests that we begin by viewing the features we want them to investigate through their freshly enquiring eyes, and not our own.

The good news is that this may well be less difficult for a 'non-specialist' than it is for a more experienced 'geographer'. It is all too easy for the latter to slip into using specialist terminology and to start presenting pupils with complex ideas. Someone for whom the work is new, on the other hand, may be able to gauge the pupils' starting points more aptly, and share in any subsequent enquiry more sincerely. It is also comforting to non-specialists to realise that at this early stage using the enquiry process itself is at least as important as the knowledge gained from it.

Geography as a subject is essentially investigative. Physical geography is less a series of facts to be learned than a series of questions about the processes that shape the environment. This is recognised in the national curriculum, which advocates direct experience, practical work, exploration and investigation. Equally the Primary National Strategy stresses the importance of pupil involvement in creatively planned activities. Fortunately all these requirements can be best served by fieldwork, especially when children are encouraged to participate in the planning of the investigation using their own enquiry questions (see pages 256-257), and the promise of such an activity immediately raises the profile of geography in the eyes of children and parents!

Like all outdoor activity, investigation of the physical environment needs careful planning. Identifying opportunities for local fieldwork can be an excellent way of providing enjoyable continuing professional development for colleagues and building the confidence of non-specialists. Teachers planning fieldwork should take account of the risk assessment and adult-child ratio stipulations of their school and LA. You also need to investigate local weather reports, tide tables, river levels or upland walking conditions (see websites, page 259), depending on the location.

This chapter is intended to support work relating to water in the landscape, especially in riverside and coastal locations, and offers starting points and activities for your own schemes of work. It does not set out to promote physical geography as a separate subject, but illustrates how physical features and processes are part of a holistic understanding of places involving other subjects and perspectives. By offering a range of possibilities loosely linked to age groups, this chapter seeks to encourage teachers to create their own field-based units of work.

It is also acknowledged that for financial reasons school-based teaching will need to supplement, and sometimes even replace, field experiences. Some of the suggestions, especially for key stage 1, are therefore based within and around the school grounds. It is in key stage 2 that more focused studies of other landscapes become appropriate and can be accomplished by developing work around one or two accessible field locations. An alternative is to build the work into a local or contrasting locality study, which should consider physical as well as human characteristics. The key to both curricular and financial economy appears to lie in making some judicious choices at whole-school planning level to ensure progression through well-designed holistic place studies. In turn, this whole-school effort would underpin specific school self evaluation (SEF) data.

Earliest encounters with the physical world

Where the school locality includes a river or stream there will be opportunities for site visits where very young pupils can talk about what they see and begin to think about the qualities of flowing water. You might also encourage them to think about how people make use of local rivers and why valleys are important routeways. Teachers sometimes take young pupils to the seaside as part of an integrated history/geography project. Using geographical terms such as beach, waves, cliffs, caves, dunes, and so forth falls naturally into such work while sand play, both in school and on the beach, offers many opportunities for early ideas about physical processes to be developed in ways accessible to the young child. There are also some excellent resources which support this work, such as the Wildgoose playmats (*www.wgoose.co.uk*). Shared literacy texts, if carefully chosen, can also be a great asset in building early physical concepts. For example, the big book *Waves* (Stott-Thornton, 2001) gives an excellent account of depositional wave action in the simplest of terms, while *Out and About* (Hughes, 1998) describes the full gamut of outdoor features and weather conditions and provides an endless source of geographical discussion points. Other relevant story books include *Webster's Walk* (Dow, 2001), which describes how a drought affects some ducks, and *Windy Weather* (Milbourne, 2007) one of a series about weather conditions. Remember too that there are now YouTube videos to go with classic tales, like *Cloudy with a Chance of Meatballs* (Barrett, 1978) which can give children great enjoyment and inspiration. Finally, *The River* (Pollard, 2003) is a descriptive account of a river from source to mouth, chronicling changes to both physical and human features encountered on the journey downstream.

There are also practical ways in which early understandings about water processes can be addressed to the benefit of both science and geography. Most children are aware that it is un-comfortable to walk in the rain and that we need special clothing to keep dry. Beginning with the question 'How does waterproof clothing work?' pupils can explore the properties of waterproof materials, and see how the shape of the surface directs water into creases and down slopes. This could lead to a detailed study of other items such as a sou'wester-style hat (whose shape directs water to flow down the back of the wearer), an umbrella whose spokes drip well away from the user, and plants whose leaves direct the water to drip onto the root base. Young pupils might even be encouraged to study their own faces and think about how the eyebrows form a barrier which directs water around the eyes, or how water flows over their body in the shower. It is a only short step from here to understanding the patterns created by flowing water on the uneven surface of a landscape. In activities like these geography offers a natural focus for creative and cross-curricular approaches to the curriculum.

Learning about coasts

The study of coastal areas in key stages 1 and 2 is an excellent way of introducing pupils to physical processes at work in the landscape. The 4425km of coastline around England and Wales offers a great variety of scenery and habitats, many of which have legal protection. Over half of all counties have varied coastlines within fairly easy reach which schools can use in their fieldwork studies. Even if your school is inland, the seashore makes an excellent contrasting locality and will offer opportunities for work across the whole range of the national curriculum.

It is difficult to conceive of any area which bears more witness to human activities which have changed or destroyed or improved the environment than the British coastline. Its popularity, and use for leisure purposes, places it at the interface of an environmental conflict between demand for an increasing range of recreational facilities on the one hand, and a desire for the conservation of the natural environment on the other.

Beaches are constantly changing owing to the sudden effects of storms and periodic high tides. We need to be aware of this in undertaking pre-visit preparations. It may be more appropriate to consider the broad possibilities offered by the site rather than details which may change before the visit. Making a video to use later can be a useful addition to classroom resources. In particular it will be important to check tide timetables. Check the internet or contact the local coastguard for tide tables and exact times well in advance. Many of the ideas which follow focus on opportunities for lower primary classes. While it is envisaged that the work may well be part of a wider history/literacy/geography package the aim here is to support only the physical geography element with which teachers are often less familiar.

Beach play

For the youngest pupils the difference between the beach and other places they know will revolve around the different play opportunities it offers. Beach play is multi-sensory. It involves the sounds of wind, waves and seabirds; the touch of spray on the cheeks, of fine and sharp sand, of smooth pebbles, silky feathers and slippery, slimy rocks; the taste of salt on the lips; the smell of drying seaweed and fish; and innumerable new sights from sparkling water to distant ships. A short period of free play on arrival is valuable. First it allows for acclimatisation and enables the children to develop a 'sense of place'. It also gives the teacher a valuable opportunity for observing individuals at play, informing assessment of their needs, and it provides pupils with the evidence to support discussion of the key question 'What is this place like?'.

Beaches are potentially dangerous because natural sound levels are high and sudden warnings are difficult to hear. You need to set clear boundaries for pupils and establish clear rules of behaviour before setting out. For example, you might use a loud whistle or bell to tell the pupils to stop whatever they are doing and gather together. A high proportion of additional adult help is required on outdoor visits and at the free-play stage it helps if these assistants form a boundary cordon rather than being involved with the play itself. Then it really is free play and the starting points it provides are securely within the pupils' remit. It need not take long; five to ten minutes is enough.

It helps to have a large tray ready to receive the objects that pupils will inevitably bring to you and which might form the focus of initial discussions. It is also worth joining hands in a long line along the shore to stare at the sea, listen to the sound of the waves and observe the action they have on the beach. You might ask pupils to close their eyes so they can concentrate on all the different sounds they can hear and the sensation of the breeze as it blows on their faces. There is plenty to talk about here.

An excellent pre-visit preparation to enhance work with any age group is to make a short video of the waves. This will be most useful if it includes mainly close-up shots, with the sea breaking over rocks as well as on sand and pebbles, and if it shows the waves operating in contrasting weather conditions. Since physical geography particularly involves considering the power of the sea, it is worth considering an out-of-season visit, especially with older pupils, provided that there is some nearby indoor accommodation to allow them, and you, to thaw out.

Photo |
Lois Gunby.

Building in sand

Sand is the feature of a beach which looms largest in children's imaginations and this will form the chief raw material of their play. Direct experience of sand, its qualities and physical properties, may also be gained by building sandcastles. Laying out the intended plan of the castle as a sand map is a useful way of practising simple cartographic skills, and photographs taken from different compass directions and looking down on the structure will demonstrate the basic idea of aerial views in a context which has personal significance for pupils.

With careful thought sand-castle building can contribute to pupils' conceptual development in other ways. For example, if you challenge them to build the walls as high as possible they will have to grapple with the way loose materials find their own angle of rest. As soon as the castle

How waves shape the coast

The principal agent shaping the coast is the sea, which reaches the shore as a never-ending series of waves of varying size, strength and frequency. Some waves are generated by storms. Known as 'swell waves' these generally diminish the further they get from the storm, as do the waves created by a passing boat. Most waves, however, are caused by the frictional drag of wind which disturbs the surface of the water as it blows. The size of these 'sea waves' depends on both the strength of the wind and the length of time (or distance) it has blown over that particular body of water. Hence waves reaching the west coast of Ireland which have had an uninterrupted passage across the Atlantic Ocean will be bigger and stronger than waves generated by the same wind on the west coast of Wales where the wind has only crossed the Irish Sea. This uninterrupted distance is known as the 'fetch' of the waves. It explains why spectacular feats of surfing can take place on some coasts, such as Bondi beach in Australia, even in good summer weather conditions.

Major exceptions to these two general types of wave include 'tsunamis', created by undersea earthquakes, and the tidal waves caused by suction of the sea into the intense low pressure of the eye of a hurricane as it comes ashore. Fortunately, we are most unlikely to meet either of these on our local beach!

The movement of waves is interesting, for while the eye tells us the water is moving forward, logically this cannot be so or the waves would keep on moving up the beach. Bear in mind they are still moving forward when the tide is going out. It is in fact the wave form that is moving, not the body of water. If we could track a single particle of water within that wave form we would find that it moves in a circular path, as shown in Figure 2. A cork or ball thrown out into the sea will bob up and down rather than travel directly towards the shore. We can demonstrate this general idea to children with a skipping rope. An up and down movement of the arm will create waves which progress laterally along the rope. A ribbon or bobbin fixed to the rope will emphasise that while the wave form moves forward, the marker bobs up and down, staying in roughly the same position.

Waves can be either constructive or destructive. Constructive waves occur in calm weather, are low in height and have a long wavelength. When they break, the energy dissipates quickly and the backwash is weak. This means that such waves tend to add new material to a beach. Destructive waves, by contrast, are stronger and larger. They are commonest in storm conditions and have a powerful backwash which can cause considerable erosion. They tend to attack headlands where the coast slopes more steeply.

Figure 1 | *Knowing about the effects of waves and how beaches are formed can help you draw pupils' attention to appropriate enquiries.*

walls become too steep then catastrophe in the form of miniature landslides will strike. This activity not only illustrates the properties of materials it also provides first-hand experience of the nature of slopes. For older pupils it is but a short step from here to considering the instability of local cliffs or the fact that sand dunes exhibit constant slope angles. This kind of open-ended activity focuses on processes rather than facts and stimulates progressive levels of thinking from infants or juniors. Whether we regard ourselves as 'geographers' or not, we can all have the confidence to raise and answer questions.

It can be particularly exciting to construct castles so close to the advancing sea that they will be attacked in the course of the beach visit. Guessing how much and which part of the castle will disappear next leads to penetrating observation and hence detailed experience of the erosion process, enhanced by emotional involvement. Allowing the children to battle in vain to save the structure with ramparts and ditches can only add to their eventual understanding of the inevitability of the sea's destructive power and makes a particularly good video sequence. This theme is explored for very young pupils in *Where is Barnaby's castle?* (Lewis, 2002) and *Barnaby Bear at the Seaside* (Jackson, 2001).

The effect of the waves

Understanding the basic effects of wave action (Figure 1) opens up another spectrum of options which we can match to the age and interest of pupils. Young children may enjoy simulating the action of constructive and destructive waves in a line dance using gentle gathering and pushing movements for the constructive waves and bolder plunging movements for destructive breakers. I have found poems about the sea invaluable with children of all ages for drawing attention to contrasting weather conditions and the effects of the waves. Maybe you already have a favourite poem of your own. If not, this might be the just the right moment to do some research!

On page 157 is another poem inspired by coastal fieldwork. This young poet's vision of people and the sea both eating rock at the seaside is a remarkable feat of lateral thinking of the kind that might identify her as a future primary teacher!

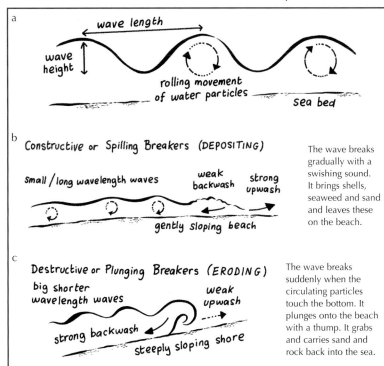

The wave breaks gradually with a swishing sound. It brings shells, seaweed and sand and leaves these on the beach.

The wave breaks suddenly when the circulating particles touch the bottom. It plunges onto the beach with a thump. It grabs and carries sand and rock back into the sea.

Figure 2 | The basic differences between wave type help to explain deposition and erosion.

You can sample beach materials using metre (or smaller) sampling squares. It is best if these have an internal grid of string or wire so that items can be taken systematically, for example at each intersection. This introduces the idea of scientific sampling and helps pupils to understand why it is unsatisfactory just to pick up attractive pebbles. If sampling grids are not available use plastic hoops instead. Being fairly robust these can be thrown across the beach to achieve something approaching a random sample. In examining pebbles and other items questions to consider include:

- Is the material natural or manufactured?
- Are all the pebbles from the same kind of rock?
- What are the similarities and differences?
- How do shapes, sizes, weights and colours compare?
- What might be the reasons for the similarities and differences?
- Where may the pebbles have come from?

Photo |
John Halocha.

The nature of these investigations and the level to which they can proceed will relate not only to the age and experience of the pupils but also to their mathematical ability, and there are fertile opportunities here for developing differentiated follow-up activities. It is not necessary to be an expert geologist to understand this kind of work. Developing observation and enquiry skills are the chief aim. However, it is helpful to use a good pictorial earth science guide. The Earth Galleries at the Natural History Museum in South Kensington have an excellent range of publications and are well worth visiting if you can.

Learning about rivers

Key stage 1

The wet sand tray is a good place to begin early work on rivers. Hilly landscapes can easily be shaped by hand, and valleys identified (Figure 3). It is quite difficult to demonstrate the flow of water simply by sprinkling 'rain' from a watering can, because the loose sand is so porous. But after trying this to show that water sinks into some surfaces, the' landscape' can be waterproofed with thin polythene film and the experiment repeated. A sprinkling of dry sand over the polythene should show that when streams develop they are capable of carrying loose material away and depositing it somewhere else. Ponds or lakes can be engineered too. Teachers of older infant classes, who might not have a sand tray on hand, will find a length of

plastic guttering and a selection of sands and gravel of different grain sizes useful for creating investigations into water flow and its capacity to move things (Figure 4).

River work might equally well begin from a study of water and how it moves around the school. Whether your school has a flat or sloping roof there will be some system for transferring rainwater to the ground. Leaky flat roofs, a scourge of many modern school buildings, can even become a temporary asset, giving

Figure 3 | *Creating a river landscape in a wet sand tray.*
Photo | John Halocha.

Pile a variety of pebbles, gravel, sand, soil, etc. at upper end of trough then watch how water moves the sediment and sorts it

Gentle trickle of water

2m length of plastic guttering sloped gently from tap to trough

Low trough to collect water and sediment

Figure 4 | *Guttering is used to show how running water can move things.*

Overfill a puddle to see which way the water flows

Cover the freshwater drain to watch how water flows on the playground

Find out where the water goes

Figure 5 | *Where water goes in the playground.*

chalk 'contour' lines

3.00 pm   2.40 pm   2.20 pm   2.00 pm

draw round drying up puddles at intervals to discover how fast they evaporate

Figure 6 | *How a disappearing puddle can be used to demonstrate evaporation and simple contour patterns.*

a good focal point for discussion of how surface water finds its way down. Models of buildings with flat, sloping and arched roofs could be undertaken as a technology project and evaluated for their effectiveness in shedding water. A sloping roof amply demonstrates the idea of a watershed, in this case the roof ridge, which separates the flow on one side of the roof from that on the other. In exactly the same way, a ridge of high ground in a real landscape, known as a 'watershed', directs water down into one river system or another.

There are many ways of illustrating the idea of a river system for young children. You could start by getting them to draw a simple pictorial diagram to show the progress of water via gutters and drain-pipes to the ground in your own school. If you can direct a flow of fresh water from a drainpipe (or any other source) onto the surface of the play-ground, pupils can watch what happens if there is no organised drainage system (Figure 5). Finding an unobstructed path, the stream of water will create a temporary river flowing down to a low point and will possibly meander on the way. It is also interesting to overfill existing puddles and watch where the water goes. Pupils might make detailed observ-ations of puddles forming and

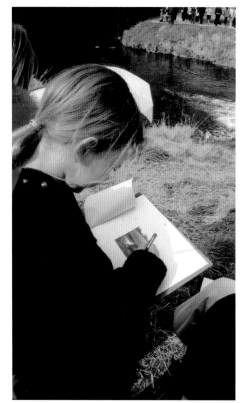

Photo | *John Halocha.*

disappearing and make maps of puddles and the likely courses of excess water in the playground – a place with which they are already very familiar (Figure 6).

If there is a small stream or river in your immediate area an opportunity to observe this will be part of the physical component of your locality study. While young pupils should obviously not be encouraged to throw rubbish into the water they could watch how the current carries a biodegradable float, such as a cauliflower floret, downstream. If the river is liable to flood, the absence of houses near the river or the presence of flood protection barriers might form a good discussion point which illustrates the interaction of people and their environment. The study of an accessible riverside environment, such as a local small park, nature reserve or public footpath, might also form part of the work and provide opportunities for simple visual investigations into how clean the water is, whether people throw rubbish into the river, who uses the riverside and how this environment might be cared for or improved. Some schools have 'adopted' a riverside area and make a real contribution to improving it with local authority help. The selection of books and websites at the end of this chapter offers further support for a range of river activities.

Key stage 2

Running water within the school grounds – in guttering and drains, overflowing from puddles and trickling down slopes, both natural and constructed – provides an initial focus for the study of rivers at key stage 2. Probably the most important single concept in this work is that water flows downhill. This may seem to be too obvious to mention but is critical to any understanding of river systems. Many pupils enter secondary school believing that rivers 'begin' at the coast and flow inland. Perhaps this is because they have seen a tidal river, or have been asked where a river 'rises', or have not fully understood the maps they have come across. The word 'mouth' adds to this confusion; after all, in the limited and personalised experience of primary pupils, things usually do go in via mouths rather than come out!

As well as shaping the physical landscape, rivers also exert powerful influences on human decisions about land use such as where to site a capital city or a chemical plant, where to graze cattle rather than grow crops, which is the best route for a new motorway, or even just where to spend next Sunday afternoon. Rivers are part of the natural water cycle, vital to industry, trade, factories and farming; needed for public water supply and transport; havens for wildlife; attractive for sport and tourism; beautiful, calming and mysteriously appealing, but also dangerously powerful and terrifyingly destructive in times of flood. So, as well as providing bridges across the geography curriculum, river studies also offer convenient routes into other subjects. From this point of view, a collection of picture books, story extracts, video-clips, news bulletins, newspaper extracts, photographs and artists' work in a number of styles will be valuable resources to support your work.

Another key idea is to think of a river as a system with distinctive 'inputs' and 'outputs'. The inputs are rain, snow and hail (collectively called precipitation); the output mechanisms of evaporation, percolation (seepage) and surface run-off ensure that water is returned as efficiently as possible to the atmosphere or oceans. As a naturally harmonious system, a river constantly readjusts itself so that it can operate efficiently. Provided its capacity is not exceeded (in which case, of course, there will be a flood) the river basin achieves a carefully adjusted water transfer operation from the hills to the sea. Many of the physical features that are of interest in a river basin can be seen as by-products of the system's effort to adjust to current circumstances and maximise its efficiency. For example, if it encounters an obstacle, in the form of either a natural feature or something dumped in the water, the river will attempt to remove it by 'erosion'. Conversely, if something slows the current so that it begins to carry more sediment than its volume and speed will allow, it will simply drop any excess as 'deposition'. This approach places the river in the context of the water cycle.

Pupils' understanding of river systems can be built up gradually over a period of time, assisted by good classroom resources and the use of the school buildings and grounds. A large sand and gravel tray or outdoor 'pit' which can be raked up to form a mountain area and 'rained on' with a spray hose, will reveal some of the features of that developing system. Pouring water onto a selection of soil, sand, gravels and small pebbles banked up in a length of guttering will illustrate how water moves and sorts its sediment load (see Figure 4). The introduction of a waterproof layer (plastic or polystyrene sheet) will demonstrate the principle of springs. Those who live near beaches can also study river systems in miniature (Figure 7). Large picture resources (for younger children) and good video sequences and websites (for older pupils) will do much to draw these practical experiments into a real context. It is not so straightforward, however, to communicate the timescale over which the system develops and operates or to consider the formation of river features inside a classroom. Ideally, then, where fieldwork is possible it should emphasise the different forms that rivers can take.

A large number of geographical terms have been used in this section, some of which will be more familiar than others. Nowhere is technical and commonplace vocabulary richer than in the description of water features – stream, burn, beck, falls, force, ghyll, puddle, pool, pond, mere and tarn are just a few examples. Most regions have a rich variety of colloquial names. There are also many problems with definition. For instance when does a stream become a river and when does a river become an estuary? You are unlikely

Figure 7 | *The Mississippi River Delta. Many river features may be seen in miniature on beaches around the UK.* **Photo** | *Courtesy of USGS National Center for EROS and NASA Landsat Project Science Office.*

to find a precise answer as there are no 'official' sizes at which these terms apply. Indeed, if there were a precise definition, say in terms of a flow rate of 'so many cubic metres per second', would it mean anything to the average person anyway? What these terminological uncertainties do imply, however, is that teaching pupils to name features is really an issue of inducting them at their own level into the whole nomenclature debate. 'What do you think we might call a feature like this?' is therefore always an appropriate question.

Many pupils, quite apart from not being able to employ a vocabulary of comparative sizes, may not even be familiar with the idea that physical features have 'proper' names like people do. We may need to be very conscious of saying 'the River Trent' rather than just 'the Trent' in the early stages of any work. Adding the three longest rivers named in the national curriculum, your own local rivers, and any others that pupils know about, to an enlarged UK map, is a simple way of raising this awareness and a good way of initiating discussion about sources, tributaries and mouths. It will help pupils if you emphasise the direction of flow by starting at the source and ending at the mouth when you draw a river on the map.

New terminology becomes easier to grapple with if it is encountered regularly. It is a case of being alert to the opportunity to 'drip feed' additional ideas whenever the chance arises. The use of appropriate stories or newspaper cuttings can greatly assist this work so the literacy hour is a good time to support geographical learning. You could, for example, ask the class to make up a name for a river that is unnamed in the story, and to relate the features of this river

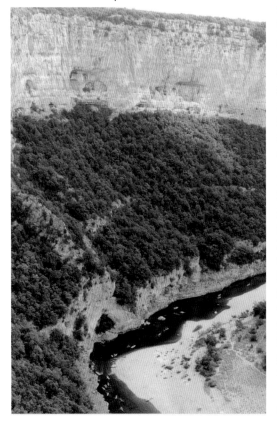

to what they have been learning by drawing an imaginary map to show where they think it begins and ends and where along its banks the story is set. Freed by the imaginary setting from the constraints of achieving locational accuracy, pupils will be able to show you what they know about rivers and maps – a useful interim assessment opportunity. It is essential, however, that we are well prepared to support their understanding of real rivers too, and this involves developing our own subject knowledge.

Rivers fieldwork

Undertaking independent fieldwork on rivers may seem daunting to anyone who does not regard themselves as a 'geographer' but it doesn't need to be. By asking key questions such as What/where is this place? How did it get like this, and how and why is it changing? you can generate ideas which you can incorporate into your initial planning. Visiting the site will also help to stimulate your thoughts. If possible you should get pupils to devise their own questions, such as those listed below. This is important as it gives them a sense of ownership and increases their commitment to the work. These questions can be

Photo | *Liz Lewis.*

Figure 8 | *How erosion and deposition can lead to the formation of an ox-bow lake.*

a) Stage 1

Current

Erosion of outer bend
River cliff

Deposition on inner bend
Slip-off slope (point bar)

b) Stage 2

The 'neck' of the
meander narrows

As the meander intensifies
the channel moves sideways
broadening the valley

c) Stage 3

The river cuts
through the 'neck'
of the meander

An abandoned meander channel
may contain an 'ox-bow lake' or
remain boggy when this
drains away

audited to demonstrate the integration of physical, human and environmental elements in a typical set of pupils' questions.

- Will it be safe to paddle?
- Is it very deep?
- Who does it belong to?
- Where does the river come from?
- Why does the river get dirty?
- How fast does the river go?
- How long is the river?
- What would happen if you fell in?
- Are there any fish in the river?
- Will we see otters and things?
- Why do rivers bend and twist?
- Where does the water come from?
- Are there any boats on it?
- Does it flood over the edges?
- How is the river bank changing?

A good place to see the physical processes at work in a river is at a bend in the channel known as a 'meander'. As the current swings round the outer side of the bend the full force of the water is thrown against the bank, loosening the soil and scouring away rock so that it becomes eroded (Figure 8). On its own water usually has little effect, so the importance of the bedload as a scouring tool needs to be highlighted once pupils begin to recognise the erosion process. The vertical bank or 'river cliff' which the river cuts on the outside of a bend can be anything from a few centimetres in height to a spectacular feature. Over time, further erosion undercuts the bank making it unstable, with the result that it collapses into the water.

When choosing a fieldwork location bear in mind that it should afford as many of the following opportunities as possible:

- A guided walk along a stretch of riverbank, ideally incorporating a photograph trail
- Opportunities to identify, describe, sketch and label landscape features
- A chance to locate features and follow the route on large-scale maps
- A stopping point which gives a vista over the whole area
- Safe locations at which to investigate the river at first hand, e.g. measuring
- A chance for groups of pupils to do their own investigation under adult supervision
- A place to have lunch, visit the lavatory and play safely

Before you go, see that the pupils are equipped with a field notebook in which they can record their observations. Over a period of time this will build up into a valuable record of work undertaken. You might also decide to take some more specific equipment such as measuring tapes, stopwatches, laminated maps of the area and biodegradable floats (e.g. cauliflower florets). Cameras of all sorts will be invaluable.

Photo | *Paula Richardson.*

Follow-up work needs to be completed quickly, while the experience is fresh. One way of presenting the work is a large interactive working display which will spawn comparative work, foster discussion and provide factual material which pupils can present to other classes. You might also use the display as a way of reporting back to parents and raising enthusiasm for more fieldwork in your school. The promise of a real audience will help to sustain interest but be wary of prolonging the follow-up beyond its natural limits. There may, however, be opportunities for developing the work by focusing on issues and changes. For example, you might challenge pupils to plan a new riverside park. This will involve them in mapwork exercises and will show how human activities relate to the physical landscape. Topics of this kind are brimming with potential not only across the geography curriculum but in other subject areas as well.

Doing geography through enquiries

I have tried, with reference to both river and coastal studies, to combine an introduction to some essential understandings in physical geography with a vision of the enquiry approach in action, some advice about fieldwork, and some suggested pupils' activities.

I have avoided matching individual activities to particular age groups because I don't believe it is possible to be prescriptive about this with any real credibility, especially in the context of someone else's class. As teachers we are all best-placed to judge the capabilities of individuals in our own teaching groups and to select well-matched activities to extend their learning. Some schools may intend to develop a single programme of work on rivers, others to integrate the work with locality studies or other curriculum areas, and yet others to visit and revisit the theme throughout the junior years in differing contexts. All these modes of organisation are possible given the flexibility of the national curriculum and the intention that we should make use of local opportunitites and adapt work to the needs of our pupils.

I have concentrated on the broad vision of field-based enquiry in the knowledge that there are already numerous published resources to assist the design of classroom-based work and individual activities, many of which can also be easily adapted to support the outdoor opportunities encountered in your own particular locality or region. For me as a teacher the beauty and strength of the enquiry approach is that it is open-ended. Once teacher and pupils have set the broad context of the investigation and defined issues of interest, individuals can enter the enquiry at their own level and pace.

Any enquiry that is worthy of the title 'geographical' must incorporate both physical and human elements. It can achieve this by examining, in the context of real places, those relationships which are at the very heart of geography – the effects of the world's varied physical conditions on human activities and of humans on their sensitive physical home, the Earth. By raising aware-ness of and fostering thoughtful responses to the many important and often politically sensitive environmental issues with which our world is currently struggling, we shall be providing the kind of learning that an informed and sensitive next generation will desperately need.

Developing understanding of the physical landscape is in some ways the most difficult aspect of geography but very worthwhile because that understanding can enrich appreciation of the natural environment and so feed the desire to protect and conserve it thoughtfully.

Sir Halford Mackinder, the prominent educationalist and pioneer of academic geography, who seems to have harboured a healthy scepticism about the sterile rote learning of the 'capes and bays' tradition, had this to say about school geography in the 1920s:

> You cannot have taught them much by way of facts, but if you send them out curious, seeking to learn, and with an idea that there is order in the world and that their experience must fit into a corresponding order in their minds, you have done all you can hope to do.

This liberating thought offers a long-standing justification for enquiry learning which has modern echoes in all the most recent curriculum directives.

Our role in primary physical geography, then, is not to present our pupils with a watered-down version of our own half-remembered or recently-resurrected, senior school experience. It is rather that we should invite and nurture the natural curiosity children have about their own world. All primary teachers, whatever their subject orientation and expertise, can surely embrace this role with confidence.

References and further reading

Barrett, J. (1978) *Cloudy with a Chance of Meatballs.* New York: Simon and Schuster.

DCSF (2007) *Primary National Strategy.* Available at *http://nationalstrategies.standards.dcsf.gov.uk* (last accessed 30 June 2010).

Dow, J. (2001) *Webster's Walk.* London: Frances Lincoln.

Hughes, S. (2002) *Alfie's Weather.* London: Red Fox.

Hughes, S. (1998) *Out and About.* London: Walker Books.

Jackson, E. (2001) *Barnaby Bear at the Seaside.* Sheffield: Geographical Association.

Lewis, L. (2002) *Where is Barnaby's Castle?* Sheffield: Geographical Association.

Mackintosh, M. (2004) 'Children's understanding of rivers' in Catling, S. and Martin, F. (eds) *Researching Primary Geography.* London: Register of Research in Primary Geography.

McKerr, L. and Matthews, C. (2007) 'Using SHEaEP to investigate rivers at KS2', *Primary Geographer*, 63, pp. 15-17.

Milbourne, A. (2007) *Windy Weather.* London: Usborne.

Pollard, N. (2003) *The River.* Brookfield, Conn.: Roaring Book Press.

Stott-Thornton, J. (2001) *Waves.* Victoria, Australia: Mimosa.

Walker, G. (2007) *Coast to Coast.* Coalville: Wildgoose.

Websites

BBC schools *www.bbc.co.uk/schools/riversandcoasts*

Coast (BBC2) *www.bbc.co.uk/coast*

Earth from space *http://landsat.gsfc.nasa.gov/earthasart*

Environment Agency *www.environment-agency.gov.uk*

Natural History Museum *www.nhm.ac.uk*

Wildgoose Education Ltd. *www.wgoose.co.uk*

Settlement

This chapter explains the key concepts used to help children understand what settlements are, what happens in them and how they change. Sections on the Early Years Foundation Stage and key stages 1 and 2 offer practical ideas for planning and teaching the settlements theme within the primary geography curriculum.

Whether they live in an isolated farmhouse, commuter village, market town or a large city, all children come to school knowing something about settlements. For example, the pupil in your class who lives on a farm may have heard how it has belonged to the family for many years and know why his/her parents are determined to continue making a living from it. Another pupil, from an inner-city area, may have a strong sense of community and identity based on their experiences within a particular ethnic culture. These two examples are particularly meaningful because they also illustrate how your pupils' experience relates closely to current issues and debates, such as community cohesion. Although farming communities may appear isolated, they are actually connected to European agricultural policy and consumer demands. Similarly, in inner-city areas, issues of social identity, integration and global migration can be found within the school catchment area.

Settlements are fascinating places and often provide really vivid examples of geographical processes and patterns at work in the wider world. They are also rich in opportunities for pupils to investigate real issues and geographical questions (Martin, 2006). They can be quite complex too! So, the first section of this chapter explains the geographical concepts which help to explain, as well as raise questions about, any settlement across the world. As you and your pupils plan geographical enquiries in your chosen settlements, you can decide how appropriate each of these concepts might be when writing your learning objectives.

Key ideas

1. Basic human needs

Studying any settlement can help pupils to understand the importance of basic needs. In the past, people tried to find safe places in which to build settlements. Living on high ground made it easier for them to spot enemies from some way off and to look out for possible food supplies. On another level, feeling 'safe' may involve being close to people similar to yourself who understand your values and beliefs, hence the growth of particular cultural communities. But geography also helps us to understand that the world is not that simple. For example, many farmers around the world have chosen to farm on the slopes of active volcanoes. It's not at all safe but they have decided that it is worth the risk as the fertile volcanic soil helps crops to grow well and ensures a regular supply of food. Human beings also need water, fuel and dry buildings in which to live. As pupils study a variety of settlements across the globe they will begin to understand that meeting basic needs can lead to all manner of outcomes. None of these responses is 'right' or 'wrong', they are simply different responses and ways of interpreting the physical environment. These ideas link directly not only with geography but also with historical and social areas of learning.

Water is an interesting example. As part of their topic or project work pupils may see images of people in dry areas carrying water over long distances. These people will be very careful how they use that water. In other cases pupils will discover that water is supplied to settlements through taps and study how much of it is wasted. Thus, by looking at contrasting settlements it is possible to introduce the issue of sustainability into your enquiries. Learning about migration can also help pupils to understand how people who are forced to leave their settlements struggle to survive, as well as helping them empathise with the lives of other people around the world (Shah, 2010).

2. Similarities and differences

As they compare settlements pupils will begin to understand that while every village, town, city or suburb is unique, it is nevertheless possible to see patterns that are repeated in settlements further afield. Take Sheffield for example. It is a unique city that houses the headquarters of the Geographical Association. Sheffield also has a unique location, history and heritage. However, it has many similarities with other large cities both in Britain and across the world. Its industries have had to adapt to changes in global demands; some parts of the city require urban regeneration; attempts have been made to improve the transportation system by introducing a tram service. You may teach in a village where most adults drive away each day to work in other places. While your village is unique, a similar commuter pattern can be seen in hundreds of other villages. By allowing pupils to investigate a range of settlements, you can help them understand how places can have special characteristics as well as illustrating more general patterns and processes.

The way that settlements are changing provides another slant for examining similarities and differences. As multinational corporations spread across the globe, it may be argued that settlements are becoming increasingly similar. In Britain, our town and city centres are now dominated by a predictable range of chain stores, while small, individual shops disappear or are driven out to areas with cheaper rents. What type of town centre would pupils want to be in when they have grown up? Do they want to identify with somewhere special, somewhere different, somewhere unique? Or do they find it reassuring to know that services of a similar type and quality can be found in many places? Exploring these kinds of questions involves using imagination, prediction and other thinking skills. It also moves geography away from factual and descriptive accounts of places to consideration of how places change and what settlements may be like in the future.

3. Context

Many schools use commercially published locality packs that focus on particular settlements, both in Britain and countries around the world. Although many of these packs are well-produced, they can lead to settlements being studied as isolated units. As a result, pupils fail to understand how the place they have studied is linked to other areas. For example, if you are studying an Indian village it is important to know how that village is linked with nearby villages and towns and places further afield. This information is not always provided with commercially published packs, but with pupils' improved ICT skills and internet access we can investigate other settlements and their wider links directly, by communicating with the pupils and teachers who live there. Understanding such links can give pupils a much more realistic appreciation of how the modern world is interconnected. Physically, people travel much more widely, and cultural links are forged by reciprocal visits; although electronic links mean some people need to travel less. More negatively, we also export our bad habits: pollution originating in one country can be transmitted by air or water to another. If geographical enquiries can help pupils understand how people and settlements are linked, they will be better equipped to understand the complex world they live in; such enquiries can also develop ideas arising from the *Every Child Matters* agenda.

4. Terminology

As pupils learn about settlements they can easily develop misconceptions about the terms they are using (Tanner, 2009). If we tell them that a village is rural and towns are urban there is a risk that we might be preventing them from developing a full understanding of the patterns and processes happening today in the landscape. A village may be in a 'rural' location but rely heavily on people visiting it as tourists from nearby towns, and have very few inhabitants who actually work in agriculture. An attractive 'rural' village may in fact have a population which mainly works in nearby towns and cities and has very few connections with the surrounding countryside. It might be interesting to investigate how a town or city can spread its 'urban' effects. For example, pupils might investigate local supermarkets to find out how far their home delivery services extend through internet shopping facilities. Ask pupils to question DIY and furniture stores to see how far out of town they will deliver goods. If you are in a village, find out where the working population actually does work. Why do they choose to travel a long way and spend money on transport when they could live closer to the town?

5. Settlement hierarchies

Settlements vary in size from individual dwellings, hamlets and villages to towns and cities (Figure 1). When you are planning settlement enquiries try to ensure that pupils are able to investigate a range of places while at primary school. This will help them make links and identify patterns. There are many ways of developing investigations. Here are some suggestions:

- How many people live in this settlement?
- What do they do?
- What types of homes can we find?
- What is the land used for?
- How is this place linked to other places?
- What facilities and services can be found in settlements of different sizes?
- Why do larger places have more facilities such as shops and places to eat?

Another way of investigating settlement hierarchy is to find out how some places specialise in certain activities. For example, seaside towns rely mainly on holidaymakers while other towns specialise in industries based on information technology. This may be taken a step further by looking at land use in settlements. Two towns may have similar numbers of people but cover very different amounts of land. So, the position of settlements within a hierarchy may not tell us all we need to know about them. Another key concept here is that there are reasons why settlements develop at specific sites. As these reasons change over time settlements need constantly to evolve. Those that fail to find new functions may decline and may even disappear.

Primary Geography Handbook

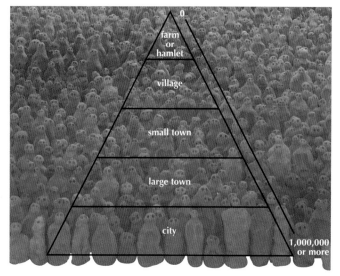

Figure 1 | Expanding settlements. **Photo** | Field for the British Isles, 1993, Antony Gormley, Terracotta. Approx. 40,000 figures, each 8-26cm tall. Courtesy of the artist and Jay Jopling/White Cube.

Settlement size
People live in settlements of different sizes. Places are called hamlets, villages, towns or cities depending on the number of people who live there. However some places are called cities because they are given special permission by a king or queen.

6. The physical setting

When we are planning investigations in settlements, it is all too easy to ignore the landscape. However, the physical setting has a crucial impact. You might think about where water flows through a town or city. Are streams and/or a river actually covered over? A topical issue would be to investigate new building on land which may flood, thus linking aspects of physical geography with demands for housing. Investigations on air quality in parts of a village, town or city could reveal interesting results. You could also bring a new dimension to your geography lessons by involving people working in environmental management. The Environment Agency has specialists who are able to support work in primary schools.

Another angle is the impact of hills and valleys on land use. Misconceptions can be addressed here by making comparisons with settlements around the world. If pupils believe people prefer not to build on very steep slopes, access data on some fast-growing cities in South America. Again on a global scale consider why people build in dangerous places. Cities such as San Francisco and Istanbul are built in earthquake zones. Why are people prepared to risk living there? To broaden pupils' understanding, the concept of lack of choice could be introduced by studying why people continue to live in villages, towns and cities of Bangladesh that are not only prone to severe flooding but, according to some predictions, could be submerged if sea level rises in future.

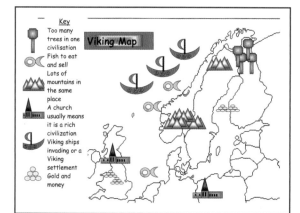

7. Issues

All the previous paragraphs contain examples of issues which pupils can investigate. They are highlighted here to demonstrate how the problems affecting settlements are constantly changing. To retain both your own and pupils' enthusiasm for geography, keep a look-out for new issues and problems. Your pupils may have good local knowledge and be able to identify suitable questions. Read local newspapers and talk to parents and local business and community people about

Pupils' work | Shelley Primary School, Horsham.

new developments. Watch regional TV news and topical interest programmes. Regularly walk your school's locality with your geographical eyes open. Can action groups, for example the local wildlife trust, highlight new issues or support pupils' investigations? Can you draw on national/international initiatives? For example, could your class investigate the case and put together a proposal for their town or city to be European City of Culture? Could they suggest reasons for holding the next Commonwealth Games there, or more controversially, in a village location? They could also investigate the impact of the London 2012 Olympics.

8. Futures education and sustainable development

As we have seen, settlements are constantly changing, sometimes as a result of things which are happening locally or because of events in more distant parts of the world. As pupils begin to understand these forces they could consider what their settlement might be like some time in the future. They could also ask what they would like to see happen. Barlow (2009) reports how studying a local village led pupils to find out about industrial heritage, citizenship and community, engaging them with real issues and living geography.

Settlements of all types and size have an effect on the environment. The amount of land needed to support a place is known as its 'environmental footprint' (Figure 2). Sustainable communities and people living in the economically developing world tend to have a relatively small environmental footprint. However, in Western Europe we can only support our current lifestyles by drawing resources from many other areas. It is estimated that the Isle of Wight has an environmental footprint around two and half times its own size. The equivalent figure for London is well over a hundred. How then could settlements become more sustainable? Is it actually possible? What happens to all the rubbish created in our town and where does it end up? Where does all the waste water and sewage go? Should towns and villages have their own wind farms? Energy is lost when generated electricity is moved a long way, but would wind turbines affect the appearance of the landscape? What do people in other European countries and around the world both think and actually do about some of these issues? Such investigations will show that many innovative ideas are being developed and that maybe we can learn from people in other places (Ballin, 2010).

9. Looking afresh at our locality

Familiarity can dull our geographical awareness! All our pupils live in a settlement of some sort and primary geography encourages them to look closely and actually question what they may well take for

Figure 2 | *Each settlement has an individual environmental footprint.*

Photo | Stephen Scoffham.

granted. Why has the village shop closed even though new homes are being built in our village? Why do our parents drive us to school each day even though we live quite close to school, and how does this affect our environment? Our streets have some unusual names: what do they tell us about what happened in our part of town in the past and why has it changed? We all know the river that flows through our part of the city, but where does it start and where does the water end up? Another valuable enquiry here might be 'and what effect do we have on that water?'.

Familiarity can also lead to pupils thinking that because their settlement operates in a certain way then all other places ought to be the same. Geography teaching in primary schools can help to dispel this misconception, largely by studying localities in a wide range of locations around the world which helps pupils to witness and value a variety of ways of life. We can also help by encouraging pupils to think about alternative ways of living in settlements. Do we really need to use so much electricity for lighting our streets? How might we make our town centre much easier and more enjoyable to use for people with various special needs? Geographical enquiries of this kind allow issues of inclusion to be developed in a practical and meaningful way within the curriculum.

Introducing settlements in the Early Years Foundation Stage

All six areas of learning in the EYFS curriculum provide opportunities for helping young children to observe and think about the world. One of the best ways of introducing them to the concepts associated with settlements is to use their own experience. You might begin by talking about their own home and people important to them. Ask pupils to think carefully about their room at home; whether they share it with a brother or sister or have a space of their own. Get them to make a model using a box (a shoe box is ideal) as a frame. They can make a model of the bed and other items or use ready-made objects such as dolls' house furniture. Ask them what they like and dislike about their room. Why are things put in particular places? Did they decide or was it done for them? How would they like to make their room better? For example, would they change the colour of the walls or make more room to play? These activities begin to get pupils thinking about different areas and spaces, or as geographers express it, land use patterns. Other questions you might consider asking pupils are:

- What can you see out of the window?
- What sounds can you hear when you are in your room?
- Where are the sounds coming from and what might be making them?
- Do you like where your room is in your home?
- Would you like a room which is sunnier, or away from a noisy brother or sister?

If you have a classroom pet such as a hamster, more key settlement concepts can be introduced by getting pupils to observe and ask questions such as:

- Why do we keep the cage in a particular part of the classroom? (It needs to be away from draughts and bright sunlight) (Concept: shelter)

- Why does the hamster move food, bedding and toys around its cage? (They are creating different areas and spaces) (Concept: land use)
- Why do we need to keep the cage clean, and provide water and food as well as interesting things for the hamster to play with? (Living creatures have a range of daily needs) (Concept: services)

If you are able to arrange walks in the school grounds and beyond, encourage people to think about why birds and animals live in particular places. For example birds build nests well away from where cats can find them and rabbits make burrows in soil that is easy to dig. Such walks are also an excellent opportunity to use geographical vocabulary linked with settlements. These words might describe different buildings – house, shop, factory – or items of street furniture – letter box, road sign, traffic lights. If you provide pupils with an aerial photograph of your school it will give them further information about your area. Research by Plester *et al.* (2003) suggests that even very young children can successfully use such resources.

Pupils at this age can be introduced to settlements further afield through story. For example, *Mia's Story* (Foreman, 2006) is a magical tale set in South America. Mia lives with her mother, father and dog Poco in a house made of bits and pieces on a rubbish dump somewhere between the big city and the white-capped mountains. The story presents a realistic view of life in a shanty town, raising many discussion questions. Why are there shanty towns? Who lives there? Questions like these raise issues about the diversity of people, lifestyles and places found in settlements all over the world.

Settlements in key stage 1

As children begin to ask questions about settlements there will be opportunities to develop their geographical skills. For example, why is there so much litter in the street outside our school? When they investigate this problem pupils may find that the litter comes from take-aways in the nearby shopping centre or that people in the car park leave litter because there are no bins. Where should new bins be placed and who could do this? This small-scale study encourages pupils to think about land use in their locality, public services and the quality of the environment. It also helps to build a sense of community and forge wider links.

Pupils of this age are capable of making quite detailed and carefully observed models. They could be given the task, in groups, of making a model of a place they visit. Arrange for them to take plenty of photographs and encourage them to look at the buildings from different angles; the front will not be enough. Can you get up high to take some oblique photographs to help add details to roofs and so on?

A variation on this activity is to divide pupils into 'expert' groups. Each group is responsible for a different task: collecting information on buildings needed for the model, on people, street furniture, vehicles, natural features such as trees, bushes and streams. As pupils are building the model, adults can ask geographical questions about how the settlement works. Why are the parent and toddler parking spaces closest to the supermarket entrance, for instance? Why have no houses been built near the river? Why are the streetlights in particular places? What is made in that factory and why does it take up so much land? One way of consolidating this work is to arrange a visit to a nearby model village. As well as enabling pupils to study a whole settlement at a manageable scale, this will also help develop geographical skills of observation (Halocha, 2007).

Pupils like to work with visitors to their school. Be on the look-out for people you know who might be visiting settlements in other parts of the world: it may be parents travelling on business, a governor visiting relations abroad, or the school's police officer going on a course in another European country. Speak to these people before they travel and explain that you want to study settlements in different parts of the world. Your class could prepare some simple questions to give to the traveller before they leave. When the traveller returns they could be invited back and become the focus of a special report. This activity naturally lends itself to, and will benefit from, the use of ICT, but the extent of this will depend on how much time your traveller can give to the project. A CD of digital photographs could be left after their visit and used to prepare a simple illustrated report written by your class. Such an ICT activity will be much more meaningful than one which is limited to simply satisfying one of the ICT objectives in the national curriculum.

Pupils' knowledge and understanding of settlements can also be developed through the use of atlas and mapping skills. Here are some questions that will focus attention on your local area:

- Working with a large-scale map, who can find all the shops?
- Who lives the furthest away from school?
- Where are the best play areas to visit?
- What's the safest place to cross the high street?

Catling (2002) suggests many more activities using atlases and globes to develop pupils' knowledge and understanding of settlements and other geographical themes.

Settlements in key stage 2

You can help to ensure that pupils investigate a range of settlements while in primary school by careful whole-school planning of fieldwork experiences. For example, if your school is in a city suburb, can you arrange a day's fieldwork to a nearby village? At some other appropriate time could a residential visit ensure that pupils experience a contrasting settlement such as a coastal town? By taking these opportunities you will provide pupils with direct experiences which will help them develop some of the key concepts discussed earlier such as settlement hierarchies and functions.

More complex geographical activities can be developed at key stage 2. You can use oblique aerial photographs to ask questions about settlements, develop geographical vocabulary and assess pupils' understanding. Collect these photographs (laminated if possible) from books, calendars and settlement study packs if your school uses these. You should then prepare a supporting set of small cards containing settlement words. Ask small groups or individual pupils carefully to place the cards on their photograph. Some of the words you write down might be 'red herrings' designed to prompt discussion. You could also have some blank cards for pupils to add their own vocabulary if not provided by you. Choose your bank of words carefully. If you include 'settlement' along with 'village', for example, you can see which term pupils use and assess their understanding. Including both 'swimming pool' and 'leisure facility' allows you to show how important collective words are in describing settlements (Figure 3).

Land use investigations often make an effective base for fieldwork at key stage 2. These involve a wide range of geographical skills such as careful observation, discussion and classification, reading and making maps, using keys, and interpreting findings using

Figure 3 | Use a bank of cards to help pupils identify features in a photo.
Photo | AirFotos Ltd.

River	Supermarket	High street	Park

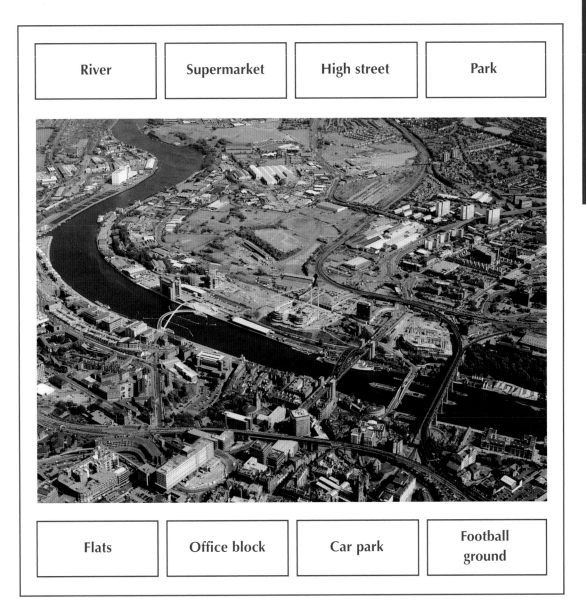

Flats	Office block	Car park	Football ground

mathematics (e.g. calculating the percentage of land used for different purposes). You will need an up-to-date large-scale Ordnance Survey map (1:1250 or 1:2500 scale) of your locality for this work. The OS website lists the range of maps. Your LA geography adviser or local Geography Champion may also be able to help.

One way of organising the work is to divide your locality into small areas so that groups of 'surveyors' can map a manageable area under close adult supervision. Decide on a range of categories and associated key colours, such as 'transport', 'housing' and 'leisure areas', before going out. This initial discussion can draw on pupils' existing knowledge and provides a real

Photos | *John Halocha (upper and middle); Ann Hamblen (lower).*

insight into their understanding of what happens in their home area. Recently, I heard a ten-year-old explain that a corner site was now derelict because it belonged to a bank which had merged and now they only needed one site in the high street. Clearly a young geographer!

When you have completed your land use survey you can go on to make further investigations. For example: How much land is given over to transport? Why are all the estate agents near each other? What might a land use survey in ten or twenty years' time show? ICT can be used to collect photographic evidence to include with your final land use map. These resources will make an excellent interactive display in your class and around the school. Finally, do ask your geography subject leader to keep these completed materials. They will provide your future colleagues in the school with an excellent historical resource to use as the basis for their own enquiries. For many more ideas on doing land use surveys, see the special issue of *Primary Geographer* Autumn 2009, which focused on 'Connecting with landscapes'.

Older people often have fascinating insights into what happens in settlements and how they have changed over time. If you can plan a geographical enquiry that includes a study of your school locality in the past, try to arrange a visit from a local resident who has known your area for many years. They may have old photographs, but if not, arrange for your pupils to find old photographs and, ideally, maps to have ready to discuss with your visitor. Ensure that questions and discussion ideas are carefully planned. If you are lucky enough to have two visitors who can come at different times, your class may find that they present two rather different versions of what happened in the past. For more ideas, Longworth (2006) is an interesting read which is both geography- and education-oriented. It is also relevant to the 'community cohesion' debate.

Activities of this kind will introduce young people to the concept that people see settlements in different ways depending on who they are, their background, family history and interests. In this way you will be helping children to understand that settlements are so much more than just the physical features we find in them; they include all the experiences, hopes, fears, pleasures, arguments, memories, beliefs and values of the people who live in them – and this is true for settlements all over the world.

References and further reading

Ballin, B. (2010) 'Making connections through school partnerships', *Primary Geographer*, 71, pp. 26-28.

Barlow, A. (2009) 'Fresh eyes on our natural world', *Primary Geographer*, 70, pp.12-13.

Catling, S. (2002) *Placing Places*. Sheffield: Geographical Association.

Foreman, M. (2006) *Mia's Story*. London: Walker Books.

Halocha, J. (2007) 'Developing investigative work/enquiry' in Johnston, J., Halocha, J. and Chater, M. (eds) *Developing Teaching Skills in the Primary School*. Maidenhead: Open University Press.

Halocha, J. (2009) 'You don't need eyes to see: you need vision', *Teaching Geography*, 34, 3, pp. 116-118.

Henshall, A. and Lacey, L. (2007) *Word on the Street: Children and young people's views on using the street for play and informal recreation*. London: National Children's Bureau.

Longworth, N. (2006) *Learning Cities, Learning Regions, Learning Communities*. London: Routledge.

Martin, F. (2006) *Teaching Geography in Primary Schools: Learning to live in the world*. Cambridge: Chris Kington Publishing.

Plester, B., Richards, J., Shevelan, C., Blades, M. and Spencer, C. (2003) 'Hunt from above', *Primary Geographer*, 51, pp. 20-21.

Shah, H. (2010) 'Critical thinking in the context of global learning', *Primary Geographer*, 71, pp. 14-15.

Tanner, J. (2009) 'Special places: place attachment and children's happiness', *Primary Geographer*, 68, pp. 5-8.

Websites

Environment Agency *www.environment-agency.gov.uk*

Ordnance Survey maps *www.ordnancesurvey.co.uk*

we use water for..

drinking

having a bath

growing things

cleaning things

flushing the toilet

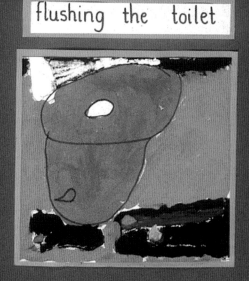

Photo | *Stephen Scoffham.*

having a shower

cooking, drinking, washing up

Environmental geography

'Let us resolve that we will not leave our children a world where the oceans rise and famine spreads and terrible storms devastate our lands. This is the moment when we must come together to save this planet.' These words, from a speech given by Barack Obama a few months before he was elected President of the United States, highlight the fundamental importance of environmental perspectives in the modern world.

This chapter offers practical help on how environmental issues can be addressed within the context of good geography teaching. It lays emphasis on practical approaches and offers a number of case studies as templates for teachers to adapt to their own circumstances/ issues/localities, including one of an eco-school. Environmental geography provides many exciting opportunities for engaging pupils' curiosity and interest in the world about them. However, to capitalise on this potential the national curriculum and EYFS requirements should be regarded more as starting points than as ends in themselves. The following considerations should underpin work in environmental geography for all ages:

1. Fieldwork is fundamental to all geographical education and involving pupils in activities outside the classroom is especially relevant to the effective delivery of environmental geography (see the Learning Outside the Classroom and Field Studies Council websites).

2. Environmental geography is an extremely useful vehicle for understanding other people's attitudes and values and for encouraging pupils to express their own opinions, develop tolerance of alternative opinions and their own ability to analyse and reconsider their own stance on a particular issue.

3. Unique opportunities are offered within environmental geography to cover issues in the context of other countries, thereby raising pupils' awareness of other cultures and values.

4. Environmental geography also offers a means by which the citizenship, sustainable development and creativity agendas may be effectively addressed within a geographical context, thereby raising the profile and appreciation of geography (see Chapters 2 and 21).

What is environmental geography?

Environmental geography examines the interactions between people and their environments, studying both how people adapt to, and how they alter, specific environments. Studying environmental geography involves using geographical skills, knowledge and understanding to explore issues affecting the quality of life on Earth. It also involves considering attitudes, values and opinions and thereby provides an ideal opportunity for pupils of all ages and abilities to contribute to *real* issues that are of *real* concern to them.

The importance of environmental geography and how, well taught, it impacts on children's education and progress, can be inferred from the 2010 geography level descriptions:

■ At level one pupils 'express their views on features of the environment of a locality'
■ At level two pupils 'show an awareness of places beyond their own locality. They express views on the environment of a locality and recognise how people affect the environment'
■ At level three pupils 'recognise that people seek to improve and sustain environments'
■ At level four pupils 'understand that people can both improve and damage the environment. They offer reasons for their own views about environmental change and recognise that other people may hold different views' (QCDA, 2010).

Thus environmental geography is wide-ranging in its scope and application. Indeed, since the inception of the national curriculum, environmental geography has steadily grown in significance: many of the initiatives that have emerged in recent years, including ECM, Citizenship, Global Development, Sustainable Schools and Learning Outside the Classroom, sit firmly within its remit. These initiatives also come together under the heading of Education for Sustainable Development (ESD), which overlaps extensively with environmental geography.

So it is important to approach environmental geography, along with sustainability and citizenship, not as 'add-ons' to an already overburdened curriculum, but as aspects of life integral to the school ethos, with an impact at every age phase. This integration could be achieved in a variety of ways:

■ engaging with national initiatives such as Eco-Schools, Healthy Schools, Forest Schools, Primary Geography Quality Mark
■ giving pupils a voice, e.g. through debates, circle time, School Councils, suggestions boxes and class and assembly presentations
■ entering competitions and awards – these help to focus the school community on a particular issue and build a whole school approach
■ making opportunities for pupil participation, e.g. gardening or other environmental clubs, speakers from relevant organisations, raising funds for charities, twinning projects with other schools, locally, nationally and internationally.

There are plenty of sources of further advice. Martin and Owens (2008) show how environmental geography and ESD can be made accessible to young children through topics such as food and farming, the school grounds and travelling to school. Martin (2006) suggests how the concepts which underpin sustainable development can form a framework for effective and enjoyable learning.

Getting started with environmental geography

One way of studying environmental geography is to start with the pupils' own environment and expand out to the wider world. All pupils need to study their local area, both in the EYFS and key stages 1 and 2. The study of more distant environments as demanded in key stage 2 does not preclude their inclusion earlier in the curriculum.

The local environment is a primary resource and has the unique quality that pupils can interact with it. It also has these advantages:

■ it is free

■ it is accessible

■ it is familiar

■ it allows opportunities for learning outside the classroom.

Local people are usually willing to be involved in pupils' activities. Indeed, fostering links with local residents is an important and often overlooked aspect of developing environmental awareness, in addition to being a significant way in which geography can contribute to the citizenship agenda and enhance community cohesion.

Working in the local area, pupils can collect their own information on a particular environmental issue through questionnaires, sound recordings, surveys, field sketches, photographs and other recording techniques. This has the advantage of developing both their enquiry skills and additional transferable skills such as those relating to ICT. When they study issues in more distant localities pupils will, of necessity, need to use secondary sources such as CDs, atlases, photographs, newspapers, magazines, links with other schools and the internet. There are many ways in which the information may be utilised, for example:

■ the creation of databases to manipulate quantitative data

■ analysis of visual material

■ developing brochures and podcasts

■ exploring specific issues, e.g. tourism/festivals/disasters.

Studying an environmental issue using information and data collected by the pupils themselves enables them to understand the issue better, how it affects both people and the environment, and how different people may hold different views from their own. It also has the advantage of giving children ownership over their learning.

The enquiry approach provides an appropriate and effective teaching technique. The strength of this technique is that it can effectively deliver almost any aspect of geography, including environmental geography.

Environmental geography is not just about collecting data and information on an issue, it is also about getting pupils to engage with and communicate their ideas on that issue. This may be achieved through such activities as:

■ the production of a report/newspaper

■ role play within the class or for wider audiences, e.g. there is an opportunity here for a special assembly or a presentation at a parents' evening

■ interviews with people involved in particular environmental issues

■ drawings, photographs and other art work to produce exciting wall displays, which offers the opportunity to use ICT

■ the production of a simulated television programme

■ the creation of a web page/site/podcast

■ using stories – the pupils could either be introduced to an issue via stories such as *Who Will Save Us?* (Morch and Hadow, 2007) and *The Trouble with Dragons* (Gliori, 2009), or encouraged to write one of their own.

Some possible themes

There are innumerable opportunities for teaching environmental geography throughout the school. The suggestions given below could be adapted and developed for all age groups, including younger children. Martin and Owen (2008) identify many further examples.

Looking after our school

Pupils could be actively encouraged to express opinions about what they feel is attractive and unattractive about their school and its grounds. Through writing and drawings they can devise plans for improvement. This theme could be part of an Eco-Schools or Healthy Schools submission (see pp. 282). Setting up a school council provides the ideal forum for pupils to share ideas of this kind, to plan their campaigns, and to give impetus to projects which involve pupils in making changes to their environment – a real lesson in citizenship.

Caring for animals

You could begin by asking pupils to consider what their pets require to survive. This might lead to a farm study/visit where pupils formulate their own opinions on the way farm animals are kept. Clearly this study might then involve more distant places, with pupils studying endangered wildlife habitats and species.

Looking after our water

Pupils could consider the various ways we use water and the absolute necessity for clean drinking water. This, of course, would naturally lead to a consideration of water supplies in other countries, encouraging children to empathise with those in distant lands and different cultures.

Trees

Pupils might research and discuss the value of trees in our world (see pages 278-9).

Other activities

- Using stories and poems to introduce or develop a theme. *What Planet are You From, Clarice Bean?* (Child, 2002) is an anarchic picture book with an eco-warrior theme. *Five Little Fiends* (Dyer, 2001) is about the interrelationship of the different elements which make up our world
- Organise an assembly to illustrate an environmental issue or dispute
- Creating a themed trail in a rural area (see the Ebchester School example on page 282).
- Creating a themed trail in an urban area. The Mywalks website offers a really interesting and interactive way of doing this using simple ICT/web-based materials
- Making a play area which pupils build themselves using resources such as bark chippings. (This has been successfully introduced into a South Tyneside school to avoid mud being brought into the school buildings.)
- Designing a butterfly garden. Engaging older pupils to help the younger ones offers an exciting way of promoting citizenship and school cohesion
- Making nesting boxes for birds and siting them in appropriate areas
- Making attractive fences and boundaries. (A school fence bordering the Tyneside Metro was transformed by a series of murals, with help from the Passenger Transport Authority and the Groundwork Trust.)

■ Improving the inside of the school with, for example, plants, signs, sculptures, paintings designed and produced by the pupils

■ Transforming the playground by introducing street furniture (Tyneside Groundwork Trust has developed several playgrounds in this way. Schools have found that this simple approach has reduced bullying in the playground.)

The above ideas may be regarded as mini-projects and may provide a sound basis for further development throughout the school and ways of engaging with the wider community.

Enquiries for older pupils

Using stories to introduce and consolidate studies in environmental geography should continue at key stage 2. As well as using picture books, such as *George Saves the World by Lunchtime* (Readman, 2006) you might use cartoon style texts. *Eco-Wolf and the Three Pigs* (Anholt, 2002), for example, is a 'seriously silly' story that reworks the tale of the three little pigs from an environmental perspective. *Will Jellyfish Rule the World?* (Hickman, 2009) adopts a similar format but has a stronger focus on facts and information.

The local area will often provide some excellent issues that pupils can investigate first-hand. The local newspaper is a useful starting point. Finding out what the children themselves think about the place where they live is also valuable. Some specific topics/ideas which you could develop and which involve a contrasting locality are suggested below. These ideas should not be regarded as being exclusively for older children – they can readily be modified for all age ranges.

Tourism – There are many examples of how tourism has had both positive and negative impacts on the environment, and these can be used to raise a variety of geographical issues. For example, there is intense visitor pressure on National Parks and mountain environments. This means that people who visit these areas often contribute to the destruction of the very things they have come to experience, i.e. unspoilt landscape, peace and tranquillity.

New roads and airports – Proposals for new roads, railways and airports affect many parts of the country. Such schemes often lead to fierce debates in which the impact on the countryside and wildlife is pitted against economic development. The wider question about whether such schemes are needed in the first place also often arises.

Rivers/coasts – The abuse of our rivers and coastal waters through misuse can, unfortunately, be all too readily studied, e.g. agricultural waste, sewage and chemical discharges and the disastrous oil spill from the deepwater Horizon rig in the Gulf of Mexico in 2010.

Green belt land – Building on green belt land is a dilemma facing most urban areas and one that impinges directly on rural areas.

Quarrying – Depending on the school's locality, resources and access to sites, quarrying can be the focus of geography topics set in a variety of place contexts, for example:

■ an open-cast coal mine within a predominantly agricultural landscape (see page 280);

■ limestone quarrying within the Peak District National Park;

■ chalk quarrying in southern England;

■ precious-metal mining in an Equatorial rainforest, e.g. the Amazon rainforest in Brazil;

■ iron-ore mining in Scandinavia.

Trees in our world

Trees provide a familiar but extremely useful focus for an exciting and wide-ranging environmental geography topic. Teachers could approach this in a number of ways but some possible aims could be:

- raising awareness of the value of trees to the environment, e.g. for landscaping, the production of oxygen and as a source of alternative medicines;
- allowing pupils to express and develop their own opinions on forest-related issues, e.g. coniferous monoculture, rainforest decimation;
- appreciating that there are different attitudes relating to the value of trees.

You might start the work with a local study. This could involve:

- mapping the school campus and/or local area to show where trees already exist, thereby raising pupils' awareness of trees and their local area;
- a visit to either a local park or woodland and/or, through a 'local expert', enabling pupils to identify suitable varieties of tree for their school, thereby increasing their knowledge and enabling them to make informed decisions;
- identifying, through discussion, the opportunities for enhancement of the environment by tree planting, thereby offering pupils an opportunity to express their opinions and ideas.

Armed with this knowledge and the opinions of a variety of people consulted by the pupils, the project could be advanced using questions such as:

Focus question	Teaching/learning outcomes
Do we want trees?	Enables the children to consider the value of trees
Why do we want them?	Offers the opportunity to express likes and dislikes
What trees will we plant?	Enables them to use their knowledge or highlights the need to find out
Which trees will grow in our environment?	This links to a consideration of weather and climate and so to other aspects of geography
How do we look after them?	Enables pupils to become conversant with how trees survive
How do we get the trees we want?	Issues of availability and scarcity
Who will plant them?	Possible involvement of the local community
How will we plant them?	Practical considerations of facilitating a change in the environment
Where will we plant them?	An excellent opportunity for pupils to produce alternative plans for the location and to present these so that a final decision can be made
Who will look after them?	Aspects of responsibility
How do we pay for them?	Considerations of costs and value

If these questions were to be formulated into a scheme to plant more trees in the school grounds, in order to achieve their aim pupils would need to develop their own ideas for raising the money, perhaps by writing letters to appropriate organisations seeking sponsorship, and organising money-raising events such as jumble sales, sponsored walks, 'swimathons' and quizzes. This could involve them in a series of community activities which would forge, develop and, it is hoped, sustain the community/school links. These activities could culminate in a high-profile event where a local dignitary takes part in the tree planting ceremony. The links between these activities and the citizenship agenda are very obvious, yet this project has clear geographical elements.

This tree project can be developed further to bring in studies of distant and contrasting localities. For example:
- the destruction of rainforests – a case study of the Amazon or the Indonesian forests would be particularly useful here
- the creation of a coniferous forest monoculture – as in the creation of coniferous forests in parts of Scotland.

Such an approach would require reference to secondary source material to resource the activities. This can be obtained from various organisations (for some suggestions see the list at the end of this chapter), many of whom have 'tailor-made' materials for just such a topic. Using such materials, pupils might be encouraged to ask and find answers to questions such as:

Focus question	Teaching/learning outcomes
What and where are the rainforests?	Raising awareness of geographic location
What is happening to them?	Understanding of the issues
Is this a problem? For whom?	Empathising with the local people
How can we influence what is happening there?	This raises major issues of empowerment
What is it like to live here?	This would encourage pupils to empathise with a different culture

Once again, conducting this study within the context of a distant locality is best achieved by using an enquiry approach. Traditional tales such as *The People Who Hugged the Trees* (Rose, 1991) highlight conflict and community issues which are ideal for exploring through simulations. *After the Storm* (Butterworth, 2003) draws attention to the damage (and opportunities) that result from extreme weather.

Photo | *Anna Grandfield.*

Mining and quarrying

Open-cast coal mining in Northumberland is a fascinating topic, highlighting many issues relating to environmental change in a UK locality. A template for making a study of this issue is outlined below. You could apply the same approach to a study of mining and quarrying in a distant locality, such as the African goldfields or the Brazilian rainforest.

Possible aims:

- raising awareness of the impact of open-cast coal mining on the environment;
- allowing pupils to express and develop their own opinions on a contentious issue;
- appreciating that there are different attitudes relating to open-cast mining in a rural area;
- development of a variety of geographical skills and techniques.

You could focus the study with the following enquiry questions:

Focus question	Teaching/learning outcomes
What types of coal mining are there?	Increasing pupils' knowledge
Why is open-cast coal mining being carried out specifically in Northumberland?	Raises awareness of specific local conditions
What does an open cast coal mine look like?	Offers the opportunity for investigation/visit
How many jobs does the industry provide and what do these jobs entail?	Puts the study into a wider context
Is the quality of the environment more important than the provision of jobs for local people?	Asks pupils to consider the impact of closing the industry
To what extent do people living around the area of coal extraction benefit or suffer from this activity and in what ways?	Empathising with different groups
To what extent do the owners of the mine ensure minimum impact in the locality?	Understanding how environmental impact may be addressed
What representation have the local people made about the effects of this industry, and to whom?	Recognition of the role of local decision making/politics
How is the landscape reinstated after mining?	Understanding of techniques of reclamation
Is the reinstated landscape better than the original?	Asking pupils to express views
Has the land use changed?	Enables the impact of change to be assessed

Suggested activities to develop the work include:

- Whole-class discussions on the nature of coal and how it may be extracted. These discussions may be reinforced through pupils' own research on coal using books, CDs, the internet and information from coal companies.
- The use of map skills involving the use of GIS to delineate the mining area and to show the extent and nature of the development. Pupils can then draw their own conclusions about land use before mining took place and develop their own opinions as to the impact the mining has had on this landscape. They can also identify the dwellings and settlements in the immediate vicinity of the coal mines and can imagine what it would be like to live in that locality.

- A site visit. Before the site visit, pupils could work in groups to develop questions that they might choose to ask their guide. During the visit they could take photographs, make field sketches and make recordings (e.g. of their interviews or the noise of lorries).
- Part of the visit may also include a period of time spent in one of the settlements close to the mine. Pupils could collect a variety of additional information that might include, for example, interviews with local inhabitants, observations on the visual and aural impact of the mine, a dust survey (using dust plates) and a traffic count. The use of environmental recording devices could enhance this study and address ICT requirements.
- If a site visit is not possible, secondary sources such as photographs, videos and the internet could be used.

Follow-up activities might include:

- Making a display of photographs, maps, newspaper cuttings, field sketches and graphs of the results of the surveys. Pupils can use these as a resource and as a focus for the classroom activities.
- Having a class discussion on what pupils have discovered about people's attitudes towards open-cast mining.
- Creative writing activities in which pupils express their opinions and attitudes about what they have seen and interacted with. This could take the form of the front page of a newspaper and involve the use of a desk-top publishing package.
- Designing and mapping a landscape that would enhance the environment after the mine has closed, perhaps using the inspirational example of the Eden Project. Pupils may choose to transform the hole into either a water park with wildlife habitats or a lake for recreational purposes; they may wish to return the area to an agricultural land use or develop a country park with woodland walks/mountain bike tracks with all the attendant facilities.
- A role play exercise centred on a proposal to start an open-cast coal mine in a new area, close to the school. The cast of characters in this scenario could include:
  - a local MP
  - a town planner
  - a conservation group representative
  - members of the parish council
  - a village shopkeeper
  - an unemployed parent of three children
  - an eight- or nine-year-old child
  - the mine owner
  - the haulage contractor
  - a farmer

This role play could take the form of a studio discussion for a television programme. It might be possible for a person from the local planning department to chair the meeting and draw together the threads of the debate. Such a person would be able to provide pupils with a considered decision as to whether or not the open-cast coal mine should go ahead. If you video the role play you could use it to stimulate discussion concerning the issues raised by open-cast mining.

Photo | *I.A. Recordings photographic archive.*

Photo | Tina Horler.

Rainforests – These provide a topical, though perhaps overused, context within which pupils can learn about our inability to sustain natural biomes. Mining and quarrying of minerals and metals in such an environment raise issues of sustainability and conflict. This opens up a wealth of views about the development of these distinctive regions.

As well as covering the environmental theme in the geography national curriculum, any work that you do on the environment will involve working at a range of scales, which is one of the other curriculum requirements. If you select your case studies carefully you may also be able to focus on a locality in a less economically developed country, thereby linking skills, places and themes in the way that was originally intended by the team that devised the curriculum.

The whole-school approach: a case study of an eco-school

Environmental geography can be taught using topics, themes and issues approaches but some of the most effective and integrated learning can be developed by taking a whole-school approach. Ebchester Church of England Primary School in County Durham provided an excellent example of how environmental geography may be delivered in holistic fashion. The head teacher, Richard Coombes, realised that the school environment, in particular the woodland, the stream and a substantial open grassed area, offered rich learning opportunities.

His enthusiasm encouraged parents, unemployed local people, local businesses and the pupils to co-operate as a cohesive body. Over a period of twelve years adults and children worked together to conserve and develop wildlife habitats in the school grounds. This provided an exciting learning experience for all those involved, forging strong links within the community which continue to flourish and develop.

At the start each class was given an area to develop. It was their task to ensure the continued progress of the project, which they did through discussion and making drawings and plans. They also identified improvements that would enhance their area in the long term. This initial planning stage then led to decisions about what was wanted and final plans were produced. The plans provided the basis for pupils to communicate their ideas to those people who could help bring them to fruition, e.g. parents, local businesses, volunteers and experts. (Note that communication of this kind can involve the use of ICT in a variety of forms, e.g. PowerPoint presentations.) Projects undertaken at the school included the following:

- woodland area
- weather station
- pond

Photo | Paula Richardson.

Figure 1 | *Trails devised by pupils at Ebchester CE Primary School.*

■ amphitheatre
■ sandpit area
■ butterfly garden
■ herb garden
■ structured play area
■ wild flower meadow
■ memorial garden
■ compost area
■ organic vegetable garden (produce from which is prepared in the school dining room).

Each year new projects and initiatives were discussed and developed. One involved the construction of an outdoor amphitheatre to stage productions. The theatre occupies what was formerly a piece of waste ground which presented a potential hazard to pupils playing near it due to its steepness. Now it offers a facility that is highly valued and utilised.

Making trails

Different areas of the school grounds, such as the butterfly garden and woodland area, were linked together by the creation of all-weather paths made from renewable materials. This improved access to and between the areas throughout the year. The trails (e.g. a bird trail and a tree trail) and the various site developments were all planned by the pupils who used their own knowledge and imagination to draw the plans, with the help of local experts (see Figure 1).

Attracting visitors

Initially, the project was quite parochial but as the plans came to fruition Ebchester School began to involve other schools which resulted in considerable valuable and enjoyable interaction. Some pupils were appointed as wardens to escort visitors around the site and were given a warden's badge. This gave pupils:

■ the opportunity to communicate information
■ confidence
■ the chance to express themselves.

Worksheets were also developed by the pupils themselves for use by visitors from other schools (Figure 2). In devising the sheets the pupils used a great range of geographical skills including learning geographical terms, making maps and plans and using symbols and keys. One of the other benefits is that they developed a better sense of their own geographical situation which helped them when they studied contrasting localities.

Ebchester School developed a curriculum which, for the most part, can be covered within the boundaries of the pupils' own environment and, as a consequence, enables all subjects within the national curriculum to be addressed in a practical and meaningful way. In addition to subject learning, the work enhanced pupils' self-esteem. As the head teacher put it, 'All of the children benefit from their interactions with children from visiting schools and take great pride in sharing their school with others.'

In a project like this, involving the lower school at an early stage can ensure the continuity of all the activities. The secret of success at Ebchester was its long-term, ongoing

FIND THREE COLOURS

What To Do

1) Take a little bit of the three colours you want.

2) Stick them on the three bits of sticky tape.

3) Tell me where you found them.

_____   _____   _____

4) Draw the whole object.

CREATURES

Go down to the woodland and see what insects are down there. Draw the insects that you have seen.

Pick out which one you like the best.

Next, draw which one you picked out.

Cut out the pictures of the insects.

Put them on a piece of paper.

Write down the names of the insects.

Figure 2 | *Worksheet for visitors, produced by pupils at Ebchester CE Primary School.*

developmental nature, which changed in emphasis from year to year because of variations in, for example:

- the pupils' interests and enthusiasm
- availability of resources
- expert help
- parental input
- curriculum developments
- contemporary environmental issues.

The pupils were central to the decision-making process and learnt a great deal from the interaction with adults and from planning the developments. This is an excellent example of the value of empowering pupils by giving them ownership of a project. This ownership also seemed to stay with the pupils as the incidence of vandalism at the school reduced to virtually zero and the older pupils who moved on to secondary school still saw the school as 'theirs'.

This scheme promoted environmental awareness in a way that links many aspects of the curriculum, including citizenship, personal well-being, health education and – particularly important for geography – sustainable development. Ebchester School's experience, recognised by their achievement of Eco-School status, shows how environmental geography can be taught in an imaginative and stimulating way. You can adapt this approach to your school; at Howe Dell School, Hertfordshire, sustainable development has been central to the creation of a new school building (Bloomfield and Stewart, 2007); Seaton Primary School, Devon's approach to sustainable energy solutions and whole-school environmental ethos won them an Ashden Award.

Teaching environmental geography – some considerations

The very nature of environmental geography means that many of the topics, such as new housing or the development of nuclear power, are likely to be contentious. Feelings about these issues can run very high and they need to be handled sensitively. Teachers therefore have a critical part to play in providing role models and it is essential that you are seen to be impartial and even-handed in dealing with the issue. It is also important that issues which create concern in young children, such as the possible extinction of animal species, are treated with particular care and that pupils are offered a final positive perspective.

Misconceptions

As in any subject, pupils are likely to suffer from a considerable number of misconceptions. In geography, these are especially significant when it comes to environmental issues as they may arise from, or lead to, prejudices. This was clearly illustrated by Palmer (1998) who was able to show that while children may be able to recognise and name unfamiliar creatures and landscapes this does not necessarily mean they understand their context or existence. Children's confusion about environmental issues can be considered as a mix of, among other things, factual errors, confusion over cause and effect and sweeping generalisations that suggest anything which is environmentally damaging contributes to every environmental problem.

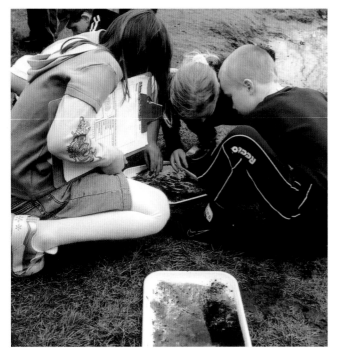

Photo | *John Halocha.*

The continuing controversy over the fish stocks in the North Sea is a case in point and a neat way of introducing a European dimension. The issue revolves around the different perceptions of the viability and sustainability of the fish stock with the fishermen arguing for their right to fish in order to preserve their livelihood and way of life, while scientists argue that without severe limitation on catch size the future of the industry is in jeopardy. This is a complex issue and before it can be fully explored in the classroom some of the following initial misconceptions need to be addressed, for example:

1. Fish start and end their lives in a supermarket.

2. Commercial fishing is done with a rod and line.

3. Fish fingers are the fingers of fish.

4. That there will always be fish to eat (i.e. children take food supply for granted).

The study of the North Sea fishing controversy offers pupils a real issue in which two opposing viewpoints are argued with both passion and evidence. The teacher's role in this study would be to facilitate the exploration of these opposing views and enable pupils to come to an understanding of the issue from which they could draw their own conclusions. The use of video clips, the internet and links with pupils in fishing ports are all ways to achieve this.

International comparisons

A very positive and exciting way of overcoming misconceptions which may arise from (mis)interpretation of secondary sources, particularly when dealing with an issue in a distant place, would be to link up with a school in that country or locality. This can be achieved via the Global Gateway website (see useful contacts at end of chapter) which offers a means of 'pairing' schools. The exchange of on-the-spot information, opinions and perceptions would enrich pupils' learning in both participating schools and would make a considerable contribution to addressing the One World issue.

It is also very constructive to consider how other countries include environmental geography in their curriculum. In France, for example, environmental education is an important part of geography, science and civic education (citizenship) and there is a strong global perspective. This is perhaps something which needs to be further developed in the UK. One of the other central concepts is the idea of *patrimoine* or heritage. This addresses not only the protection of the natural environment, e.g. sustainability, but also the protection of relics of the past and the protection of the cultures of a group, a region or country. Older pupils in France are also taught about the role of the United Nations but, as in the UK, when studies of litter, waste, recycling and sorting are undertaken, the pupil tends to be the starting point.

Conclusion

There is a wide range of resources available to enhance the teaching of environmental geography. To begin with, the local surroundings offers rich possibilities for fieldwork. Secondary sources include internet resources, teaching packs and colourful and inviting information books. Many texts, however, focus on environmental education as opposed to environmental geography. It is therefore all too easy to be drawn into environmental education without fully appreciating the wealth of geographical opportunities that also lie along this route.

When it comes to finding out about issues, newspaper cuttings, local news footage, planning applications, information from pressure groups such as Greenpeace, and photographs collected over a period of time are all extremely valuable. So is the internet; one option is to enable pupils to identify the issues they want to study for themselves and to help them search for and appraise appropriate resources. Flexibility and responsiveness on the part of the teacher is essential. It is important to remember that pupils need the opportunity to explore their own feelings, values and thoughts on environmental issues and to do so within a clear geographical framework. The best outcome of good teaching in environmental geography is perhaps that the pupils are able to feel that they can *really* make a difference, no matter how small.

References and further reading

Bloomfield, P. and Stewart, C. (2007) 'Howe Dell: Sustainable school'. *Primary Geographer*, 64, pp. 42-3.

Hicks, D. (2009) 'Naturally resourceful: could your school be a transition school?'. *Primary Geographer*, 70, pp. 19-21.

Martin, F. (2006) *Teaching Geography in Primary Schools*. Cambridge: Chris Kington Publishing.

Martin, F. and Owens, P. (2008) *Caring for our World*. Sheffield: Geographical Association.

Martin, H. and Davis, C. (2006) 'Eco-warriors take a learning journey'. *Primary Geographer*, 60, pp. 7-9.

Palmer, J. (1998) 'Environmental cognition in young children', in Scoffham, S. (ed) Primary Sources: *Research findings in primary geography*. Sheffield: Geographical Association.

QCDA (2010) *The National Curriculum Level Description for Subjects*. Coventry: QCDA.

See also *Primary Geographer*, 64, Autumn 2007, which focuses on sustainable schools; and the think piece 'ESD at KS1 and 2' on the Geographical Association website *www.geography.org.uk/gtip/thinkpieces*

Picture books and stories to do with the environment

Anholt, L. (2002) *Eco-Wolf and the Three Pigs.* London: Orchard Books.

Butterworth, N. (2003) *After the Storm.* London: Harper Collins.

Child, L. (2002) *What Planet are You From, Clarice Bean?* London: Orchard Books.

Dyer, S. (2001) *Five Little Fiends.* London: Bloomsbury.

Foreman, M. (2004) *One World.* London: Andersen Press.

Gliori, D. (2008) *The Trouble with Dragons.* London: Bloomsbury.

Hickman, L. (2009) *Will Jellyfish Rule the World?* London: Orchard Books.

Morch, R. and Hadow, P. (2007) *Who Will Save Us?* Newton Abbott: Rebecca Morch Publishing Ltd.

Readman, J. (2006) *George Saves the World by Lunchtime.* London: Random House.

Rose, D. (1991) *The People Who Hugged the Trees.* Laneham, MD: Rinehart.

Websites

Ashden Awards *www.ashdenawards.org*

Campaign to Protect Rural England *www.cpre.org.uk*

Centre for Alternative Technology *www.cat.org.uk*

Eco-Schools *www.eco-schools.org.uk*

English Heritage *www.english-heritage.org.uk*

Field Studies Council *www.field-studies-council.org*

Forest Schools *www.forestschools.com*

Global Gateway *www.globalgateway.org.uk*

Learning Outside the Classroom *www.lotc.org.uk*

Learning Through Landscapes *www.ltl.org.uk*

Mywalks *nuweb.northumbria.ac.uk/mywalks/intro.php*

Natural England *www.naturalengland.org.uk*

Teachernet Sustainable Schools *www.teachernet.gov.uk/sustainableschools*

World Wildlife Fund *www.wwf.org.uk*

School grounds improvement schemes

Groundwork *www.groundwork.org.uk*

Keep Britain Tidy *www.keepbritaintidy.org*

The Tree Council *www.treecouncil.org.uk*

The Wildlife Trusts *www.wildlifetrusts.org*

World Wildlife Fund *www.wwf.org.uk*

Acknowledgement

The authors wish to thank Richard Coombes and the staff and pupils at Ebchester Church of England Primary School, County Durham.

Say Yes for Gatwicks Runway

Gatwicks New Runway has made more uses for the Airport and flights are cheaper for abroad.

Luggage

Less people come on each plane so you can bring 1 – 2 more bags on the, the Plane to HoLiDay!!!!!

Once your there and on the plane celebrate and EnJoy your HOLiDaY!!!!!

CELEBRATION

Pupils' work | Y6, Salford's Primary School, Redhill.

CHAPTER COVERAGE:
CITIZENSHIP • DISTANT PLACES • ENQUIRIES • FIELDWORK
• ISSUES • LITERACY/STORIES • PROGRESSION • TRANSITION

Citizenship and primary geography

Many primary schools accord high priority to citizenship and values education. Programmes such as Social and Emotional Aspects of Learning (SEAL) prepare pupils for their lives at school and in the future, developing their self-knowledge and their ability to understand and manage their feelings and relationships with others. Similarly, responsible behaviour, the importance of ethos, codes of conduct and the role of the individual as an effective member of the school community are also emphasised.

'If the aspiration is to create pupils who are active and well-rounded citizens, there is no more relevant subject than geography.' (Ofsted, 2008.)

There is a strong connection between primary geography, its content, teaching and learning strategies, and all aspects of children's lives and experiences. Not only is it difficult to separate them, it is also undesirable, as real life does not come in compartmentalised boxes. Our lives intertwine with those of others, both through space (locally, nationally, globally) and through time (past, present and future). As they plan their curriculum, schools need to take account of this interconnectedness.

Primary geography investigates real contexts and real-life issues and situations. The curriculum encourages pupils to study places at a range of scales from local to global and to explore the interdependence of society, economy and the natural environment. Pupils study how people are influenced by and affect their environments and they are encouraged to develop a sense of responsibility for personal and group actions. As they explore 'live' issues pupils are encouraged to listen carefully to arguments from different viewpoints and to reflect on these points of view. Primary geography questions the values on which decisions are based and explores alternative ways of providing for human needs and wants.

Citizenship education also starts from the pupils and draws on their backgrounds, beliefs and concerns. It seeks to explore different values and attitudes, promote self-respect and tolerance of others, encourage respect for democracy, justice, law and human rights and develop social and moral responsibility. Pupils have the opportunity to compare values and beliefs, to examine evidence and opinions critically, to form conclusions, discuss differences and resolve conflicts. Real life and relevance helps to motivate the pupils, thereby creating more effective learning that involves communication, collaboration, self-directed learning, problem solving, researching and publishing findings. Pupils feel their work has purpose and a goal. Education for citizenship and community cohesion involves not only pupils, but the whole school, their families and the communities in which they live, so strong links between home, school and community are essential.

Active learning

It is widely accepted that children learn in different ways (Gardner, 1999) so it makes sense to employ a wide range of methodologies in classroom teaching. Engaging pupils' interest through exciting, active learning is a very effective way of making the learning experience more memorable and effective. The official review of the primary curriculum emphasised this point:

Local Issues
- Transport – development of bypass, cycle routes, bridleways, pedestrian walks, safe routes to school, school travel plans
- Development & redevelopment: Brown field/green field issues
- Housing/industrial development
- Siting of new supermarket
- Waste – litter, vandalism etc., waste disposal, landfill sites, incineration, siting of collection points etc.
- School grounds development
- Children's playground issues

Global Issues
- Fair trade (bananas, clothes, coffee etc.)
- Global warming, destruction of rainforests
- Energy resources
- Poverty, hunger, homelessness, refugees
- Human-rights, racism, children's rights
- Water resources
- Waste

Figure 1 | *Exploring local and global issues.*

The touchstone of an excellent curriculum is that it instils in children a love of learning for its own sake. This means that primary children must not only learn what to study, they must learn how to study, and thus become confident, self-disciplined individuals capable of engaging in a lifelong process of learning.
(Rose, 2009, p. 9.)

If you want to promote active learning in geography and citizenship there are a number of factors to take into account. In particular you need to:

- Plan activities which help pupils to develop the knowledge, skills and understanding to enable them to act as responsible citizens
- Investigate issues at a range of scales from the local to the global
- Employ a wide variety of organisational strategies, from teacher-led, whole-class activities and discussion, to children working as individuals, in pairs and in groups
- Use a number of different teaching and learning methods including role play, creative problem solving, critical thinking, communication, geographical enquiry including mapwork, fieldwork, analysis of photographs and links with the local community

Investigating issues

There are numerous issues which might be explored in a combined geography and citizenship topic. Figure 1 indicates some of the possibilities.

Whether the issue is local, national or global, pupils will need to develop strategies to find out who the stakeholders are, who has the power to make the changes and who can influence the decision-makers (Figure 2). Pupils also need to think about who they feel they need to inform about the issue. The people will vary according to the issue.

Teaching activities

The following teaching activities illustrate how the principles outlined above can be applied in practice. They cover a range of topics, involve studies at different scales and are aimed at specific key stages.

As well as relating to the geography curriculum, these activities support community cohesion, the enhanced Healthy Schools programme and the SEAL programme. The links to the eight doorways from the Sustainable Schools strategy will also be apparent, especially travel and traffic, food and drink, local well-being and inclusion and participation. All the activities can be adapted and applied to other issues, not just the ones identified in this chapter.

Figure 2 | How investigating an issue can lead to change and action.

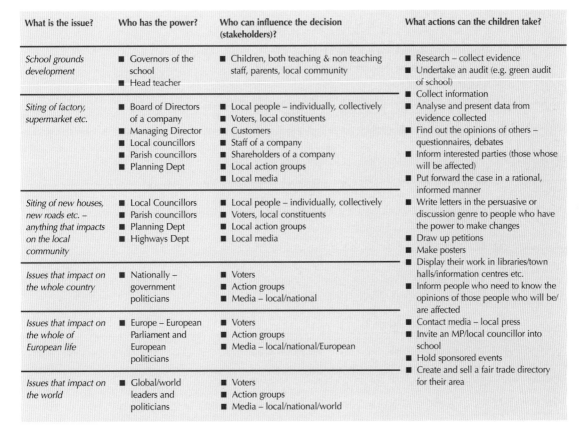

What is the issue?	Who has the power?	Who can influence the decision (stakeholders)?	What actions can the children take?
School grounds development	■ Governors of the school ■ Head teacher	■ Children, both teaching & non teaching staff, parents, local community	■ Research – collect evidence ■ Undertake an audit (e.g. green audit of school) ■ Collect information
Siting of factory, supermarket etc.	■ Board of Directors of a company ■ Managing Director ■ Local councillors ■ Parish councillors ■ Planning Dept	■ Local people – individually, collectively ■ Voters, local constituents ■ Customers ■ Staff of a company ■ Shareholders of a company ■ Local action groups ■ Local media	■ Analyse and present data from evidence collected ■ Find out the opinions of others – questionnaires, debates ■ Inform interested parties (those whose will be affected) ■ Put forward the case in a rational, informed manner
Siting of new houses, new roads etc. – anything that impacts on the local community	■ Local Councillors ■ Parish councillors ■ Planning Dept ■ Highways Dept	■ Local people – individually, collectively ■ Voters, local constituents ■ Local action groups ■ Local media	■ Write letters in the persuasive or discussion genre to people who have the power to make changes ■ Draw up petitions ■ Make posters ■ Display their work in libraries/town halls/information centres etc. ■ Inform people who need to know the opinions of those people who will be/ are affected
Issues that impact on the whole country	■ Nationally – government politicians	■ Voters ■ Action groups ■ Media – local/national	■ Contact media – local press ■ Invite an MP/local councillor into school ■ Hold sponsored events ■ Create and sell a fair trade directory for their area
Issues that impact on the whole of European life	■ Europe – European Parliament and European politicians	■ Voters ■ Action groups ■ Media – local/national/European	
Issues that impact on the world	■ Global/world leaders and politicians	■ Voters ■ Action groups ■ Media – local/national/world	

Caring for the environment (key stage 1)

Aim: To help the pupils investigate the impact of people's actions on the environment, both locally and globally, and on the lives of others as well as their own.

As a stimulus, read the story *George Saves the World by Lunchtime* (Readman, 2006) which focuses on the four environmental strategies all starting with the letter 'R'– 'Reduce, Reuse, Repair, Recycle'.

Activities:

■ Whole class: Select one of the pupils to take George's role. The rest of the class ask him questions about one of the things he does to protect the environment. How does it help? What advice has he got for other pupils? Alternate the role so that other children have the chance to focus on different strategies. This activity helps to develop questioning skills and helps children to clarify their thinking.

■ Use *The Trouble with Dragons* (Gliori, 2009). This delightful story uses quirky pictures and rhyming couplets to put across the message that we need to work together and share what we have in our efforts to care for the planet. There are good opportunities for dramatic wall displays based on the illustrations, as well as for detailed discussions of the issues raised.

The world of work (key stage 1)

Aim: To introduce pupils to the world of work

Activities:

■ Using the class role-play area, ask pupils to act out the different jobs done by adults (e.g. travel agent, post office counter clerk, shopkeeper, lorry driver). As they play encourage them to talk about their work, the clothes they have to wear and what they like and dislike about their job. Provide a dressing-up box, or simply hats, which the pupils wear when they are in role, to help bring the activity to life.

■ Give pupils a job with a geographical context to perform (e.g. booking a holiday, packing the suitcases and travelling to a certain destination). Ask them to choose a destination and to find out something about the place they want to visit, the type of clothes they will need and how they are going to get there.

■ Instruct each pupil in the group to take on a role and to behave in a certain way all the time (e.g. sulky, bossy, lazy, bad tempered, nasty, and so on). The pupils then explore, through role play, what would happen if they set about their given task as a group, but behaved in their allotted manner.

Settlements (key stage 2)

Aim: To introduce pupils to the concepts of settlements and routeways.

Activities:

■ Introduce pupils to road playmats, construction kits and other similar resources.

■ Build a model village or town with certain buildings and features using a variety of materials (junk modelling as well as commercially produced equipment). How do you get from A to B? What is this building? What is it used for? Who works there?

An island development (key stage 1)

Aim: To help pupils to investigate the impact of change on people's lives using *Katie Morag and the New Pier* (Hedderwick, 1994). As the new pier is built on the Isle of Struay, Katie Morag feels both excited at the prospect of seeing Granny Mainland more often and sad when she realises that her friend the ferryman will lose his job.

Activities:

■ After reading the book, ask pupils to discuss (in groups) who lives on the island and what work they do.

■ Compare the pictures on the first and the last two pages of the story. What things are changing on the island? Why? How do you feel about the changes? How do you think the islanders feel about the changes? Encourage pupils to express views about these changes.

Photo | *Greg Walker.*

- Using a scaffolding frame put forward the case for and against building the new pier.
- In role (e.g. Struay parish councillor, islanders, ferryman, travel agent, Katie Morag, fisherman, conservationist) debate the issue of the new pier and the changes it will bring. Who is in favour of the changes and who is against?
- Discuss how the pier will change the lives of the islanders. Compare the jobs people did before and after its construction. Who is now better or worse off?
- Make a tourist map and brochures advertising a visit to the island covering a range of topics such as weather, landscape, buildings, jobs, wildlife and environmental issues.
- List the types of foods that are produced by the farmers and fishermen on the island. The pupils then write a menu for the ferryman's café using local produce from the farms and the sea, giving the dishes appropriate names. Discuss how you think visitors will respond to them.

Safe routes to school (key stages 1/2)

Aims: To consider the impact of traffic on our lives, whether at a local, regional, national or global scale; to investigate issues of safety, pollution, health, management of scarce resources and sustainability and use the information to develop a school travel plan; to find out how places are connected and how people move between those places.

Activities:

- Group work: Devise a questionnaire to find out how most pupils travel to school. Ask them to carry out a survey and then analyse the data (use ICT if appropriate).
- Individual work: Using a local map (use Local Studies software or pictorial maps with younger children), ask each pupil to mark his/her route to and from school showing the places where they cross a road with an 'X'. Now get them to conduct a safety audit (risk assessment) of the route they take and means of travel that they use. Can they identify danger spots (e.g. junctions, corners, parked cars), or hazards (cracked pavements, potholes, bad parking, speeding)? Are there any hazards that affect a particular group of people (disabled, elderly, people with pushchairs)?
- Group work: Ask pupils to look at each other's routes to school and the danger points. Discuss how the danger could be reduced.
- Group work: Ask the pupils to plan a safe walking route with safer crossing places (pelican and zebra crossings, bridges, islands, school crossing patrol points) and measures to reduce traffic speed (speed humps, speed restrictions). Ask your local Road Safety Officer to come to school to work with pupils on the project.
- Involve local councillors and show them the safe routes, explaining the danger spots. If pupils feel it is appropriate, they could ask the councillors to act on their findings.

Fieldwork visits (key stages 1/2)

Aims: To focus on specific geographical themes or topics (fieldwork, contrasting locality, rivers, settlements); to develop investigative skills; to build co-operative and teamwork skills and to encourage greater independence and self-confidence.

Activities:

- Whole class: Before the visit, ask pupils to reflect on the environment in which the visit is taking place, using geographical enquiry questions (Where is this place? What is this place like?). Exchange ideas, discuss and anticipate areas of danger.

Primary Geography Handbook

Categories	Possible issues and problems
■ Pollution	■ litter and dog mess – health hazards ■ exhaust fumes – health problems ■ CFCs (chlorofluorocarbons) – destroying ozone layer – cancer
■ Conservation of energy	■ use of exhaustible fossil fuels (coal, oil, gas) ■ excessive burning of fossil fuels – acid rain, greenhouse effect, global warming ■ use of nuclear fuels
■ Waste	■ wasting energy in the home ■ disposable society ■ use of plastics and material which is not biodegradable ■ unhealthy and unsightly disposal of plastics
■ Protection of wildlife and nature	■ destruction of woodlands and rainforests ■ destruction of animal habitats

Figure 3 | *Local environmental issues fall mainly into one of four categories.*

- ■ Group work: Ask pupils to design their own rules and own codes of practice for the visit.
- ■ Whole class: Discuss emergency first aid procedures with personnel from St John's Ambulance.
- ■ Group work: List the contents of a first aid box. Get pupils to design one of their own.
- ■ Group work: Find out about the weather data for the place to be visited, given the time of the year, as well as the terrain, and likely fieldwork activities. Either develop a kit list for the visit and pack a bag, or describe what will be needed.

Change in the local area (key stage 2)

Aim: To make pupils aware that they can make important contributions to environmental issues and to remedying problems.

Activities:

- ■ Whole class: Exchange ideas about environmental problems affecting your locality. Figure 3 shows the kind of issues pupils are likely to raise: they all create links between geography, citizenship, sustainability, community cohesion and social issues.
- ■ Whole class: Discuss what is likely to happen in five, ten and fifteen years' time. What would the pupils like to happen? If the future is to be different, what needs to change?
- ■ Group work: Ask pupils to discuss and list the actions they could take to help ensure the future quality of the Earth and the health and safety of the people who live there.

New developments (key stage 2)

Aims: To explore different ways to improve the area (e.g. derelict site), by looking at different views of the issue and its resolution; to investigate how developments affect local people, for example, the impact on existing shopkeepers of building a new shopping mall; to encourage pupils actively to engage in the improvement of their local environment.

Activities:

Photo | *Anna Grandfield.*

- ■ Introduce pupils to the Development Compass Rose (see p. 210). This framework helps pupils to discuss any issue, resource, photograph or artefact in a balanced manner at either a local, regional, national or international scale.
- ■ Get pupils to debate the development by putting them in role (e.g. developers, parents, children, supermarket company, local wildlife trust, local councillor, house-building company). Give the pupils role cards with the different opinions, ensuring there is a strong emphasis on health and safety issues (e.g. dangerous unlit site, stranger danger, traffic,

Enquiry questions	Learning Activities
■ Domestic waste: What sort of waste do we produce at home and school? ■ What sort of waste is found in a modern dustbin? ■ Do we produce less/more/the same/different waste than in 1900? ■ Why?	**In groups:** Pupils design a questionnaire to use at home and at school. Research work to find out the percentage by weight and volume of rubbish found in a modern bin. Comparison of above information with the same information from 1900.
■ Is all the packaging used on goods really necessary? ■ How do supermarkets and markets dispose of their waste? ■ How much waste and packaging is there in a packed lunch?	**Whole class:** Visit local supermarkets and markets to find out about how they dispose of their waste. Look at the compacters. **In groups:** Undertake a waste audit. Write ten 'top tips' for reducing waste in the classroom. Design a poster to encourage children who bring packed lunch to school to use reusable containers and packaging.
■ Industrial Waste: Why do we produce more hazardous industrial waste today than we did in 1900? ■ What are the problems of disposing of industrial waste?	**Whole class:** Arrange for a spokesperson from a local place of employment to talk about their efforts to minimise the effect of their waste on the atmosphere, rivers and so on.
■ Where is our nearest landfill site? ■ How do we get from school to the landfill site? ■ How can I ensure I am safe when I visit the site?	**In groups:** Locate the site on maps and on aerial photographs. Plan a route to the site. **Whole class:** Discuss the safety aspects of a visit to the site. **In groups:** Design a set of safety rules for the visit.
■ What happens at the landfill site? ■ How are the cells on the landfill site made? ■ Does the site affect the local community? ■ What will happen to the site when it is full?	**Whole class:** Make a site visit if possible. Listen to a talk by the site manager, relating to site management, how the cells are made and filled in, any affects the site has on the local community and how the land will be rehabilitated in the future.
■ How can we all help to reduce the amount of waste we throw away? ■ How does reduce, reusing, recycling, composting and minimising help the environment?	**Whole school:** Arrange a visit to school by 'Cycler' Robot. Contact UK Waste or your local Groundwork Trust to make your request. **In groups:** Sort cleaned waste into four categories (reuse, recycle, compost, minimise) and discuss how this will help the environment
■ Make a sculpture out of waste products. ■ Can you make a fruit bowl, to hold apples, bananas, oranges & grapes, out of paper?	**In groups, pairs or individually:** Make a sculpture or model out of waste. **In groups, pairs or individually:** Make a fruit bowl out of newspaper. (Use any technique, papier-mâché, weaving and so on.)
■ Can we design and make clothes out of waste products? ■ Can we put on a fashion show of our clothes?	**In groups or pairs:** Design and make clothes out of waste products. **Whole class:** Produce a clothes show presentation.

Figure 4 | *Enquiry questions and activities for a unit of work on waste management.*

pollution). Try to reach a consensus. Discuss who the most powerful stakeholders were and why they were powerful.

■ If possible, debate a real 'live' issue within your locality such as the re-development of a brown field site and involve personnel from different groups with interests in the development.

Waste management (key stage 2)

Aims: To learn about waste and its management (RRR – reduce, reuse, recycle); to increase awareness of the role of minimisation within school, the wider community and the industrial and business community; to help pupils to understand that everyone (including themselves) can make a difference to global environmental problems.
Activities: See Figure 4.

Tourism and travel (key stage 2)

Aims: To develop sensitivity towards other cultures, challenge bias and make pupils more aware of stereotyping and the differing viewpoints; to investigate the environmental impact of tourism (litter, traffic congestion, footpath erosion) and review its impact on the local economy (jobs, income, new building work).
Activities:
Travel and tourism links to the geography national curriculum (investigating real people in

real places and the impact they have on the environment) and provides a context for the following enquiry questions:

- Who are tourists?
- Why do tourists travel?
- Where do tourists travel?
- When do tourists travel?
- How do tourists travel?
- Why do tourists travel to particular places?
- What effects do tourists have on environments, economies, societies, cultures and host populations?
- What differing attitudes are held about tourism and its effects?
- What are the possible futures for tourism?

Extension activities:

- Extend the above activities by using holiday images found in tourist brochures.
- Give each group of pupils a collection of images showing (a) well-behaved tourists (b) tourists who show no respect for the host population. Ask pupils to discuss and list behaviours under 'good holidaymaker' and 'bad holidaymaker'. Compare lists. Compile a cartoon strip which shows examples of good and bad behaviour. Write a code of behaviour for tourists.

A hotel in the rainforest (key stage 2)

Aims: To explore the impact of tourism on a community and to recognise that change can have both positive and negative effects on different sectors of the community; to explore concepts of fair play, power relationships and invasion of territory; to extend the children's knowledge and understanding of people and places.

Activities:

- Read *Where the Forest Meets the Sea* (Baker, 1987), a story about when a boy and his father take a boat to reach a remote tropical beach and an ancient rainforest in North Queensland, Australia.
- Locate this rainforest on the globe. Now look for other rainforest areas. Discuss the vegetation and animal habitats found in the rainforest.
- Create a rainforest environment in the role-play area.
- In groups of three or four, give pupils a photograph of an unspoilt tropical beach scene. Ask them the following questions: What is this place like? How is this place changing? Why is it like it is? How do you feel about this place? Who might use the area shown in the photograph? Share responses with the whole class.
- Discuss arguments for and against the development of tourism in this area of tropical beach/rainforest. Which groups of people support and oppose the development and why? How do you think the native Australians (Aborigines) feel about the changes?

Photo | *Diane Wright.*

1. Ask pupils to study a photograph of an unspoilt tropical beach and to discuss who might use it.
2. Divide the pupils into six groups each assuming one of the following roles: local resident, local person who earns living from the sea, local child, local government official, travel company representative, holiday maker.
3. To enable the pupils to get into role, ask them to discuss in their small groups: Who they are? What job they do? How they might use the beach in the photograph? How do they spend most of their time? Are they rich or poor? What parts of the beach might they need for work? What parts might they use for pleasure?
4. Ask each group to imagine that a hotel is going to be built by the travel company. How does the hotel change things? Will their way of life be affected? Will some changes be for the better? Will some changes be for the worse? Do they want the hotel to be built?
5. Ask each group to list three statements which express their views (in role) about this proposed development.
6. Ask the pupils to form six new groups, each comprising representatives from the original groupings.
7. In new mixed groups and still in role, children take it in turns to give views and discuss their statements, to listen to the views of others and to consider whether their view has changed.

8. Pupils return to their original groups, discuss what they have heard and then and then elect a spokesperson.
9. Organise a mock public enquiry and allow each spokesperson to speak for two minutes.
10. Ask pupils to vote 'for' or 'against' the hotel and discuss the idea of 'rated' votes: that the local government and travel company groups votes are rated at two compared to the votes of the local residents, local child, local person who earns living from the sea and holiday maker, who are rated at one.
11. The rating provides an opportunity for discussion of who holds the power and why this might be so. In some countries groups, such as women and youths, have virtually no say in their country's development. Discuss whether this is fair.
12. Out of role, as a whole class discuss the following: Do they feel their group had a fair say? How much did their own group's interests affect the decision to build or not to build the hotel? What issues did the groups raise? Who held the power? Why do they think this was?
13. Write an account of the role-play activity in the role of a journalist attending the public meeting.

Activity adapted from Mason, 1992.

Figure 5 | *How to explore an issue in role.*

■ Ask pupils to study the photograph of the unspoilt tropical beach and to discuss who might use it. Put them in role, e.g. Melanie Forest (conservationist), Darren Plant (botanist), Lesley Fortune (Director of Grandiose Hotel Developments Ltd), Peter Campaign (town councillor), Jeremy Beach (barrier reef coastal ranger), Miranda Holidayinn (Midsummer Hotel), Danny (the local boy), Polly (wind-surfing club), Melanie Law (local resident) and debate how building a new holiday complex on the tropical beach will affect the area. Who is for the changes and who is against?

■ Use a writing frame to put forward the cases for and against the building of the new holiday complex (note taking, discussion and persuasion genres).

■ Make a tourist map and brochures advertising a visit to the rainforest hotel. Include all the information and pictures of what you can see and do.

Extension activity:

■ Who has the power? These activities can easily be extended to look at the most powerful stakeholders (Figure 5) or adapted for other development situations: e.g. new supermarket, bypass, building or extending a regional airport, building a theme park at the coast.

Wants and needs (key stage 2)

Aim: To develop pupils' understanding of the differences between 'wants' and 'needs', and 'quality of life' and 'standard of living'.

Activities:

■ Whole class: Explore with pupils what they think they need to lead a happy, healthy life.

■ Work in pairs: Ask pupils to select nine items from the previous activity and rank them according to which they feel are most important. Use diamond ranking with the most important at the top, the least important at the bottom and the others in between.

■ Compare the results from different groups and agree a class list.

- Group work: Ask pupils to reflect on what they really need to be happy and healthy and to have a good quality of life. Ask them to revise their original lists of wants and needs. Do they wish to move some items up or down the list?

Extension activities:

- Whole class: Have a class discussion about the meaning of 'quality of life' (open spaces, pure air, friendship, leisure time etc.) and 'standard of living' (bigger house, better car etc.).
- Group work: Ask pupils, in their groups, to produce a poster illustrating 'quality of life'.
- Whole class: Explore with pupils who is responsible for our quality of life and reflect on how increasing our standard of living could have an impact on the environment and other people's lives, both now and in the future.

Children's rights (key stage 2)

Aims: To identify basic human rights such as food, shelter, clothing and love; to consider how rights need to be balanced with responsibilities.

Activity:

- Group work: Look at a simplified version of the UN Convention on the Rights of the Child and think about a contrasting locality or place you are studying. Do the children there have the same rights as you do? Discuss the reasons for any differences.

Cultural diversity (key stage 2)

Aim: To explore similarities and differences between the two cultures.

Activities:

- Read *Shanyi Goes to China* (So, 2006). On a visit to her Chinese grandparents Shanyi finds out the customs and daily life of her Chinese relatives.
- Ask the pupils to make a list of the places Shanyi visits and the things that she did.
- Using both the photographs and the text, make a list of similarities and differences between the UK and China.
- Ask pupils to imagine they are Shanyi and write a postcard to their family in the UK.
- Use the internet, books and videos to find out more about people's lives in China.

Going to secondary school (key stage 2)

Aim: To ensure pupils are confident when starting at the secondary school.

Activity:

- Arrange for year 6 pupils to work with year 7 pupils from the secondary school to produce a new induction booklet for the secondary school. This will give pupils a stronger sense of ownership and team membership and increase their confidence. It should include maps and plans of the secondary school and a route showing how to get there. It could also include bus timetables, information about sports facilities and drawings of the buildings.

Visualisation and relaxation (key stages 1/2)

Aim: To celebrate the beauty of the earth and encourage a sense of awe, wonder and mystery.

Activities:

- Whole class: Ask pupils to close their eyes and relax and imagine they are on the seashore (or any other environment being studied in geography). Look carefully at the sea and the way it moves. What colour is the sea? How is the water moving?

■ Look carefully at the shore. Is it made of sand, stones, shingle or a mixture? Pick up a stone or a shell. Feel its shape, size, texture and weight. Touch two other things you find on the beach. Look at their shape ... and colour ... and size ... and feel their ... then put them back on the beach. Sit on the beach and listen. What two sounds can you hear? Who or what is making the sounds? Feel the elements of the weather on your body – is it sunny/windy/rainy?

■ In pairs: Ask pupils to open their eyes and then with a partner discuss parts of their visualisation, make notes about their feelings and share ideas with the class.

Assemblies (key stages 1/2)

Many assemblies address elements of citizenship education and PSHE linked to geography. They also celebrate the community of the school and its ethos, and draw on the backgrounds, traditions and cultures of pupils and the communities in which they live. Common themes are the differences and uniqueness of people, preparation for adult life, giving something back in return for everything one has, and caring for others. Assemblies may be times when outside speakers such as council officers, charity workers and environmental campaigners visit the school to discuss issues with the pupils. By taking a global as well as a local perspective and by thinking about the future of the planet in its largest sense it is possible to reinforce and revisit the topics and activities outlined above.

References and further reading

Gardner, H. (1999) *Intelligence Reframed: Multiple intelligences for the 21st century*, New York: Basic Books.

Mason, P. (1992) *Learn to Travel: Activities for travel and tourism in primary schools.* Godalming: WWF UK.

Ofsted (2008) *Geography in Schools: Changing practice.* London: Ofsted.

Rose, J. (2009) *Independent Review of the Primary Curriculum.* Available at *www.dcsf.gov.uk/primarycurriculumreview* (last accessed 1 July 2010).

Websites

Action Aid *www.actionaid.org.uk*

Oxfam *www.oxfam.org.uk*

Save the Children *www.savethechildren.org.uk*

Teachers in Development Education *www.tidec.org.uk*

Picture books about citizenship and identity (see also Chapter 16)

Baker, J. (1987) *Where the Forest Meets the Sea.* London: Walker Books.

Castle, C. (2000) *For Every Child.* New York, NY: Phyllis Fogelman Books.

Dunn, J. (2008) *ABC UK.* London: Frances Lincoln.

Edwards, L. (2004) *An African Princess.* London: Doubleday.

Gliori, D. (2009) *The Trouble with Dragons.* London: Bloomsbury.

Hedderwick, M. (1994) *Katie Morag and the New Pier.* London: Red Fox.

Hoffman, M. (2006) *The Colour of Hope.* London: Frances Lincoln.

Readman, J. (2006) *George Saves the World by Lunchtime.* London: Random House.

So, S. (2006) *Shanyi Goes to China.* London: Frances Lincoln.

Velthuijs, M. (1995) *Frog and the Stranger.* London: Andersen Press.

Section 5

Managing the curriculum

Chapter

22. Planning the curriculum

23. Assessment for learning

24. Inclusion and special needs

25. The subject leader

26. The inspection and accreditation of geography

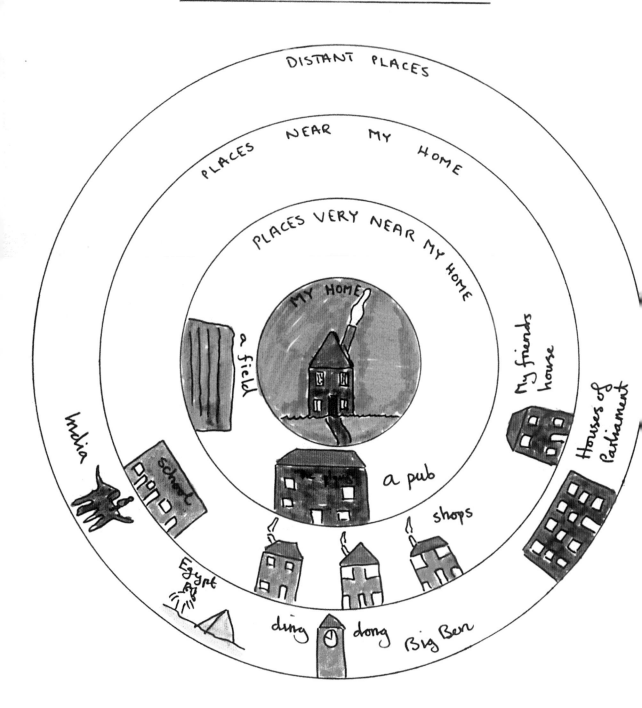

Photo | Stephen Scoffham.

CHAPTER COVERAGE:
CREATIVITY • CROSS-CURRICULAR LINKS • GOOD PRACTICE • PLANNING • PROGRESSION

Planning the curriculum

G eography teaching and learning should be an enjoyable, creative, stimulating and magical experience for pupils and teachers alike. Geography is about places, people and issues both locally and globally, all of which are of interest and concern to everyone. After all, we all live in the same world!

First-hand experience and practical work should underpin much of what we do in the name of geography and the wide boundaries of the subject should allow us to provide pupils with a wonderful learning opportunity. Over the past few years, however, for many and varied reasons geography has not had the time or the space in the primary curriculum to allow it to develop to its fullest extent. However, a new air of optimism nationally about what is important in the curriculum has stimulated a more flexible approach to developing and choosing what we teach. In particular, there is a recognition that historical, geographical and social perspectives can work together to help children understand not only how the present is shaped by the past, but also that we all have a responsibility to live more sustainable lives to preserve our world for the future. In this context, teachers' professional knowledge and personal enthusiasm are important factors in helping to develop a curriculum which matches the needs of individual schools.

Creativity is a central feature of many government curriculum directives. Initiatives such as *Excellence and Enjoyment* (DfES, 2003) and *Every Child Matters* (DfES, 2004) encourage primary teachers to be more imaginative and flexible in their planning and to decide for themselves what opportunities and experiences they want to offer their pupils. However, this increased freedom means we must plan our geography to ensure it provides the best possible experience for our pupils. Successful planning enables teachers to devise coherent and exciting lessons that promote continuity and progression in children's learning. Planning can take several forms; many schools have devised their own standard format for all subjects/areas of learning. The suggestions and advice in this chapter are designed to offer stimulus and leadership to teachers who wish to create an exciting geography programme in their school.

The planning process

The planning process is best seen as an ongoing cycle in which all staff take part (Figure 1). Naturally the subject leader has a key role in developing plans and units of work, updating resources and helping colleagues to devise a policy for the subject. Nevertheless, it is important that all teachers in the school have a sense of ownership and shared understanding of this process. It is equally important that once any plans and policies have been developed they are kept under review, are evaluated from time to time and revised as necessary. As Figure 1 indicates, many people are involved in curriculum planning and important decisions will be taken at each stage about how to deliver geography in your school.

In devising and modifying the curriculum you would be wise to take into account current government curriculum guidance, as the parameters are subject to frequent change.

Primary Geography Handbook

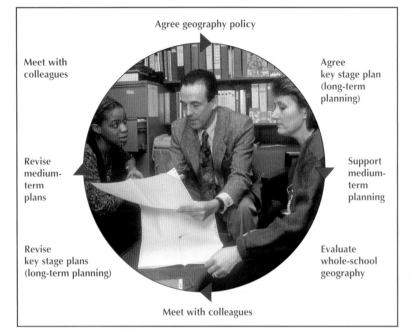

Agree geography policy

Meet with
colleagues

Agree
key stage plan
(long-term
planning)

Revise
medium-
term
plans

Support
medium-
term
planning

Revise
key stage plans
(long-term planning)

Evaluate
whole-school
geography

Meet with colleagues

Figure 1 | *The planning process.*
Photo | *www.JohnBirdsall.co.uk*

The annual subject reports produced by Ofsted are a useful source of information and ideas. From their inception, these have stressed the importance of fieldwork, enquiries and local investigations. They also emphasise the value of geography's wider world perspective. However, some reports (Ofsted, 2008a, 2008b, 2009) also register a number of concerns about the way schools are teaching geography. These include poor use of ICT, insufficient attention to fieldwork and the global dimension, weaknesses in management and leadership and problems with assessment and progression. Teachers' lack of subject knowledge was also a concern. We should view these concerns not negatively, as criticism, but as positive, useful signposts to help us devise a creative and exciting programme of geography for each of our schools. So what other factors should we consider as we plan our geography work?

1. The needs of the children

One of the best starting points is to think about what pupils actually need. What previous experiences have they had both within school and in their pre-school time? How do we build on these experiences and extend them? As well as exploring their own locality, pupils should experience a different environment from the one in which they live, be it city, suburb, village or rural area. We may also need to consider the smaller things in life. For example, have the pupils had the opportunity to travel on a train or bus?

2. The local area

The local area is an important resource for geography teaching and we need to use it fully. Remember that it includes the school building, school grounds and local streets and buildings. Ask yourself a few questions. How can we define our local area and what features does it contain? How best can we use it? What is missing? It may be helpful to talk to other schools working with children of different ages about how they use the same area, so that a range of different and progressive activities can be developed at each key stage to engage and challenge pupils. Many children have their first experience of fieldwork in the local area, and the experience is essential in helping them to learn about the real world. Practical experiences outdoors underpin classroom knowledge and skills and provide a context for learning about the real issues facing every community, wherever it may be.

3. Skills and resources in the school

Many teachers feel very insecure about their own personal knowledge in geography and

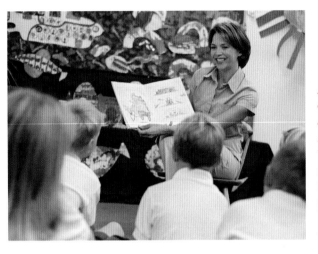

about their skill and ability to teach it. Continuous professional development (CPD) is one way of strengthening subject knowledge and can help to introduce new teaching ideas. Your own personal enthusiasm, e.g. for map reading, rock collecting or travel is also likely to be infectious. Resources collected from distant places or contrasting environments can provide real ingredients for teaching, bringing a little of the magic of the place into the classroom.

4. Time and pressure on the subject

The school day always seems packed with activities, and the core subjects, together with literacy and numeracy, dominate the curriculum. It is essential to be creative when planning geography and to find 'spots' or opportunities to enhance the time that has been officially allocated during the year. You might like to think about teaching geography in the following ways:

- As part of an integrated topic or theme
- As a smaller element within a topic led by another subject
- In a talk or session with a visiting speaker
- In assembly
- In class discussion – Who saw the news on TV last night?
- During story time or when reading books
- In displays both in the classroom and around the school
- In a concentrated block of teaching time such as a 'Europe Day' or an 'Environment Week'
- As a homework task or holiday activity

Continuous topics, such as 'What's in the news?' are also well worth considering, as they allow you to discuss geographical issues on a regular basis.

5. Linking geography with other areas of the curriculum

Geography's makes a significant contribution to so many aspects of the curriculum: literacy, numeracy, sustainability, thinking skills and social and emotional learning. Some geography topics integrate with and support other areas relatively easily; for example, geography, science and art combine naturally in a topic on water. The best units of work combine a number of subjects which contribute different perspectives. After all, as Barnes (2007) argues, our experience of the world is cross-curricular.

Using schemes of work

Most schools have carefully planned schemes of work, many of which have been adapted to suit local circumstances. Teachers have also often built up a range of resources, including the Geographical Association *SuperSchemes* series (Geographical Association, 2005-06, 2008-09) and developed out of classroom experiences which support their teaching. However, it is important to remember that the curriculum is dynamic and change is a key geographical concept. You will need to keep the topics taught in your school under review and encourage

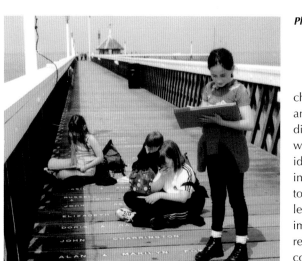

Photo | Paula Richardson.

changes which will enhance the children's learning and enjoyment. This might mean teaching about a different country or creating a more integrated topic where environmental, historical and geographical ideas come together naturally to help children investigate the world around them. The length of topics can vary: some might cover only a few lessons, while others might take several weeks. The important thing is to revise your schemes on a regular basis so the freshness and vitality of the content is maintained.

What are the features of a good geography curriculum?

While the curriculum identifies the range of material to be covered at different levels, good practice in geography teaching requires a far wider reach than this. Some of the features of creative planning include:

■ Recognising that pupils have their own experiences and knowledge of the world
■ Giving the pupils vital concrete experiences outside the classroom, and in a variety of locations
■ Helping pupils use the internet, GIS and other ICT resources to learn about people and places
■ Giving pupils access to a wide range of tangible resources, including pictures, artefacts, data, maps and atlases
■ Enabling pupils to learn to use a range of ways to describe and investigate the world, e.g. specialist vocabulary, maps, diagrams, models
■ Integrating skills, themes and real places
■ Providing activities which are enquiry-based and encouraging pupils to look for issues, ask questions, and analyse their findings
■ Encouraging pupils to link together different aspects of geography using key ideas such as pattern, change, process and interaction
■ Including studies of a range of places on a global scale

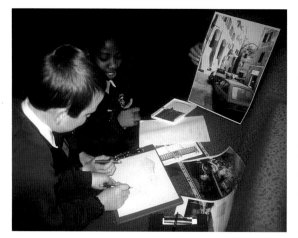

Developing a curriculum plan

It is generally helpful when planning the geography curriculum to think in terms of long-, medium- and short-term plans (Figure 2). These should stem naturally from the school geography policy which in turn identifies the features of the subject that you feel are important. More advice about creating a geography policy will be found in Chapter 25. Some helpful examples of long-, medium- and short-term plans are usually available on official government websites.

Photo | Paula Richardson.

Figure 2 | *Planning geographical work at key stages 1 or 2.*

Whole-school planning

Produce a policy statement for geography which addresses:

- the aims of geographical education and geography's distinctive contribution to children's learning at this key stage
- geography's role in reinforcing literacy, numeracy and ICT (basic skills) and links to other subjects such as history and citizenship
- geography's contribution to personal and social education and primary languages, and other initiatives such as Sustainable Schools and Every Child Matters
- opportunities for a wide range of teaching and learning experiences, including fieldwork
- how much time will be devoted to geography in the key stage.

Long-term planning (key stage)

Produce a key stage plan for geography which outlines:

- how often and in what depth geographical work will feature during the key stage
- whether geography will be taught separately or linked with other subjects
- progression from previous geographical work
- the enquiry focus and the broad sequence of content
- how places, themes and skills will be integrated
- development of the skills of geographical enquiry.

Medium-term planning (e.g. half a term)

Produce a plan for a unit of work which includes:

- a more detailed list of specific enquiry questions
- a sequence of teaching and learning activities
- learning objectives (knowledge/understanding/skills) and assessment opportunities
- resource needs and fieldwork arrangements
- the amount of time needed.

Short-term planning (e.g. lesson)

Produce a lesson plan which clarifies:

- the lesson focus or question and the learning objectives
- the way in which skills are integrated with place studies and thematic work
- learning activities and, if appropriate, assessment opportunities
- how the pupils should be grouped, how resources are to be used, how other adults can be involved
- additional strategies for teaching the most and least able pupils
- opportunities for feedback to and from pupils.

Long-term planning

Traditionally a school develops a long-term plan for each year group to show how the requirements of the national curriculum will be covered through a range of topics and discrete subjects. This long-term plan is vital as it gives an overview of what is to be included and helps to check that a balanced curriculum is being delivered. It is also useful in identifying overlap or where gaps in provision occur and as a way of checking continuity and progression in topics through different key stages.

Medium-term planning

The medium-term plan sets out the body of the topic to be taught and is concerned with the details within each unit of work. Broad learning objectives are central to medium-term plans. These specify the concepts, knowledge, skills and attitudes we expect pupils to acquire during the work done on a unit. They also provide a focus for assessment. The medium-term plan should:

- Focus on the unit of work and suggest timings
- Ensure equal access to the curriculum for all pupils in the group and identify ways of differentiating the material
- Relate to the programmes of learning
- Specify broad learning objectives and suggest some assessment activities

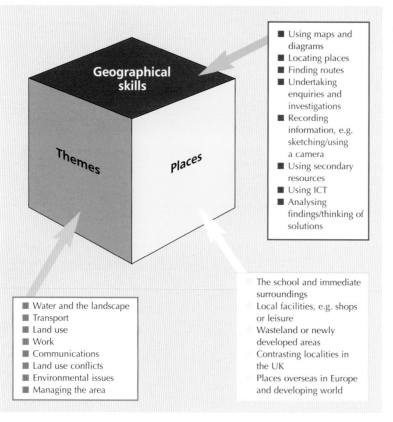

Figure 3 | *The integration of geographical skills, themes and places.*

Geographical skills

- Using maps and diagrams
- Locating places
- Finding routes
- Undertaking enquiries and investigations
- Recording information, e.g. sketching/using a camera
- Using secondary resources
- Using ICT
- Analysing findings/thinking of solutions

Themes

- Water and the landscape
- Transport
- Land use
- Work
- Communications
- Land use conflicts
- Environmental issues
- Managing the area

Places

The school and immediate surroundings
Local facilities, e.g. shops or leisure
Wasteland or newly developed areas
Contrasting localities in the UK
Places overseas in Europe and developing world

- Pose key questions and encourage an enquiry approach to learning
- Identify activities to deliver the objectives
- List appropriate teaching resources
- Identify how ICT can be incorporated into a unit
- Identify possible links to other areas of the curriculum

You need to ensure that the work you do relates to real places and that wherever possible a global dimension is included. When pupils learn specific mapwork skills, for example, they should be encouraged to apply these to an actual context so that they have meaning, rather developing them as a free-standing skill. One of the principles underpinning the national curriculum is the notion that skills, places and themes should be integrated. This idea can be expressed diagrammatically using a cube to represent the geography curriculum (Figure 3).

Some of the questions you might want to consider as you draw up your medium-term plans are:

- Which aspects of the work will be enhanced by the use of ICT, including digital cameras?
- What geographical vocabulary can be developed?
- Where are the best opportunities for fieldwork and practical work?
- How can the use of maps, atlases and globes be developed most effectively?
- Is there an opportunity to include a global dimension?
- Which key questions will develop enquiry skills and provide a direction for the work?

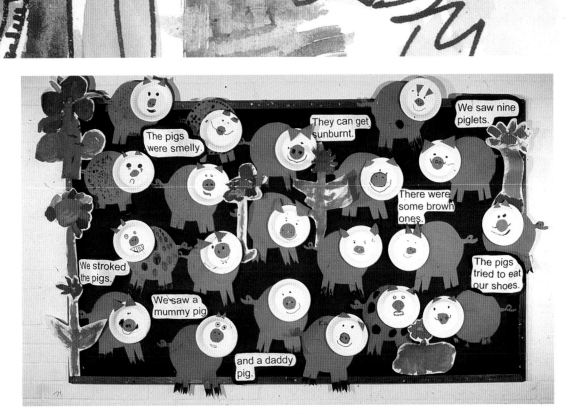

Children's responses after encountering pigs on a farm visit. **Photo** | *Stephen Scoffham.*

Short-term planning

Short-term planning or lesson planning is very detailed and personal to the teacher. It should reflect and maximise the individuality and personal flair and enthusiasm of the person concerned. Having said this the lesson plan should indicate:

■ The learning objectives and content for the lesson – what the pupils will be able to do, know and understand by the end of the lesson

■ What sort of assessment will take place

■ Differentiated learning experiences linked to individual children

■ Classroom organisation/grouping

■ Links with the classroom assistants/support teacher if appropriate

■ Resources needed

Progression and continuity

Progression is a key part of any curriculum. In geography, pupils should be introduced to greater breadth and depth as they move through their studies. They will also need to be provided with opportunities to examine increasingly complex issues and have the chance to develop an understanding of the attitudes and values people hold about a range of issues and places. For instance, how do people in their area feel about the proposed location of an incinerator? How varied will the views be that are expressed?

You will also need to think about how your pupils will increase their knowledge and understanding of other parts of the world. Think about how best to introduce, establish and develop this from EYFS right through to year 6.

Photo | Kate Russell.

Summary

The points below provide a summary to help you create a well-constructed curriculum plan for geography across the key stages.

1. Make geography real by studying actual places and the issues and problems that affect them.
2. Combine work on places, skills and themes rather than teaching them in isolation.
3. Think about the order in which pupils study topics. Allow for pupils to return to key ideas and aspects several times during their primary years.
4. Build progression into your planning by introducing more demanding skills and widening the range, complexity and methods of study.
5. See that you use assessment and findings from any research you have read to inform your planning.
6. Adopt an enquiry approach by structuring your teaching units around a series of key questions. Share these with your pupils.
7. Exploit natural links between geography and other subjects, especially ICT.
8. Try to provide a mix of local and global material in all years. For younger pupils 'local' can mean in their known world, while 'global' means any new experience which extends beyond it.
9. Increase the proportion of distant place work as children progress through the years.
10. Ensure that the pupils have regular exposure to geography throughout the primary years. They should have some, even if only brief, contact every term.

The Geographical Association declares in a statement circulated to all primary schools that 'geography makes a major contribution to our physical, intellectual, social and emotional development' (Geographical Association, 2004). The statement also identifies a number of aspects of learning which help to place geographical learning at the heart of the curriculum. Good geography teaching offers many opportunities to ensure this contribution by stimulating pupils' interest in both their surroundings and in the variety of physical and human conditions on the Earth. In turn, good planning will help to achieve a geography curriculum which will help pupils to understand more about their world and their place in it.

References and further reading

Barnes, J. (2007) *Cross-curricular Learning 3-14.* London: Chapman.

Catling, S. and Willy, T. (2008) *Teaching Primary Geography.* Exeter: Learning Matters.

DfES (2003) *Excellence and Enjoyment: A strategy for primary schools.* London: DfES.

DfES (2004) *Every Child Matters: Change for children in schools.* London: DfES.

Geographical Association (2004) *Finding time for things that matter: geography in primary schools.* Sheffield: Geographical Association.

Geographical Association (2005-06, 2008-09) *SuperSchemes Units 1-26* and *SuperSchemes Basics Units 1-4.* Sheffield: Geographical Association.

Martin, F. (2006) *Teaching Geography in Primary Schools.* Cambridge: Chris Kington Publishing.

Ofsted (2008a) *Annual Report of HMI of Schools: Standards and quality in education.* London: Ofsted.

Ofsted (2008b) *Geography in Schools: Changing practice.* London: Ofsted.

Ofsted (2009) *Improving Primary Teachers' Subject Knowledge Across the Curriculum.* London: Ofsted.

QCA (2009) *Cross-curriculum Dimensions: A planning guide for schools.* London: QCA.

Websites

Woodlands Junior School *www.woodlands-junior.kent.sch.uk/index.html*
Staffordshire Learning Net *www.sln.org.uk/geography/primary.htm*

See also the Early Years and Primary section of the Geographical Association website for the latest news and discussion on planning and the curriculum: *www.geography.org.uk/eyprimary*

Pupils' work / St Matthew's Primary School, Redhill.

Chapter 23: Assessment for learning

Assessment for learning

A ssessing geography in the school curriculum can be made into a very complex operation. The purpose of this chapter is to provide advice to teachers and subject co-ordinators about realistic approaches to assessing pupil progress in geography that will enhance pupil learning in ways which will not place unrealistic demands on teachers. Assessment for learning (AfL) is based on the idea that:

> ... pupils will improve most if they understand the aim of their learning, where they are in relation to this aim and how they can achieve this aim (or close the gap in their knowledge) (DCSF, 2007).

Teachers face continual demands to raise standards at both pupil and whole-school level in all school subjects. There is also an expectation that procedures for monitoring teaching standards will be in place. While it is very positive always to strive for improved performance, the measurement of performance should not become such a priority that it detracts from the vital processes of planning and teaching. It needs to be recognised that when so much emphasis is placed on the core curriculum it is often only possible for co-ordinators to negotiate minimal time for geography. Assessment procedures need to be manageable within the teaching situation. Also, teachers will be more prepared to promote and enhance assessment initiatives if they actively contribute to the process of learning. One of the key messages in this chapter is that most useful assessments take place during normal teaching periods and assessment procedures need to be relevant to both pupils and teachers alike.

What is assessment for?

Assessment can fulfil many purposes within the geography curriculum. Co-ordinators and teachers need to be aware of these diverse purposes in order to determine which assessment procedures can enhance individual and whole-school standards.

It is important for a school teaching staff to have a common understanding about how assessment procedures can have diverse functions. They need to agree which assessment procedures will enable their school to achieve its objectives. The list in Figure 1 is not exhaustive and co-ordinators and teachers may find it useful to explore ways in which assessment procedures can be used to support the geography curriculum. Once the underlying purposes of assessment are agreed, the next stage will be to develop appropriate procedures.

As far as geography is concerned, recent Ofsted reports have repeatedly drawn attention to weaknesses in assessment, which they regard as unsatisfactory in many primary schools. As one report puts it, 'assessment focuses insufficiently on giving constructive feedback to pupils about their geographical knowledge, skills and understanding' (Ofsted, 2008, p. 5).

Assessment can be used to:

1. help motivate pupils to learn
2. inform planning
3. raise standards
4. find out what pupils know and understand
5. inform general standards within a school
6. fulfil statutory requirements
7. provide evidence of progress to external agencies
8. evaluate teacher performance.

Figure 1 | Functions of assessment.

Ten principles of assessment for learning

Assessment for learning should:

- be part of effective planning and teaching
- focus on how students learn
- be recognised as central to classroom practice
- be regarded as a key professional skill for teachers
- be sensitive and constructive, because any assessment has an emotional impact
- take account of the importance of learner motivation
- promote commitment to learning goals and a shared understanding of the criteria by which they are assessed
- be organised so learners receive guidance about how to improve
- develop learners' capacity for self-assessment so they can become reflective and self-managing
- recognise the full range of achievements of all learners.

Figure 2 | *Assessment is a powerful tool for raising standards (after QCDA, 2010).*

The assessment process

Assessment can take many forms – from formal testing to discussion with individual pupils. The system of national testing within the core curriculum (i.e. English, mathematics and science) has tended to equate assessment with testing and grading pupils according to their performance within a standardised framework. Not only does this approach help to formulate the level of performance of a cohort of pupils, it also provides information to teachers, parents and pupils about individual pupil success or lack of it. This formal approach to assessment can significantly influence the attitudes pupils develop towards learning.

An alternative approach is to view assessment not as a labelling and sorting procedure but rather as a procedure that can aid teachers to enable pupils to achieve their potential (Figure 2). It cannot be emphasised too much that teacher/pupil-centred assessment can enhance both individual pupil and whole-school standards. As the Assessment Reform Group (1999) notes, it has been 'proved without a shadow of doubt' that informal assessment with constructive feedback to the pupil will raise attainment.

Primary school geography is not subject to the pressures of external assessment procedures and national league tables and thus there is opportunity to use assessment as a vehicle to promote learning and understanding. Assessment can also be used to encourage positive attitudes to learning geography among pupils of all abilities whether they are slower learners or gifted and talented. In short, pupils' assessment needs to:

- promote learning
- promote success
- provide active involvement of the pupils in their own learning
- provide positive feedback to the pupils
- aid the development of positive attitudes among the pupils
- inform future planning.

Photo | *Paula Richardson.*

The learning process

If assessment is specifically designed to facilitate pupil learning it is necessary for the teacher to know what needs to be learnt. The curriculum defines the content which has to be covered in geography. For notions of progression it is best to turn to the level descriptions (see page 318). However, as all practising teachers will be aware the sequence of learning adopted by individual pupils fails to fit into neat categories. The art of successful teaching is to promote an environment that facilitates diverse approaches to learning and successful classroom dynamics. It is also imperative to engender positive attitudes and provide pupils with the potential for success. Assessment procedures can provide teachers with the information they need to create stimulating and challenging lessons that match the needs of the pupils with whom they are working. Generally, it is best to pitch activities at a level where the majority of the pupils will achieve the learning targets. The minority who will find this work challenging can be identified and their learning targets tactfully modified, while at the opposite extreme those who are exceeding the targets can have planned extension activities.

There is a further problem. How best can we accommodate the links and connections between subjects? Dividing the curriculum into areas of learning is one solution, but this too runs the risk of creating separate blocks of knowledge and understanding which fail to interact. For instance, pupils who undertake a geographical activity often need skills, knowledge and understanding in a number of curriculum areas (e.g. a river study will draw on mathematical and scientific ideas). It is important to consider if pupils will need these prior to developing new learning in geography. This is achieved by assessing the pupils and continuing the assessments while they are working. In order to create a positive learning environment teachers needs to:

■ identify clear learning objectives – i.e. know what is to be taught
■ provide pupils with information about what they are aiming to learn
■ have a strong notion about what pupils already know and understand
■ be aware of any misconceptions pupils may already hold. about the subject
■ have a strong notion of progression
■ be able to assess the learning that has taken place in order to organise future planning.

Successful learning takes place when pupils have ownership of their learning, understand the goals they are aiming for, possess the skills they need, and are motivated. Thus for any successful learning to take place it is essential that the teacher is aware of the learning needs of their pupils.

Different forms of assessment

Any assessment process needs to be efficient, informative and require the minimum amount of time to administer. Primary teachers have difficulty simply meeting all the requirements of the national curriculum within the school day. In addition, the assessment requirements for the core curriculum can be quite onerous for many schools. It would be extremely difficult for a co-ordinator to advocate any assessment and recording procedures in geography that are time-consuming or complex. It is therefore important that both geography co-ordinators and class teachers have a clear view about the purposes of assessment within the context of teaching geography. There are many simple assessment procedures. These include:

■ Observing pupils, not only watching but also listening to them recount how they carried out their work and what they found out.
■ Asking pupils open-ended questions that give them the opportunity to develop their own ideas.
■ Providing pupils with tasks that demonstrate that they have acquired skills or new learning.

■ Providing pupils with opportunities to present their work in different ways, e.g. maps, diagrams, writing, drawing, speaking, role-play.

Assessment will both be formal and informal, formative and summative. We often under-estimate the amount of informal assessment that goes on in the classroom through observation and discussion with pupils during day-to-day teaching and learning activities. This professional judgement is an important component in, and starting point for, more formal assessments which might include written work, mapwork, oral presentations, group work, posters, role play and fieldwork. A range of assessment techniques is necessary to assess a pupil's full range of ability; some pupils are better at mapwork, others may find oral presentations easier. Also, some types of assessment lend themselves to a particular topic; role play and simulation are often good ways to explore an environmental issue such as a local bypass; posters are effective in allowing pupils to express their views of a locality and can be an ideal way of illustrating geographical patterns. Whatever approach you adopt it is important to remember that assessment tasks should be an integral part of a unit of work. Assessment is not a bolt-on extra. As Black and Wiliam (2003) remind us, 'there is no "quick fix" that can be added to existing practice with promise of rapid reward' (p. 629).

Pupil self-assessment

Self-assessment can help to develop children's understanding and encourage them to take a positive attitude towards their learning. It can also provide valuable evidence of their learning. However, teachers need to take due regard of the pupils' maturity and level of ability in setting self-assessment tasks. Pupils must also be encouraged to apply their learning to new situations.

As the Primary National Strategy concludes, 'peer assessment and self assessment are most effectively promoted as part of a systematic approach to developing the social and emotional aspects of learning. They require children to take increased responsibility for their learning and develop as independent learners. This has fundamental implications for a school's learning ethos.' (DCSF, 2007.)

Example

A group of Y6 pupils were carrying out a topic about Spain. One of the key targets was to be able to determine the location of Spain using atlases and maps. The pupils were told their targets and they discussed appropriate achievement indicators. They then had to define where different places were using their newly acquired skills. At each attempt the pupils were encouraged to reflect critically on how they could further improve their work. A similar self-assessment activity was carried out in a Y1 class where children were learning how to draw a picture showing the location of their home and different routes in the local area. Each time they carried out an activity they were asked to consider alternatives. As a result the pupils were better able to transfer their learning to other mapwork exercises involving features such as shops and parks. Some even managed to develop this skill further by using simple symbols on their maps.

What do I need to record?

The opportunities for assessment will vary according to the school's own scheme of work. Similarly, the school's policy on assessment and recording may determine the amount of

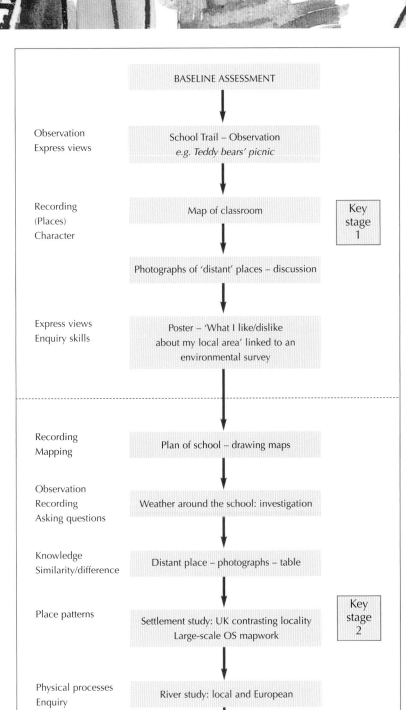

Figure 3 | *A model of possible assessment and recording opportunities.*

recording undertaken. It is neither possible nor necessary to keep or record every piece of work that a pupil produces. The records you keep will depend on the purpose of the school's recording system.

Records have a number of purposes. Among other things they can:

- aid planning
- inform parents
- inform teachers
- record progress
- provide data for curriculum coverage.

The key element in any recording system is that it is manageable and relevant to the teaching and learning processes. For example, if a scheme like the one in Figure 3 was used it would be sufficient for you simply to indicate whether a pupil could or could not do certain things, like recognise the countries of the UK or be aware of places beyond their own locality by the end of year 2. All the staff could decide on a few basic skills they agree to assess at some point during the year, e.g. map skills. In schools with more than one class per year group, class teachers might decide to carry out the same activity and compare performance. One of the most effective tools in helping to assess pupils' performance and progression is the subject portfolio.

Two pie charts and commentaries about shops on the High Street, from children of different abilities.
Photo | *Stephen Scoffham.*

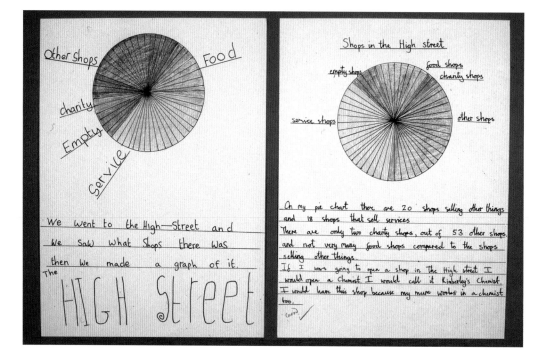

Level descriptions

The 2010 level descriptions provide a useful reference point for both assessing and reporting pupil progress. Other government websites give useful examples of children's work. Assessing and recording pupils' attainment will help you plan for progression in their learning and for continuity in their experience across the key stages. Remember, though, that level descriptions are not intended for the detailed assessment of individual pieces of work; rather, they provide end-of-key-stage summative judgements that serve as a 'best fit' description of a pupil's ability. The programme of learning and level descriptions can be broken down into four main aspects:

1. Geographical enquiry and skills
2. Knowledge and understanding of place
3. Knowledge and understanding of pattern and process
4. Knowledge and understanding of environmental change and sustainable development

Assessment involves combining these different aspects. Pupils carrying out an enquiry into changes in their local area, for example, will be using a range of geographical skills and studying a range of geographical physical or human processes. Similarly, pupils who are learning about an overseas locality may be developing their mapwork and photograph interpretation skills as well as enhancing their ability to use the internet and ICT packages as sources of information.

Different children's responses to being asked to describe their local area.
Photo | *Stephen Scoffham.*

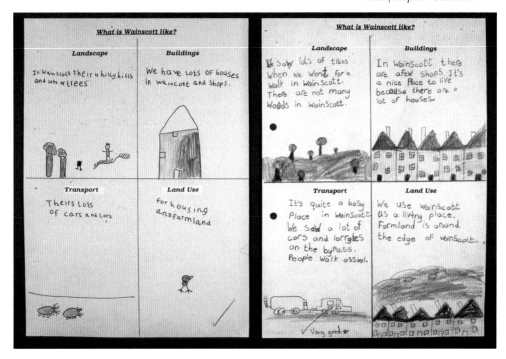

How can assessment can help me in my planning?

Assessment of pupils' attainment can be used to inform any stage of the learning process, when planning, teaching or learning. You might have information regarding the pupils' experience and ability that you can use in your initial planning. The teacher then builds up a hypothesis about what the pupils know and the activities that will lead to further progressive learning. The activities planned will relate to ability levels within the class. The differentiation will be by either outcome or by task. The assessments will be continuous as the teacher interacts with the pupils and there may also be a finished body of work that will also provide information about the success of the pupils in achieving learning targets.

Good assessment, recording and reporting systems will:

■ allow you to assess the standard that pupils are reaching at any one point in time;

■ help pupils to know how well they are doing and what they need to do better;

■ provide information to help you plan more appropriate teaching and learning activities;

■ provide information on pupils' progress for parents, colleagues in the school and for any transfer documentation to other schools.

Monitoring standards

The argument thus far has been that assessment needs to be continuous because the primary function of assessment is to facilitate planning and also to provide positive reinforcement to individual pupils. However, schools are also required to maintain and improve standards and

Testing

The school will need to decide what to test and what criteria to use. It will be very hard to construct tests that could accurately indicate a level as defined in the level descriptions. There is a requirement for pupils to be formally assessed in the Foundation Stage as part of their Foundation Stage Profile.

Monitoring pupil work

This is a strategy where the co-ordinator reviews work carried out by pupils. The co-ordinator can ask to see all work or ask for a sample. A process for recording the results of such a process will need to be in place.

Monitoring planning

The co-ordinator receives teachers' medium-term and/or short-term planning. This will enable the co-ordinator to monitor implementation of the school geography policy and scheme of work. In addition, areas of development identified by individual teachers resulting in modification of planning can be monitored by the co-ordinator.

Observing teaching

This can be a very positive and beneficial approach. It is expensive to apply because some form of teaching cover is required as well as training for the 'observer' on how to observe positively yet critically.

Reporting on individual progress

Reporting to parents is a legal requirement at the end of the academic year. Report documents relate to individual pupils and it would be difficult to utilise them for whole-school assessment of standards unless, within the document, teachers are required to enter a level of attainment. It is not a legal requirement for a child to be allocated a level in the three primary key stages.

Teacher assessment of levels

This can be achieved by using the level descriptions and the 'best fit' approach. It is a time-consuming process, especially if in the cause of consistency 'levelling' is required for all national curriculum subject areas.

Exemplification portfolios

Samples of pupil work are kept centrally. They indicate the standards of achievement and also the expectation of the standards within the school.

Figure 4 | *Some possible strategies for monitoring standards.*

it is the role of the geography co-ordinator to decide how to monitor these standards. Figure 6 indicates some of the options but schools may develop others. Whatever processes are used they need to have a logical cohesiveness that is contained within the school's geography and assessment policies.

Do I need to keep a portfolio of pupils' work?

You do not have to keep a portfolio of each pupil's work. However, developing a geography portfolio for the whole school is a good idea because it allows the co-ordinator/ subject leader to:

- develop consistent judgements across year groups
- come to a common understanding of level descriptions
- help 'new' teachers in the school or year group to develop appropriate expectations
- show aspects of progression and continuity across the key stages/school
- monitor the quality and standards of geography across the school.

A portfolio might include examples of pupils' work from different year groups to show progression, or it might have pieces of work from different abilities within the same year group to show differentiation. As well as pupils' work you could include photographs and teachers' notes, annotations to the work, and so forth. These annotations to pupils' work might include the following:

1. Details of the instructions given, resources used, amount of teacher support and whether the work was undertaken individually or in groups.

2. Brief commentary on what the work shows in terms of geographical knowledge, understanding and skills.

3. Other evidence of the pupils' work – discussion, comments to the teacher and so on.

4. Comments about how this work could be taken further and whether the work is in line with expectations.

Such a portfolio would make an invaluable tool for INSET activities related to geography and an excellent record to show to parents, visitors and visiting Ofsted inspectors. Subject leaders are playing an increasing role in monitoring their subject area and, for them, a good portfolio is an ideal alternative to visiting colleagues' classrooms to observe their teaching, particularly given the normal time constraints.

Teachers might also be encouraged to complete a proforma for their pupils' work using the headings in Figure 4. Staff could then discuss the relative merits of individual pupil's work and perhaps relate these to aspects of the level descriptions.

Conclusion

Assessment plays a crucial role in the learning process. It helps us to appreciate the different ways in which pupils learn, identify what they know already, and take account of any misconceptions they may possess. This information gathering process should take place within an environment where the pupils want to learn. Formative assessment has a particular value in supporting new learning.

Seen in the broadest terms assessment has two main functions. It can:

1. Provide a 'snapshot' of the knowledge and understanding achieved by pupils.

2. Be an aid to determine the next stage for planning areas of learning for pupils.

Within these two broad functions, assessment procedures can affect the learning processes that take place within the classroom. It is important to appreciate the crucial link that exists between assessment in the classroom and these learning processes. As an anonymous saying expresses it:

> *If you want a plant to grow it is no good just measuring it, you need to give it the things that will make it grow. Children are the same, measuring them is not enough! They need to be given learning that makes them grow.*

References and further reading

Assessment Reform Group (1999) *Assessment for Learning: Beyond the black box*. Cambridge: Cambridge University School of Education.

Black, P. and Wiliam, D. (2003) 'In praise of educational research: formative assessment', *British Educational Research Journal*, 29, 5, pp. 623-637.

Catling, S. and Willy, T. (2008) *Teaching Primary Geography*. Exeter: Learning Matters.

DCSF (2007) *Primary National Strategy*. Available at *www.nationalstrategies.standards.dcsf.gov.uk/primary*. (last accessed 1 July 2010)

Ofsted (2008) *Geography in Schools: Changing practice*. London: Ofsted.

Owens, P. (2008) 'Level headed geography: planning achievement', *Primary Geographer*, 65, pp. 15-18.

QCA (2007) *Teacher Assessment Activities: Geography foundation stage and key stage 1*. London: QCA.

QCA (2007) *Teacher Assessment Activities: Geography key stage 2*. London: QCA.

QCDA (2010) *The National Curriculum Level Descriptions for Subjects*. Coventry: QCDA.

Till, J. (2007) 'Assessment matters', *Primary Geographer*, 63, pp. 24-27.

Websites

National curriculum level descriptions *www.geography.ndo.co.uk/natcurric.htm*

Our front doors

Photo | Stephen Scoffham.

with contributions from Stephen Scoffham

CHAPTER COVERAGE:
CREATIVITY • DIFFERENTIATION • FIELDWORK • GOOD PRACTICE • INCLUSION/SEN • ISSUES

Inclusion and special needs

O ver the past few decades there has been a huge shift in public attitudes towards inclusion. Physical and mental disabilities are no longer seen as barriers to achievement but as different points on the spectrum of human experience. As a society we are increasingly tolerant towards differences of race, sexual orientation, religion and culture. Much more progress still needs to be made in promoting international understanding, but the rigid social attitudes which once dominated the way people thought and behaved have been replaced by a greater willingness to embrace diversity.

These societal changes have been paralleled by developments in education. Special educational needs (SEN) legislation, to remove barriers to participation and learning, led to the formulation of an *SEN Code of Practice* (DfES, 2001). As well as setting out detailed procedures and policies, the SEN Code established some general principles, including the stipulation that children with special educational needs should have access to a broad, balanced and relevant curriculum, to be delivered normally in mainstream schools or settings.

Subsequent directives have built on these principles. *Excellence and Enjoyment* (DfES, 2003) makes it clear that learning should be focused on individual children's needs and abilities. Another key document driving educational policy, *Every Child Matters* (DfES, 2004), also stresses a holistic approach to learning. It recommends multi-agency working and extended school services that respond to all a child's needs. The *Social and Emotional Aspects of Learning* (SEAL) programme (DCSF, 2005) drew attention to the way social and emotional skills help children deal with everyday situations within a framework that respects diversity and values the rights of others. Inclusion is also highlighted in a general sense in the *Disabilities Discrimination Act 2005* and more specifically in the *National Framework for Sustainable Schools* (DCSF, 2008) where it is one of the eight 'doorways' that make up the framework. There is a clear vision for the future. By 2020 the government would like all schools to be models of social inclusion. All pupils should be able to participate fully in school life in an ethos that respects human rights, freedoms, culture and creative expression.

These initiatives have direct relevance for geography teaching and give both SENCOs/Inclusion Managers and class teachers more scope to be flexible and creative. *Excellence and Enjoyment* (DfES, 2003) includes a case study from an area of severe deprivation, St Joan of Arc School, Bootle, whose head teacher says: 'The curriculum needs to be exciting. In our case, this means building in quality, not quantity, so children learn first-hand' (DfES, 2003, p. 19).

The distinction between quality and quantity is a key point, particularly for those pupils who are unable to participate fully in school life, and will be returned to later. One of the implications is that SENCOs and Inclusion Managers are now empowered to devise an exciting geography curriculum based on the school locality and tailored to pupils' needs. This view is reinforced in the *Excellence and Enjoyment* (DfES, 2003, p.12) where it states that schools will be encouraged to 'take a fresh look at their curriculum, their timetable and the

Primary Geography Handbook

Photo | *Paula Richardson.*

organisation of the school day'.

Most primary school teachers know from experience how different teaching approaches can add quality and enjoyment to their pupils' learning. Inevitably, pupils have varying strengths and experience different learning difficulties. Good, effective teaching involves matching the creativity of the educator with personal knowledge of the capabilities of pupils. This pedagogical approach is likely to provide equality of opportunity and curriculum access. Subsequently, barriers to participation will be minimised and all pupils will be able to demonstrate their abilities and achievements.

When we are close to teaching it is easy to miss the progress a pupil is making, particularly if they are accessing the curriculum in smaller steps than their peers. Learning achievements are often clearer to regular visitors so it is important to adopt a team approach, involving other teachers, the SENCO, Teaching Assistants (TAs) and parents. Where a culture of team work prevails, teachers benefit from the support they obtain and can confirm that their particular approach is appropriate to the situation. This also helps to ensure consistency across the school and fosters the achievement and enjoyment of all. This approach is also vital to avoid the perception that only 'specialist adults' can cope with certain pupils – we need to develop the expertise of all staff for the benefit of all pupils.

Fieldwork

Fieldwork is crucial in geography and ensures first-hand memorable experiences for all pupils because it involves all the senses. The examples in *Excellence and Enjoyment* (DfES, 2003) can be used to argue the case for allowing more time for fieldwork activities. The head teacher of St Joan of Arc, Bootle mentioned earlier made the point that his school acquired two minibuses 'so that classes can make visits and build opportunities for enrichment'. Not every school can acquire a minibus, which is clearly a valuable asset – particularly if it is built to take wheelchairs – but one can often be borrowed from secondary schools, special schools or charities. A local university that has a geography department or trains teachers can also be a useful source of 'labour and transport' and help to support both residential trips and local fieldwork. An alternative is to establish links and relationships between a range of schools to share resources, teachers and pupils. Many special schools are delighted to join in partnerships with other schools as they all too often become isolated and the expertise and experience they have is not shared. The LA advisory team or local Geography Champion should be a good starting place for developing such partnerships.

Fieldwork, though, does not need minibuses in order to be effective. A primary school in Islington planned regular fieldwork for its nursery class in the local area. This culminated in a trip on the underground to a local park for a picnic and gave pupils the chance to experience a different environment. The nursery teacher, nursery nurses, a member of staff trained in geography and senior staff at the school were all involved in the planning. The crucial aspect of this type of work, particularly for those pupils who experience barriers to learning, is careful preparation. You need to walk the route, identify suitable learning opportunities and carry out a risk assessment. If you take pictures, perhaps using a video, you will be able to use these as material to prepare the pupils before they go. When you return, the images will provide a valuable resource for pupils who either missed the trip or who need a visual reminder of what they saw. Other useful tools are digital cameras and dictaphones, as both can be used to record material for use back in school. Using ICT equipment also gives pupils a sense of ownership and pride in what they are doing.

When you are doing your planning you need to ensure that you are fulfilling your responsibilities under the *Special Educational Needs and Disabilities Act, 2001*. This involves taking into consideration generic questions such as 'Who will describe the environment for blind pupils?' and 'Are there any problems regarding wheelchair access?'. You will also need to consider how to support pupils who are challenged by changes in routine or the freedom of relatively unstructured situations. Remember that each pupil is unique and that many pupils have undiscovered strengths which they can offer or contribute. Good planning involves assessing the needs of the class, groups and individuals.

Well-planned fieldwork enables pupils to build on previous skills and knowledge. Remember also that the work that develops as a result can be used as a school resource and put in the library on the geography shelves. This means that videos, ICT material, maps, plans and photographs will be available for all pupils and parents. This will be valuable because it:

1. Demonstrates to the pupils that their work is valued and is used again. (A key issue in the area of sustainable development.)
2. Enables pupils to revisit the work – to recap, remember, go back over and extend ideas. (This is important for pupils who learn more slowly or more quickly than their peers.)
3. Allows parents to see what their pupils have done. (Their children's work has a purpose.)
4. Means that others can use the work as a starting point in future years.
5. Enables the school to build its own quality resources for geography and special needs when there is a paucity of quality material in the market place.

You could make use of initial teacher training students, in school on teaching practice, to help develop local fieldwork material in conjunction with the Inclusion Manager and geography co-ordinator. For example, a school in the north-west of England recently used school experience students, in conjunction with the college tutor, to develop work related to mapwork and orienteering. Everyone benefited. The students involved gained valuable experience, the pupils, particularly those considered to have special or additional needs, extended their learning, and the school added to its resources. One of the other outcomes was that the material provided evidence of how the pupils were progressing in relation to geographical skills and enquiry.

This approach means that fieldwork and the results of the fieldwork investigations can become part of the school's learning resource. It also means that the parent of a pupil who is

Photo | www.JohnBirdsall.co.uk

a wheelchair user or is blind or deaf, for example, can see what pupils did last year and perhaps make suggestions about how to modify the visit. Making the results part of the school resource means that pupils can also explore the notion of change using their own archive. Studies which help pupils to recognise that local environmental issues are complex and contested could include the redevelopment of wasteground sites, new traffic management schemes and the loss of local play space.

In one school, for example, year 5 and 6 pupils examined the issue of safety outside their school. The pupils were convinced that, because of a recent accident, there ought to be a zebra crossing. They collected information in a number of ways including traffic surveys, interviews and questionnaires, and wrote letters to local councillors and MPs. Scrivener (2003) describes this type of work as action-orientated learning. In essence, the pupils examined what they saw as a real issue. This can be crucial in bringing geographical learning to life for pupils who have barriers to participation and who may not be 'switched on' by a more formal or academic approach.

Practical enquiries and investigations of this type provide meaningful activities over which pupils can exercise a sense of ownership. They also help pupils examine and clarify their values and attitudes which in turn helps to stimulate their involvement in the future of the environment. It is important that within the geography curriculum pupils are helped and enabled to recognise the personal role they have in the future of their planet. This sometimes begins with an investigation of a local issue that the pupils have identified and then moves out from the locality through the region to national and global questions. Relating the work to the Sustainable Schools agenda is another way of helping the pupils to recognise that their voice is valued. If schools can build their own resources as a result of action-orientated fieldwork over a number of years they will enable pupils to feel that their work is valued. This surely means, as suggested by the head of St Joan of Arc School, that we need to go for a quality and not a quantity model of the curriculum and learning.

Basic principles

Following this discussion about geography fieldwork it is now possible to establish some fundamental principles regarding inclusion and pupils with special learning needs. These are:

1. All pupils are entitled to receive a geography curriculum that enhances their ability to be part of a democratic society now and in the future.

2. All pupils are entitled to receive a geography curriculum that increases their geographical knowledge in a manner that (a) increases their self-esteem (b) opens their minds to future geographical exploration.

3. All pupils have geographical knowledge. It is our task as teachers to:
   – recognise their existing knowledge
   – build/extend and develop this knowledge
   – enable pupils to use their knowledge in present and future debates about the world we live in. *Visions of the Future* (Hicks and Holden, 2007) is a valuable resource in this area.

4. All pupils have a right to enjoyment which, as *Excellence and Enjoyment* (DfES, 2003) declares, is their 'birthright'.

These are the fundamental principles: setting suitable learning challenges; responding to pupils' diverse learning needs; and overcoming potential barriers to learning and assessment. These basic principles and the ideas can also be matched directly to the concept of inclusion and the requirements of the *Special Educational Needs and Disability Act, 2001. The Code of Practice* (DfES, 2001) makes it clear that:

> *From September 2002 schools will be required not to treat disabled pupils less favourably for a reason relating to their disability and to take reasonable steps to ensure that they are not placed at a substantial disadvantage to those who are not disabled* (DfES, 2001, p. v).

This places the emphasis firmly on adapting the environment to suit the pupil rather than trying to make the pupil fit an inappropriate context. It also provides a clear definition of SEN that can be used as a base line for planning and thinking. The definition makes it clear that pupils have a learning difficulty if they:

■ have significantly greater difficulty in learning than the majority of pupils of the same age; or

■ have a disability which prevents or hinders them making use of educational facilities of a kind generally provided for pupils of the same age in schools within the area of the local education authority (DfES, 2001, p. 6).

The basic principles and the statements regarding disability and learning difficulty need to be placed within the context in which you are working – your primary school, its pupils and staff, its geographical location and its existing resources. To this must be added, I would suggest, the time available for geography and geography-related activities, especially fieldwork, given the importance attributed to the core subjects in the National Strategies and SEF. It is also important to consider the needs of those pupils who might be described as 'gifted and talented'. The key principle as always is responding to the pupils with regard to individual and collective learning needs and to build on strengths. It is for this reason that the term 'AEN' (Additional Educational Needs) is now gaining wider acceptance.

Research by the author in the north-west of England suggests that the time generally available for geography in many primary schools amounts to less than one hour per week. This raises the very difficult issue of the balance between time for curriculum coverage and time for understanding subject matter. This problem is likely to be especially acute for pupils with particular learning needs. It also raises the question of how to find time to extend a study of geographical issues both for those pupils who might be described as 'gifted and talented' and those who are enthusiastic about geography even if they are not high achievers.

Whatever subject is involved, education requires balancing curriculum requirements on the one hand with pupils' learning needs on the other. In order to keep self-esteem and motivation levels of both staff and pupils high, it is essential that this match is appropriate and that all involved achieve success. This means that in the primary school it will be crucial for the SENCO, the geography co-ordinator, the age-phase managers and senior mangers to work together to examine the following key questions:

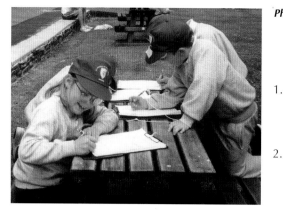

Photo | Paula Richardson.

1. What do we believe we can reasonably explore at either first or second hand with our pupils, within the environment in which we live, to develop their geographical understanding?

2. How can we ensure that all pupils are introduced to a fundamental core of geographical understanding – with clear possibilities for extension and breadth – in the time we are prepared to give it?

3. How can we minimise the barriers that some pupils experience in geography, including physical and sensory disabilities?

4. What resources, both human and physical (books, maps, videos, ICT, CDs, DVDs etc.), do we need in order to achieve the above?

5. Do we have an efficient and effective recording system that follows the pupils through from nursery to year 6 that will enable the secondary school to build on the skills and concepts the pupil has acquired and which identifies the fieldwork they have undertaken?

6. What are the possibilities for action research relating to geography and special needs that might involve a range of staff and relate to the school's CPD and staff development plan?

7. What links can we establish outside the school – special schools, primary and secondary schools, industry, colleges and universities that will enhance the quality experience in geography?

It is to be hoped that these guidelines will provide a framework within which pupils with special educational needs can undertake geography in a manner that opens doors, eyes and imagination. The alternative is to risk closing down their natural wonder about the world because we decide they are not capable of understanding aspects of the subject due to a low reading age or a behavioural, a physical or sensory difficulty.

An inclusive approach

Many specialist organisations can provide specific and detailed learning material for a range of learning needs. You can find out about these from the websites listed at the end of this chapter. However, it is also important to recognise that terms such as dyspraxic, dyslexic, ADHD (attention deficit hyperactivity disorder), blind and autistic do not delineate homogeneous groups: they simply infer a continuum of learning issues. So, for example, when a blind student made it clear to me that he would let me know if he needed help and asked me not to make generalised comments, he was in fact asking not to be categorised.

It is therefore crucial in applying fundamental principles that we always focus on the individual learner and not the so-called 'disability with learning'. When examining the physical environment of the school, for example, we need to take two standpoints: general issues to do with education and teaching; and specific issues related to individual pupils.

This, I would suggest, is the hallmark of quality teaching. The principles that underpin quality teaching are the same for all pupils, not just those described as having learning difficulties. Educational thinking and research confirm the validity of this approach. Gardner's theory of multiple intelligences (1993), the notion of emotional and social intelligence (Goleman, 1996, 2007) and the idea that learning is culturally mediated (Rogoff, 2003) all suggest that we need a broad teaching repertoire, based on a careful assessment of individual learning needs at any precise moment in time.

An example of this 'catholic' approach can be where pupils are put into groups of three. One pupil closes their eyes, another gives directions and the third acts as scribe noting the instructions word for word. The 'director' navigates the pupil from A to B in the classroom, the playground or the school field using simple instructions – right, left, forwards, backwards – using paces as the unit of measure. On completion of the journey the pupil who had their eyes closed draws the journey and the three compare notes. Each pupil gets a chance to play each part. It is fascinating for sighted pupils to see how accurate many pupils with sensory impairments can be in recounting their journey – whether via drawing or speech. This type of work can help in the development of graphicacy and spatial ability and illustrate the value of maps drawn to a uniform scale. One school in the north-west of England uses a large-scale street map of the area around the school projected and drawn on a wall to encourage pupils to tell and draw their journey to school. Pupils are encouraged to discuss a range of possible routes and give reasons for their choices. No route is necessarily wrong, but some may be better for specific purposes.

Clearly the work can be extended by the use of a compass and the use of games such as treasure hunts and orienteering. Activities like these also help to build trust and self-confidence. You might get pupils to draw and describe real and imagined journeys. If they have heard the story of *The Hobbit* they will be aware of a journey through different landscapes, or you might discuss the film version of *Lord of the Rings*. These stories could also be used as a stimulus for drawings (and maps) of an imaginary journey to a specific place or destination. Again this idea lends itself to pupils working in groups. Some pupils are particularly good at drawing real and imagined maps, some might provide the words and some could provide the illustrations. The final result might even be enacted as role play or drama.

In terms of problem solving it can be valuable to start at the local level. This allows pupils to bring some initial knowledge to the issue or problem. You might then extend the scope to include problems which, while they may not be evident in your locality, still involve pupils and will be perceived as relevant. For example, when you plan a day trip for infants to a castle think about how each group could be presented with different geographical problems. What is the best route? What is the quickest route? What is the cheapest route? What is the most interesting route? Other questions to consider are whether the pupils need a map, what they need to wear and where they could find shelter if it rains. By posing geographical questions you will be challenging pupils to use literacy, numeracy and other skills in seeking the answers or solutions.

The problems that you select can either be open-ended or set within parameters decided by staff. Environmental issues and sustainability provide a particularly useful focus and have the advantage that they can be illustrated locally, e.g. graffiti. The Millennium Development Goals could be the platform for moving on to wider national and international issues. Try to encourage pupils to see that politicians and policy makers struggle to find answers as there are often no quick solutions. It can be difficult for pupils to recognise complexity and it can be salutary for them to recognise that teachers too may not have the answer and that our ideas change with 'new knowledge'. This is part of the essence of geographical thinking.

A variation on this theme is for pupils to collect used plastic bottles from the school and home over a specific period of time and store them in rubbish sacks. Speculate on how many sacks would fill the room. This can then lead to a debate on the impact of rubbish on the future of our planet and ways we might deal with it. Another example comes from a small village school in Wales. When the only newsagent in the village closed, pupils were asked 'How might we get newspapers?'. Working in groups they came up with a range of possible ideas. (For further ideas and suggestions look at the Eco-Schools handbook or website (*www.eco-schools.org.uk*) which provide a range of resources and ideas which place pupils at the centre of the decision-making process.)

Practical activities of this kind which involve learning through the senses can be vital for some pupils and awaken their sense of awe. Again it is possible to move from local to national to global, particularly by using the internet and television material. Video news clips that pupils can go back to again and again are ideal for stimulating, reinforcing and extending learning, especially when combined with stories about the lives of people in other countries. Your school needs to reflect on how best to build a resource collection for geography, catalogue the material and place it in the library for future use. This material can also inform the debate with regard to the past and the future. Video clips and media articles collected over a period of time are an invaluable tool for helping pupils to recognise that ideas, values and feelings in geography change over time.

It is also important to consider the way the school and classroom are organised. We need to do this from a standpoint not of guilt or pressure from a government initiative but because we recognise how the learning environment we create has an impact on pupils, the subjects, the environment and our teaching in general. We also need to acknowledge that as teachers we have an 'emotional link' to our teaching and that some pupils will test this emotional link. Pupils who present challenges in behaviour and/or learning can put pressure on our personal credibility and resolve. It is easy to feel guilty and to say to yourself 'I don't think the pupil is learning. Help, what do I do next?'. An idea in one school has been to get a Teaching Assistant to take a pupil who presents a particular challenge within the ADHD spectrum out of the classroom with a digital camera to take some geographical pictures of the locality. This intervention works because some pupils need to engage in a task more physically than others and require the reassurance of one-to-one support. We need to recognise that giving pupils the occasional opportunity to work outside the classroom environment does not contravene the principles of inclusion. Inclusion is not so much about a pupil's physical location as accepting and valuing the unique contribution they can make. These tensions are part of everyday school life. It is our role as teachers to see that pupils are provided with a supportive learning environment.

A good example of this approach was developed in a year 5 and 6 class in an inner-city school where a significant number of pupils had learning difficulties that resulted in challenging behaviour. Here the class teacher developed, over an extended period of time, the notion of peer support and collaborative learning. Pupils were encouraged and expected to help and support each other on both a cognitive and affective level. One particular boy who was prone at times to become upset, aggressive and throw objects was supported by a group of girls on his table. The year 5 boy might have several outbursts a day. The girls were helped to recognise the signs of distress – usually because he was becoming frustrated with his work – and would offer help, distraction or seek adult assistance. The crucial fact was that the behaviour was not seen as naughty but as something that was understood but not

Photo | Anna Grandfield.

acceptable. It was also making the boy unhappy and he would often end up in tears and then become the subject of fun. The class teacher saw this as a class issue and enabled the pupils and the boy to take increasing control of his behaviour, which gradually improved over the period of a year. Two factors were crucial in addressing this problem: the trust between the pupils and all the adults involved; and the deliberate use of class discussion to help the class community recognise the role that they had in supporting each other in the management of learning and behaviour.

The same approach was also used during geography fieldwork where the boy would be in a group to provide support (and record data) but not do his cognitive work. Placing the emphasis on assistance meant that any questions posed to the group needed to be open ended to enable him to contribute ideas. In a different situation a pupil with learning difficulties might need very specific questions. Again, other pupils and support assistance could be used to create an affirmative environment. This approach, which includes using circle time, peer tutoring and mediation, contributes to a number of curriculum areas. The main point is that by discussing the learning environment pupils become involved in a collaborative process. This is not dissimilar to the notion of action-orientated learning except that the centre of the action is not a particular subject or activity but the learning environment itself.

This approach has important ramifications for the notions of collaborative learning and fieldwork. I have observed a PGCE primary student who happened to be blind teaching in a city centre school where the pupils and the student managed the environment and interacted successfully, each using their strengths in a supportive manner. The key questions are:

1. How do we maximise the staff expertise in geography?
2. How do we combine staff expertise in geography and SEN to meet teaching and training needs?
3. How do we allocate time and space for geography?
4. How do we systematically build up a range of resource material, some based on pupils' work, so that it is available for all over the coming years?
5. How do we make maximum use of parents, outside speakers and visits to establish a notion of continuity and development in relation to geography?
6. How do we manage the physical environment to ensure that we comply with the *Special Educational Needs and Disability Act, 2001*?

Specific issues

All pupils will have specific issues or difficulties at certain times, in certain subjects and with individual teachers. We need to try different approaches, recognise we will make mistakes and discuss problems with pupils as they arise. Pupils can often give you valuable insights into why something has not worked but they need to trust you first and you need to listen to them. This will take time, so be patient. In order to examine specific learning problems a team approach works best, especially if you have an agreed common philosophy. Once you have examined the physical environment of the classroom and the school has begun to build resources, then you need to build on pupils' strengths and individual learning styles.

It can be difficult and time-consuming to ascertain what skills and knowledge pupils with SEN have if we are too focused on the notions of literacy and numeracy as discrete skills. It is important that we create time and space to discuss and listen to our pupils. The Cognitive

Acceleration through Science Education (CASE) group developed an approach to science that might well prove valuable with geography (Simon, 2002). My simplistic interpretation is that the building blocks for learning depend on the respect and value which teachers accord to pupils' views. So, for example, the traffic crossing issue discussed earlier would be an ideal vehicle for this approach. The use of open-ended questions which the teacher builds on and extends is also crucial, for example 'I see what you are saying but what if… 'Suppose we did this what might be…'. The aim is to provide a scaffold which helps pupils explore their thoughts and ideas rather than pupils trying to provide the right answer that they think we want.

The notion of providing a scaffold, which is something as primary teachers you do already, can be extended with regard to the learning needs of specific pupils. The scaffold might involve:

- changing the font, colour or font size of printed material;
- providing a visual timetable for pupils on the autistic spectrum;
- the use of a TA, parent or another adult/pupil;
- the physical adaptation of the classroom or environment you wish to work in.

Some pupils require a very specific routine that provides the security in which they can work. A pupil who is described as having Autistic Spectrum Disorder (ASD), for example, may have problems in organising themselves and materials in both space and time. They can manage the familiar better than novelty and seem to prefer activities and routines that they have experienced before. Other pupils may require a range of strategies with regard to managing the behaviour which should be covered within the school's behavioural policy – but again a collaborative approach is crucial.

The increasing role of TAs should also have a positive impact on the organisation of learning. There is also much to be said for a learning log in which pupils record their work using a file, video clip, computer disc or some other electronic format. Not only does this provide feedback and a record for the teacher, it also helps to open a geographical dialogue which can stay with the pupil and take them through the junior years and into secondary school.

Corbett and Norwich (1999) have explored the links between general learning pedagogy and specific learning programmes for individual pupils. They recognise that the programmes are difficult to write, and argue that individual programmes can isolate pupils, suggesting that teachers need to plan creatively for a range of different needs. Problem solving, key to geography, can be particularly hard to include. Some of the examples provided here offer opportunities for pupils to be creative within the geography curriculum. The important thing is to find ways of promoting geographical literacy. Children whose reading age is not yet commensurate with their chronological age may have other geographical strengths on which you can build: it is our job to discover and use these talents to build for success. Be patient, because it can take time; and always plan for quality, not quantity.

References and further reading

Corbett, J. and Norwich, B. (1999) 'Learners with special educational needs' in Mortimore, P. (ed) *Understanding Pedagogy and its Impact on Learning.* London: Paul Chapman.

DCSF (2005) *Social and Emotional Aspects of Learning (SEAL): Improving behaviour, improving learning.* London: DCSF.

DCSF (2008) *National Framework for Sustainable Schools.* London: DCSF.

DfES (2001) *Special Educational Needs Code of Practice.* London: DfES.

DfES (2003) *Excellence and Enjoyment.* London: DfES.

DfES (2004) *Every Child Matters.* London: DfES.

Gardner, H. (1993) *Multiple Intelligences: The theory in practice.* New York: Basic Books.

Goleman, D. (1996) *Emotional Intelligence: Why it can matter more than IQ.* London: Bloomsbury.

Goleman, D. (2007) *Social Intelligence: The new science of human relationships.* London: Arrow Books.

Great Britain. *Disabilities Discrimination Act 2005: Elizabeth II. Chapter 13.* London: The Stationery Office. Available at *www.opsi.gov.uk/acts/acts2005/ukpga_20050013_en_1* (last accessed 26 April 2010).

Great Britain. *Special Educational Needs and Disabilities Act 2001.* Elizabeth II. Chapter 10. London: The Stationery Office. Available at *www.opsi.gov.uk/acts/acts2001/ukpga_20010010_en_1* (last accessed 4 May 2010).

Hicks, D. and Holden, C. (2007) 'Remembering the future: what do children think?', *Environmental Education Research*, 13, 4, pp. 501-512.

Rogoff, B. (2003) *The Cultural Nature of Human Development.* Oxford: Oxford University Press.

Scrivener, C. (2003) 'Getting your voice heard and making a difference: using local environmental issues in a primary school as a context for action-orientated learning', *Support for Learning*, 18, 3, pp. 100-106.

Simon, S. (2002) 'The CASE approach for pupils with learning difficulties', *School Science Review*, 83, p. 305.

Slaymaker, J. (2007) 'How can we put inclusion into practice in geography?' in Cooper, H., Rowley, C. and Asquith, S. (eds) *Geography 3-11: A guide for teachers.* London: David Fulton.

Websites

Eco-Schools *www.eco-schools.org.uk*

Every Child Matters *www.dcsf.gov.uk/everychildmatters*

Gifted and talented *www.qcda.gov.uk/resources*

Inclusion and National Strategies *http://nationalstrategies.standards.dcsf.gov.uk/inclusion*

Millennium Development Goals *www.un.org/millenniumgoals*

National Association for Special Educational Needs (NASEN) *www.nasen.org.uk*

Special Educational Needs Code of Practice *www.teachernet.gov.uk/wholeschool/sen/sencodeintro*

Social and Emotional Aspects of Learning (SEAL) *http://nationalstrategies.standards.dcsf.gov.uk/primary/behaviourattendanceandseal/primaryseal*

Sustainable Schools Framework *www.teachernet.gov.uk/sustainableschools/framework/framework_detail.cfm*

CHAPTER COVERAGE:
ASSESSMENT • GOOD PRACTICE • CPD/INSET • INSPECTION • PLANNING • TRANSITION

The subject leader

Most primary teachers deliver the full range of national curriculum subjects so it is expected that they will have a working subject knowledge of both the core and foundation subjects. However, it is also expected that teachers will co-ordinate one or more curriculum areas and be responsible for developing it/them across the school. These can be very considerable demands.

As a teacher you will possess more extensive subject expertise in some curriculum areas than others. However, the subjects you are asked to co-ordinate are not always the ones in which you are strongest. This chapter provides guidance to all who co-ordinate geography whether or not they have specific subject expertise. It sets out the responsibilities of the subject leader/subject co-ordinator and will help you match your background and experience with your responsibilities, your school's agreed agenda for action and your own professional development needs. Acting as a subject co-ordinator is an integral part of the leadership and management structure of a primary school. It also provides you with the opportunity to develop your skills at middle-management level.

The role of the co-ordinator is crucial to the success of geography teaching in a primary school. As a co-ordinator you will need to champion the subject and demonstrate its importance to pupils and staff. In addition, geography lends itself to cross-curricular work and provides a context for exploring many other subject areas. Teachers are increasingly encouraged to be creative in how they plan and deliver all that is expected of them within specific time constraints. Therefore the more flexible and creative teachers become, the more effective the cross-curricular work will be.

Superior subject knowledge is not necessarily a criterion for the choice of a co-ordinator. In some cases, particularly in small schools, geography is co-ordinated by the head teacher or deputy head teacher in addition to their other responsibilities. In larger schools, teachers have responsibility for co-ordinating only one subject. However, geography is also frequently linked with history or citizenship, with one co-ordinator responsible for a broad area of learning. Typically, while senior teachers co-ordinate the core subjects and receive responsibility allowances, geography is

---

Which of these descriptions best matches the position you find yourself in?

- You were appointed this year as an newly-qualified teacher and were asked whether you would co-ordinate geography.
- You are in a small school where everybody has to carry a wide range of curriculum responsibilities and there was no one else to take responsibility for geography.
- You are the head teacher and no one else felt able to do the co-ordinator job so it fell to you.

- You last studied geography when you were 14, but you are interested in outdoor education so it seemed natural to give the co-ordinator job to you.
- You are already the history co-ordinator and geography and history are seen as being very similar.
- You are a geography graduate and it was assumed that made you an ideal co-ordinator.
- You have attended INSET or further study linked to the work of geography co-ordinator and feel quite confident about the role.

Figure 1 | *Geography co-ordinators come from a range of different backgrounds.*

often co-ordinated by the least experienced newcomer who receives no responsibility allowance at all.

Geography subject co-ordinators come to their posts in a great variety of ways. The descriptions in Figure 1, derived from conversations with teachers in Cheshire, give a sense of the diversity of backgrounds.

So it is that the teaching experience and subject expertise of geography co-ordinators may vary considerably. You are likely to teach most of or the entire curriculum, although you may combine a generalist role with advice and support for geography; you may be a semi-specialist; you may teach geography full-time. Whatever your background, to be a successful curriculum co-ordinator you will need the following:

■ the professional skills to work with colleagues collaboratively, sharing curriculum expertise
■ a clearly defined role backed up by a job description which is linked to the school management structure
■ a sound working knowledge of the geography curriculum and access to appropriate INSET for professional development
■ a perspective of the geography curriculum in the context of the whole curriculum framework
■ the ability to produce a key stage plan or plans which meet statutory and school requirements
■ the ability to produce detailed topic, theme or unit plans
■ the support of the head teacher and governing body and full recognition in the school development plan
■ clearly identified budget provision.

The responsibilities of the geography co-ordinator

These are shown in Figure 2 and expanded in the paragraphs that follow. The order in which they appear is not intended to indicate importance. The first thing to do if you are appointed to this post is take stock of your situation: your priorities are likely to emerge from that process. Look at where your school is now, where you want to be in the future and how you are going to get there. The self evaluation model offered by the Primary Geography Quality Mark could help you with this audit (see Chapter 26 for further details).

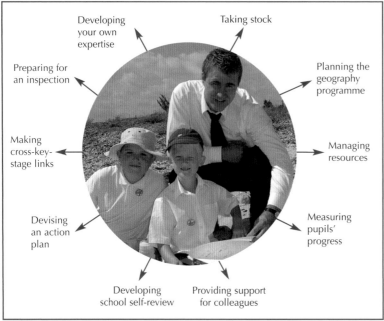

Developing your own expertise
Taking stock
Preparing for an inspection
Planning the geography programme
Making cross-key-stage links
Managing resources
Devising an action plan
Measuring pupils' progress
Developing school self-review
Providing support for colleagues

Figure 2 | The responsibilities of the geography co-ordinator.

Taking stock

Discover what is expected of the geography co-ordinator in your school. There should be a 'job description'; if not, ask the head teacher for one. Find out what geography is already being done, and what is going well. Talk to colleagues to find out what they expect of you, and what confidence/expertise they already possess. Consider your curriculum coverage – many schools have adopted, then adapted, published schemes of work; others have devised their own. Look too at previous Ofsted inspection reports and ask for a copy of your school's current SEF, highlighting areas that relate to geography. Find out what work is done in geography; talk to the children, and look for links between geography and other curriculum areas. This will show you what the pupils actually do in geography, and where it is taught well. This evidence will support you when you assess your professional needs and those of your colleagues.

Bear in mind that some of your colleagues will require more support than others. For example, if you have an NQT in school, focus specific attention on supporting this colleague. An audit of resources will also be very valuable. Don't forget to look for resources such as information books and 'big books' which can be used to support geography in a cross-curricular way.

Examine the long-, medium- and short-term plans for geography. These will indicate progression and continuity of the subject. Remember that pupils should have a recurring experience of geography throughout the primary years, so if there are any gaps you will need to make plans to fill them. Make sure that colleagues are using the enquiry approach (see Chapter 7), and integrating the study of places, themes and skills. Think also about what geography you want the school to be doing next year – and in three years' time.

Planning the geography programme

The programme for geography should be clearly set out and subdivided into teaching units. You should also ensure that the programme sets out how continuity and progression in geography are to be achieved both across and within the key stages. *The Children's Plan* (DCSF, 2007) and sections of *Every Child Matters* (DfES, 2004) (particularly those on 'enjoying and achieving' and 'making a positive contribution') are especially important to consider when planning the geography curriculum. Don't feel you have to reinvent; make sure you keep what works.

Geography lends itself extremely well to the development of thinking skills such as information processing, enquiry and evaluation. As a school, consider how you can develop other vital skills through your geography work. *Excellence and Enjoyment* (DfES, 2003), the government's strategy for primary schools, encourages teachers to be more flexible in their approach to teaching by making use of a wider range of teaching styles and strategies. This could form the basis for a valuable early evening INSET session.

The programme should also identify links with other curriculum areas and the opportunities to reinforce literacy, numeracy and ICT through work in geography. Pupils should be able to enjoy geography in a variety of ways (fieldwork, visits, visitors, ICT, videos, DVDs) and these will have to be planned into appropriate points in the programme. It should also be possible to take opportunities for 'incidental geography' (e.g. current events, school assemblies, displays).

Managing resources

Your school should possess enough teaching resources to deliver the geography programme to pupils of different abilities through a range of varied learning experiences. The first thing to do is check which resources you already have and identify any gaps; consider the need for a good balance of books, maps, photographs, videos, DVDs and software when deciding how to file them, prioritising expenditure sensibly by concentrating first on the main teaching units. The school library may contain resources which will support geographical work so include these in your survey; both fiction and non-fiction geography resources should support the literacy programme. Be aware of local and national priorities and make good use of the internet by compiling a list of useful websites both for teachers and pupils to use.

Ensure that your resources support active, investigative learning. In particular, ensure resources take account of different learning styles – this is required to support inclusion. Don't forget local resources – people, buildings, environments – which may support fieldwork, but remember the need for risk assessments and careful planning. Make sure that your resources are easily accessible and that all your colleagues know what and where they are. Keep your resources up-to-date and ensure that you receive a good range of product catalogues and resource lists. Joining the Geographical Association will give you access to up-to-date ideas via *Primary Geographer* and the GA website as well as member's discount on a range of teaching resources. If you do nothing else, you should make subscribing your priority.

Measuring pupils' progress

It is the co-ordinator's job to ensure that colleagues are clear about how to assess geography, and that their judgements are in line with the whole-school policy and practice (see Chapter 23). Teaching plans should identify clear learning targets; work across classes should be compared, and work recorded and reported to parents. Staff meeting time should be devoted to this assessment. Achievement should inform the planning of future work. Feedback to pupils is important; they should know their strengths and weaknesses and have the opportunity to assess their own work. Think about how to identify SEN and Gifted and Talented pupils and consider how to meet their needs and any special provision which may be required.

Providing support for colleagues

One of the most important roles of the co-ordinator is to facilitate INSET for colleagues. INSET sessions can range from 'one-to-one' advice and support; to the staff meeting after school; to a half day or whole day involving all your colleagues and sometimes including the support staff. Clusters of schools can be effective for networking. Make use of the LA Advisers if available and consult the GA website to see what other local expertise is available. Finding informal time to chat to colleagues always pays off in terms of generating mutual support.

Here are some thoughts about planning activities for your colleagues. It is recognised that this offers quite a challenge and may make you feel quite uneasy as someone who will be expected to have 'all the answers'!

■ Good research and preparation are essential – you may not be the expert, but you should be able to refer colleagues to an appropriate source of help. The Geographical Association website and publications, especially *Primary Geographer*, can be very useful here.

Photo | *Wendy North.*

■ One-to-one support is time consuming, but can be well targeted to need. It is particularly successful when combined with 'team teaching'; for instance, when you visit an outdoor centre for the day or overnight.

■ Staff meetings after school tend to be time-pressured so aim for a crisp start. The golden rule is don't try and cover too much in the time available.

■ Half and whole days are undoubtedly best. They work particularly well when you can involve your colleagues in devising curriculum materials themselves. Try and show your colleagues that geography, as Martin (2006) puts it, is within their grasp and that they can use it imaginatively as a 'lens' for making sense of everyday experiences.

■ Inviting an adviser or someone from a college to run a session can be very effective, but they need careful briefing – make sure they address your agenda!

Developing school self-review

Most schools have some system for reviewing whole-school issues, in particular the effectiveness of curriculum management and teaching. However, evidence from inspections suggests that school self-review is one of the weakest parts of a school's planning cycle. Ofsted reports indicate that monitoring is a very powerful tool for improving the learning environment and for raising standards of pupil achievement, but that most co-ordinators are not able to monitor directly or even indirectly the quality of geography in their schools.

It would be helpful if the senior management team could monitor geography teaching throughout the school. As a co-ordinator you should be involved in this process. Conducting peer reviews, where colleagues observe each other in a supportive manner, is also very valuable. This monitoring process can effectively tie in with performance management. Furthermore, if geography is a priority within the school SEF, then it would be completely justified to focus on geography for performance management objectives, either at whole-school or class level or for your own professional development. Some of the areas a self-review should investigate are:

■ the quality of learning and teaching
■ the pupils' achievements
■ the pupils' response to particular activities such as fieldwork visits
■ geography's contribution to pupils' spiritual, moral, social and cultural development
■ leadership and management, staffing, accommodation and resources
■ provision for gifted and talented/SEN pupils
■ safeguarding children, including health and safety issues (fieldwork risk assessment)
■ action research in the classroom.

It is best to identify specific areas for review to make the process manageable and to avoid superficial treatment of important issues. Evidence for the review will come from a variety of sources depending on the item being covered. It should be qualitative and professional, not solely quantitative. You might include discussions with teaching and non-teaching staff including the head teacher, parents and pupils past and present; book scrutiny; an evaluation of resources, including the library; a review of industry visits and fieldwork; and the efficiency of financial planning.

Ultimately self-review is intended to help schools create a balance between consolidation and innovation. It needs to be built into curriculum management to ensure the effective delivery of a stimulating and challenging curriculum.

Devising an action plan

The outputs of review will help you devise an action plan for geography. The plan will need a three-year overview and a detailed one-year programme. You will need to consider the following:

- Objective: What are we going to do?
- Rationale: Why do we need to do it?
- Success criteria: What do we expect to achieve?
- Action plan: How are we going to do it?
- Personnel: Who will do the different parts of the action plan?
- Resources: How much will we need to spend?
- INSET: What are our training needs?
- Timescale: When will it be completed?
- Monitoring: Who will monitor progress, to whom will progress be reported?
- Evaluation: How will we measure success?

The completed action plan will identify priorities for geography and contribute to the SEF. Given the right climate, drawing up the plan will provide an opportunity to celebrate success – something which can often be overlooked in these times of constant change.

Making cross-key-stage links

The geography co-ordinator has an important role in ensuring that pupils receive a coherent geographical education as they move through their school life. Prior learning must be acknowledged, celebrated and assessed at the start of pupils' formal education, and at all points of transfer throughout their school life. As Catling and Willy (2008) argue, to have meaning and relevance primary school geography needs to connect to children's lived experience. When children enjoy what they are doing and are actively committed to it then effective learning will take place as 'a matter of course' (p. 4).

Both pastoral and curriculum-related information needs to be exchanged, especially when pupils move school. This is most important at the key stage 2/3 boundary, which often marks a significant change in the style and organisation of the geography curriculum. The following suggestions will help ensure a smooth transition:

- sharing resources between your partner secondary school(s) to enable you to begin a curriculum dialogue;
- forwarding information about the localities, in addition to the local area, which your pupils have studied;
- acknowledging that secondary schools tend to use concepts or themes rather than places (localities) as the main curriculum building block;
- the high school acknowledging that your pupils will have a good working knowledge of their local area which can be shared with pupils from other schools in year 7.

Developing your own expertise

It is now recognised that continuous professional development (CPD) is essential to effective curriculum leadership. Your personal programme should be agreed in your appraisal and/or form part of the school's development plan. Most geography co-ordinators need two main things: externally provided INSET and the help of a curriculum adviser. The former will offer broad-brush advice, applicable to all schools, whereas the latter can be tailored to your individual needs. The problem is that both can be expensive. One way round this difficulty is to attend the Geographical Association Annual Conference which is held in a different location each Easter and offers both broad advice and specific support at a modest cost.

Your professional development can also be enhanced by action research. Finding out about the problems which pupils encounter in geography is both fascinating and rewarding. If you and your colleagues focus on a particular aspect of teaching you will be able to analyse your respective skills. This also gives you an opportunity to assess the work of your colleagues in a supportive and non-threatening manner.

Another approach to CPD is to use networks and cluster groups. Other schools will have the same problems as you have. By working with colleagues in similar schools you can develop an informative and supportive liaison with relatively no outlay. Cluster groups can often work well with feeder schools working with the local secondary school. This cluster work can also support transition between key stages 2 and 3. Work carried out by a co-ordinator can also be tied into performance management objectives.

The Geographical Association, recognising that curriculum leadership is a demanding role, has developed a number of online courses which will help support your professional development. If you choose to take this route it could lead to an award from the Teacher Learning Academy. You can access these courses on the CPD area of the GA website.

In addition you might investigate the RGS-IBG Chartered Geographer (Teacher) accreditation scheme which similarly focuses on professional advancement and raising standards.

Preparing for an inspection

In preparing for an inspection, the geography co-ordinator is best placed to make sure that the presence of geography in the school is clear (plenty of geographical work on display) and well integrated into the whole curriculum. Make sure that colleagues recognise the distinctive contribution that geography makes to the school curriculum (world knowledge, sense of place, pattern and process, environment, skills), and that they understand how it also contributes to basic skills and provides effective learning opportunities for all pupils.

You will need to find out if there was a reference to geography in the main findings in your last school inspection report and if your school prepared an action plan for this area. Reviewing the curriculum using the Ofsted framework and SEF will also help to identify those aspects of geography which could be better organised. The inspectors will certainly review the progress your school has made since their last visit. The inspectors will also be checking that teachers are working to clear plans and have proper resources and that the pupils are challenged and motivated. This aspect of the work of a co-ordinator is discussed more extensively in Chapter 22.

How do I construct a geography policy?

The purpose of a geography policy is to inform parents, governors and other interested people about how geography is taught in your school and how it contributes to pupils' development. The policy should reflect a consensus of staff views on the place of geography within the whole-school ethos. Schools have a statutory obligation to provide a policy for each area of the curriculum.

Your policy should contain clear and simple statements about the nature and importance of geography. It should be brief and jargon-free, and supported by a scheme of work. The main elements of a geography policy are given in the outline below. It is included as an example of good practice, but your school will need to respond in its own particular way to match its own needs. It is based on the geography national curriculum programme of study, and although the specific requirement to follow the programme of study has been relaxed, it is important for any policy to offer viable schemes of work which deliver geography as part of a broad and balanced curriculum.

An example of a geography policy statement

Introduction

This policy outlines the purpose and management of the geography taught and learned in the school. The school policy for geography reflects the consensus of opinion of the entire teaching staff, brought about through discussion in staff meetings.

A structured framework has been designed, allowing for progression and continuity across the primary sector. The implementation of this policy is the responsibility of all the teaching staff.

The nature of geography

Geography is concerned with the study of places, the human and physical processes which shape them and the people who live in them. Pupils study their local area, and contrasting localities in the United Kingdom and other parts of the world.

Geography helps pupils to gain a greater understanding of the ways of life and cultures of people in other places. The study of the local area forms an important part of the geography taught at our school, particularly at key stage 1. Enjoyable geographical activities are planned to build upon the pupils' knowledge and understanding of the local area. Through our teaching of geography we aim to:

- stimulate the pupils' interest in and curiosity about their surroundings;
- create and foster a sense of wonder about the world;
- inspire a sense of responsibility for the environments and people of the world we live in;
- develop pupils' competence in specific geographical skills;
- increase the pupils' knowledge and awareness of the world;
- help pupils acquire and develop the skills and confidence to undertake investigation, problem solving and decision making.

We hope that pupils will increase their knowledge and understanding of the changing world and will want to look after the Earth and its resources. We hope that they will begin to develop respect and concern for, and an interest in, people throughout the world regardless of culture, race and religion.

Roles and responsibilities

Each member of the teaching staff will have responsibility for the teaching of geography and they will need to ensure that their own knowledge is continually updated. The school has a geography co-ordinator to assist this process, and take specific responsibility for geography issues in the school. The geography co-ordinator should be a member of the teaching staff who has been trained to lead the teaching of geography. It is his or her responsibility to:

- support colleagues in teaching the subject content and to demonstrate good teaching where required;
- audit current practice;
- instigate and organise teaching programmes, planning documents and schemes of work where necessary;
- develop a school policy;
- resource the curriculum by:
  - keeping abreast of the latest teaching methods and materials by subscribing to the Geographical Association termly magazine, *Primary Geographer*, and storing up-to-date publishers' catalogues and information about new software and equipment in the geography curriculum file;
  - renewing, updating and complementing resources where necessary, and drawing up action plans accordingly;
  - building up a collection of video and audio recordings;
  - ensuring that colleagues are made aware of the resources available in school and their location;
- facilitate the standardised assessment of pupils' work at moderation meetings;

- be a consultant to colleagues, and plan the geography content of their teaching on a termly basis. Copies of the medium-term plan are located in the geography curriculum file;
- keep people informed of possible visits, exhibitions and courses.

Entitlement

Geography is one of the national curriculum foundation subjects with designated programmes of study linked to descriptions of attainment levels. Schools have been advised that as a starting point they might spend 33 hours per year on geography at key stage 1 and 36 hours at key stage 2.

At key stage 1 and 2 the programme of study is divided into a number of areas including:

- geographical enquiry and skills
- the study of key ideas such as change, patterns and processes
- the study of localities
- the study of themes.

At key stage 1 pupils study their school locality and a contrasting locality either in the UK or overseas. At key stage 2 pupils study a locality in the UK and a locality in a country that is less economically developed. There are three themes at key stage 2 — water and the landscape, settlements and an environmental issue.

All pupils are entitled to access the geography programme at a level appropriate to their individual needs. Those pupils who work below the levels defined by the geography national curriculum for their key stage will be given additional assistance by the class teacher. Progress will be carefully monitored; if necessary, and with full parental understanding and support, internal special needs help will be made available. We aim to meet all the needs of individual pupils in the school, whether the pupils are designated as having special educational needs or are gifted and talented. The school fully supports the policy of inclusion.

Leadership

The geography co-ordinator will be given non-contact time in order to develop geography throughout the school. She/he will be expected to report back to the SMT in school of her/his findings. It will be expected that the co-ordinator will scrutinise planning and books, audit resources, examine CPD for the staff, observe lessons, model exemplar lessons, write and implement the geography action plan and deliver staff meetings and INSET.

The geography co-ordinator will be expected to develop the subject according to the school development plan and will work to develop learning and teaching according to the ethos of the school. The co-ordinator will work within any local and national priorities.

Implementation procedures

The national curriculum programmes of study define the content of the school curriculum for geography. In our school geography is the main focus for teaching for one term each year. However, wherever possible, some geographical skills or place knowledge will be included in studies with other foci. Current events ranging from local issues to floods and earthquakes overseas are used sensitively and appropriately to promote learning.

Places

As well as undertaking specified place studies, pupils at key stage 2 also need to learn to locate significant places and environments in the UK, Europe and wider world. Whenever possible we develop this locational knowledge in the context of our work on places and themes. We also seek to give emphasis to the lives of real people in order to avoid stereotyping, give equal emphasis to the roles of men and women at all levels in society and create positive images of parts of the world that may be much poorer economically than ourselves.

Skills

The geographical skills outlined in the programme of study at both key stages are integrated with work associated with places and themes. Throughout the school pupils are encouraged to use appropriate geographical vocabulary to promote their thinking. We encourage practical activities and investigations within the classroom and further afield, together with the use of ICT equipment.

Themes

The study of places and themes are linked at both key stages. However, to allow in-depth study and ensure that the work is undertaken at a range of scales from local to national some studies are discrete. An investigative approach to geography involving pupils' active participation in enquiry, fieldwork, mapwork and the use of ICT is promoted throughout.

Where does geography occur in the curriculum?

- As a major focus for a topic.
- As a smaller element within a topic.
- As a discrete lesson/talk.
- As part of an assembly.

- In discussion (who saw the news last night?).
- During story time.
- In displays both in the classroom and in other areas of the school.
- As an integral part of residential visits. The school visits outdoor educational centres where geographical skills can be confirmed in a practical way. (All risk assessments are held with the head teacher, the teacher in charge, the governing body and the educational visits co-ordinator.)

Classroom organisation and teaching methods

Classroom organisation will depend on the needs and abilities of the pupils and also on the aims of the lesson. However, a variety of approaches such as whole-class lessons, group, paired and individual work are experienced by pupils in their geographical work. Access to resources is sometimes a determining factor in classroom organisation. Teachers are mindful of the ways in which pupils learn. The teaching of geography reflects different learning styles to ensure full inclusion.

We believe fieldwork helps to promote learning in all aspects of geography and we seek to incorporate it in all aspects of the curriculum plan. When they are engaged in fieldwork pupils are expected to behave in a considerate and responsible manner, showing respect for other people and their environment.

All pupils have opportunities to use ICT as part of their geographical work. They also have opportunities to use the following resources: globes, maps, atlases, pictures, aerial photographs, compasses, measuring equipment, cameras, books and games. Most of these items are kept in the resource area and are readily accessible to staff, who will select resources appropriate to the needs of the pupils. The interactive whiteboards are an excellent resource enhancing pupils' learning.

Assessment and recording

Pupils' progress is assessed and monitored during the year through normal teacher planning and observation. Individual records, and portfolios of pupils' work, will chart progress. A class record of areas/topics is kept to assist with future teaching and planning for continuity and progression. Parents are informed of their child's progress at termly parents' evenings and via the annual reports which are sent home in the summer term.

Special needs

Differentiation in terms of learning objectives, tasks, teaching methods and resources will be planned for pupils with special educational needs. All pupils should have access to materials and opportunities suitable to their specific needs. Exceptionally able pupils need to be challenged with open-ended tasks which provide opportunities to tackle more complex issues and use a wider range of resources.

Review and revision

This policy was drawn up by the geography co-ordinator and is based on the school's understanding of the geography national curriculum. It will be reviewed annually by the geography co-ordinator who will collect and collate the experiences and ideas of colleagues that arise during staff meetings and any designated INSET time.

References and further reading

Catling, S. and Willy, T. (2008) *Teaching Primary Geography*. Exeter: Learning Matters.

DCSF (2007) *Building Brighter Futures: The children's plan for families*. London: DCSF.

DfES (2004) *Every Child Matters: Change for children in schools*. London: DfES.

Martin, F. (2006) 'Everyday geography', *Primary Geographer*, 61, pp. 4-7.

Tauk, A. (2008) 'How to bluff your way as a geography co-ordinator', *Primary Geographer*, 65, pp. 19-20.

Websites

Chartered Geographer (Teacher) *www.geographyteachingtoday.org.uk/chartered-geographer/introduction*

Geographical Association CPD *www.geography.org.uk/cpdevents*

Laura Murray   2nd May

What new would a bird
have of snawsdowns walk?

Lowerway

Grass

Footpath

Footpath

E ← → W

S

N

well done!   *Pupils' work* | Y5/6, Parsons Down Junior School.

CHAPTER COVERAGE:
ASSESSMENT • GOOD PRACTICE • INCLUSION/SEN • INSPECTION

The inspection and accreditation of geography

Despite all the changes of the last few decades, geography has retained its unique role as a subject which promotes active learning and develops children's understanding of the world and the way it is changing, from local to global scales. Until 2005 primary schools received detailed Ofsted geography inspections from time to time, usually as part of whole-school inspections. With the general improvement in the quality of teaching, and teachers' increased skills in classroom observation, the importance of school self evaluation has grown. Since 2005, Ofsted has implemented a much shorter inspection process which includes a self-evaluation process. Geography no longer has a specific focus in inspection reports, but is part of the cluster of foundation subjects contributing to the whole school curriculum and quality of learning and teaching. So judgements about a school's geography curriculum are no longer simply left to an outsider in the form of an inspector.

In addition, with fewer local authority specialist subject advisers, teachers who oversee geography now need more than ever to develop their skills and confidence in the subject. There are three main opportunities for schools to develop their evaluation skills and gain recognition for the work they are doing with children and staff in geography. These are:

■ Ofsted surveys and specialist subject inspections
■ the Geographical Association Primary Geography Quality Mark
■ the Geography Champions' network.

Ofsted survey and specialist subject inspections

In addition to whole school primary short inspections, Ofsted carries out separate subject inspections and surveys. The purposes of these are:

■ to contribute to the Chief Inspector's annual schools' report, giving a national picture of strengths and areas for development
■ to enable Ofsted to disseminate findings including good practice, through its website, conferences, talks and articles
■ to provide useful feedback to individual schools
■ to support the school's own self evaluation.

Although compared to whole school inspections individual subject inspections are relatively rare, teachers often want to know what the process involves so they can be well prepared. The school may be chosen for a visit through random sampling methods or because it is known for having good practice in the subject. Such inspections are at short notice (not more than two weeks) and usually last a day. They will be carried out by the specialist geography HMI or by an additional inspector with expertise in the subject. Feedback will be given to the school at the end of the visit. The school can be inspected once every three years under the current whole-school inspection system. However, survey inspections are likely to be less frequent.

Photo | Paula Richardson.

What is the focus of a survey or inspection?

Inspectors evaluate geography achievement, provision, leadership and management, using the same Ofsted self-evaluation framework and criteria (SEF) used for whole-school inspections. In addition, the inspection visit includes a specific focus on a current issue of national importance. In 2009/10, for example, as well as the key areas of geography, visits evaluated how effectively geography teaching and the geography curriculum promoted community cohesion. Useful guidance on Ofsted findings is embedded in a range of Ofsted publications, such as *Improving Primary Teachers' Subject Knowledge Across The Curriculum* (Ofsted, 2009). Use the search function to locate relevant topics, for example sustainable schools, or CPD.

So how does a school prepare for a geography survey or subject inspection?

Since the inspection visit will only last one day, it is clearly important to see that geography is being taught at the time and to ensure that the subject leader or other key staff are available for discussions during the day as necessary. The inspector, as well as observing teaching, will want to talk to pupils and look at pupils' work. He or she will want to have access to subject documentation, such as the geography subject action or development plan, curriculum plans/schemes of work, the standards portfolio of pupil work and the relevant policy. As well as lessons, the inspector may attend an assembly if it is relevant to your subject area. He or she will want to give you feedback at the end of the day, and will subsequently also provide a written report. In other words, the inspector will want to evaluate the teaching, documentation and processes which an effective subject leader should have no trouble making available or accumulating over time. However, for an inspector this is all concentrated into the space of one day!

Self evaluation leading to accreditation: the Primary Geography Quality Mark (PGQM)

The Geographical Association recognised as early as 2004 that schools needed support to develop self evaluation and accreditation for geography. With hardly any local authority advisers left to offer help in the subject, and no specific requirement to cover geography in whole-school inspections unless it was identified by the school, there was a danger that the largely non-specialist geography subject leaders would receive no external support at all. At the same time, the high priority accorded to literacy and numeracy meant that many foundation subjects were struggling for curriculum time, and geography had tended to become marginalised. The Department for Education and Schools (DfES), now the Department for Education, was similarly aware of these risks. As a result the Geographical Association and RGS-IBG were jointly awarded funding for a new programme of help for schools – the Action Plan for Geography.

The Geographical Association devoted part of this funding to developing the PGQM – a nationally recognised quality mark which would enable schools to recognise and celebrate their own achievement and inspire them to further develop their geography. To develop the PGQM a small team of primary geography consultants and teachers developed a set of criteria which were specific to geography but also aligned to the whole School Evaluation Framework (SEF). Written for three levels – bronze, silver and gold – the draft criteria were trialled with 30 volunteer schools in 2005/6 and amended according to feedback. The PGQM went live nationally as an award scheme in 2006/7. Like other awards such as Artsmark, Healthy Schools, Eco-Schools and the ICT Mark, the Primary Geography Quality Mark formally accredits the work a school has done, and in the scheme's first four years over two hundred schools achieved a PGQM award.

How can the award help my school?

The Primary Geography Quality Mark helps schools achieve recognition for the quality of their geography leadership, curriculum development, learning and teaching. The self-assessment framework relates to the four principal SEF areas:

- the characteristics of geography in your school
- how well pupils enjoy and achieve in geography
- the quality of provision
- subject leadership and management.

Entering for the award can:

- provide guidance for school leadership teams who want to engage in a process of whole-school supported self-review
- support teachers who are new to the co-ordinating role by showing how geography can be developed in their school
- identify and celebrate what is already good in a school, which can greatly encourage both the subject leader and colleagues.

How can the award help me as an individual?

In order to apply for the award you or your school need be a member of the Geographical Association. You can then download the framework and other appropriate tools, such as the audit form, from the GA website (*www.geography.org.uk/pgqm*). The website resources will help you, as a non-specialist subject leader, build your knowledge and confidence until such time as you feel ready to go to your head teacher and suggest that the school should tackle the award formally. At this point it must become a whole-school project. In addition there are opportunities for personal accreditation through the Teacher Learning Academy (TLA). You can do this by keeping a brief 'open learning journal' to document work in progress. Working to achieve the PGQM award could contribute significantly towards TLA accreditation assessed at level 2 or level 3. The TLA website (*www.teacherlearning academy.org.uk*) contains further information.

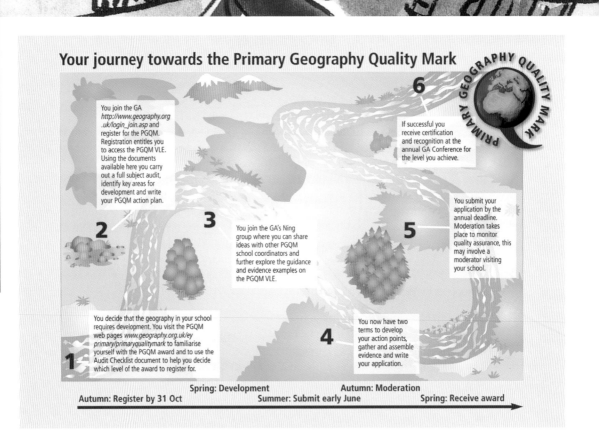

Figure 1 | *The Primary Geography Quality Mark timeline summarises the actions involved in applying for and submitting the award.*

How does my school apply for the award formally?

Once you have decided that you do want to work for the award formally, you will need to register for it through the website. This gives you all relevant documents and some excellent exemplification from accredited schools so you know what is expected when you come to fill in your application. You may register for an award up to six months before you intend to present your evidence. You may need about two years to assess and develop the subject from your starting point to the point of submission. The award process from registration to award notification takes 16 months (Figure 1).

You can reapply, to maintain the same level or progress to the next level of silver or gold, every three years. There is a clear progression across the three levels:

■ A bronze award recognises the school's commitment to ensuring lively and effective learning in geography.

■ A silver award recognises the importance of whole-school approaches that support excellence in geography.

■ A gold award recognises the school's capacity to embed excellent and innovative geography throughout the school.

At bronze level, the school is developing its geography and moving on, even though good practice may not yet have become embedded in every class of the school. By the time a school achieves the gold award, it is likely to have begun to have an impact with geography beyond its own institution. (See the section on Geography Champions below.)

Photo /
Salisbury
Journal.

What is the key to successfully presenting my evidence for the award?

When you write up your evidence you will need to:

- show how effectively children learn geography and whether they enjoy their learning
- communicate how you provide for quality learning in geography and whether your provision is having an impact on children as learners
- demonstrate how effectively the subject is led and managed
- celebrate the characteristics of geography in your school.

The key to successful evidence presentation is to demonstrate the impact that your leadership and the school's teaching and learning have had, rather than just describing what it looks like. The most successful entries have usually, in addition to having done the actual development work on geography in the school, spent a significant amount of time looking at the exemplification on the PGQM VLE to see how to present the information effectively. As well as writing about what you have being doing and its impact on children's learning, you will probably want to include photographs and examples of children's work.

How is my award entry assessed?

Most of the bronze and silver awards are gained through the submission of paper/electronic evidence which is then moderated by a GA nominated moderator. Occasionally a bronze or silver level school may be visited to satisfy the GA's own quality assurance procedures. Such visits will be cost free.

Gold awards are open to schools which demonstrate that geographical learning is truly embedded across the whole school and where the geography subject leader contributes to the development of primary geography beyond their school, e.g. to GA or LA conferences or publications. In addition to the submission of the paper/electronic evidence, a GA-nominated moderator makes a half-day visit to the school. Schools on the silver/gold borderline may also request a visit if they are aiming for gold.

You could begin by thinking about how geography is organised:

- Do you as subject leader have a vision for the subject in your school?

- What is the place of geography within the school improvement plan and the school self-evaluation process?

- Does geography feature in the school development plan?

- Is geography clearly identifiable within your cross-curricular and creative units of work?

- If you have discrete units of geography work, have they been updated in line with relevance to local needs?

- Have you considered the standards pupils can reach in different years or key stages? (To help with this, use *www.ncaction.org.uk* and the examples of pupils' work to be found in many sections of *www.geography.org.uk/eyprimary*.)

- How is pupils' progress in geography assessed against standards, rather than just coverage?

- What are your expectations about geography in your school as a whole?

- Do you know how much continuity and progression are built into pupils' geographical learning, especially in map and atlas knowledge and skills?

- How does the school monitor and evaluate geography standards?

- What do you do with the information you acquire from assessments?

- How do staff and pupils feel about the subject? Do they enjoy it? Do you have evidence for this, e.g. feedback from pupils interviewed? Are parents or governors consulted and involved?

- Is geography fieldwork an entitlement for all classes?

- Is it clear to all how geography contributes to the *Every Child Matters* agenda?

- Have you recognized how geography can contribute to teaching and learning about sustainability, global citizenship, community cohesion and diversity?

- Do you know how geography has improved over time?

In addition you need to ensure that geography has a visible and valued presence in your school. For example:

- Are there geography displays in classrooms and corridors which act either as a stimulus to enquiry or to celebrate pupils' work?

- Are resources adequate – globes and atlases, as well as story books and reference books?

- Is there access to digital mapping in addition to Google Maps?

- · Have there been dedicated geography days or weeks, or themed weeks or days in which some clear geography objectives have been found?

Finally, you need to establish to what extent you are able to lead staff:

- Do staff really know about the resources available? (High staff turnover can have a bad impact on resource awareness.)

- Can you give examples of how you support colleagues in their geography teaching?

- Have you led any staff development sessions on geography, even sharing ideas while looking at pupils' work to assess coverage and standards?

Figure 2 | *Developing an awareness of the state of geography teaching in your school.*

Geography Champions network

What is a Geography Champion and how can they help with the accreditation of geography?

The Geography Champions project aims to develop local networks to support primary teachers with responsibility for geography across England. The Champions are a mix of primary teachers, many of whom have attained PGQM accreditation, and some are headteachers, local authority and independent consultants and initial teacher education trainers. They all have a passion for geography, can recognise good practice and know how to inspire teaching and learning in the subject. The Champions run network meetings around the country, providing continuing professional development for those responsible for leading geography in their schools. Those belonging to the network can also communicate online via a dedicated Champions networking site known as the Champions Ning (*http://geographychampions.ning.com*), sharing ideas, questions and advice. If you belong to such a network you are bound to increase your knowledge and expectations through exposure to the experiences of other practitioners. You can take back the ideas you will gain into your own school which will help you with the development,

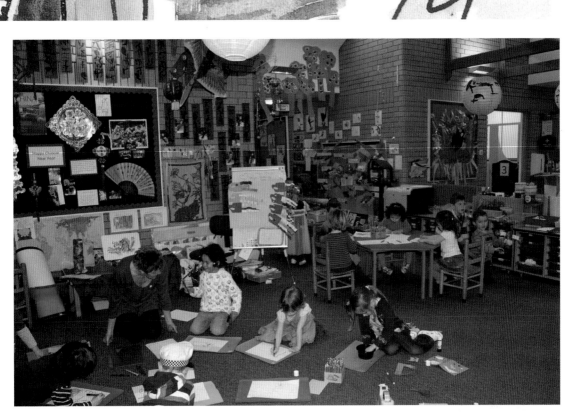

Photo | *Paula Owens.*

evaluation and accreditation of your own geography curriculum. Any Ofsted survey or subject inspections are likely to comment on the impact of your participation in the Champions' network on geography in your school, endorsing your work. You will likewise have the chance to contribute ideas to your network, enabling other teachers to develop and celebrate their work with their school.

Building a picture of strengths and weaknesses

Successful evaluation and eventual accreditation of the geography curriculum and its teaching and learning is all about developing awareness of the strengths and weaknesses of the subject in your own school. Whether your concern is to prepare for an inspection or to submit a Quality Mark Award entry, Figure 2 lists the kinds of questions which you need to be asking yourself and your colleagues. These prompts will help you build up a picture of the strengths and weaknesses of geography within the whole school curriculum in your school.

See *www.geography.org.uk/eyprimary/geographysubjectleaders* for more ideas.

Do you know what the children think about geography?

One of the most useful ways to start evaluating the impact of geography in your school is to talk to children. Can they tell you what geography is about? Even within creative and cross-curricular work, it is still important for children to identify different subjects and know what they are called. In addition to any knowledge, understanding or skills that they are able to tell you about, find out what they like and dislike about geography and what they would like more or less of. It is usually easier for the subject leader to carry out this kind of monitoring and evaluation, with the permission of colleagues of course, than it is to observe lessons. However, if you can observe lessons just as a 'finding out' activity for yourself it can be a

In good geography teaching and learning there is/are:

- properly planned lessons with specific learning objectives related to geographical knowledge, understanding and/or skills
- activities which challenge pupils to use and transform geographical information in some way, not just to transfer it from one place to another
- lesson plans which relate back to the scheme of work and which explore cross-curricular links
- lesson objectives which are shared with pupils at the start of the lesson
- fun starters and/or finishers to lessons, including short place-knowledge quizzes, for example mapwork linked to real places
- an approach which promotes the skills of geographical enquiry through fieldwork and practical activities within the classroom, in addition to the use of secondary sources
- well-prepared, stimulating, up-to-date resources, ready at the beginning of the lesson, e.g. artefacts and/or music of distant or local places, photopacks, maps, books, atlases, globes
- good use of ICT at all stages of learning, e.g. websites, video-clips, digital cameras, e-mail, DVDs and other ICT tools such as Geographical Information Systems
- resources matched to the age, ability and learning styles of pupils in the class, e.g. type and scale of map or photograph, text, worksheet, writing framework
- reference to specialist geographical terms and vocabulary where appropriate, e.g. 'hill' in year 1, and 'landscape' in year 6
- studies which relate to topical examples and real situations of relevance to pupils' lives whenever possible
- an approach which helps children to develop overarching ideas such as pattern, change, sustainability and the application of skills
- an expectation that pupils will work through geographical questions for short or longer periods to collect, record, represent, communicate and analyse data, be it information collected during fieldwork or in class
- planned opportunities for pupils to discuss, recognise and weigh up environmental, aesthetic and cultural attitudes and issues
- the incorporation of thinking-skills techniques into activities
- a creative approach to the subject
- a good pace to the lesson – with pupils aware of timings
- teaching assistants who support learning effectively
- a clear summary to the lesson, involving pupils in explaining or showing what they have learned
- an understanding that pupils develop their attitudes and values.

Figure 3 | *Twenty features of good geography teaching and learning.*

brilliant way of learning about geography in the school. If you can do some lesson observation in a more formal way then Figure 3 offers some advice on what to look for. Clearly you will not expect to see all of this in every lesson but such pointers may help you in working on strengths and weaknesses to develop the subject with your colleagues.

What are the features of good geography teaching and learning?

Good teaching is teaching that promotes effective progress and high standards, fun and enjoyment. In the case of geography it has many of the features identified in Figure 3.

In addition the teacher should either already have reasonable subject knowledge, or know how to develop their knowledge through, for example, referring to *Primary Geographer*, the GA website and of course, the *Primary Geography Handbook*!

By focusing on these issues over a period of time you will gradually gather the information that you need and be in a position to articulate the strengths and weaknesses of geography teaching in your school. You will be able to speak with confidence to an inspector or your headteacher and devise a plan that is appropriate to your needs. You will be able to celebrate the progress you are making. Perhaps the quality of your school's geography will have already been accredited through an Ofsted inspection. You may be working towards the Primary Geography Quality Mark, if you are not already. And if you are moving up through the awards maybe you will be able to help others as a Geography Champion too!

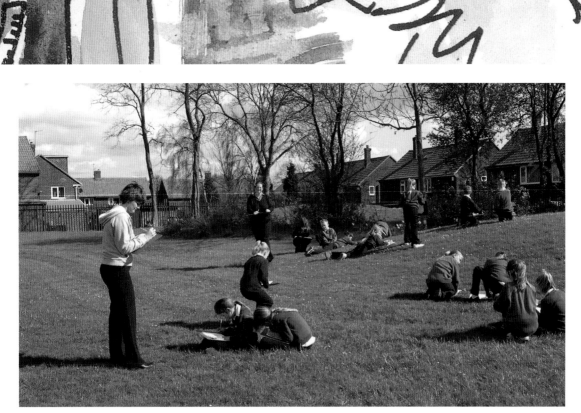

Photo | Wendy North.

References and further reading

Catling, S., Bowles, R., Halocha, J., Martin, F. and Rawlinson, S. (2007) 'The state of geography in English primary schools', *Geography*, 92, 2, pp. 118-136.

Catling, S. and Willy, T. (2009) *Teaching Primary Geography*. Exeter: Learning Matters.

Martin, F. (2006) *Teaching Geography in Primary Schools*. Cambridge: Chris Kington Publishing.

Ofsted (2008) *Geography in Schools: Changing practice*. London: Ofsted. Available at *www.ofsted.gov.uk/publications* (last accessed 2 July 2010).

Ofsted (2009) *Improving primary teachers' subject knowledge across the curriculum* (Thematic report no. 070252). London: Ofsted. Available at *www.ofsted.gov.uk/publications* (last accessed 2 July 2010).

Tauk, A. (2008) 'How to bluff your way as a geography co-ordinator', *Primary Geographer*, 65, pp. 19-20.

Websites

National curriculum in action *www.ncaction.org.uk*

Ofsted *www.ofsted.gov.uk*

Primary Geography Quality Mark *www.geography.org.uk/pgqm*

Geography Champions *http://geographychampions.ning.com* (GA members only).

Teacher Learning Academy *www.teacherlearningacademy.org.uk*

Resources

Good geography teaching requires a wide range of supporting resources. In an ideal world teachers and pupils might collect their resources themselves. In practice the use of prepared teaching materials will considerably enhance the delivery of the subject. There are a huge range of resources available. Commercial publishers, charitable bodies and the media all produce structured materials designed to meet the latest curriculum requirements. The Geographical Association has an extensive catalogue for primary schools (*www.geographyshop.org.uk*).

While there are plenty of materials from which to choose, schools often find themselves severely restricted when it comes to funding. What is the best way of using limited amounts of money and what approaches will help appraise what is available? The information here is not intended to be comprehensive. However, it will serve as a prompt and help you make some informed choices. Over a period of time an enterprising teacher can assemble an impressive range of resources for little or no cost. Equally there are some resources which simply have to be purchased, such as:

maps at various scales	aerial photographs	atlases
globes	contrasting locality packs	textbooks
IT software	teachers' guides	magnetic compasses
thermometers	digital recorders	cameras (digital/video)

Given the pace of change there is little point in listing specific products or titles here. For up-to-date information, consulting the educational press, visiting the Geographical Association website (www.geography.org.uk) and subscribing to *Primary Geographer* will prove invaluable. *Primary Geographer* is the only journal aimed at primary school geography teachers and it contains a wealth of ideas, articles, reviews and comment.

Maps and fieldwork equipment

Ideally any maps that you use regularly should be laminated to make them more durable.

Resource	Comment
Large scale OS maps (1:1,250 urban areas) (1:2,500 rural areas)	At this scale individual houses and gardens can be easily discerned. Invaluable for local area studies, fieldwork and enquiries
Medium scale OS maps (1:10,000)	A black and white map showing the pattern of roads, street names and main buildings which is ideal for land use surveys
Standard scale OS maps (1:25,000 Pathfinder series)	A coloured map that shows field boundaries and more detail than the classic Landranger series (see below) making it ideal for walking
Standard scale OS maps (1:50,000 Landranger series)	The most popular OS series, accessible to upper KS2, which provides an overview of the features in the local area and surrounding region
Street maps	Useful for tracing local routes and journeys
Road maps	A good way of providing an overview of UK towns and cities and the transport links between them
Historical maps	Useful for studying changes. Availability varies according to area

Atlas maps	Invaluable for developing a knowledge and understanding of key places in the UK, Europe and wider world. Many atlases now contain satellite images and information
Globes	An indispensable aid for all ages and the only way of showing the true proportions of the Earth. Can be used to illustrate planetary motion and to qualify two-dimensional atlas maps
Wall charts	Available at a variety of scales and for different locations. Useful in class displays and for research
Plastic floor maps	Outlines of the world, UK and other areas. Particularly useful with younger pupils
Jigsaw maps	Provide colourful images and symbols for places around the world. Particularly useful for interaction and reflection
Satellite images	Great variations in impact and quality of image
Magnetic compasses	A simple but vital instrument to be used alongside maps or independently in fieldwork
Thermometers	Maximum-minimum thermometers have the advantage of recording variations over a day
Weather recording equipment	Simple recording equipment can be improvised or made by the pupils. Suppliers have a range of instruments for school use including wind vanes and barometers
Measuring height and distance	Long tape measures or trundle wheels for measuring distance and clinometers for angles and heights

Books, photographs and artefacts

Resource	*Comment*
Textbooks	Bring together a wide range of resources. Often have the advantage of being graded and designed to meet the needs of the national curriculum
Reference books	Can be very valuable in supporting individual or group projects but be careful pupils do not simply copy them
Stories, fairytales and rhymes	A useful way of developing empathy, motivation and creative mapwork. Very effective for theme or topic work with younger pupils
Locality packs	Provide detailed information, useful for in-depth studies but best used alongside other resources
Teachers' guides and resource books	A useful way of gleaning resources and ideas for self-designed lessons. Often contain activity sheets which are useful if linked to practical enquiries and investigations but rather sterile if used in isolation
CDs	Increasingly available on a range of geographical themes and topics. Ideal for integrating with ICT skills
Photopacks	Collections of photographs on a theme, often with supporting activities. Useful for stimulus displays
Aerial photographs	An excellent resource for amplifying and extending local area work especially if centred on the school. Best used alongside a map of the same scale for comparison
Colour prints and digital photographs	Provide additional information about places and themes. Can be assembled from holiday snaps, especially if focused on specific themes. Digital photographs can be imported into PowerPoint presentations and stored for later use
Postcards	A cheap way of adding to a photograph collection
Photographs in brochures, magazines and calendars	Best grouped thematically and added to over time

Artefacts	Can range from tourist souvenirs and craft items to fresh food, plants and flowers from a supermarket or used tickets and labels on paper bags from other countries
Newspapers and brochures	Provide information about current events and issues as well as local language and customs
Rock, fossil and plant samples	Another cost-free way of collecting geographical 'clues'. Preserve leaves by pressing in a heavy book
CDs	An excellent way of introducing music from around the world as well as songs and nursery rhymes. Your own sound recordings are another approach
DVDs	Shoot your own, virtually cost-free videos or record news items and other relevant programmes
Educational TV programmes	An extremely effective way of bringing images of distant places into a classroom. Usually supported by teachers' notes and activities

Websites

The most useful websites for specific themes and areas of learning are listed at the end of each chapter.

Geographical Information Systems

Geographical Information Systems (or GIS) are a way of representing the world using layers of data. In a sense a GIS is an electronic map for the 21st century: it can be used to study anything that has a position on the Earth's surface. By drilling down through the layers of information, GIS reveal patterns and connections that may not be immediately obvious. Exploring the link between current and historic settlement patterns is just one example of how you could use GIS with primary school children. You may find the following sites useful.

Provider	Description
Geograph *www.geograph.org.uk*	An interactive project to which you and your pupils can contribute, this aims to collect geographically representative photographs and information about every grid square in the UK
Geographical Association *www.geography.org.uk/gtip/thinkpieces/gis*	An introduction to GIS and how to teach it
Google *http://earth.google.co.uk*	Not strictly speaking a GIS, Google Earth is a very stimulating way of introducing the idea of aerial views and zooming down on a location
Infomapper *www.ulearn.infomapper.com*	Free online resources accessed through postcode, place name or grid references to enable pupils to create their own GIS
Ordnance Survey *http://mapzone.ordnancesurvey.co.uk/mapzone/giszone.html*	The GIS zone of the Ordnance Survey website contains simulations of GIS applications along with teacher guidance
Soft Teach Educational *www.soft-teach.co.uk*	A number of applications aimed at key stage 2 including Local Studies, in which pupils can build up maps of their local area
TrackLogs *www.tracklogs.co.uk*	A wide range of tools for route planning, profiling, 3-D views and printing
Wildgoose *www.wildgoose.ac*	An educational GIS (Vista) combining coloured vertical aerial photography and OS digital map data

Index

A

accreditation   349-57
Action Plan for Geography   165, 350
active learning   289-90
activity sheets   see worksheets
aerial photographs   16, 105, 106, 112, 126-8, 187, 199
affective domain   36
Africa   31-2, 59, 131, 210, 222, 225
aims of primary geography   77
airport visit   169
Alcock, Kathy   49
Amazon rainforest   40, 210, 279
art, and emotional literacy   40
artefacts, distant places   207, 212, 213
assemblies   299
assessment   307, 310, 313-21
   distant places   202-3
   Early Years Foundation Stage   72
   geography subject leader and   338, 346
   mapwork skills   109-11
   pupil self-assessment   316
   ten principles   314
atlases   106, 107, 114-15, 240, 268
attachment to place   37-9
awareness of wider world   19-21, 79, 87-9, 205

B

Barlow, Anthony   335
Barnaby Bear   58, 157, 168, 202, 206, 251
Barnes, Jonathan   25
beach play   249-50
Beaufort Scale   236
Bee-Bot   168
'big' geography and 'little' geography   192-3
Bing maps   167, 168, 170
Blow, David   323
Bowles, Rachel   231
brain   22, 33, 36-7
Brazilian rainforest   224
Bridge, Colin W.   105
British Council   202-203, 241
Bruner's spiral curriculum   21
'bubble-wrap' generation   18-19
building materials   185, 189
   see also school and grounds

C

CABE (Commission for Architecture and the Built Environment)   190
CASE (Cognitive Acceleration through Science Education)   332
Catling, Simon   75
CDs   168, 170, 171, 191, 197, 268

change   25, 26, 29, 33
   see also environmental change; futures education
child development stages   15
child protection issues   140-43
childhood memories of places   37-9, 147
Children's Plan   337
children's rights   298
choice, motivation through   56
citizenship   31-2, 51, 54, 56, 70, 89, 197, 217-18, 242, 273, 276, 289-99
   and emotional literacy   37, 41
   local area fieldwork   188-90
   national curriculum   75, 86, 89, 217, 289
classroom observation   350, 356
classroom plans   106
climate   see weather and climate
climate change   244
coal mining and quarrying case study   280-81
coastal areas   200-201, 202, 248-52, 258-9
communication, language and literacy (CLL)   67, 70, 71
community cohesion   190, 271, 289, 294
community facilities projects   189, 191
compass directions   108-9, 186, 233, 329
computers   see ICT
concepts   19-21, 72, 76, 132, 152, 306
conflict and war   217, 218
confluent education   199
conservation   224, 294
continuity and change   25, 26, 29, 33
   see also futures education
contrasting localities   195-203, 268, 277, 279, 292-3, 305 see also distant places
CPD (continuing professional development)   155, 159, 160, 305, 341, 349-57
   see also INSET
creativity   25-33, 40, 273, 303, 323
   creative development (CD)   67, 70, 71
   fun and games   49-61
cross-curricular links   32, 40, 84, 183, 197, 206, 248, 305, 307, 335, 349
   and assessment   315
   environmental geography themes   231, 234, 237, 254, 274
   in fieldwork   136
   in games   55-6
   see also English and geography links
cultural issues   20, 222-4, 298
curriculum   149-50
   see also cross-curricular links; national curriculum; planning
cycle of learning   66-72
Czech Republic   202

D

dance and movement   28, 40, 251
data handling   *see* ICT
DEA (Development Education Association)   214, 219, 221
definitions of geography   75-6, 149-50, 342-3
describing places   26-7
developing world   *see* economically developing world
Development Compass Rose   209-10, 294
Development Education Centres   225
DfES   303
   see also Excellence and Enjoyment; national curriculum; Ofsted
diagrams   129-30
differentiation   170-171, 315, 326-7, 328, 332
digital photography   137, 165, 167, 171, 198, 268, 308, 325
digital video   170
Dinkele, Geoff   95
Disabilities Discrimination Act   323
displays   161, 337
   distant places   213-14
   environmental geography   275, 281
   local area   191-2
   river studies   258
   settlement   270
   weather   235
distant places   19-21, 31-2, 195-203, 205-15, 217-27, 266
   assessment   202
   choosing a study locality   206-8, 209
   citizenship   290, 296-7, 298
   designing own study   208-9
   and emotional literacy   41
   environmental geography   279
   EYFS (Early Years Foundation Stage)   65
   farm planning (Tanzania)   31-2
   games   56, 57, 59
   ICT   199
   images   20
   imaginary journeys and places   156, 329
   and language development   156
   maps   213-14
   perceptions   19-21
   photographs   20-21, 65, 130, 198-9, 207, 211, 222
   planning   208-9, 221-5
   promotion of global dimension   221-5
   reasons for studying   205
   resources   197-9, 207, 225, 227
   story   211
   weather and climate   209, 232, 233, 236-41
   websites   172-3
   see also names of *individual places*; and school links
diversity   28
drama   40

E

Earth Galleries, Natural History Museum   252
economically developing world   31-2, 197, 208, 220, 221, 225
   distant places   214
   weather and climate   233
Eco-Schools   190, 224, 274, 276, 282-4, 330
email   167-8, 170
emotional learning   36-7
emotions   22, 25, 26, 33, 35-47
English and geography links   30-31, 149, 153
   see also literacy and numeracy
enquiry approach   95-103, 275
   citizenship   290-99
   distant places   31-2, 195-6, 206-8, 211
   focused enquiry   97-8
   general enquiry   98
   and ICT   167
   and literacy development   151-3, 158-9
   local area   56, 98-103
   mapwork skills   109-15
   progression   97
   rivers, coasts and landscape   30-31, 258-9
   school and grounds   182
   settlement   261-71
   see also questions
environment   273-87
   and emotional literacy   40, 42-3
   exploration of   17-19
   perceptions of   17-19, 220-21
   understanding and caring for   77-8, 182, 183, 188, 190, 291
   see also environmental issues
environmental change   33, 188, 199, 236, 258, 318
environmental enquiries   98-103
environmental footprint   265
environmental improvement project   102
environmental issues   25, 33, 42, 81, 83, 98-103, 145, 158-9, 261, 264-5, 273, 326
   citizenship   290-99
   distant places   31-2, 202, 208-9, 217-27
   national curriculum   86
Essex-Cater, Liz   273
Europe   52, 197, 202, 209, 305
   assessment   316
   environmental issues   265, 285
   mapwork   106, 115
Every Child Matters   36, 197, 263, 303, 307, 323
Excellence and Enjoyment   36, 303, 323, 324, 327, 337
experiences
   opportunities for   67, 68-72
   see also outdoor experiences
Explore Kent   116
Eye in the Sky   199

EYFS (Early Years Foundation Stage)   63-73, 76
  concepts in   65, 71
  and creativity   26-7
  cross-curricular links   67
  curriculum   76
  distant places   202, 205
  environmental geography   274-6
  fieldwork and local area studies   136, 181,
184-8, 325
  framework   68
  games   55, 64
  Geographical Association's three core principles
63-4
  global dimension   218
  good practice   72
  home to school journey   19
  local area   86
  mapwork   118-19
  opportunities for experiences   67, 68-72
  planning   68
  principles   66
  rivers, coasts and landscape   248
  sensing   65, 184
  settlement   266-7
  statutory framework   181
  stories and poetry   156-7, 276
  understanding pictures   122

F
Facebook   168
fair trade   218-19, 224
family life   46, 289
farm planning project (Tanzania)   31-2
favourite places   17-18, 37-9
feedback after inspection   349, 350
feelings   39, 40, 43
  see also emotions
fiction   45, 157, 200, 277
field sketching   129-30, 146, 199
field studies centres   111, 139
Field Studies Council   43, 273
fieldwork   135-47
  activities   138, 146-7
  activity sheets   136, 144
  citizenship   293-4
  contrasting locality fieldwork   199
  and creativity   28-31
  distant places   139
  early years   325
  and emotional literacy   43
  environmental issues   273-87
  equipment   145
  games   59
  and graphicacy   123, 130
  guidelines   139

health and safety issues   140-43, 183, 247, 249
  hierarchy of suitable locations   137
  and language development   151-2, 153
  local area   17-18, 28-9, 69, 138, 143-4, 146-
7, 184-90
  planning   135-7, 140
  progression   143-4
  questions   135-6, 144, 182, 258-9, 329-30
  recording   137, 141, 144, 191, 257
  resources   144-5, 325
  risk assessment   140-43
  rivers, coasts and landscape   247-9, 256-8
  school and grounds   19, 137-8, 183, 184-8,
233, 235, 236, 241
  settlement   267, 268
  and special educational needs   324-6, 331
  weather and climate   233, 235, 236, 241
financial budgets   89, 336, 337, 340
Flip video   166, 170
Foley, Marcia   349
food   27-8, 214
Forest Schools   274
Foundation Stage
  see EYFS (Early Years Foundation Stage)
futures education   25, 132, 220-21, 242, 265,
294, 326, 327, 330
  see also continuity and change

G
games   49-61, 329
  and emotional literacy   39-40
  local area   50-51, 60, 184-8
  mapwork   111-15
Gardner, Howard   35, 50
gender differences   16, 118
Geograph   198
Geographical Association   26, 310, 338, 341,
350, 351
  core principles for EYFS   63-5
  ICT   165
  and language development   154, 157
  online gallery   203
  see also Primary Geographer
geography
  aims of primary geography   77
  definitions of geography   75-6, 149-50, 342-3
  and ICT   165-7
Geography Champions   157, 269, 349, 354,
357
geography subject leader   303, 315, 320, 335-
47, 350, 351, 354
  geography action plan   340
  geography policy statement   342-7
  and inspection   341-2, 349-57
  responsibilities   336-42
Getmapping   199

Ghana   59
GIS (geographical information systems)   90, 137, 165, 306, 360
global dimension   31-2, 217-27, 290-91
   10 strategies to promote   221-5
   using photographs   222, 223
   see also distant places
global interdependence   28
global warming   220, 244
GLOBE project   241
globes   106, 114-15, 233, 268, 308
globe games   52
Goleman, Daniel   35
good practice   84-9, 342-7, 349, 354, 356-7
   citizenship   289-90
   distant places   208-9
   EYFS   63-5
   fieldwork   135-47, 181-3
   geography and language development   149
   and the global dimension   217-27
   ICT   169-170
   planning   306
   special educational needs   329
Google Earth   115-16, 128, 191, 192, 199
Google Maps   115, 170
GPS (global positioning systems)   78, 170
graphicacy   121-33, 329
greenhouse gases   244
Groundwork   190

H

Halocha, John   261
health and safety
   fieldwork   140-43, 183, 247, 249
   e-safety   171
   pupils' projects   43, 98-101, 293, 326
Healthy Schools   36, 274, 276
historical maps   29, 199
historical understanding   133
history   29, 188, 261
holidays   53, 58-60
home corner area waste management project 70-71, 72
home data collection   137
home life   46, 289
home to school journey   19, 98-101, 112, 266, 329
homework involving fieldwork   137
human rights   217, 218, 298

I

ICT   165-77, 304, 337, 346
   computers and peripherals   165, 170
   data handling   137, 167, 168, 170, 171
   distant places   199
   and enquiry approach   167
   environmental geography   275
   and graphicacy   121-33
   and mapwork   167, 168, 170, 175, 199
   multimedia software   166
   national curriculum   166
   programmable toys   168, 170
   schools linking   225
   settlement   262, 268, 270
   supporting the geography curriculum   166
   teachers' guidance and advice   176-7
   travel guide creation   57
   weather and climate   169, 170, 237, 241-2
   see also CDs; digital photography; internet; websites
identity   17, 37, 66
imagination   25, 26-7, 29, 156, 329
in-service education and training   see INSET
inclusion   27-8, 40, 50, 323-33, 326-7
   see also special educational needs
India   27-8, 56, 225
industrial heritage   265
InfoNation   168
Information and Communications Technology see ICT
INSET   336, 337, 338-9, 340, 341, 347
   geographical question sequence   153
   geographical vocabulary   154
   interpreting photographs   131
   local area studies   41, 183
   portfolio of pupils' work   320-21
   and schemes of work   57
   see also CPD
inspection   320, 341-2, 349-57
intelligence
   emotional   35-6
   multiple intelligences   35, 49, 50
interactive whiteboards (IWBs)   165
interdependence   25, 217, 218-19
International School Award   200
internet   89, 105, 106, 123, 124, 165, 191, 197, 241-2, 286, 306
   see also websites
internet shopping   263
interpersonal skills, and emotions   36, 43-5
iPhones   170
Isle of Coll (Scotland)   200-201, 292-3
issues   28, 42, 217-27, 289-99
   see also cultural issues; environmental issues; special educational needs

J

Jackson, Elaine   289
Jewson, Terry   181
jigsaws   53
jungle   26-7

K

Kent, Gemma   195
Kenya   16
Kenyon, John   313
key geographical concepts   71, 132, 306
key questions   71-2, 96-101, 152, 308
  see also enquiry approach; questions
key skills   32, 54-7
key stage 1
  citizenship   289-99
  contrasting localities   196-7, 202
  curriculum   79-82, 166, 344, 349
  distant places   206-8
  environmental geography   274-6
  fieldwork equipment   145
  global dimension   218
  local area   19, 39, 181, 247
  rivers, coasts and landscape   252-4
  settlement   267-8
  weather and climate   231-5
key stage 2
  citizenship   289-99
  contrasting localities   196-7, 202
  curriculum   80-84, 166, 169, 344, 345, 349
  different types of environment   39
  distant places   206, 208-9
  environmental geography   277
  fieldwork equipment   145
  global dimension   218
  landscapes   247-8
  local area   98-101, 181
  planning geography work   307-10
  rivers, coasts and landscape   247-8, 254-8
  settlement   268-71
  weather and climate   236-41
key stage 2/3 links   84, 89-90, 298, 340
knowledge and understanding of the world
  (KUW)   67, 70, 71, 181
Krause, Jeremy   335

L

LA/Governors
  fieldwork   139-40, 182, 247
  LA websites   174-5
land use projects   158-9, 199, 254, 263, 268-70
landscape   56-7, 188-9, 264
language development   149-63
laptops   165-170
Learning Outside the Classroom   135, 199, 273
learning process   15, 36-7, 66-8, 95, 289-90
  and assessment   314-15, 319, 321

learning log   332
learning theory   15-16, 35-7, 50-51, 66, 110, 116-18
lesson observation   356
lesson planning   21, 307, 338
  language development through geography 161-2
  using games   51
  see also planning
level descriptions   202, 274, 314, 318
Lewis, Liz   149, 247
library for geography   159-60
links   see cross-curricular links; school links
literacy and numeracy   149-63, 183, 248, 249, 305, 337, 350
litter   184, 267, 286, 295
Llandudno (Wales)   202
local area   181-93, 274-5, 304
  attachment to   38-9
  citizenship   290, 293, 294-5
  and contrasting localities   196-7
  and emotional literacy   39-40
  exploring   17-18, 28-9, 66, 69-70
  fieldwork   17-18, 28-9, 69, 138, 143-4, 146-7, 184-8
  games and activities   51-3, 60, 184-8
  and language development   158-9
  local issues   98-103, 143, 146-7, 158-9
  mapwork   29, 187, 191-2, 293
  photographs   127, 130-31, 137, 146, 186
  planning   182-3
  resources   86, 106, 160, 168, 262
  settlement   268-71
  story books   157
  using ICT   167, 168, 169
  weather and climate   185, 189, 241
locality definition   181
locational knowledge   15-19, 57-8, 105-19, 135-47, 199, 206, 213, 345
London 2012 Olympics   265

M

Mackintosh, Margaret   121
mapwork   105-19, 155, 308
  cards, games and activities   51-2, 53, 108, 111-15
  compass directions   108-9, 186, 233
  contrasting locality   199
  conventions   108, 112-13
  and creativity   29, 31-2
  digital mapping   115
  distant places   213-14
  early years   15-16, 118-19
  and graphicacy   122, 125, 126
  and ICT   115-16, 167, 170, 175, 199
  and learning and thinking skills   116
  local area   29, 181-8, 191-2, 293

open-cast mining and quarrying case study 280-281
  pictorial maps   125
  plans   106, 107-8, 109, 112, 329
  questions   111-15
  research   117-18
  resources   105-6
  scale and distance   108, 113-14
  settlement   268-9
  skills assessment   109-11, 316
  skills progression   15-16, 65, 109-11
  surveying   186
  websites   167, 168, 175, 199
  vocabulary   109
Martin, Fran   63
Maudsley, Philip   181
mental maths   55
Millward, Jane   335
Milner, Angela   181
misconceptions   15, 21, 27, 109, 121-32, 321
  distant places   195, 205, 209-10, 219-20
  environmental issues   284-5
  rivers   155, 254
  settlement   263, 266
  weather and climate   242, 243
  see also stereotypical thinking
mobile phones   137
models   121, 127, 129, 266, 267, 292
monitoring   319-320, 339-40, 346, 356
Montage Project   241
motivation   56, 68, 328
mountains   172-3
MovieMaker   171
Mozambique   131
Multimap   116, 167, 168, 199
multiple identities   224
multiple intelligences   35, 49, 50
multi-sensory teaching   36
music   27-8, 40, 54, 58, 214

N
national curriculum   76, 79, 95, 150, 268, 274, 344
  see also primary curriculum
National Framework for Sustainable Schools 323
National Languages Strategy   150
natural places   38-9
Netbook   170
Neuroscience   36
news media   89, 207, 208, 225, 236, 264-5, 305, 330
North Sea fish stocks issue   285

O
Obama, Barack   273
Ofsted   135, 165, 304, 313, 337, 349-50, 354, 357

see also inspection
open-cast mining and quarrying case study 280-81
oral activities   39-40
Ordnance Survey
  Get-a-map service   115
  maps   89, 106, 107, 187, 199, 269
  map symbol flashcards   52
  Mapzone website   52, 115
outdoor experiences   65, 151, 156, 188, 247, 248
Owens, Paula   63
Oxfam   220

P
painting activities   26-7, 68
parking projects   167
patterns and processes   28-9, 236, 318
PDA (personal digital assistant)   170
personal involvement, EYFS   72, 79
personal, social and emotional development (PSE)   67, 70, 71
PGQM (Primary Geography Quality Mark)   274, 336, 349, 350-53, 355, 357
photographs   122-8, 131
  contrasting locality   198
  digital photopacks   171
  distant places   20-21, 65, 130, 207, 211, 222
  and emotional literacy   44
  fieldwork   137, 146
  internet sources   123, 124, 125, 128, 133
  local area   131, 137, 146, 186
  photopacks   106, 125, 130-31, 197, 200, 207
  weather and climate   232
  see also aerial photographs; digital photography
PhotoStory 3   171
physical development (PD)   67
physical geography   247, 264
Piaget's theories   15
pictorial maps   125
picture books   26, 45
picture postcard games   53
pictures   122, 123-6, 133
  and emotional literacy   44
  fieldwork activities   146
  and ICT   168, 174
  and vocabulary   156
  weather and climate   233
places
  attachment to   37-9
  childhood memories of   37-9, 147
  children's experiences of   65
  and creativity   25-33
  describing   26-7
  developing sense and perception of   130-31, 136, 195, 203, 249
  and emotions   35-47
  level descriptions   318

understanding   77, 86-7, 236
planning   80-83, 303-11, 327-8
  and assessment   307, 308, 310, 319
  contrasting localities   195-203
  distant places   208-9, 221-5
  early years cycle of learning   66-73
  fieldwork   135-7, 140, 147
  geography subject leader and   336, 337, 338
  ICT   169
  and inspection   350
  linking with literacy work   153
  local area   182-3
  long-term planning   306
  medium-term planning   306-8
  rivers, coasts and landscape   249-50, 256-9
  short-term planning   309
  special educational needs   325, 328-33
  see also lesson planning
play   54, 64, 68-73, 249-50
  see also sand play
Plowden Report   135
poetry   30-31, 251, 276
  and language development   156-7,
pollution   294
portfolios of pupils' work   320-21, 346, 350
Potts, Ruth   49
PowerPoint   137, 172, 192
prejudices   21, 89, 205, 209-10, 219, 223-4
primary curriculum
  contrasting localities   196-7
  distant places   87-9
  enquiry approach   95
  fieldwork   86
  ICT   166
  level descriptions   314, 318
  literacy   150
  local area   79, 86, 87, 183
  school and grounds   79, 87
  and special educational needs   327
  see also curriculum; EYFS; key stage 1; key
stage 2
Primary Geographer   58, 89, 147, 163, 215,
227, 270, 286, 338, 343, 356
primary languages   150, 197, 307
Primary National Strategy   247, 316
prior knowledge   21, 66, 68, 69
  see also misconceptions
private geographies   17-18, 37-9
problem solving   56, 329-30, 332-3
problem solving, reasoning and numeracy (PSRN)
67, 71
progression   21, 79-84, 86, 89-90, 306, 309, 337
  and assessment   319
  distant places   203
  in enquiry   97, 318
  fieldwork   143-4
  graphicacy   122, 125
  language development   152-4

map skills   15-16, 109-11, 117
  rivers, coasts and landscape   247, 248, 252, 258
  weather and climate   232-41
puppets   55

Q
QCDA   197, 314
quality of life   296-7
questionnaires and interviews   98-103, 137,
275, 326
questions   72, 79, 96-101, 315
  contrasting localities   195-6, 199
  fieldwork   135-6, 143, 144, 182, 258-9, 329-
30
  games involving   52, 53
  mapwork skills   109-15
  open-cast mining and quarrying case study
280-81
  river studies   256-7
  trees case study   278-9
  weather and climate   233-4
  working with photographs   123-4, 131
  see also enquiry approach
Quikmaps   167, 170
quizzes and puzzles   52

R
Race Relations Act   219
rainforests   26-7, 40, 210, 224, 279, 282, 296-7
Rawlinson, Steve   273
record keeping
  for assessment   316-17
  geography subject leader and   346
  for inspection   350
recording
  fieldwork   137, 144, 191, 257
  see also weather and climate
recycling   190, 220, 286, 295
relaxation   299
remote sensing   see satellite-based technology
research, local area   191
resources   89, 305, 330, 338, 358-60
  contrasting localities   197-9
  distant places   197-9, 208, 225, 227
  environmental geography   286
  fieldwork   144-5, 325
  ICT   167, 170-76, 325
  library for geography   159-60
  local area   106, 168
  mapwork   105-6
  promotion of global dimension   225
  rivers, coasts and landscape   248, 251, 254, 255
  settlement   267, 269, 270-71
  visual images   123-6, 133, 168
  weather and climate   236, 237, 241, 244-5
Richardson, Paula   135, 303
risk assessment   140-43, 182, 183
river studies   30-31, 155, 167, 202, 209, 247-59

role models, practitioners as 64, 284
role play 40, 44, 55, 159, 281, 290, 292, 294, 297, 316
rural locations 138, 195, 263
Russell, Kate 165

S

safety *see* health and safety
sampling, beach material 251-2
sand play 55, 248, 249, 250-51, 252, 255
satellite-based technology 78, 165
  images 105, 106, 128, 240
scaffolding 72, 332
schemes of work 53, 57-8, 183, 305
school cohesion 276
School Development Plan 169-70, 337, 340
school and grounds 181-93
  and emotional literacy 40
  environmental geography 276, 278
  fieldwork 19, 137-8, 183, 184-8, 233, 235, 236, 241
    school plans 106
    settlement 267
    weather and climate 233, 235, 236, 241
school journeys and visits 111, 113, 139, 169, 197, 281, 324-5, 329-30
  see also fieldwork; local area
school links
  for CPD 341
  distant places 197, 202, 214, 221, 225-6, 262-3
  environmental geography 285
  for fieldwork activities 139
  role of ICT in 225
  weather and climate 233, 241
  see also secondary school links
school travel plan 293
Scoffham, Stephen 15, 35, 95, 205, 181, 313, 323
Scotland 200-201, 292-3
SEAL (Social and Emotional Aspects of Learning) 36, 37, 289, 290, 323
  and emotional literacy 37
seaside *see* coastal areas
secondary school links 84, 89-90, 298, 340
self-assessment (pupils) 316-17
SEF (self evaluation framework) 197, 248, 339, 349, 350, 351, 354
  see also self-review (schools)
self-review (schools) 347, 350, 351
  see also monitoring
sensing and sensory games 17, 27-8, 30-31, 184, 249, 299, 329, 330
settlement 209, 261-7, 292
shopping projects 143, 167, 169, 189, 218-19
signs and symbols 121-2, 128-9
  weather 233, 235, 237

simulations 279
singing 27, 54
sketches 129-30, 146, 199
skills awareness, early years 68
skills progression 80, 83, 84, 307-8, 318, 354
  maps and mapwork 15-16, 65, 78
  weather and climate 232-41
Skype 165, 166
slavery 220
social justice 217
social learning 22
South America 267
Spain 316
spatial awareness and understanding 15-16, 77-8, 168
special educational needs 323-33, 346-7, 356
  and assessment 314, 315
  Code of Practice 323
  and emotional literacy 36-7
  fieldwork 324-6, 331
  geography subject leader and 338
  good practice 329
  ICT 170-171, 325
  issues 328
  sensing 27-8, 30, 329, 330
  see also inclusion
standard of living 296-7
standards 320
  see also assessment
stereotypical thinking 20, 65, 160, 205, 219-20, 222, 225, 295
  see also misconceptions
stories and story books 26, 45, 200, 207, 232, 248, 267, 275, 276, 277, 279
  and language development 156-7, 159-61
story telling games 54-5, 56
street maps and plans 106, 167, 329
subject co-ordinator *see* geography subject leader
sustainable development 25, 70, 81, 220-21, 242, 265, 273, 284
Sustainable Schools 190, 274, 290, 307, 326
sustainability 76, 294, 330
symbols *see* signs and symbols

T

Tanner, Julia 35
Tanzania 31-2
teachers 85
  ICT guidance and advice 174, 176-7
  student teachers 326, 331
  team approach 324
  see also geography subject leader
teaching assistants (TAs) 324, 330, 332
thematic studies 85, 202
  see also specific themes
think pieces 47, 61, 119, 147, 163, 227, 286